ANGLO-CHINESE RELATIONS
1839–1860

宇和先生編

雅片戰爭時代
中葉外内内伴提供

戊午秋秦琴生題

ORIENTAL DOCUMENTS VII

ANGLO-CHINESE RELATIONS 1839–1860

A Calendar of Chinese Documents in
The British Foreign Office Records

J. Y. WONG

Published for **THE BRITISH ACADEMY**
by **THE OXFORD UNIVERSITY PRESS**

Oxford University Press, Walton Street, Oxford OX2 6DP

LONDON GLASGOW NEW YORK TORONTO
DELHI BOMBAY CALCUTTA MADRAS KARACHI
KUALA LUMPUR SINGAPORE HONG KONG TOKYO
NAIROBI DAR ES SALAAM CAPE TOWN
MELBOURNE AUCKLAND
AND ASSOCIATE COMPANIES IN
BEIRUT BERLIN IBADAN MEXICO CITY

Published in the United States by Oxford University Press, New York

ISBN 0 19 726014 4

British Library Cataloguing in Publication Data

Anglo-Chinese relations 1839–1860 – (Oriental documents; 7)
1. Great Britain – Foreign relations – China
2. Great Britain – Foreign relations – 1837–1901
3. China – Foreign relations – Great Britain
4. China – Foreign relations – To 1912
I. Wong, J. Y.   II. Series
327.41051   DA47.9.C5

PRINTED IN GREAT BRITAIN BY
LAMPORT GILBERT PRINTERS LIMITED
WANTAGE ROAD, READING, BERKSHIRE

In Honour
of
J. R. EDE, cb
Some Time Keeper of Public Records
and
First Chairman
of the
British Academy Oriental Documents Committee

CONTENTS

ACKNOWLEDGEMENTS

I wish to thank the British Academy, which has financed much of this project through its Oriental Documents Committee and has made possible the publication of this volume. The Australian Academy of the Humanities/Myer Foundation awarded me a travel grant to enable me to do more work in London in 1976. The Department of History in the University of Sydney generously offered me typing assistance in the preparation of a camera-ready script for publication. The Public Record Office in London has given me every facility to do my work.

Professor W.G. Beasley, CBE, of the School of Oriental and African Studies in the University of London, has given this project his close attention and unflagging support. Our numerous discussions have clarified many difficult points. Without his interest and encouragement this project would never have been completed.

J.R. Ede, CB, some time Keeper of Public Records and the first Chairman of the British Academy Oriental Documents Committee, played an important role in the inception of this project. His colleagues in the Office, Mr E.K. Timings, Dr R.F. Hunnisett and Mr N.E. Evans have gone out of their way to help me. Mr N.E. Evans, in particular, read my early drafts. Messrs M. Roper, A.A.H. Knightbridge, C.D. Chalmers, and J.L. Walford, successive Principal Assistant Keepers who supervised the project, also devoted much time to it; especially in evolving an acceptable format for an unusual archive.

Mr John Lust, Principal Assistant Librarian in the School of Oriental and African Studies, kindly let me borrow trolley-loads of reference books for elucidating the documents. Mr Adrian Roberts of the Bodleian Library in Oxford, Dr F. Taylor and Miss G. Matheson of the John Rylands University Library of Manchester, Mr P.J. Gautrey and Miss M.I. Scott of the University Library in Cambridge, as well as Mrs Felicity Strong, formerly of the Royal Commission on Historical Manuscripts, have all done more than their fair share to assist me in the course of my research.

I also wish to thank the Master and Fellows of Churchill
College in Cambridge for having elected me, during my year of
sabbatical leave in 1980, to a Fellow Commonership, as well as
Professor F.H. Hinsley and the Centre of International Studies in
the History Faculty in Cambridge for having elected me to a Visiting
Fellowship in the same year; both of which have enabled me to complete
the ground work for this project in a congenial environment. My work
has also benefited greatly from the discussions with Professor D.C.
Twitchett of the Oriental Faculty at Cambridge.

Mr P.D. Coates' timely advice about the importance of the
registers has saved me from significant blunders. Our numerous
discussions in the Public Record Office in Chancery Lane, in his
study in Lewesland Cottage at Barcombe, in my study at Churchill
College in Cambridge, and our voluminous correspondence have been
most beneficial. His advice about the existence of F.O. 230/74-75
has enabled me to incorporate some of the information therein in my
list. His assistance in obtaining for me copies of some documents
on which to work in Sydney, and in physically re-arranging on my behalf
the sixty or so documents discovered after 1980, is much appreciated.
Mr Coates has also checked my final typescript.

My life-time friends Dr Janet Hunter, Dr Stephen Hickey and Dr
Andrew Purkis have offered their warmest hospitality each time I
visited London. Our discussions about my work over coffee in the
comfort of their homes have been most refreshing. They have also
read drafts of my Introduction and have made valuable suggestions.
The Introduction also benefited from the advice of Mr Howard Nelson,
Assistant Keeper in charge of the Department of Oriental Manuscripts
and Printed Books in the British Library, who recommended that I
describe the physical appearance of the documents and the mechanism
of cataloguing them.

Over the years, my wife, Linda 曹昭蓮, has assisted in all technica
matters. So have Mr Beng-tat Ee 余明達 , Dr Lance Eccles, Mr D.K.Y.
Kwan 關一球 , and Dr Lee Tzu-wen 李子文 , in various degrees. Over
the years, too, Professor M.G. Jacobs has been most generous in
letting her secretaries, Miss Helen Knight, Mrs Kay Donoghue and
others type different parts of the initial drafts. The Book Binding

Section of the School of Graphic Art, Sydney Technical College, have kindly let me use their facilities to bind up endless notes and loose papers.

In 1980, Mr Jack Aldridge of the Public Record Office in London proof-read all my cards before they went to the typist, Mrs E. Goode. Mr Aldridge also proof-read that first typescript in its entirety. This script was subsequently proof-read again in Sydney with the help of Mr Beng-tat Ee and some of my students, particularly Christopher Nailer and Robert Vines. Heavily scored by my emendations, it was then re-typed by Mrs Gabriele McPhedran, without whose patience and skill the camera-ready script would never have been ready. Mrs Jaya Thuraisingam and others have also helped in the task of re-typing.

Mr Grahame Harrison has put far more time into assisting me with checking the final typescript than I have any right to expect of a colleague. Other colleagues in the Department of History, University of Sydney, have also read either the Introduction or parts of the Calendar and have made useful comments. They are Professor Deryck Schreuder, Mr Tony Cahill and Dr Jim Waldersee.

The Chinese characters on the front cover and on the title page are the work of two Cantonese artists, Mr Hu Ken-t'ien 胡根天 and Mr Ch'in O-sheng 秦咢生, who are respectively ninety and eighty years of age. All the other Chinese characters in this volume were written by my wife.

Mr Hagan Powell of the British Academy has taken much trouble over the publication of this volume.

To all others, too numerous to mention individually, who have helped to bring this project to a successful conclusion, I offer my grateful thanks.

FOREWORD

The Chinese-language archive of the British embassy in Peking, which included material dating from the time of the Superintendency of Trade at Hong Kong in the mid-nineteenth century, was returned to England in 1959 and deposited at the Public Record Office. A preliminary list was made of the many bundles of documents contained in the boxes, but it soon became clear that something much more detailed was required in order to make the collection fully available to research-workers. A start was made by Dr David Pong, whose list of the Kwangtung Provincial Archives (captured during the hostilities of 1857-8) was published in 1975. Work on the diplomatic papers had by that time also begun, under the auspices of the British Academy's Oriental Documents Committee. The present volume, covering the years 1839 to 1860, is the first result. It was originally intended to produce similar volumes for the later diplomatic documents, but this now appears to be un-necessary, since it has proved possible for Mr P.D. Coates, who has been working on that part of the archive, to reconstitute it in accordance with the original Chinese registers, which therefore serve as a guide to the papers. The Public Record Office plans to make these registers available on microfilm.

An archive undertaking on this scale cannot be carried out without financial support, made available over a period of years. The British Academy has been generous in providing it. Nor could the work have been done without the active cooperation of the Public Record Office in affording facilities for it. Valuable support has also been given by the University of Sydney. Nevertheless, I am sure that all who have been concerned with the preparation of this volume would agree that the key role, and the major contribution, have been those of its editor, Dr John Wong. The listing of nineteenth-century Chinese documents needs many skills, not only linguistic ones. Equally important, it requires exceptional qualities of care and commitment. In demonstrating how fully he possesses them, Dr. Wong has put other scholars under a lasting debt of gratitude.

London
January 1982   W.G. Beasley

INTRODUCTION

This volume contains summaries in English of the diplomatic correspondence in Chinese between the British and Chinese authorities during the years 1839 to 1860. The documents were originally kept by the Chinese Secretary [*cheng ṣan-i-kuan*正繕譯官][1] of Her Majesty's Plenipotentiary in the Far East; they are now deposited in the Public Record Office in London.

In so far as these summaries are arranged in a chronological order, they may be read as a partial documentary history of a crucial period of Anglo-Chinese relations. They offer insight into the problems peculiar to this era, an era in which Great Britain and China twice went to war. China's defeat on both occasions decided the fate of this state for the next hundred years or so, until she was given the chance of a fresh start in 1949.

The dramatic changes in the tone of the diplomatic language of the documents is perhaps indicative of the changing relationship between the two states. Before the First Opium War, for example, Imperial Commissioner Lin Tse-hsü wrote out edicts to be transmitted by his very junior officials to Her Majesty's envoy in China, Captain Charles Elliot, RN. Between the two Opium Wars, the representatives of the two governments communicated with each other on apparent equal terms. But it is important to observe that increasingly H.M. Plenipotentiary took the initiative to write, and

---

[1]*F.O.682/1987/21, Bowring to Yeh Ming-ch'en, 9 May 1854. Ibid., 11 May 1854, 12 May 1854, 17 May 1854, 19 May 1854, 22 May 1854. However, there is evidence to suggest that by 1859, the Chinese Secretary had begun calling himself han-wen cheng-shih* 漢文正使 *(F.O.682/1992/25b, Undated draft comment on a Chinese despatch dated 24 Jun 1859.)*

that his language became more and more belligerent as time went by.
The tone of successive Imperial Commissioners was sometimes
conciliatory, sometimes sarcastic, but invariably defensive. On the
other hand, it should be pointed out that these communications took
place between Canton, where the Imperial Commissioner was posted,
and Hong Kong, where H.M. Plenipotentiary was stationed. Peking
continued to ignore the envoy from London. Even after Canton had
been captured by the Allied British and French forces towards the
end of 1857, Peking still refused to reply directly to Lord Elgin's
despatch.[1] Instead, the local authorities of Kiangsu were asked to
transmit the reply which urged Elgin to go back to Canton, where a
new Imperial Commissioner would be sent to meet him. Elgin responded
by 'showing the guns' rather than the 'flag'. Thereafter he and even
his interpreters such as Harry Parkes and Horatio Lay virtually
dictated to the high mandarins what to do. This was a far-cry from
even the inter-war years when, for example, Acting Imperial
Commissioner Po-kuei reacted to a British complaint about the use of
the character 夷 by professing ignorance of the classics and
dictionaries and consequently found it novel that the character 夷
could prove to be a source of anger and dispute.[2] In the space of
twenty-two years, therefore, the Celestial Empire declined in status
to what has been described as a semi-colony.

---

[1] *F.O. 682/1991/31a, Ho Kuei-ch'ing and Chao Te-ch'e to Elgin,
21 Mar 1858.*

[2] *F.O. 230/75, Hsü Kuang-chin and Po-kuei to Bonham, 27 Jul 1852.
The great irony in this extremely cutting despatch in terms of
Chinese humour was apparently wasted on the Chinese Secretary.*

Most British historians have accused the Chinese officials of intransigence and evasiveness. Chinese historians have always been loud in their denunciation of British aggression. Both have a point, but neither acknowledges the other's arguments. The summaries presented here might provide much food for thought. The documents are fairly complete and they give a comprehensive picture of the day-to-day relations between the representatives of the two governments. It is clear that both parties were arrogant, although their respective arrogance was different in nature and expression. The despatches from the Chinese after 1839 leave little doubt that the writers treated the addressees with a combination of fear and contempt. The British despatches were often designed to strike fear into the hearts of the Chinese, reflecting the spirit of Lord Palmerston's remark of 1850, 'These half civilised Governments, such as those of China, Portugal, Spanish America require a dressing every eight or ten years to keep them in order.'[1] In the end, might was right. Chinese pride succumbed to British gunboats.

The pride and the might revolved round the major issues of the period. They were issues which the British authorities had not anticipated while dictating the Treaty of Nanking to the Chinese towards the end of the First Opium War in 1842. For example, the opening of four ports in addition to Canton had been considered sufficient. However, it was soon discovered that British manufactures were not selling as well as had been expected. The

---

[1] F.O. 17/173, *Domestic Various*, Palmerston's remark on Bonham's despatches 65, 67, 72. 29 Sep 1850.

assumption was that if more ports had been opened, more British manufactures would have been sold; hence the demand to open the interior of China, principally the Yangtze River area, for trade. British diplomatic efforts concentrated on having the Treaty of Nanking revised to incorporate this and other new demands. The Chinese government responded by adhering strictly to the terms of the treaty. Nor had the British authorities anticipated the hostility of the Cantonese after the First Opium War. From all accounts, the Cantonese before the war were friendly and helpful to foreigners. The atrocities of war appear to have changed them. Somehow they came to regard the walled city of Canton as their bastion of independence and self-respect. They were determined to keep the foreigners out of it. Equally determined were the British authorities to subdue this symbol of Cantonese defiance. Thus, the so-called Canton city question occupied much space in the diplomatic correspondence of this period. Yet another issue was the legal-isation of opium, an issue over which the Chinese negotiators in 1842 absolutely refused to compromise whatever the consequences. Subsequent and constant British efforts at persuasion proved equally futile.

In so far as the summaries are made as an attempt to catalogue the documents, this volume does not pretend to be any different from the printed catalogues daily used by searchers in the Public Record Office in London, or in similar institutions around the world. Indeed, I am much indebted to the editorial staff of the Public Record Office for their advice on technical matters. Two pieces of such advice have proved particularly useful. One is to

use suffixes, such as 'a' and 'b' when a certain reference number
has to be duplicated. The other is to use the description 'number
not used' when a number has been omitted. This volume is perhaps
more liberal than is usual in its use of such devices because of
the circumstances in which it was compiled. The project began in
1972. But since 1974, I have been teaching in Australia, and apart
from the periodic visits I made back to London in 1976, 1977, 1978
and 1980, much of the work has been done in Sydney. On more than
one occasion was it thought that the catalogue was complete and the
reference numbers were treated as final, and indeed typed as such.
In 1980, I even re-arranged the documents physically according to
the new reference numbers. But always some new material came to
light just in time to prolong the project and increase the suffixes.
Part of the difficulty arises from the fact that the documents had
been kept in the loft of the British Legation in Peking for about a
hundred years and in time were mixed with a multitude of other
papers before the entire bulk of papers was shipped back to London in
1959. Indeed, until all the papers have been identified and sorted
out, one is not in a position to say that *all* the documents which
should have been summarised in this volume have been so included.

The Uniqueness of the Documents

One consolation to me has been the knowledge that this
collection of documents is very rare indeed. One rival could have
been a similar collection kept by the clerical staff of the Chinese
Imperial Commissioner for Foreign Affairs. But in 1857 the Imperial
Commissioner, Yeh Ming-ch'en himself, together with his own official
and private archives, was captured by the Allied British and French

forces.[1] An examination of the captured papers indicates that
very few of the despatches have survived. It is possible that many
of them were burnt when the Allied Forces bombarded the Commissioner's
yamen, which subsequently caught fire. It is also possible that
when the Commissioner fled from his *yamen* with boxes of selected
papers, not all the despatches were among those selected. This is
not surprising as the Commissioner was concurrently Viceroy of
Liang-Kuang and had been very active in suppressing rebellions in
South China since 1851.[2] The papers that would have concerned
him most if they fell into the hands of foreign foes would hardly
have been those despatches which he had sent to them or received
from them, but rather those containing state secrets.

Even if the collection kept by the Commissioner had survived,
it could not have been as large as the one kept by the Plenipotentiary.
The latter communicated not only with the Commissioner but also with
the Viceroys and Governors on the China coast in peace time, and then
during the hostilities, with various Imperial Commissioners who came
directly from Peking.

As for the other Powers, none of them was as involved with
China in this period as Great Britain. Consequently, their collections may be patchy. Denmark is perhaps not a fair comparison, but
as far as one can ascertain this is the only country that has had the

[1] D. Pong. A *Critical Guide to Kwangtung Provincial Archives Deposited
at the Public Record Office of London*. (Camb., Mass., 1975),
pp. 2-4.

[2] J.Y. Wong. *Yeh Ming-ch'en: Viceroy of Liang-Kuang, 1852-58*.
(Cambridge, 1976), pp. 81-155.

catalogue of its collection published. There are very few entries indeed for the same period 1839-1860.[1]

Historians who have consulted the British Foreign Office records which are also deposited in the Public Record Office and classified as F.O. 17 may wonder about the completeness of this class in terms of the diplomatic correspondence between the two governments. It will be most interesting to compare the Chinese documents with the English versions which appear as enclosures in F.O. 17, to determine the extent and the accuracy of the translations. But one thing appears certain. The Plenipotentiary is likely to have enclosed only those documents (or translations of them) which he considered significant enough to be reported to Whitehall in full. Furthermore, it is important to remember that the Chinese documents are the originals that *were exchanged* between two govern- ments. Western historians, in all good faith, have used English translations, in F.O. 17, of despatches from the Chinese; they have also used the English originals in the same series, of despatches to the Chinese.[2] What is not often grasped is that, although the British government acted on these English translations and English originals, the Chinese government acted on neither. The Chinese

---

[1]Baark, Erik. *Catalogue of Chinese Manuscripts in Danish Archives: Chinese diplomatic correspondence from the Ch'ing dynasty 1644-1911.* London, 1979.

[2]*See, for example, Sargent, A.J. Anglo-Chinese Commerce and Diplomacy. Oxford, 1907. Costin, W.C. Great Britain and China, 1833-1860. Oxford, 1937. Nolde, John, J. 'The "Canton City Question", 1843-1849: A preliminary investigation into Chinese antiforeignism and its effects upon China's diplomatic relations with the West.' Ph.D. thesis, Cornell University, 1956. Wakeman, Frederic, Jr. Strangers at the Gate: Social disorder in South China, 1839-1861. University of California Press, 1966.*

government knew only the Chinese originals of their own despatches, and recognised only the Chinese translations of those prepared and presented to them by the British. Therefore, Western historians who have so far used only the English translations and English originals may have to reconsider their conclusions based on evidence of the despatches written in a language that was not the medium of communication between the British and Chinese diplomats.

On the other hand, historians in China have at times found it necessary to use re-translations (into Chinese) of those English versions of the Chinese originals which are no longer extant in their own country. It is hardly necessary to elaborate on the difficulties involved in using such double-translations. One example is perhaps sufficient to illustrate the point. On 27 April 1853, the Taiping Generals Lo Ta-kang 羅大綱 and Wu Ju-hsiao 吳如孝 jointly sent a despatch to Sir George Bonham, who was then on his way to Nanking aboard the steamer Hermes. In this despatch, the Taipings recalled their intimate friendship with two British friends, whose names appeared in the re-translation as Pai-lai-mu 白萊姆 and I-li-wang-k'en 伊利旺肯.[1] They went on to praise the nobleness of the former and to wish the latter good health, expressing, at the same

---

[1]Ts'ao Shu-chü 曹聚仁 re-translated the English version of the document from the British Parliamentary Papers of 1853, a blue book entitled Papers Respecting the Civil War in China, 1853, and had it published in I-ching 逸經 , No. 11 (5 Aug 1936), pp. 9-10. This re-translation was collected in Hsiang Ta 向達 et al. (eds.), T'ai-p'ing t'ien-kuo 太平天國 (Shanghai, 1952), Vol. 4, pp. 9-11, as well as in Yang Sung 楊松 et al. (eds.), Chung-kuo chin-tai-shih tzu-liao hsüan-chi 中國近代史資料選輯 (Peking, 1954), p. 210.

time, an irrepressible anxiety to see their old friends again.[1] A
great deal of importance has been placed on this document, which
appears repeatedly in published collections of materials on the
Taiping Rebellion.[2] If it is true that patriotism plays a part in
the study of the Taiping Rebellion in China, little do the
specialists on the Taipings realise that they may contradict their
colleagues who specialise on the First Opium War, the study of which
in China also appears to have patriotic overtones. In Chinese
historical writing on the First Opium War, the villains of the piece
were Commodore Sir Gordon Bremer and Captain Charles Elliot, RN.
These are the men referred to in the double-translation I have cited.
The translator was obviously not aware of the fact that Chinese
literature on the First Opium War refers to Gordon Bremer as 伯麥
[Po-mai] and Charles Elliot as 義律 [I-lü].[3]

Chinese was used as the diplomatic language because the Ch'ing
government persistently refused to train its own interpreters.
Consequently, H.M. Plenipotentiary was obliged to correspond with

---

[1] *See note on previous page.*

[2] *Idem.*

[3] *See, e.g. Ting Ming-nan* 丁名楠 *et al., 'Ti-i-tz'u ya-p'ien chan-cheng
___ wai-kuo tzu-pen chu-i ch'in-lüeh Chung-kuo te k'ai-tuan'* 第一次鴉片戰爭
___ 外國資本主義侵略中國的開端 *Chung-kuo k'o-hsüeh-yüan li-shih
yen-chiu-so ti-san-so chi-k'an* 中國科學院歷史研究所第三所集刊
*Vol. 1 (1954), pp. 114-52. I myself had been eagerly searching in the
Public Record Office in London for the original Taiping despatch, if
only to check the accuracy of the translation made by the Chinese
Secretary in order to find out if G. Bremer and C. Elliot were the men
in question. I am indeed grateful to Professor Ch'en Hsi-ch'i* 陳錫祺
*who wrote to tell me that the despatch had been found in China recently
and published in Wen-wu* 文物 *(1979) No. 8, pp. 72-73.*

the Chinese officials in their own language. This partly accounted
for the continued existence of the position of Chinese Secretary
[cheng fan-i kuan　正繕譯官] in the British establishment, a
position that dated back to the time of the British East India
Company's monopoly in China. As mentioned before, it was in the
Chinese Secretary's Office that these documents were originally
filed.

The Chinese Secretary and his Office

This Office was originally created by the British East India
Company in China. It was the British merchants who had travelled
half way round the globe in order to trade in China. It was also
the British merchants, rather than the Chinese, who took the
initiative of trying to overcome the language barrier by employing
a fellow European who had received some training in the Chinese
language as Chinese Secretary. In 1833, the monopoly of the British
East India Company to trade in China was abolished. A Superintendent
of Trade was appointed by the Crown to look after British commercial
interests in China. The Superintendent inherited the Chinese
Secretary from the Company.

During the period under review, the staff of the Chinese
Secretary's Office was small. It consisted mainly of the Chinese
Secretary, who was invariably a European. Successive Chinese
Secretaries of this period were J.R. Morrison (from 1834), K.
Gutzlaff (from 1843), W.H. Medhurst (from 1854) and T.F. Wade (from
1855). They were pioneer interpreters whose proficiency in the
Chinese language was, to say the least, not perfect. Then there
were the supernumerary interpreters who were also Europeans,

nominally studying Chinese under the supervision of the Chinese
Secretary. But as often as not they were hard at work in H.M.
Plenipotentiary's Office copying despatches rather than working in
the Chinese Secretary's Office.[1] Finally there were the native
Chinese scribes. They risked capital punishment for helping the
barbarians read and write Chinese. Consequently, the recruits were
often second rate 'scholars' whose calligraphy and literary style
were quite inadequate.

Not surprisingly, the British despatches inspired little respect
from the high mandarins. When the mandarins sued for peace during
the hostilities[2] or asked the British authorities for a favour,[3] they
polished the language employed in conveying the British conditions
for peace or conditions for doing such a favour. Otherwise, they
simply amused themselves by replying in highly sophisticated
bureaucratic language, which occasionally succeeded in irritating the
British authorities. In 1849, for example, Sir George Bonham protest-
ed that Hsü Kuang-chin's despatch ended with an impolite note. Hsü
Kuang-chin expressed surprise at the accusation, adding that perhaps
the interpreter's knowledge of Chinese was poor, and that Hsü himself
would appreciate it if an educated man were found to point out where
the despatch was improper.[5] Bonham quoted the allegedly offending

---

[1] I am most grateful to Mr P.D. Coates for this inside information.

[2] F.O. 682/1974/31, Ch'i-shan to Elliot, 5 Feb 1841.

[3] F.O. 682/1988/Cb, Chi-erh-hang-a and Wu Chien-chang to [Bowring],
15 Feb 1855.

[4] F.O. 682/677/26, Bonham to Hsü Kuang-chin, 11 Jun 1849.

[5] F.O. 682/1982/26, Hsü Kuang-chin to Bonham, 15 Jun 1849.

sentence.[1] Hsü Kuang-chin then explained the sentence, that it was common knowledge in China to use such a sentence to address equals, and that again, Bonham's complaint showed the ignorance of the interpreter.[2] One wondered how the Chinese Secretary took it. Apparently, successive Chinese Secretaries reacted in such a way as to prevent them from using the Chinese despatches as models for their own. The standard of British despatches improved very little during the twenty-two years under review.

It is to be expected, therefore, that instances of more serious misunderstanding would occur. On 9 April 1849, Sir George Bonham drafted a despatch to Hsü Kuang-chin in which he said that 'the question [i.e. Canton city question] at issue rests where it was and must remain in abeyance.'[3] Historians have always been anxious to find out the exact Chinese characters used by the Chinese Secretary in his translation, because subsequent Chinese circulars in Canton alleged that Bonham had pledged he would never enter the city ['yung puh juh ch'ing 永不入城'].[4] Indeed, Lord Palmerston reprimanded Bonham for having used the above English expression, 'I must observe with regard to the phrase in your letter of the 9th April, 1848, "the question rests where it was, and must remain in abeyance", that

---

[1] F.O. 682/677/26, Bonham to Hsü Kuang-chin, 25 Jun 1849.

[2] F.O. 682/1982/28, Hsü Kuang-chin to Bonham, 2 Jul 1849.

[3] F.O. 17/154, Bonham - Palmerston, Desp 45, Encl., Bonham to Hsü Kuang-chin, 9 Apr 1849.

[4] Chinese Repository, 18 (1849) 224, quoted in Huang Yen-yü, 'Viceroy Yeh Ming-ch'en and the Canton Episode (1856-1861), Harvard Journal of Asiatic Studies, 6 (1941).

though the meaning of that phrase is sufficiently intelligible to an English reader, it might, without much straining, be made, by translation into a foreign language, to bear the meaning which the Chinese have attached to it; namely, that Her Majesty's Government has entirely abandoned all discussions connected with their right of entry into the city of Canton'.[1]

It is indeed fortunate that the Chinese Secretary kept a copy of the despatch, and that the copy has survived, albeit in very bad condition. Apparently, the key sentence in the translation was not the one quoted above, but the sentence which immediately followed it, viz., 'The discussion of it cannot, at present, be farther prosecuted between Your Excellency and myself'.[2] When this sentence was translated, the expression pu-te pien-lun 不得辯論 [3] [must not discuss] was used. Small wonder that Hsü Kuang-chin took it to mean that Bonham had dropped the question altogether. Hsü Kuang-chin and his successor, Yeh Ming-ch'en, continued to use the Chinese version of Bonham's despatch to deny British entry into the city of Canton. So much frustration was generated among British authorities that in 1856 an entirely unrelated event, the so-called Arrow incident,[4] was used to demand entry into the city.[5] When Yeh Ming-ch'en

_____

[1] F.O. 17/164, Palmerston to Bonham, 8 Oct 1850.

[2] F.O. 17/154, Bonham - Palmerston, Desp 45, Encl., Bonham to Hsü Kuang-chin, 9 Apr 1849.

[3] F.O. 682/1982/20, Bonham to Hsü Kuang-chin, 9 Apr 1849.

[4] For a detailed account and assessment of the Arrow incident, see J.Y. Wong, 'The Arrow Incident: A re-appraisal', Modern Asian Studies, 8, no. 3 (1974), pp. 373-89.

[5] See J.Y. Wong, 'Sir John Bowring and the Canton City Question', Bulletin of the John Rylands University Library of Manchester, 56, no. 3 (1973), pp. 219-45.

still refused to open the city gates, Admiral Sir Michael Seymour ordered his gunboats in the Canton River to bombard Yeh's *yamen*.[1] But even Seymour had to acknowledge the mistake made by Bonham's Chinese Secretary. Replying to Yeh's reference to Bonham's famous despatch of 9 April 1849, Seymour had to resort to saying that his demand to enter the city was 'not related in any way to previous agreements and promises'.[2]

Historians have attributed the difficulties surrounding the Canton city question either to the obstinacy of the mandarins, or to the unruliness of the Cantonese populace, or both. The contribution made by the Chinese Secretary's Office has so far escaped attention.

In the end, Lord Elgin's interpreters had their revenge on the high mandarins. T.F. Wade had been Chinese Secretary since 1855, and H.N. Lay was one time supernumerary interpreter in the Chinese Secretary's Office.[3] Both were recruited by Elgin as interpreters. On 9 June 1858 they visited Commissioner Ch'i-ying who had just arrived at Tientsin from Peking the day before. Ch'i-ying recalled his friendly relations with the British authorities during his years as Imperial Commissioner for Foreign Affairs at Canton. Abruptly, H.N. Lay produced a copy of a memorial which Ch'i-ying had written to the Emperor towards the end of 1850, and

---

[1] *F.O. 230/74, Seymour to Yeh Ming-ch'en, 30 Oct 1856.*
[2] *Ibid., 1 Nov 1856.*
[3] *J.J. Gerson. Horatio Nelson Lay and Sino-British Relations, 1854-1864. (Camb., Mass., 1972), pp. 22-23, 70-78.*

in which Ch'i-ying explained that he had only been friendly with the
British authorities in an attempt to 'keep the barbarians in hand'.[1]
Ch'i-ying hastily excused himself, leaving the other two Imperial
Commissioners Kuei-liang and Hua-sha-na to see off the guests.   The
Emperor commanded Ch'i-ying to 'put an end to himself'.[2] The other
two Imperial Commissioners must have wondered whether, in fact, they
were more fortunate than Ch'i-ying to have survived: in all
subsequent negotiations for a peace settlement, they were not met by
the British and French Plenipotentiaries but only by the interpreters.
From all accounts, 'Mr Lay had a temper; and being the mouthpiece of
a conquering power imposing terms on a defeated nation, he gave free
play to his natural disposition and assumed a domineering tone
designed to beat down Chinese opposition by force of vehemence rather
than of argument'.[3] The difficulties experienced by the Imperial
Commissioners were surely compounded by the fact that H.N. Lay's
command of the Chinese language was apparently not adequate.   In 1854
Sir John Bowring went to Shanghai and sought an   interview with
Viceroy I-liang of Liang-Chiang.   In the absence of the Chinese
Secretary, W.H. Medhurst, whom Bowring had sent to Tientsin for
negotiations,[4] H.N. Lay translated Bowring's despatch to I-liang.
The Chinese version, alas, could only be described as a flat refusal

---

[1]L. Oliphant. *Elgin's Mission to China and Japan*. *(London, 1860)*,
p. 366.
[2]*North China Herald*, 3 Oct 1858.
[3]*H.B. Morse*. *The International Relations of the Chinese Empire*.
Vol. 1, *(Shanghai, 1910)*, p. 522.
[4]*J.J. Gerson*. *Horatio Nelson Lay*. p. 38.

to see the Viceroy.[1] The high mandarin must have been greatly intrigued by the foreign devil who wrote to reject an interview which he had never granted.

One is reminded of the English translations of official despatches from Russia in the sixteenth and seventeenth centuries, made to their own advantage by British merchants who had traded in that country.[2] The Chinese Secretaries and interpreters did not have similar motives. Perhaps the mistranslations in the negotiations between the British and Japanese in the nineteenth century are closer analogies.[3] At any rate, one must remember that the Chinese Secretary's Office at this time was still young, and the difficulties it encountered were enormous.

The Entry-Books and the Registers

The entry-books and the registers also reflect the immaturity of the Chinese Secretary's Office which prepared them.

There are three entry-books relevant to the period under review, all of them deposited in the Public Record Office in London.[4] The first is classified as F.O. 677/26; the second and third as F.O. 230/74 and F.O. 230/75 respectively.

F.O. 677/26 contains copies of the despatches sent to the

---

[1] F.O. 682/1987/39, Bowring to I-liang, 10 Jul 1854.

[2] I am grateful to Mr N. Evans, Principal Assistant Keeper of the Public Record Office in London, for this information.

[3] I am grateful to Professor W.G. Beasley of the School of Oriental and African Studies, University of London, for this information.

[4] It appears that after Thomas Wade became Chinese Secretary in 1855, he had some of the in-coming despatches of 1841-50 copied selectively, and the copies bound into nine volumes, for his own use. These volumes were not entry-books of the time. They are now deposited in the University Library at Cambridge as part of the Wade Collection, and classified as F80-F88.

Chinese authorities as well as those received from them.[1] In other

words, the in-coming despatches and out-going despatches were copied

into the entry-book each time a document was sent or received. This

entry-book covered the years 1848 to 1851.

The second and third entry-books are sister works. F.O. 230/74

contains copies of the out-going despatches of the years from 1852

to 1862, the date of the last despatch being 22 December 1862.

F.O. 230/75 consists of copies of the in-coming despatches of the

years 1852 to 1862. The date of the last despatch is missing but

that of the last but one is 10 February 1862.

One obvious difference between the two sets of entry-books is

the separation of in-coming and out-going despatches in the second

set. This may be regarded as an improvement in the working of the

Chinese Secretary's Office. The other difference is that the second

set contains copies of letters as well as despatches. Here, a few

words about the technical names used in this volume will be in order.

Despatches, or *chao-hui* 照 會 in Chinese, were the official

communications. The term *chao-hui* 照 會 was agreed upon in the

Treaty of Nanking. As the British and Chinese authorities had been

communicating with each other in Chinese, and expected to continue

doing the same, the Chinese terminology was the crucial one. The

English equivalent mentioned in the Treaty was 'communication',

which was never used. In any case, it was standard British practice

---

[1] *It also contains miscellaneous papers such as* shang-yü 上諭 [impérial
decrees], tsou-che 奏摺 [memorials to the Emperor], and
despatches (also in Chinese) from H.M. Plenipotentiary to the
authorities in Japan, Annam, and Liu-ch'iu.

to call such official communications 'despatches', which is the term
used in this volume.

Hsin 信 , or letter, is here used not as a result of a formal
agreement between the British and Chinese authorities at the time.
Indeed, it was not the character *hsin* 信   but its variants *han*
函 [1] and *shih* 示 [2] that appeared in the letters themselves. As
the Chinese Secretary's Office gradually standardised its usage of
technical terms in later years, the character *hsin* 信   was adopted;[3]
hence its use in this volume. A letter in this period was an informal means of communication, was seldom signed, but was always
accompanied by the writer's calling-card. The earliest letter extant
appears to be one written at Shanghai jointly by Governor
Chi-erh-hang-a and Intendant Wu Chien-chang to Sir John Bowring. In
this letter, they endorsed Bowring's draft terms of an agreement in
which Bowring had apparently offered to persuade the rebels to
evacuate the city of Shanghai in return for the public pardon of two
of the rebel leaders.[4] Neutrality was the official British policy
in China. Bowring's action directly contravened this policy. One
could easily understand why he wanted the communications about this
matter to take the form of informal letters. Indeed, the letter in

---

[1]*F.O. 682/1991/119c, Kuei-liang et al. to Elgin, 18 Oct 1858, and
F.O. 682/1993/55b, Prince I and Mu-yin to Elgin, n.d. [1860].*

[2]*F.O. 682/1988/6b, Chi-erh-hang-a and Wu Chien-chang to Bowring,
15 Feb 1855.*

[3]*F.O. 937/6,   Register of in-coming letters, 1865-1871, and
F.O. 932/7,   Register of out-going letters, 1865-1871.*

[4]*F.O. 682/1988/6b, Chi-erh-hang-a and Wu Chien-chang to Bowring,
15 Feb 1855.*

question was not recorded in the entry-book F.O. 230/75. It was an oversight on his part to have left the letter in the Chinese Secretary's Office. Other letters were recorded, but they were mainly about courtesy visits made to each other by the British and Chinese authorities. As a matter of interest, it should be noted that at Canton, throughout this period, appointments for meetings appear to have been made in official despatches.

Besides the entry-books, there were also the registers. Registers were obviously intended as a means of quick reference and of logging documents instead of keeping copies of them. But like the entry-books, they offer some information as regards the gradual sophistication of the Chinese Secretary's Office. One of the registers recorded that all the out-going despatches of 1849 were either *mi-lan pu-ch'üan* 糜 爛 不 全 [incomplete due to decay] or simply *mi-lan* 糜 爛 [reduced to a pulp]. The section for the year 1850 was left entirely blank.[1] All the in-coming and out-going despatches for 1850 had possibly suffered the same fate. It is remarkable, therefore, that I should have come upon three in-coming despatches of that year. The section for the out-going despatches of 1856 was also a complete blank.[2] If a despatch had been register- ed each time it was sent or received, one would not expect the above comments and blanks. Obviously, some of the registers were compiled retrospectively; but when?

There are two sets of registers pertinent to this period. They

---

[1] *F.O. 932/1, Register of in-coming and out-going despatches, 1840-1856.*
[2] *Idem.*

are both deposited in the Public Record Office in London. The first set is classified as F.O. 932/1. It consists of two volumes, one being the register of in-coming despatches for the year 1840 to 1856, and the other being the register of out-going despatches intended for the same period. The titles given to these two registers are revealing. They are called *Chiu lai-wen mu* 舊來文目 [Old Register of In-coming Despatches] and *Chiu ch'ü-wen mu* 舊去文目 [Old Register of Out-going Despatches].[1]

The next set of registers does not have Chinese titles, only Chinese dates and Gregorian dates written in Chinese script. But they *do* have very prominent English titles, although their contents continue to be in Chinese. F.O. 932/3 bears its original title of *Register Despatches Sent, 1857-1864*. F.O. 932/2 bears its original title of *Register Despatches Received, 1857-1864*. In addition, the entries in these two registers are in a numerical sequence within a given year, such as *Ti-i-hao* 第一號 [Despatch No. 1] *Ti-erh-hao* 第二號 [Despatch No. 2] and the like, of the year 1857. Similar numbers are not to be found in the first set of registers which covers the period 1840-1856. Furthermore, the second set of registers does not contain comments about certain documents having decayed; nor does it have conspicuous blanks.

---

[1]*F.O. 932/1. These registers also bear an English title, namely, Register Letters Sent and Received, 1840-55. This title is misleading in two ways. Firstly, the registers do not stop at 1855, but at 1856. Secondly, 'letters' is technically a wrong word to use because the registers have logged despatches. One may attribute these to the lack of professionalism on the part of whomsoever was responsible for penning such a title.*

Comparing the two sets of registers, one may wonder if the
first set was compiled retrospectively in 1857, and if the Chinese
Secretary began logging the documents each time a despatch was
received or sent, from 1857 onwards. But, as mentioned before,
there is a complete blank in the register for the out-going despatches
of the previous year. It would have been too soon for the despatches
to be 'reduced to a pulp'[1] or to be lost. Therefore, although one
might conclude that the first set of registers was compiled retrospectively, it would be difficult to conclude that it was so
compiled in 1857.

One's thoughts naturally turn to the second set of registers,
which covers the period 1857 to 1864. At the beginning of the
register for in-coming despatches, there is an interesting piece of
evidence. It is a list of the total number of despatches received
each year during the period 1857 to 1867, with some annotations.
One will observe that, although this register ends in 1864, it offers
information up to the end of 1867. This may be taken as an
indication that even the second set of registers was compiled
retrospectively. This theory is supported by two other pieces of
evidence. The annotation for 1860 reads, *nei ch'üeh i-chih-shih
chien* 内缺一至十件 [one to ten despatches this year are
missing].[2] In the sister register, for out-going despatches 1857 to
1864, there is also an interesting annotation. It reads, *'ch'ien
wu-shih hao* 欠五十號 ...*ch'ien liu-shih-pa hao* 欠六十八號

---

[1] F.O. 932/1, *Register of in-coming and out-going despatches, 1840-1856.*
[2] F.O. 932/2, *Register of in-coming despatches, 1857-1864.*

.... [Despatch No. 50 is missing ....Despatch No. 68 is missing...].[1]

Although the date of this annotation is not specified, it clearly

falls within the period 1857 to 1864.

Thus, one may assume that the two sets of registers relevant to

this volume were both compiled retrospectively, possibly in 1868.

It is less likely that they were compiled much later than 1868 because

in 1865, a new set of registers for the despatches, as well as the

first set of registers for the letters, was started.[2] This suggests

that the Chinese Secretary's Office had become quite professional in

the keeping of its records by the mid-1860s. The question remains,

however, as to why the first set of registers has the character *chiu*

舊 [old] in its title whereas the second one does not, especially

if both were compiled retrospectively at different times. Perhaps

it was because the entries in the second set were numbered in sequence,

which was a *new* way of compiling registers. As regards the decay or

possible loss of some of the documents, it should be remembered that

the British Legation was established in Peking towards the end of

1860 and the Chinese Secretary's Office was moved there from Hong

Kong. Some of the papers could have become wet or lost during the

removal. In addition, it is likely that the Chinese Secretary had

far more important matters to attend to in the new situation than

the inspection of old and possibly irrelevant papers. Perhaps, he

did not even open the parcels packed in Hong Kong for a good many

---

[1]*F.O. 932/3, Register of out-going despatches, 1857-1864.*

[2]*F.O. 932/4, Register of in-coming despatches, 1865-1871;*
F.O. 932/5, Register of out-going despatches, 1865-1871;
F.O. 932/6, Register of in-coming letters, 1865-1871;
F.O. 932/7, Register of out-going letters, 1865-1871.

years. When at last he did, some of them would surely have been 'reduced to pulp', which probably prompted him to have registers compiled of those which had survived.

Physical Description of the Documents

With a few exceptions, the despatches were written on a long piece of Chinese paper stretching from right to left but folded in a concertina manner for easy handling. Thus one fold would have two pages, and about two and a half pages might go into a frame of microfilm. In a particularly lengthy document, two or sometimes three such pieces of paper were joined with glue and the official stamp[1] of the writer was used to make an impression across the join. When folded, a despatch chosen at random measured 25 cm long and 11 cm wide. Generally speaking an in-coming despatch was slightly longer and wider than an out-going despatch. The number of columns of Chinese characters on each page was, however, the same for both in-coming and out-going despatches, viz., five. So was the number of Chinese characters in each column, viz., twenty-three. When the Chinese characters meaning 'country', 'royal', 'imperial' and the like were used, a new column was started and the characters elevated by two spaces, augmenting the number of characters in that column by two. When the Chinese Emperor or the British Sovereign was mentioned, the characters were elevated by three spaces. The scribes of the Chinese officials, however, did not always pay the British

---

[1] *Strictly speaking, the Chinese mandarins used their official stamps (or seals), and H.M. Plenipotentiaries their private coats of arms. See explanation later.*

authorities the respect that was their due, causing endless complaints, the return of the despatches for corrections, and sometimes the sacking of the scribes in question.[1]

The columns were written vertically, from right to left, and on one side of the paper only. An enclosure was usually attached to the reverse side of the paper towards the end of the despatch. The first page of the concertina-folded paper was in effect the front cover of the document. In the centre of the upper half of this front cover were written or stamped the characters *chao-hui* 照 會 [a despatch]. An impression of what was understood to be the official seal of the writer was made in the same position over the characters *chao-hui* 照 會 , the same impression as those made across the joins of documents mentioned earlier. It was standard Chinese practice for the mandarins to make the impressions of their official seals on their documents. The equivalent British practice was for the bureaucrats to sign their papers. Successive British Plenipotentiaries tried to conform to the Chinese usage by making impressions of their own coats of arms on the despatches. In 1852, Dr John Bowring, who was Acting Plenipotentiary in the absence of Sir George Bonham, asked the Foreign Office for some money to make an official seal in the Chinese fashion for the office of Her Majesty's Plenipotentiary in the Far East.[2] His request was rejected on the ground of economy.[3] Consequently, successive Plenipotentiaries

---

1
  See the entry entitled 'format' in the Index-Glossary for references to the numerous cases of dispute.

2
  F.O. 228/133, Bowring to Malmesbury, 19 May 1852. I am grateful to Mr P.D. Coates for this reference and the one in the next note.

3
  F.O. 228/138, Malmesbury to Bowring, 21 Jul 1852.

continued to use their coats of arms. In 1854, Dr John Bowring became 'Sir John', and H.M. Plenipotentiary. He then attempted to change the practice of using seals by sending a signed despatch in English to Commissioner Yeh Ming-ch'en. The English text was accompanied by a Chinese translation, written on the usual folded paper, but not bearing his coat of arms. In his reply, Commissioner Yeh completely ignored the English text bearing Bowring's signature. He regarded the Chinese translation as the substantive document, and took pains to point out that Bowring had forgotten to put his official stamp on the despatch.[1] Bowring explained that he was only following British practice. Nonetheless, he agreed to send his Chinese Secretary, Mr W.H. Medhurst, to Canton with the 'seal' to make amends.[2]

Apart from the characters *chao-hui* 照 會 , which was the title of the document, and the stamp, which made it official, there was a third aspect about the front cover worthy of note. Very often, there was a docket glued to it. A docket almost always bore an Arabic numeral, and usually but not invariably a summary in English of the content of the document. This was obviously penned by the Chinese Secretary. Some of the numerals bore suffixes 'a' and 'b', such as those in this volume. Others were crossed out and replaced by new ones. A Chinese numeral might be found on the front cover, too, though seldom on the docket. It was always written with a brush and ink, undoubtedly by a Chinese scribe. This Chinese numeral

---

[1] *F.O. 682/1987/18, Yeh Ming-ch'en to Bowring, 7 May 1854. See also next note.*

[2] *F.O. 682/1987/21, Bowring to Yeh Ming-ch'en, 9 May 1854.*

did not necessarily tally with the Arabic numeral penned by the
Chinese Secretary. As far as one can judge, much of this confusion
occurred in the despatches dated before 1857. Small wonder that the
registers, compiled retrospectively, for the period 1840 to 1856,
contained entries that did not have a numerical sequence.

As for the English summaries in the dockets, some of them were
informative. One despatch, for example, referred to a certain
san-wei-kan yang-ch'uan 三桅杆洋船 [foreign ship with three masts].
The docket gave the name of the ship as Gevant Packet.[1] Another
despatch referred to a foreign ship called Ta-wei 大威 . Historians
who had experienced much frustration while using Chinese books which
contained transliterations of English proper names only but not the
English originals would really appreciate the docket which gave the
name of the ship as HMS Driver.[2] Again, despatches that alluded to
pai-t'ou-jen 白頭人 [white head man] and hei-jen 黑人 [black man]
did not make much sense without the dockets which revealed them as
Parsee[3] and lascar.[4] However, a docket with a summary such as 'Reply
to despatch no. 35' would be a different story. Indeed, given the
splendid state of confusion in which one found the numerical
sequence of the despatches, one wondered whether such a summary would

---

[1] F.O. 682/1976/117, Ch'i-ying to Pottinger, 25 Sep 1843.
[2] F.O. 682/1978/19, Davis to Ch'i-ying, 17 Apr 1843.
[3] F.O. 682/1982/3, Hsü Kuang-chin to Bonham, 11 Jan 1849.
[4] F.O. 682/1974/22, C. Elliot to Ch'i-shan, 16 Jan 1841.

have helped the Chinese Secretary himself.[1] Worse still, some
dockets appeared to have fallen off the despatches because the glue
had aged, and somebody in the Chinese Secretary's Office took it
upon himself to glue them back to the documents. Alas, the summaries
in the dockets did not always tally with the actual contents of the
despatches. Subsequently, somebody else in the same office discovered some of these mistakes, crossed out the dockets, and pencilled new
summaries so hard on the front covers as to pierce the fragile
Chinese paper.

   As mentioned before, the first page of a despatch, folded in a
concertina manner, constituted the front cover of the document. The
second page was the place where the actual despatch began. On it, the
first column contained the complete title (i.e. the rank, decoration,
office &c) and surname (or the first syllable of the surname if he was
British, Manchu or Mongolian) of the writer. An example would be
illuminating. *Ta-Ying ch'in-feng ch'üan-ch'üan kung-shih ta-ch'en
tsung-li wu-kang Ying-shang mao-i shih-i tsung-tu Hsiang-kang teng-
ch'u shui-lu chün-wu nan-chüeh Pao* 大英欽奉全權公使大臣總
理五港茉商貿易事宜總督香港等處水陸軍務男爵包
[Her Great Britannic Majesty's Plenipotentiary, Superintendent of
Trade in the Five Ports, and Governor of Hong Kong, Baron Bowring].
Bowring was, of course, only a knight, not an aristocrat. Possibly,
he directed his Chinese Secretary to be deliberately liberal in the

---

[1]*It certainly does not seem to have helped Mr Sasaki Masaya* 佐々木正哉
*who felt desperate enough to give his own reference numbers, without
authority, to the despatches et al. which he copied in the Public
Record Office and subsequently published in a volume entitled
Ahen sensō go no Chū-Ei kōsō, shiryō kenkō* 鴉片戰爭後の中英抗爭資料稿
Tokyo, 1964.

translation of this part of his title in order to make it sound as impressive as that of the addressee, which was *Ta-Ch'ing ch'in-ch'ai ta-ch'en t'ai-tzu shao-pao ping-pu shang-shu Liang-Kuang tsung-tu pu-t'ang shih-hsi i-teng nan-chüeh Yeh* 大清欽差大臣太子少保兩部尚書兩廣總督部堂世襲一等男爵葉 [His Great Ch'ing Imperial Majesty's Commissioner, Junior Guardian of the Heir Apparent, Minister of War, Hereditary Baron of the First Class, Yeh Ming-ch'en]. Indeed, it was this title that concluded the despatch,[1] followed by the date of the document. As mentioned before, a despatch from the Chinese authorities bore the date in the Chinese lunar calendar only, while a despatch from the British authorities bore the date in the Gregorian calendar as well. The last page of the despatch was, in effect, the back cover of the document. It bore the official stamp of the writer as did the front cover.

The letters were far less formal. None of them bore official stamps or titles, but they were accompanied by the calling-cards of the writers. The addressees appear to have had a habit of throwing away the calling-cards on receipt of the letters, not knowing how often archivists of later years would have to tear their hair in an attempt to identify the letters as well as the writers and addressees. Besides, whereas a despatch normally bore the year, month and day as its official date, a letter, as a rule, bore only the month and day. A letter was always written on a piece of red paper, made in China. Consequently, a letter was sometimes referred to as a 'red note'. A piece of red paper of this kind usually measured 12.2 cm wide and

---

[1] *F.O. 682/1987/74, Bowring to Yeh Ming-ch'en, 23 Dec 1854.*

25 cm long. One might say that a letter was not designed to be
lengthy; it seldom went on to a second piece of red paper.
Searchers who dreaded the cost of photocopying documents obviously
thought that the brevity of the letters was good news, until they
found out that black Chinese ink on red Chinese paper often produced
only dark blank pages on photocopying machines.

The Mechanics of Cataloguing

If the papers of the Chinese Secretary's Office had arrived at
the Public Record Office in their original order, or simply as one
collection, the task of cataloguing would have been less time-
consuming and the result more satisfactory. As it was, the papers
were mixed with thousands of other papers accumulated over a period
of more than a hundred years. With the benefit of hindsight, one
could argue that it would have been better for the archivist to go
through all the Chinese papers in the Public Record Office, separate
the diplomatic correspondence from the rest, arrange the diplomatic
correspondence in chronological order, read it from beginning to end
to acquire an overall picture, and then begin to summarise individual
documents. I would be the first to agree that ideally this would
have been the best approach. But there were practical difficulties.
As mentioned before, until *all* the Chinese papers in the Public
Record Office were identified, it would not be possible to say with
certainty which was which. Even if it were possible to separate the
diplomatic correspondence from the rest, to do so would mean putting the
diplomatic correspondence out of circulation while it was being
properly catalogued. This would not have been in the interest of
the public, particularly as the process of cataloguing turned out to

be a protracted struggle which took over ten years to conclude.[1] By
coincidence, Dr D. Pong, who has prepared a similar piece of work
for another section of the Chinese papers, also appears to have spent
ten years on his project.[2] Mr P.D. Coates is the third person now
engaged in dealing with yet another section. It is to be hoped that
slowly but surely, comprehensive guides will eventually be provided
for all the Chinese papers.

Since it was not possible to have the luxury of all the pertinent
documents in front of me for the purpose of cataloguing, I could only
rely on whatever clues were available to locate them, and prepare a
summary each time a document was found. In 1962, and in the space of
less than ten days, the late Professor Chang Hsin-pao 張歆保 and
Mr Eric Grinstead jointly compiled a preliminary list of *all* the
Chinese papers in the Public Record Office,[3] in most cases copying
the title on the wrapping paper of each bundle of documents. I
depended on this list for much of my information (and misinformation).
The alternative was to search the bundles one by one, which I did
subsequently, more than once, when I had exhausted the information
in the Chang-Grinstead list. Mr P.D. Coates, who began working on

---

[1] *This project started in 1972.*

[2] *D. Pong. A Critical Guide to the Kwangtung Provincial Archives
Deposited at the Public Record Office of London. Camb., Mass., 1975.*

[3] *See their article, entitled 'Chinese Documents of the British
Embassy in Peking, 1793-1911', in Journal of Asian Studies, Vol. 22,
no. 3 (1963), pp. 354-6. In fact, the Chinese papers go beyond the
year 1911. The article stopped in 1911, possibly because it was
written in 1962 and the fifty-year rule still applied in the United
Kingdom at that time.*

[4] *On page 44 of that list, for example, where one would expect to find
all the despatches of 1842, there were only five entries. In fact
there were almost two hundred despatches for that year, dispersed in
numerous boxes.*

the Chinese papers in 1978, also provided valuable information in
the course of his work. Mr Coates had worked in the Chinese
Secretary's Office in the 1940s and consequently was able to offer
much insight into the manner in which that institution functioned.

The fact that a summary was made on a card each time a document
was found, instead of having all the pertinent documents to hand and
reading them chronologically from beginning to end before summarising them, meant that the summaries could have been made out of
context. When the cards were subsequently re-arranged in a
chronological order, every attempt was made to provide a sense of
continuity by editing the summaries. But editing the summaries was
not the same as summarising directly from documents which had
already been arranged in a chronological order.

The Chinese bureaucratic practice had been to refer to a
certain official by his title or position, followed by his surname
only. The British diplomats had conformed to this practice. As
far as possible, therefore, I tried to find out the true identity
of the official, to spell out his name in full in the summary, and
to provide the Chinese characters in the Glossary-Index. The
Wade-Giles system of romanisation was used because back in 1972,
when the first summaries were made, this system, whatever its faults,
was very much in currency.

Format of Entries in the Calendar

The present text has six columns.

The first column contains the new reference number given to each
document. Unless otherwise specified, a document may be requisitioned
only by this number.

The second column gives the Gregorian date of the document, arranged in the order of year, month and day.. The third column gives the lunar date arranged in the same order. Despatches from the British authorities usually contain both Gregorian and lunar dates. Despatches from their Chinese counterparts contain only lunar dates, which are hereby converted into Gregorian dates. Square brackets are used in both columns to indicate what, in my opinion, the correct date of the document should be. Three more symbols are used in the third column. TK stands for Tao-kuang, HF for Hsien-feng, and i for intercalary month. Thus TK19 stands for the nineteenth year of Emperor Tao-kuang's reign, and HF1 stands for the first year of Emperor Hsien-feng's reign. An intercalary month is a month inserted in the calendar to make the calendar year correspond to the Chinese lunar year. This is done by repeating a certain month of the year. Thus, i3 is a repetition of the third month of the year. During the period under review, an intercalary month occurred in the years TK21, TK23, TK26, TK29, HF1, HF4, HF7 and HF10, which correspond roughly to the years 1841, 1843, 1846, 1849, 1851, 1854, 1857 and 1860. It appears that the British and Chinese bureaucrats were industrious enough to have written some despatches during the intercalary months of all these years except HF1 and HF7.

The fourth column contains the summaries of the documents. The Wade-Giles system of romanisation is used, except for well-known Post Office spellings such as Kwangtung, Canton, Nanking and Peking. In addition, words such as plenipotentiary, imperial commissioner and magistrate, which normally appear in the lower case, are here put in the upper case, if only to give some idea of the importance attached to such positions by the diplomats of the time, particularly the British. The titles and positions of Chinese officials are rendered into English according to the examples set by *Present Day Political Organisation of China*, written jointly by H.S. Brunnert and V.V. Hagelstrom, and translated jointly by A. Beltchenko and E.E. Morgan. This standard work was first published in 1911 and reprinted in Taiwan in 1963. To economise on space, articles are generally omitted in the summaries.

The fifth column gives the length of the document in pages. Generally speaking, one and a half pages may fit into a frame of microfilm.

The last column is the old reference of the document. Unless otherwise specified, the old references should not be used for the purpose of requisition.

A summary of this format of entries is provided on a separate page for quick reference.

For the benefit of those who have used the documents before they were properly catalogued, cross-references are provided at the end of this volume. In addition, a list of dates at which successive British Plenipotentiaries and Chinese Imperial Commissioners took office has also been provided to assist searchers. The Index-Glossary was prepared at the same time that the documents were summarised Since it was not possible to know the exact *new* references of the documents at that early stage, the dates of the documents, the only constant factor, were used as guides. Searchers using the Index-Glossary *must* remember that these dates are *guides* to the documents, not the actual *dates*

at which events occurred. The Chinese characters in the Index-
Glossary have been copied from the documents, reflecting the
degree of sophistication (or lack of it) of the writers. Not
all the entries have Chinese characters. For example, *Thency*,
the name of a ship, appears in the docket but not in
transliteration in the document itself. Consequently, it has
no Chinese characters. When I provide an entry of my own,
such as the famous word 'insults', I sometimes give what I
think is a fair Chinese translation, in square brackets.

I am, by training, an historian, not an archivist or editor.
By an historical accident, I was called upon to catalogue the
documents mentioned above, and to prepare a camera-ready typescript
for publication. It has been a beneficial and humbling experience.
In particular, marking the documents in pencil, transcribing the
same reference numbers onto acid-free envelopes, and then putting
the documents judiciously into their respective envelopes, as I
did for much of the year 1980,[1] inspired boundless respect in me
for the archivists who spend their lifetime making it possible
for other scholars to do their research. The mechanical and
time-consuming task of preparing a camera-ready typescript makes
one realise how much authors are indebted to professional editors.

Sydney
3 February 1983   J. Y. *Wong*

---

[1] *Just before this volume went to press, Mr D.K.Y. Kwan
spent December 1982 and January 1983 meticulously checking
the documents and the envelopes to make sure that everything
was in order. To him I offer my most grateful thanks.*

SUCCESSIVE BRITISH PLENIPOTENTIARIES AND[1]
CHINESE IMPERIAL COMMISSIONERS
1839-1860

Dates	Plenipotentiaries	Imperial Commissioners
5 Mar 1839	Captain Charles Elliot, RN [Superintendent of trade]	
12 Apr 1839		Lin Tse-hsü
20 Feb 1840	Rear-Admiral Sir George Elliot	
2 Jan 1841	Captain Charles Elliot, RN	Ch'i-shan
27 Jun 1842	Sir Henry Pottinger	
4 Aug 1842		Ch'i-ying & I-li-pu Joint Commissioners
5 Nov 1842		I-li-pu
23 Apr 1843		Ch'i-ying
8 May 1844	Sir John Davis	
28 Feb 1848		Hsü Kuang-chin Acting Commissioner
28 Mar 1848	Sir George Bonham	
4 Jul 1849		Hsü Kuang-chin
31 Jul 1851		Yeh Ming-ch'en Acting Commissioner
29 Mar 1852	Dr John Bowring Acting Plenipotentiary	
28 Feb 1853	Sir George Bonham [returned from leave]	

---

[1]This table is arranged in the order of the pertinent names appearing for the first time in the despatches.

Dates	*Plenipotentiaries*	*Imperial Commissioners*
25 Mar 1853		Yeh Ming-ch'en
17 Apr 1854	Sir John Bowring [formerly Dr John Bowring]	
17 Dec 1857	Lord Elgin	
3 Jun 1858		Kuei-liang & Hua-sha-na Joint Commissioners
14 Feb 1859		Ho Kuei-ch'ing [office formerly held concurrently by the Viceroy of Liang-Kuang but now held concurrently by the Viceroy of Liang-Chiang]
3 Mar 1859	Hon. Frederick Bruce	
6 Aug 1860	Lord Elgin	
25 Aug 1860		Kuei-liang & Heng-fu Joint Commissioners
10 Sep 1860		Prince I & Mu-yin Joint Commissioners
21 Sep 1860		Prince Kung
8 Nov 1860	Hon. Frederick Bruce	

NOTE ON THE FORMAT OF ENTRIES IN THE CALENDAR

The entries in the calendar provide the following information:

Column 1

The piece-number of the document in F.O. 682, as now re-arranged.

Some of the items summarised in the calendar exist only as copies in entry-books, which are classified as F.O. 677/26, F.O. 230/74, and F.O. 230/75. Summaries derived from these entry-books are not given a piece-number. Hence nothing is shown against them in this column. Instead, their provenance is indicated in square brackets in column 6.

Column 2

The date of the document according to the Gregorian calendar.

Column 3

The date according to the Chinese lunar calendar.

(a) The column heading indicates the year by reign-title (*nien-hao*) and serial number, making use of the following abbreviations:

TK   Tao-kuang
HF   Hsien-feng

(b) The entry in the column gives the number of the month and the day, in that order. In years in which an intercalary month was inserted in the calendar, this is indicated by the letter *i*, preceding the number of the appropriate month.

Column 4

Summary of the document or of the copy in the entry-book.

Column 5

The length of the Chinese text in pages.

Column 6

The former piece-number in F.O. 682, i.e. before re-arrangement of the material. Where the item is to be found in the entry-books, not in F.O. 682, this column gives the entry-book reference in square brackets.

[*NOTE. For additional information about the entries, see the final section of the Introduction.*]

F.O. 682/ 1972	Date 1839	TK 19	Description	pp	Old F F.O. 682/

NOTE: *For an explanation of the format of entries, see NOTE on p. 37*

/1a   n.d.   n.d.   Captain C. Elliot to Viceroy [Teng   1   116/2
     [Feb -] [01 -] T'ing-cheng] of Liang-Kuang. Has
                    heard that a British merchant has
                    been arrested. Asks that custody
                    of said merchant be transferred to
                    him. Guarantees to produce said
                    merchant for questioning by Chinese
                    authorities if necessary. Would
                    take full responsibility if said
                    merchant should escape from his
                    custody.

/1b   n.d.   n.d.   C. Elliot to Teng T'ing-cheng. Is   2   116/
     [Feb -] [01 -] disturbed to hear that execution
                    of a criminal will again take place
                    near factory area. Crowd of spect-
                    ators might   turn into a plunder-
                    ing mob. Besides, if the place of
                    execution were chosen with a view
                    to intimidating British subjects,
                    this would be tantamount to insult-
                    ing Britain which had done nothing
                    to offend China.

/1c   n.d.   n.d.   C. Elliot to Teng T'ing-cheng. Again   1   116/
     [Feb -] [01 -] requests that execution of criminal
                    does not take place near factory
                    area [incomplete].

/1d   Mar 5   01 20 C. Elliot to [Viceroy Teng T'ing-cheng 4   426/
                    of Liang-Kuang]. Execution of
                    criminal near factory area has great-
                    ly upset foreigners, who feel terribly
                    exposed. Requests that no further
                    executions be carried out in factory
                    area.

/2   Mar 25 02 11 Prefect Chu-erh-hang-a of Canton and 16 426/
                    Colonel Han of Canton Regiment to
                    C. Elliot. Transmit Viceroy Teng
                    T'ing-cheng's edict reiterating
                    Commissioner Lin Tse-hsü's
                    determination to besiege factory
                    area until all opium is surrender-
                    ed and wondering what Elliot means
                    when referring to "two countries"
                    as England is a tributary state.

/3   Mar 26 02 12 Chu-erh-hang-a *et al.* to C. Elliot. 20 426/
                    Transmit Lin Tse-hsü's edict:
                    rejects Elliot's request to let
                    Britons and their ships leave

Date		Description	pp	Old Ref.
				F.O.
1839	TK 19			692/

		Canton; condemns him for collaboration with opium smugglers and for having tried to escape from Canton with [Mr] Dent; demands speedy signing of bond pledging not to import any more opium.		
Mar 26	02 12	Chu-erh-hang-a *et al.* to C. Elliot. Transmit Lin Tse-hsü's edict: in response to Elliot's request, sent Chu-erh-hang-a *et al.* to meet him in factory area and Provincial Treasurer and Provincial Judge to wait for news in New City; is shocked to learn that they have been waiting from morn till night in vain. Condemns Elliot for having tried to escape with [Mr] Dent and for preventing British merchants from surrendering opium.	19	426/4
Mar 27	02 13	Chu-erh-hang-a to C. Elliot. Transmits Lin Tse-hsü's edict: is pleased to learn that Elliot is willing to surrender opium; orders him to make detailed account of all opium stock.	10	426/5
Mar 28	02 14	Chu-erh-hang-a to C. Elliot. Transmits Lin Tse-hsü's edict: accepts Elliot's figure of 20,283 chests of opium in stock and agrees to receive them in instalments as they come in. Will go with Viceroy [Teng T'ing-cheng] to Hu-men to supervise delivery of opium.	19	426/6
Mar 28	02 14	Chu-erh-hang-a to C. Elliot. Transmits Lin Tse-hsü's edict specifying manner in which opium is to be surrendered: (1) opium in factory area to be put outside buildings on 29 March; opium in Whampoa to be delivered on 30 March; (2) opium at Lintin to be delivered at Hu-men on 31 March and on 1 and 2 April; (3) British opium in Macao to be delivered at Sha-chiao; (4) opium clippers on high seas to be ordered to sail to Sha-chiao.	10	426/7
Apr 1	02 18	Chu-erh-hang-a to C. Elliot. Transmits Lin Tse-hsü's edict: rejects Elliot's request to send deputy to	10	426/8

F.O. 682/ 1972	Date 1839	TK 19	Description	pp	Old F F.O. 682/
			Lintin to acknowledge receipt of account of opium stock before delivery to Chinese authorities, as Elliot can order merchants to hand over account and stock to Chinese authorities directly.		
/9	Apr 5	02 22	Chu-erh-hang-a to C. Elliot. Transmits Lin Tse-hsü's edict: has sent officials to escort Elliot's deputy to go to Lintin and to lead opium hulks to place of opium delivery; Elliot must order merchants to sign opium bond.	10	426/
/10	Apr 8	02 25	Chu-erh-hang-a to C. Elliot. Transmits Lin Tse-hsü's edict: foreigners in China must obey Chinese law; opium bond must be signed.	20	426/
/11	Apr 12	02 29	Lin Tse-hsü and Teng T'ing-cheng to C. Elliot. Opium hulks may now come all at same time instead of in twos, as more ferries have been hired to receive opium at Hu-men.	5	426/
/12	Apr 13	02 30	Chu-erh-hang-a to C. Elliot. Transmits Governor I-liang's edict: rejects Mr Daniell's plea to go to Macao to look after his sick child, regarding this as attempt by Elliot to test out attitude of Chinese authorities towards siege of factories.	10	426/
/13	Apr 13	02 30	Chu-erh-hang-a to C. Elliot. Transmits edict by Lin Tse-hsü and Teng T'ing-cheng: they return letter which Elliot wrote to his deputy Johnston asking Johnston to wait for instructions if in doubt; such a letter would delay process of handing over opium at Hu-men. Foreign sailors in hulks are pleased with [Chinese] presents of cows and foodstuffs.	10	426/
/14	Apr 19	03 06	Lin Tse-hsü and Teng T'ing-cheng to C. Elliot. Condemn delay in delivery of opium at Hu-men; one hulk arrives with only 80 chests while its fresh water-mark shows that it has just unloaded some of its cargo; meanwhile Chinese opium	7	426,

. / 2	Date 1839	TK 19	Description	pp	Old Ref. F.O. 682/
			smugglers just captured admit having bought opium from hulks on 10 April.		
5	Apr 20	03 07	Lin Tse-hsü and Teng T'ing-cheng to C. Elliot. Johnston has written to Elliot proposing to stop delivery of opium after 10,000 chests unless he begins to see sampans ferrying foreigners from Canton. This is blackmail. Elliot must order Johnston to deliver all opium without delay.	9	426/15
6	Apr 21	03 08	Prefect Designate She Pao-shun to Johnston. Transmits Lin Tse-hsü's edict: has requested Canton authorities to allow foreigners to leave Canton after half of estimated opium stock has been surrendered. Would have done so even before this if only all opium hulks had arrived at Hu-men; there is evidence to show that delay in arrival of many hulks is caused by desperate attempt to sell stock; condemns Johnston for having had letter delivered directly to him rather than through Chinese merchants as required by regulation.	16	426/16
7	Apr 22	03 09	Lin Tse-hsü and Teng T'ing-cheng to C. Elliot. Will not release foreigners from Canton until all opium hulks [in Chinese waters] have reported at Hu-men. Condemn Johnston's attempt at blackmail. Encl. Edict ordering Johnston to get all opium hulks to Hu-men, n.d.	10 7 ff.	426/17
8a	Apr 22	03 09	Lin Tse-hsü's public notice. Has reversed earlier decision to release foreigners from Canton because of Johnston's attempt at blackmail. Now that Johnston refuses to let hulks unload any more opium, has decided not to receive opium and to return to Canton.	1 poster	426/18
8b	n.d. [Apr 27]	n.d. [03 14]	C. Elliot to Lin Tse-hsü and Teng T'ing-cheng. Has instructed Johnston to resume delivery of opium.	1	1438/2

F.O. 682/ 1972	Date 1839	TK 19	Description	pp	Old Re F.O. 682/
/19	May 4	03 21	Chu-erh-hang-a *et al.* to C. Elliot. Transmit edict by Lin Tse-hsü and Teng T'ing-cheng: as more hulks have come to surrender opium, foreigners in Canton will be allowed to leave except [Mr] Dent and fifteen others who are wanted for questioning.	14	426/19
			Encl. List of names of Dent and fifteen others, n.d.	2	
/20	May 4	03 21	She Pao-shun to Johnston. It is total number of chests of opium surrendered that counts, not number of hulks with small quantities of opium. Johnston must urge that all stocks in Nan-ao be delivered at Hu-men promptly.	11	426/20
/21a	May 8	03 25	Chu-erh-hang-a to C. Elliot. Transmits edict by Lin Tse-hsü and Teng T'ing-cheng: Englishman En-i-t'u [Endicott?], caught smuggling opium into Canton, has been expelled to Macao, where he has again been caught smuggling opium; demand that he be sent back to England.	13	426/21
/21b	May 9	03 26	Lin Tse-hsü and Teng T'ing-cheng to Cantonese merchants for James Matheson *et al.* Accuse Matheson *et al.* of being among most notorious opium smugglers, who should have been severely dealt with. Considering the fact that all opium has now been surrendered, Matheson *et al.* are hereby ordered only to leave China, but they must sign pledge never to return.	2	39/10
/22	May 9	03 26	Chu-erh-hang-a to C. Elliot. Transmits edict by Lin Tse-hsü and Teng T'ing-cheng: on basis of 17,000 chests of opium surrendered and on Elliot's guarantee that remaining 3,000 or so chests will arrive from Nan-ao within fifteen days, siege of factory was lifted; so far 3,000 chests are still wanting and deadline is set for end of month [Chinese month].	12	426/22
/23a	May 10	03 27	Chu-erh-hang-a to Superintendents of Trade from Britain, U.S.A. and Holland. Transmits joint edict by	10	426/2

.0. 82/ 972	Date 1839	TK 19	Description	pp	Old Ref. F.O. 682/
			Lin Tse-hsü, Teng T'ing-cheng and I-liang granting their request to leave for home, adding that they must do so for good. Anyone bringing opium in the future will be liable to the death penalty.		
/23b	May 12	03 29	Lin Tse-hsü and Teng T'ing-cheng to Cantonese merchants for James Matheson *et al.* Reject plea by Matheson *et al.* to delay departure from Canton. Again command them to sign pledge never to return once they have left China.	3	39/10/2
/24	May 12	03 29	Chu-erh-hang-a to C. Elliot. Transmits edict by Lin Tse-hsü and Teng T'ing-cheng: demand that Elliot reports on ship newly arrived from Ko-ssu-ta [Calcutta?].	7	426/24
/25	May 12	03 29	Chu-erh-hang-a to C. Elliot. Transmits edict by Lin Tse-hsü and Teng T'ing-cheng: En-i-t'u [Endicott?] must be sent back to England as soon as possible; Chinese authorities in Nan-ao reported seven foreign vessels raising anchor but only two have arrived at Hu-men; they have stayed at Hu-men for over one month and Johnston should go in person to urge their captains to go to Hu-men to surrender opium.	9	426/25
/26	May 12	03 29	She Pao-shun to Johnston. Transmits Lin Tse-hsü's edict: seven foreign vessels are reported to have left Nan-ao but only two have arrived at Hu-men; demands explanation; also demands report on vessel newly arrived from India.	11	426/26
/27.	May 13	04 01	Chu-erh-hang-a to C. Elliot. Transmits Lin Tse-hsü's edict: requires Elliot to state if clipper newly arrived from Indian subcontinent is under British or Portuguese protection.	10	426/27
/28	May 18	04 06	Joint edict by Lin Tse-hsü and Teng T'ing-cheng to Chinese merchants, forbidding them to trade with a certain U.S. vessel which has tried	7	426/28

F.O. 682/ 1972	Date 1839	TK 19	Description	pp	Old Re F.O. 682/
			to avoid being measured for tax purposes.		
/29	May 21	04 09	Chu-erh-hang-a to C. Elliot. Transmits edict by Lin Tse-hsü and Teng T'ing-cheng: foreign vessel *Chia-li-yin* claims that it has transferred its opium cargo to another vessel for surrender at Hu-men; require Elliot to report on opium still on board *Chia-li-yin*, or name of ship on which opium has been transferred and amount of opium subsequently surrendered at Hu-men.	8	426/29
/30	May 24	04 12	Chu-erh-hang-a to C. Elliot. Transmits Teng T'ing-cheng's edict: grants Elliot's request to leave Canton for Macao on grounds of ill health; commands him to see to illness quickly and to find out if foreigners in Macao have stocks of opium.	7	426/30
/31	May 26	04 14	Acting Sub-Magistrate Liu K'ai-yü of Fo-shan to C. Elliot. Transmits edict by Lin Tse-hsü and Teng T'ing-cheng: are pleased with Elliot's performance in surrender of opium; will write separately transmitting Imperial Edict of amnesty; all empty hulks will be rewarded with tea so that an alternative living may be found on returning home.	10	426/31
/32	May 26	04 14	Lin Tse-hsü *et al.* to C. Elliot. While opium was being surrendered, requested Emperor to pardon British opium dealers and to reward them with tea. Request was granted by Emperor and now that all 20,283 chests of opium are surrendered, will reward them with 1,640 chests of tea. Praise Elliot for having acted in interests of foreign merchants.	11	426/32
/33	Jun 1	04 20	Liu K'ai-yü to C. Elliot. Transmits edict by Lin Tse-hsü and Teng T'ing-cheng: are shocked to learn that British ships, ostensibly exercising their cannon, have damaged a Chinese war junk in three places; as Elliot is still	14	426/3

0. 2/ 72	Date 1839	TK 19	Description	pp	Old Ref. F.O. 682/

			in Canton and probably not expecting such an incident, they are reluctant to act except to require a report on the incident and the handing over of offenders.		
34	Jun 7	04 26	Liu K'ai-yü and Sub-Magistrate Chiang Li-ang of Macao to C. Elliot. Transmit Teng T'ing-cheng's edict: endorses Elliot's view that opium smugglers are damaging the cause of proper trade, and his proposal to lay down regulations to put legal trade on sound footing; will send official to Macao to discuss formulation of regulations with British and Portuguese authorities.	13	426/34
35	Jun 7	04 26	Liu K'ai-yü and Chiang Li-ang to C. Elliot. Transmit edict by Lin Tse-hsü and Teng T'ing-cheng: clippers wishing to load before leaving must come to Whampoa without delay and those not wishing to do so must leave Chinese waters immediately.	9	426/35
36	Jun 8	04 27	Liu K'ai-yü and Chiang Li-ang to C. Elliot. Transmit edict by Lin Tse-hsü and Teng T'ing-cheng: have formulated regulations to revive *pao-chia* system to stamp out opium in Macao but will be interested to know what proposals Elliot has in mind to achieve same goal.	10	426/36
37	Sep 20	08 13	Chiang Li-ang to C. Elliot. Re Elliot's request for amicable relations, transmits terms for peace from Lin Tse-hsü and Teng T'ing-cheng. [See next entry.]	7	426/37
38	Sep 20	n.d. [08 13]	[Lin Tse-hsü and Teng T'ing-cheng to C. Elliot]. Set out terms for peace: (1) opium newly arrived must all be destroyed; (2) murderer of Lin Wei-hsi must be handed over; (3) opium dealers must be sent back to England; (4) as Elliot claims he is waiting for instructions from home, he must specify when he may expect to receive such instructions.	11	426/38

F.O. 682/ 1972	Date 1839	TK 19	Description	pp	Old Re F.O. 682/
/39	Sep 28	08 21	Lin Tse-hsü and Teng T'ing-cheng to Chiang Li-ang for C. Elliot: (1) accept Elliot's opium bond but insist that following sentence be added: "henceforth any opium found will be confiscated and smuggler executed"; (2) give new deadline of ten days to hand over murderer of Lin Wei-hsi; (3) notorious opium dealers who have been expelled from Macao are given six days to return and pack up belongings; (4) traitors still in British service must be handed over.	30	426/39
/40	Oct 8	09 02	Lin Tse-hsü and Teng T'ing-cheng to C. Elliot: (1) reject Elliot's plea that exact wording of opium bond must wait for another three or four months; (2) extend deadline for handing over of murderer of Lin Wei-hsi for another ten days; (3) threaten to destroy any foreign vessel which is in Chinese waters without permission; (4) notorious opium dealers who have been expelled from Macao and are still in Chinese waters must be made to leave immediately.	24	426/40
/41	Oct 27	09 21	Lin Tse-hü and Teng T'ing-cheng to C. Elliot. Reject Elliot's suggestion to replace signing of opium bond with careful search of each vessel coming into port. Demand report on Britons who shot dead one Chinese (Li Hsiang-hsien), wounded three and cut hair of seven on 26 Sep 1839. As opium smuggling is again rampant with Hong Kong as a new centre of distribution they are preparing to attack British vessels gathered there.	26	426/41
/42	Nov 3	n.d. [09 28]	[Commander-in-Chief of marines Kuan T'ien-p'ei] to C. Elliot. Will not stop military action until murderer of Lin Wei-hsi is handed over.	4	426/43
/43	Dec 19	11 14	Colonel Li of Ch'eng-hai [Ch'ao-chou area] to C. Elliot. Transmits edict by Lin Tse-hsü and Teng	16	426/42

No.	Date		Description	pp	Old Ref.
2/					F.O.
72	1839	TK 19			682/

T'ing-cheng: reject Elliot's request to be allowed to live in Macao while waiting for instructions from home, as Elliot has refused to sign opium bond or to hand over murderers, has prevented foreign merchants from engaging in legal trade, and has fired on Chinese war junks.

F.O. 682/ 1973	Date 1840	TK 19	Description	pp	Old Re F.O. 682/
/1	Jan 1	11 27	Prefect Chu-erh-hang-a of Canton to Cantonese merchants for British merchants. If Chi-li-pu [Gribble] is proved innocent, he will be released in due course.	6	39/4
/2	Jan 6	12 02	Colonel Li of Ch'eng-hai to C. Elliot. Returns Elliot's second letter to Lin Tse-hsü and Teng T'ing-cheng as it is superfluous: if arrested Briton Chi-li-pu [Gribble] is innocent he will be released in due course.	7	483/2,
/3	Jan 9	12 05	Colonel Li of Ch'eng-hai to C. Elliot. Chi-li-pu's [Gribble's] letter forwarded to Elliot yesterday must have indicated date of his release; if not, Li himself does not know any more than Elliot does.	5	483/2,
/4	Jan 9	12 05	Colonel Li of Ch'eng-hai to C. Elliot. Transmits edict by Lin Tse-hsü and Teng T'ing-cheng: had ordered release of Gribble when Elliot's letter threatening military action unless Gribble was released was received; consequently they decided to continue to detain Gribble in order to show that on no account would they yield to blackmail.	13	483/2,
		TK 20			
/5	Aug 11	07 14	G. Elliot to Viceroy Ch'i-shan of Chihli. Has been appointed Joint Plenipotentiary with C. Elliot. Has attempted to deliver letter at Amoy to be forwarded to Peking but was fired upon by Chinese soldiers. Has again attempted to do so at Ningpo but Chinese authorities have refused to forward it. Is now in Peiho and hopes Ch'i-shan will forward it.	6	845
/6	Sep 13	08 18	Ch'i-shan to G. Elliot. Has transmitted Elliot's letter to Emperor. Commissioner Lin Tse-hsü will be heavily punished for ill-treatment of foreigners. Compensation for burning of opium is out of question. Britons can still reap huge profits through legal trade.	11	290/2

). :/ 73	Date 1840	TK 20	Description	pp	Old Ref. F.O. 682/
7	Sep 13	08 18	Ch'i-shan to G. Elliot. Reiterates that compensation for burning of opium is out of question. China is well prepared if Britain should decide to resort to arms. China wants nothing from Britain but Britain needs Chinese tea and rhubarb.	35	290/3
8	Oct 1	09 06	Viceroy I-li-pu of Liang-Chiang to G. Elliot. Two Britons are detained because one went inland surveying, and other disturbed civilians. Will release them if Elliot withdraws to Canton to negotiate with Ch'i-shan.	9	102

F.O. 682/ 1974	Date 1841	TK 20	Description	pp	Old Re F.O. 682/
/1	Jan 2	12 10	Commissioner Ch'i-shan to C. Elliot. In China, do what the Chinese do. Rejects all Elliot's demands.	22	867
/2	Jan 5	12 13	C. Elliot to Ch'i-shan. Dismissal of Commissioner Lin Tse-hsü *et al.* does not benefit Britain. Insists on equality of nations, payment of indemnity etc., or else will not agree to evacuate occupied areas.	12	886
/3	Jan 5	12 13	Commodore Sir Gordon Bremer to Ch'i-shan. Notifies resumption of war.	5	887
/4	Jan 8	12 16	Commander-in-Chief Kuan T'ien-p'ei to Bremer. Has forwarded letter to Ch'i-shan and should have his reply soon. Asks Bremer to withdraw from Sha-chiao and Ta-chiao.	8	866
/5	Jan 8	12 16	C. Elliot and Bremer to Kuan T'ien-p'ei. Set out terms for truce: (1) Sha-chiao, now under British occupation, remains under British control as a place where Britons may live and trade; (2) Canton be re-opened as a port but trade should henceforth be conducted at Sha-chiao; (3) customs duties be levied at Sha-chiao instead of Whampoa; (4) present programme to build new forts or re-arm existing forts be stopped; (5) previous agreement with Ch'i-shan about indemnity, opening of new ports and evacuation of British forces from Ting-hai etc. be honoured. Will resume war if there is no reply from Ch'i-shan within three days.	7	889
/6	Jan 8	12 16	Bremer to Kuan T'ien-p'ei. Has released prisoners of war taken yesterday. Explains some European rules of war.	6	888
/7	Jan 9	12 17	Ch'i-shan to C. Elliot. Protests about attack on Sha-chiao and Ta-chiao which was carried out without waiting for his reply.	10	865
/8	Jan 10	12 18	C. Elliot and Bremer to Kuan T'ien-pei. Ask Kuan to forward letter to Ch'i-shan. Will suspend hostilities while waiting for reply.	4	891

Date		Description	pp	Old Ref. F.O. 682/
1841	TK 20			
Jan 10	12 18	C. Elliot to Ch'i-shan. Has attacked because all demands were rejected.	9	890
Jan 10	12 18	Kuan T'ien-p'ei to C. Elliot and Bremer. Much time is needed for messages to travel between Hu-men and Canton: impossible to have Ch'i-shan's reply in three days.	6	864
Jan 11	12 19	Ch'i-shan to C. Elliot. Sha-chiao, where many Chinese soldiers have been slain, is an inauspicious place for Britons to live and trade; will forward British request for an island to the Emperor. Trade at Canton will resume when Ting-hai is returned.	10	863
Jan 11	12 19	C. Elliot to Ch'i-shan. Will take Hong Kong and Chien-sha-tsui [Kowloon] instead of Sha-chiao; if allowed Hong Kong and Kowloon, will waive demand for other ports for trade. Canton must be re-opened before evacuation of Ting-hai.	9	925
Jan 11	12 19	Bremer to Kuan T'ien-p'ei. Kuan should stop all preparations for war during truce; promises not to attack unless provoked.	4	892
Jan 11	12 19	Kuan T'ien-p'ei to Bremer. Will order remaining troops to strike their tents.	6	862
Jan 13	12 21	Bremer to Kuan T'ien-p'ei. Demands a comment within two hours on reports that forts have been re-inforced at night.	4	926
Jan 13	12 21	Kuan T'ien-p'ei to Bremer and C. Elliot. Denies reports about re-inforcements; marines cannot be withdrawn all at once because they lack sufficient transport.	7	861
Jan 13	12 21	Ch'i-shan to C. Elliot. Insists that Ting-hai must be evacuated before trade can be resumed at Canton.	6	859
Jan 14	12 22	C. Elliot to Ch'i-shan. Has ordered evacuation of Ting-hai.	5	893

F.O. 682/ 1974	Date 1841	TK 20	Description	pp	Old R F.O. 682/
/19	Jan 14	12 22	C. Elliot to Ch'i-shan. Resumption of trade at Canton must not be delayed any longer. Sha-chiao and Ta-chiao will be evacuated on cession of Hong Kong and Chien-sha-tsui [Kowloon].	6	894
/20	Jan 15	12 23	Ch'i-shan to C. Elliot. Will re-open Canton for trade and release prisoners of war. Will cede Hong Kong or Chien-sha-tsui [Kowloon] but not both.	10	860
/21	Jan 16	12 24	C. Elliot to Ch'i-shan. Accepts Hong Kong.	6	875
/22	Jan 16	12 24	C. Elliot to Ch'i-shan. Requests release of French missionary, M. Taillandier, and a lascar.	5	876
/23	Jan 17	12 25	C. Elliot and Bremer to Viceroy I-li-pu of Liang-Chiang. Have come· to understanding with Ch'i-shan. Hereby orders evacuation of Ting-hai and Chusan and release of prisoners of war; British merchants with stocks in occupied areas should be allowed to sell them at Ningpo.	8	877
/24	Jan 18	12 26	Pass issued by Ch'i-shan to HMS *Columbia* to purchase supplies *en route* to Ting-hai. Valid until 6 Feb 1841	5	857
/25	Jan 18	12 26	Ch'i-shan to C. Elliot. M. Taillandier and lascar are hereby released.	5	858
/26	Jan 20	12 28	C. Elliot to Ch'i-shan. Thanks for release of M. Taillandier and lascar. Has ordered evacuation of Sha-chiao and Ta-chiao. Requests that agreement to re-open Canton be honoured: proclamation should be issued to placate Cantonese.	6	878
		TK 21			
/27	Jan 28	01 06	Bremer to Colonel Lai En-chüeh of Ta-p'eng. Is proceeding to occupy Hong Kong. Advises evacuation of all military personnel and warns against intervention.	5	874

. / 4	Date 1841	TK 21	Description	pp	Old Ref. F.O. 682/
8	Jan 30	01 08	C. Elliot to Ch'i-shan. Chinese troops must be withdrawn from Kowloon and forts destroyed, so that British authorities need not garrison more troops or build more forts in Hong Kong than are necessary.	6	879
9	Feb 1	01 10	C. Elliot to Ch'i-shan. Encloses translation of Queen's letter investing Elliot with pleni-potentiary powers to negotiate. Threatens war if treaty is not forthcoming.	7	880
0	Feb 5	01 14	Ch'i-shan to Elliot. Will withdraw troops from Kowloon. Cannon may be removed only by sea and will take some time. Hong Kong should not be garrisoned.	9	856
1	Feb 5	01 14	Ch'i-shan to Elliot. Has not ignored agreement: has taken some time to polish its language. Has despatched this polished version to Elliot yesterday.	8	855
2	Feb 7	01 16	Elliot to Ch'i-shan. Accepts proposal (conveyed verbally) to meet on 11 February.	5	881
3	Feb 13	01 22	Elliot to Ch'i-shan. Encloses draft treaty. Requests date and place of meeting to sign it. Encl. Chinese version of draft treaty: (1) Chinese government will protect British merchants; (2) Chinese and British officials of equal ranks will correspond with one another as equals; (3) Hong Kong Island will be ceded to Great Britain; (4) rules of extradition will be observed by both parties; (5) indemnity and debts must be paid within three years, whereupon Co-hong monopoly will be abolished; (6) Britons caught smuggling opium must either be handed over to British authorities or be deported, although their vessels and goods may be confiscated by Chinese authorities ; n.d.	4 9	882
4	Feb 16	01 25	Elliot to Ch'i-shan. Evacuation of Ting-hai is under way. Will resume	5	884

F.O. 682/ 1974	Date 1841	TK 21	Description	pp	Old F F.O. 682/
			war if treaty is not speedily concluded.		
/35	Feb 16	01 25	Elliot to Sub-Magistrate Chiang Li-ang of Macao. Requests letter be forwarded to Ch'i-shan.	4	885
/36	Feb 17	01 26	Elliot to Chiang Li-ang. Returns Chiang's letter in which Elliot's title has been omitted. Threatens to ask Ch'i-shan to discipline Chiang.	5	895
/37	Feb 18	01 27	Ch'i-shan to Elliot. Will reply in detail on recovering from illness.	6	853
/38	Feb 24	02 04	Bremer to Kuan T'ien-p'ei. Claims it will be useless to resist him: if forts are surrendered, soldiers will be spared.	6	896
/39	Mar 4	02 12	Elliot to commanding officer of Erh-sha-wei. During truce, all preparations for war must cease.	4	898
/40	Mar 5	02 13	Elliot's revised and expanded terms for truce: (1) as regards payment of indemnity and of debts owed British merchants totalling twelve million dollars, half must be paid within three days while rest should be paid in a year's time, whereupon all territories occupied by British forces except Hong Kong and Chien-sha-tsui [Kowloon] will be returned; (2) previous agreement should stand except cession of Hong Kong should include Chien-sha-tsui; payment of indemnity and debts must be completed within three years, after which Co-hong monopoly must be abolished; in future, privileges granted to other nations must be extended to Britain; disagreements over text of treaty be referred to the English version; (3) Canton must be re-opened for trade within three days.	5	897
/41	Mar 7	02 15	Elliot to Ch'i-shan. Is going to attack maritime provinces as Emperor has been intransigent. If Canton continues to be hostile, it too will be punished.	5	899

. / 4	Date 1841	TK 21	Description	pp	Old Ref. F.O. 682/
2	Mar 9	02 17	Elliot to Intendant I Chung-fu of Kao-Lien. Encloses letter for Ch'i-shan. Protests about ill-treatment of Britons and foreigners in and near Macao.	4	901
3	Mar 9	02 17	Elliot to Ch'i-shan. Demands proclamation be issued to prohibit ill-treatment of foreigners travelling between Canton and Macao; otherwise will attack Hsiang-shan.	7	900
4	Mar 16	02 24	Elliot to Ch'i-shan. Gives ultimatum for meeting within one day. [Envelope marked 'returned unopened'.]	3 / 1	1599A
5	Mar 16	02 24	Copy of previous entry.	4	902
6	Mar 16	n.d. [02 24]	[Elliot's] proclamation. All foreigners should be allowed to leave Canton freely or British troops will advance on city.	2	903
7	Mar 18	02 26	Elliot to Commissioner Yang Fang. Demands meeting today and reply to this letter within one hour.	4	904
8	Mar 19	02 27	Elliot to Yang Fang. Is determined to fight on until all his demands are met.	4	905
9	Mar 29	03 07	Elliot to Yang Fang. Requests return of three Britons abducted near Macao.	4	253A/4B/15
0	Apr 3	03 12	Elliot to Governor Liu Yün-k'o of Chekiang. Demands safe return of Mr Stead, master of British ship, kidnapped by Chinese soldiers in civilian clothes. [Envelope marked 'returned unopened'.]	9 / 1	1599B
1	Apr 3	03 12	Copy of previous entry.	6	870
2	Apr 14	03 23	Elliot to Yang Fang et al. Demands to know if General I-shan and Minister Lung-wen, just arrived from Peking, want war or peace.	4	907
3	Apr 15	03 24	Yang Fang to Elliot. Has forwarded request to Emperor. Arrival of I-shan and Lung-wen will not affect	4	854

F.O. 682/ 1974	Date 1841	TK 21	Description	pp	Old R F.O. 682/

NOTE: The symbol *i* in the third column stands for intercalary month, *i.e.* a month inserted in the calendar to make the calendar year correspond to the Chinese lunar year.

			truce: both are waiting for instructions from Emperor.		
/54	May 2	*i*3 12	Elliot to Yang Fang. Returns herewith Yang's private note: Yang's communications should be conveyed in official manner, and signed by I-shan and Lung-wen as well.	4	908
/55	May 11	*i*3 21	Elliot to She Pao-shun. Demands speedy withdrawal of troops from Canton to reduce risks of breaching truce.	6	909
/56	May 11	*i*3 21	Elliot to She Pao-shun. Demands removal of cannon from West Fort and proclamation to calm populace.	4	906
/57	May 11	*i*3 21	Elliot to She Pao-shun. Is leaving for Macao next day: asks for quick reply, otherwise it will have to be delivered to Macao.	4	910
/58	May 22	04 02	Elliot to population of Canton. Will attack their city within a day unless they put pressure on their authorities to yield.	7	911
/59	May 26	04 06	Elliot's draft Convention of Canton [agreed upon next day]: (1) the three Imperial Commissioners will leave Canton with their troops to places no less than two hundred *li* from Canton; (2) Canton authorities will pay indemnity of six million dollars over a period of six days from tomorrow onwards; (3) if Canton authorities take more than six days but less than fourteen days to pay, indemnity will be increased to seven million dollars; then to eight million dollars if they take fourteen days to pay, and to nine million dollars if they take twenty days to pay; but once indemnity is paid, British forces will withdraw from Canton area; (4) compensation for losses suffered by foreign factories in Canton, and for the burning of a Philippine ship in 1839 will be paid within seven days;	5	913

. / 4	Date 1841	TK 21	Description	pp	Old Ref. F.O. 682/
			(5) Prefect of Canton must have joint authorization from the three Imperial Commissioners, Tartar-General of Canton, Viceroy and Governor to sign convention.		
0	May 27	04 07	I-shan *et al.* to She Pao-shun. Authorize him to negotiate Canton Convention.	5	912
1	Jun 3	04 14	Elliot to Cantonese. Peace is restored. All should return to city to do business as usual.	4	914
2	Jun 5	04 16	Elliot to Sub-Magistrate Hsieh Hsiao-chuang of Macao. Asks enclosed be forwarded to [Viceroy Ch'i Kung of Liang-Kuang].		
63	Jun 5	04 16	Hsieh Hsiao-chuang to Elliot. Has forwarded letter to [Ch'i Kung].	5	852
64	Jun 5	04 16	Elliot to Ch'i Kung. Protests about continued posting of joint declaration by I-shan and Lung-wen calling upon Chinese to exterminate Britons. Will not evacuate Heng-tang and other forts until Ch'i Kung issues proclamation to opposite effect.	6	916
65	Jun 7	04 18	Elliot's proclamation to maritime provinces. Hong Kong is free port. All traders will be protected. Chinese ports will be blockaded if Chinese government prevents subjects from trading with Hong Kong. Anyone with information about pirates will be rewarded.	4	915
66	Jun 8	04 19	Ch'i Kung to Elliot. Looting and raping by British soldiers cause disturbances; they must be restrained.	5	849
67	Jun 9	04 20	She Pao-shun to Elliot. Requests return of forts, junks and accessories according to Canton Convention.	10	848
68	Jun 10	04 21	Elliot to Hsieh Hsiao-chuang. Has heard that Chinese troops have assembled in Macao. Will put matter in hands of Admiral in case	3	918

F.O. 682/ 1974	Date 1841	TK 21	Description	pp	Old R• F.O. 682/
			of incidents.		
/69	Jun 10	04 21	Hsieh Hsiao-chuang to Elliot. Denies reports that Chinese troops have assembled in Macao for offensive: merely groups of disbanded militia passing through Macao on way home.	10	851
/70	Jun 10	04 21	Elliot to Ch'i Kung. Will return Heng-tang and other forts as soon as notice of departure of Yang Fang *et al.* is received: but forts are not to be repaired, re-armed or garrisoned by more than one hundred soldiers.	4	919
/71	Jun 10	04 21	Elliot to Ch'i Kung. Declares Hong Kong free port. Attempts to prevent Chinese going there to trade will lead to British blockade of Canton.	3	920
/72	Jun 11	04 22	Hsieh Hsiao-chuang to Elliot. Forwards reply from Ch'i Kung and letter from She Pao-chun. Urges withdrawal from Hu-men.	5	850
/73	Jun 11	n.d. [04 22]	Hsieh Hsiao-chuang to Elliott. Has forwarded two letters to Ch'i Kung. Declines to forward any more.	3	847
/74	Jun 15	04 26	Elliot to Hsieh Hsiao-chuang. Asks him to continue to forward letters to Canton.	4	921
/75	Jun 16	04 27	Hsieh Hsiao-chuang to Elliot. Agrees to forward the letters delivered to him; declines to forward any more as Co-hong is the usual channel.	7	846
/76	Jun 17	04 28	Elliot to She Pao-shun. Requests meeting in Macao: should [Canton] Convention be disregarded, will resort to war.	3	922
/77	Jun 17	04 28	Elliot to Ch'i Kung. Misconduct of British soldiers is caused by desire to avenge ill-treatment of foreigners by Chinese. Will restrain soldiers but Chinese must behave themselves.	9	924
/78	Jun 17	04 28	Elliot to Hsieh Hsiao-chuang. Poster inciting local people against	3	923

). 2/ 74	Date 1841	TK 21	Description	pp	Old Ref. F.O. 682/
			foreigners must be removed.		
79	Jun 17	04 28	Copy of previous entry.	4	1595B
80	Jun 19	05 01	Elliot to Ch'i Kung. Bremer has returned from India and is invested with plenipotentiary powers to be exercised jointly with Elliot.	4	869
81	Oct 16	09 02	British Plenipotentiary Sir Henry Pottinger to Chinese Minister for Foreign Affairs. Demands Imperial Commissioner of status equal to his be despatched to negotiate treaty.	9	871
			Encl. Chinese version of Palmerston's letter, 3 May 1841. H.M. Government has ordered occupation of Chusan until all demands are met. Elliot has returned Chusan contrary to orders and is recalled. Pottinger is new Plenipotentiary and will proceed to re-occupy Chusan. It will be useless to resist.	10	868
82	Oct 16	09 02	British Commander-in-Chief to Governor and Commander-in-Chief of Chekiang. Demands ransom for Hangchow and other cities captured: otherwise will attack more places.	5	872
3	n.d. [Oct 17]	n.d. [09 03]	Copy of Imperial Edict appointing Ch'i-ying Viceroy of Liang-Chiang and I-li-pu Imperial Commissioner at Canton.	2	996B
4	Dec 5	10 23	Proclamation by Colonel Craigie. Chinese army has suffered numerous defeats and has not won victories as reported in Peking Gazette. Warns inhabitants of Chen-hai against sheltering Chinese agents.	11	873

F.O. 682/ 1975	Date 1842	TK 22	Description	pp	Old Re F.O. 682/
/1a	Feb 14	01 05	Commodore Sir Gordon Bremer and General Sir Hugh Gough to [Chinese Authorities at Ningpo]. Will treat only with Imperial Commissioner sent directly from Peking [2 copies].	4	258
/1b	Feb 16	01 07	Proclamation by Sir Henry Pottinger. Henceforth Hong Kong and Chusan are free ports. Those who wish to trade there will be protected. Should Chusan be evacuated in the future, merchants would be given every opportunity to complete their business before leaving [2 copies].	4	259
/1c	May 7	03 27	Proclamation by Bremer and Gough. Have decided to accept offer of one million dollars as ransom for city of Ningpo so as to avoid destruction of life and property. Citizens of Ningpo should feel grateful and should do all they can to facilitate foreign trade [2 copies].	6	260
/1d	May -	04 --	Proclamation by British authorities to citizens of Cha-p'u in Chekiang. Demand immediate surrender of their city to avoid destruction [2 copies].	2	261
/1e	May 20 [Rec'd]	04 11 [Rec'd]	Former Viceroy I-li-pu of Liang-Chiang to British authorities. Great Britain wants trade and China wants customs revenue. Urges resumption of peace and trade.	6	262
/1f	May 20	04 11	Acting Tartar General Ch'i-ying of Hang-chow to I-li-pu et al. Commands them to inquire why the British have decided to attack Cha-p'u.	10	264
/1g	May 21	04 12	Gough to I-li-pu. Remembers with gratitude the kindness with which I-li-pu treated British prisoners of war. Will gladly receive I-li-pu at Cha-p'u and will guarantee his safety. Only H.M. Plenipotentiary has been authorised to negotiate peace settlement, but China can be certain of peace if she accepts all British demands as conveyed in previous communications [2 copies].	5	263

O. 2/ 75	Date 1842	TK 22	Description	pp	Old Ref. F.O. 682/
1h	May 26	04[17]	Draft of next entry.	8	265
1i	May 26	04[17]	Commodore Sir Gordon Bremer and General Sir Hugh Gough to I-li-pu [Assistant to Chi'i-ying]. Agrees to the truce. Will release prisoners of war, expecting I-li-pu to do the same. H.M. Plempotentiary will soon arrive in Chusan.	8	113/1
2	Jun 7	04 29	I-li-pu to Bremer and Gough. Will consult Emperor on terms of lasting peace. Is releasing sixteen prisoners of war; thanks for good treatment and release of Chinese prisoners.	7	114/2
3	Jun -	04 -	I-li-pu to Gough. Agrees that hostilities should stop. Is willing to meet Gough after intentions of Sir Henry Pottinger are known.	7	114/1
4	Jun 20	05 12	Bremer to Acting Deputy Lieutenant-General I-li-pu. Thanks for release of prisoners of war. Cannot stop hostilities until all demands are met.	8	113/2
5a	Jun 20 [Rec'd]	05 -	I-li-pu to Gough. Is startled to learn that Royal Navy has bombarded Shanghai after prisoners of war have just been exchanged.	4	114/3
5b	Jun 20	05 12	Bremer and Gough to I-li-pu. Are pleased to read that I-li-pu has been appointed Manchu Brigade-General of Cha-p'u. H.M. Plenipotentiary Sir Henry Pottinger arrived at Chusan some time ago and has now proceeded to Wu-sung. If China wants peace, she must send Imperial Commissioner to meet Sir Henry Pottinger.	8	266
6a	Jun 27	[05 19]	Bremer to Tartar-General Ch'i-ying of Canton and I-li-pu. H.M. Plenipotentiary Sir Henry Pottinger has arrived at Wu-sung.	6	113/3
6b	Jun 27	05 19	Bremer and Gough to Ch'i-ying and I-li-pu. Have forwarded all diplomatic correspondence Sir Henry Pottinger, who has arrived at Wu-sung.	2	267
7a	Jun 27	05 19	Draft of next entry.	4	268

F.O. 682/ 1975	Date 1842	TK 22	Description	pp	Old Ref F.O. 682/
/7b	Jun 27	05 19	Sir Henry Pottinger to Ch'i-ying and I-li-pu. Will not stop hostilities until Imperial Commissioner is despatched by Emperor to negotiate peace treaty.	6	113/4
/8	Jun 27 [Rec'd]	05 -	Ch'i-ying and I-li-pu to Pottinger *et al.* Are willing to treat, suggesting either Chen-hai or Sung-chiang as meeting place.	5	114/4
/9	Jun 28	05 20	Draft letter [Pottinger to Chinese government]. Argues for legalisation of opium. Contains two instructions from cabinet : to Elliot (27 Feb 1841) and to Pottinger (28 Jun 1841).	14	929
/10	Jul 4	05 26	I-li-pu to Pottinger. Trade brings profits and war brings sufferings. Sues for peace and requests resumption of trade.	9	114/5
/11a	Jul 5	05 27	Draft of next entry.	6	269
/11b	Jul 5	05 27	Bremer and Gough to Commander-in-Chief of Kiangnan and Intendant of Su-Sung-T'ai. Demands ransom of one million dollars for city of Shanghai. Threatens to increase ransom if payment is delayed.	6	113/5
/11c	Jul 5	05 27	Proclamation by Pottinger to Chinese populace. Britain has decided to make war on China because : (1) Commissioner Lin destroyed British opium and threatened lives of British subjects; (2) I-shan attacked British forces near Canton; (3) Chinese officials abducted British sailors, particularly shipwrecked sailors, and reported to Emperor as having captured them in action; (4) Co-hong system at Canton was restrictive and damaging to trade. Britain now demands : (1) suitable indemnity; (2) equality with China; (3) cession of an island. Hostile actions by Chinese populace will invite retaliation.	11	270
/12	Jul 6	05 28	Captain Ho's [Hope's] Proclamation at Wu-sung : (1) misdemeanours of British sailors should be reported to him; (2) local people should bring poultry, meat, eggs, milk and vegetables to British man-of-war for	5	253B/2

No.	Date		Description	pp	Old Ref. F.O.
2/ 75	1842	TK 22			682/

			sale; should attempts be made to stop such supplies, sailors will help themselves; (3) should British sailors be assaulted or abducted while on shore, villages nearby will be burnt down.		
3	Jul 8	[06 01]	Pottinger to I-li-pu. Proposes meeting at Nanking. Reiterates that hostilities will not stop until Imperial Commissioner is appointed to grant all British demands.	5	113/6
4	Jul 19	06 12	Proclamation by Bremer and Gough. Chinese vessels must stop crossing Yangtze River in Chen-chiang and Nanking areas or they will be fired upon. If fire boats are used to attack Royal Navy, any Chinese vessel captured will be destroyed.	4	253B/20
5	Jul -	[06 -]	Pottinger to Ch'i-ying. Acknowledges receipt of Ch'i-ying's letter that bore no official seal. Cannot discuss national matters on private basis. Ch'i-ying must get himself appointed Imperial Commissioner with full powers to grant all British demands before hostilities will stop.	7	113/7
6	n.d. [Jul -]	n.d. [06 -]	Copy of previous entry.	7	253B/23
7	Jul -	06 -	Ch'i-ying and I-li-pu to Pottinger. Suggest meeting to negotiate peace settlement instead of endless discussion by correspondence.	5	114/6
8	Jul 26	06 19	Bremer and Gough to Viceroy Niu Chien of Liang-Chiang and Tartar-General Te-chu-pu of Nanking. Are going to attack Nanking unless ransom is paid.	6	113/8
9	Jul 26	06 19	Draft of previous entry.	6	253B/29
0a	Jul 27	06 20	Niu Chien to British Commanders-in-Chief. Has sent two messengers to take letter to Sir Henry Pottinger. Requests that they be given free passage.	5	253A/4B/2
0b	Jul 27	06 20	Niu Chien to Pottinger. Expostulates with Pottinger about the waging of war on China. [Incomplete]	10	327/5/115

F.O. 682/ 1975	Date		Description	pp	Old Re F.O. 682/
	1842	TK 22			
/21	Jul 30	06 23	Bremer to Niu Chien and Te-chu-pu. Has forwarded letter to Pottinger. In case previous note is lost, copy of it is enclosed herewith.	4	113/10
/22	Jul 30	06 23	Draft of previous entry.	4	253B/5
/23	Jul 30	06 23	Pottinger to Niu Chien. Will not stop hostilities until Imperial Commissioner is appointed to negotiate peace treaty.	8	113/9
/24	Jul 30	06 23	Draft of previous entry.	6	253B/1
/25	Aug 1	06 25	Pottinger to Ch'i-ying. Will not stop military action until Ch'i-ying or some other official is given plenipotentiary powers to negotiate peace settlement.	6	113/11
/26	Aug 1	06 25	Draft of previous entry.	4	253B/8
/27	Aug 2	06 26	Proclamation by Bremer and Gough. Four hundred thousand dollars is not enough: until one million dollars is paid as ransom for Shanghai, blockade of Wu-sung will not be lifted.	4	253B/6
/28	Aug 3	06 27	Ch'i-ying and I-li-pu to Pottinger. Re previous letter in which their names were not prefixed with title *Ch'üan-ch'üan* (Plenipotentiary), in China *Ch'in-ch'ai ta-ch'en* (Imperial Commissioner) is equivalent to Plenipotentiary.	6	114/18
/29	Aug 4	06 28	Niu Chien to [Captain Morrison]. Has despatched two messengers to take letters to Pottinger, Bremer and Gough. Requests safe passage for them.	5	114/1C
/30	Aug 4	06 28	Niu Chien to Pottinger. Ch'i-ying and I-li-pu have been appointed Imperial Commissioners with full plenipotentiary powers to negotiate peace settlement. Whatever Pottinger does he must bear in mind *vox populi vox Dei;* and he must keep his word whenever agreement is reached.	13	114/7
/31	Aug 4	06 28	Niu Chien to Bremer and Gough. Their demand for ransom for Nanking contradicts Pottinger's request for Imperial Commissioner to negotiate	15	114/8

0. 2/ 75	Date 1842 TK 22		Description	pp	Old Ref. F.O. 682/
			peace settlement. Government revenues are ear-marked for specific expenditures and it is not up to Niu Chien to use any of them as ransom money.		
2	Aug 4	06 28	Niu Chien to Bremer and Gough. Although government cannot pay ransom, citizens of Nanking have in fact begun donating money for it. Sudden appearance of Royal Navy will only frighten away citizens and their money. Requests that Royal Navy withdraw for about ten miles, promising news of ransom within five or six days.	7	114/9
3	Aug 5	06 29	Niu Chien to Pottinger. Only three hundred thousand taels have been collected from citizens of Nanking as most rich people have been frightened away by appearance of Royal Navy. Requests that Royal Navy withdraw for about ten miles from Nanking so that rich people may be summoned to contribute another three hundred thousand taels for ransom.	9	114/11
4	Aug 5	06 29	Niu Chien to Bremer and Gough. Again urges Royal Navy to withdraw for about ten miles from Nanking so that rich people may be persuaded to contribute another three hundred thousand taels for ransom.	7	114/12
5	Aug 5	06 29	Niu Chien to Pottinger. Notes that Pottinger wishes to meet him and I-li-pu. As I-li-pu is at Wu-hsi, five hundred li away and is certain not to make it in day or two, suggests that he and Pottinger meet first at Ching-hai-ssu.	7	114/13
36	Aug 6	07 01	Niu Chien to Pottinger. Of all officers involved only Niu himself dared request permission from Emperor to negotiate peace settlement. If Emperor knows Royal Navy's sudden threat to Nanking, he will accuse Niu of lying. Wonders why Pottinger declines to meet him. Encl. Copy of Imperial Edict to Niu Chien appointing Ch'i-ying and I-li-pu Imperial Commissioners to negotiate peace settlement, n.d.	9 2	114/14 A+B

F.O. 682/ 1975	Date 1842	TK 22	Description	pp	Old Re F.O. 682/
/37	Aug 6	07 01	Bremer and Gough to Niu Chien. Refuse to withdraw Royal Navy from Nanking until ransom of three million dollars is paid. No point in meeting until Chinese official with plenipotentiary powers is appointed to negotiate peace settlement.	9	113/12
/38	Aug 6	07 01	Draft of previous entry.	8	253B/7
/39	Aug 6	07 01	Pottinger to Niu Chien. Acknowledges receipt of letters. Reply is being translated and will be despatched the following morning.	4	113/12
/40	Aug 6	07 01	Draft of previous entry.	4	253B/1
/41	Aug 6	07 01	Imperial Commissioner I-li-pu to Pottinger. Hostilities must stop and peace be concluded on terms satisfactory to both British and Chinese monarchs.	6	114/15
/42	Aug 6	07 01	Copy of previous entry.	6	114/16
/43	[Aug -]	06 -	Pottinger to I-li-pu. Agrees to meet and proposes Nanking as meeting place. But until I-li-pu and Ch'i-ying have been given plenipotentiary powers to negotiate peace settlement, hostilities will not stop.	5	253B/2
/44	Aug 6	07 01	Pottinger to Niu Chien. Is pleased to read that Ch'i-ying and I-li-pu have been appointed Imperial Commissioners with full powers to treat. Much destruction could have been avoided if such appointments had been made earlier.	16	113/14
/45	Aug 6	07 01	Copy of previous entry.	16	113/16
/46	Aug 6	07 01	Draft of previous entry.	14	253B/5
/47	Aug 6	07 01	Draft of previous entry.	14	253B/1
/48	Aug 7	07 02	Niu Chien to Pottinger. Messenger reported yesterday that translation of reply may be completed today. Is now sending messenger to fetch reply.	7	114/1

Date			Description	pp	Old Ref. F.O. 682/
1842		TK 22			
Aug 8	07 03		Pottinger to I-li-pu. Is concerned that I-li-pu and Ch'i-ying have not yet received appointments as Imperial Commissioners, but is prepared to send deputy for preliminary negotiations. Draws attention to letter in which [Queen of England] is put one space below Emperor [of China].	8	113/15
Aug 8	07 03		Draft of previous entry.	8	253B/9
Aug 8	07 03		Copy of previous entry.	7	253B/55
Aug 8	07 03		Copy of previous entry.	9	113/17
Aug 9	07 04		Niu Chien to Pottinger. Nanking has been impoverished by floods and war. Six hundred thousand taels is maximum it can afford. Offers one million dollars as present to British forces but not as ransom, as ransom is an improper term. Sum of three million dollars demanded as ransom will be impossible to meet; if Pottinger insists, Niu Chien will be punished in same way as Ch'i-shan by Emperor.	19	114/19
a	Aug 10	07 05	Draft of next entry.	7	271
b	Aug 10	07 05	Bremer and Gough to Niu Chien. Even if Imperial Commissioners have been appointed, peace treaty is not concluded. Therefore unless ransom is paid Nanking will be attacked.	8	113/18
Aug 10	07 05		I-li-pu to Pottinger. Does not possess seal of Imperial Commissioner but Ch'i-ying does. Since both have been appointed Joint Commissioners, Ch'i-ying's seal is as good as his. Scribe is to blame for wrong format in previous despatch.	9	114/20
Aug 11	07 06		I-li-pu to Pottinger. Reiterates that he, jointly with Ch'i-ying, has plenipotentiary powers to settle all points of dispute. Expects Ch'i-ying will arrive soon. Encl. Copy of Imperial Edict appointing Ch'i-ying and I-li-pu as Joint Imperial Commissioners with plenipotentiary powers to conclude peace treaty, n.d.	7

2 | 114/21 A+B |

F.O. 682/ 1975	Date 1842	TK 22	Description	pp	Old R< F.O. 682/
/57	Aug 11	07 06	Niu Chien to Pottinger. Wonders why there is no reply to his offer of one million dollars as present to British forces. Any message Pottinger may feel reluctant to put on paper may be conveyed to messenger verbally.	5	114/2.
/58a	Aug 11	07 06	Draft of next entry.	7	272
/58b	Aug 11	07 06	Pottinger to Niu Chien. There will be no peace until all British demands are met. If Emperor is sincere in his willingness to treat, ransom placed on Nanking may be included in final indemnity.	8	113/1
/59	Aug 12	07 07	Ch'i-ying and I-li-pu to Pottinger. Ch'i-ying arrived yesterday. Chang Shih-ch'un and T'a-feng-pu are sent as deputies to conduct preliminary negotiations.	7	114/2
/60	Aug 12	07 07	Pottinger to Ch'i-ying and I-li-pu. Has deputed Mr Malcolm and Mr J.R. Morrison to meet their Chinese counterparts.	4	113/2
/61	Aug 12	07 07	Copy of previous entry.	4	253B/
/62	Aug 12	[07 07]	List of terms to be included in Treaty of Nanking, [prepared by Sir Henry Pottinger].	11	113/2
/63	Aug 14	07 09	Ch'i-ying et al. to Pottinger. Deny accusation, conveyed verbally by T'a-feng-pu and Chang Shih-ch'un, that preliminary negotiations are delaying tactics. Agree to most of Pottinger's demands. Encl. Replies to Pottinger's demands.	9 6	114/2
/64	Aug 14	07 09	Niu Chien to Pottinger. Is pleased to learn of proposal to include ransom of Nanking in final indemnity. Denies accusation that Niu Chien has mobilised troops for another battle.	13	114/2
/65	Aug 15	07 10	I-li-pu to Pottinger. Encloses copy of terms for peace agreed upon in preliminary negotiations. Encl. Copy of peace terms.	5 8	114/2

Date		Description	pp	Old Ref. F.O. 682/
1842	TK 22			

[Aug 15]	[07 10]	Copy of enclosure to previous entry.	6	114/27
Aug 15	07 10	Pottinger to Niu Chien. Denies rumours that British forces intend to attack Nanking while negotiations are under way.	8	113/22
Aug 15	07 10	Draft of previous entry.	8	253B/13
Aug[16]	07 11	Draft of next entry.	5	273B
Aug 16	07 11	Pottinger to Ch'i-ying, I-li-pu and Niu Chien. Encloses draft Treaty of Nanking.	4	113/23
Aug 31	07 26	Ch'i-ying *et al.* to Pottinger. Are forwarding five hundred thousand taels from Nanking. Request receipt for it.	5	114/28
Aug -	07 -	Draft of next entry.	8	273A
Aug -	07 -	Pottinger to Ch'i-ying *et al.* Has had draft Treaty of Nanking translated into Chinese and is confident language used conforms with Chinese practice. Requests Imperial seal be stamped on to it to signify its perpetually binding effect. Details of customs duties and question of opium are to be translated and settled afterwards.	8	113/24
[Aug -]	[07 -]	Statement of different sums paid at Yangchow, Nanking and Wu-sung that make up total of six million dollars of indemnity.	4	113/25
[Aug -]	[07 -]	Draft of previous entry.	3	113/26
[Aug -]	[07 -]	By-law proposed by Chinese concerning consular courts: Consuls are to be stationed at five treaty ports to supervise conduct of Britons. In a dispute, if offender is Chinese, he is to be punished by Chinese officials; if British, he is to be punished by Consul.	1	113/27
n.d. [Aug -]	n.d. [07 -]	[Intendant at Shanghai to Niu Chien]. French Embassy has arrived requesting permission to sail to Nanking to ascertain if British forces have been committing atrocities in China and if so to report back to French [King] so he can reason with British authorities. Has tried to	3	253B/25

F.O. 682/ 1975	Date 1842	TK 22	Description	pp	Old Re F.O. 682/
			persuade Embassy to return to Canton in vain.		
/75	n.d. [Aug -]	n.d. [07 -]	Report by Intendant at Shanghai on his conversation with French Embassy: France is afraid China might cede territory to a victorious Britain; in West, Ambassadors are sent to other countries to cut down risk of war; Embassy wishes to hire junks to go to Nanking to see what Pottinger and Chinese officials are doing.	8	253B/2
/76	n.d. [Aug -]	n.d. [07 -]	Draft of Proclamation by Pottinger to Chinese populace. Outlines British version of Opium War up to negotiations at Nanking. Warns Chinese not to be misled by their ignorant officials into provoking further hostilities.	5	253B/3
/77	Sep 1	07 27	Ch'i-ying *et al.* to Pottinger. Are forwarding four hundred thousand taels from Soochow. Request receipt for it.	5	114/2
/78	Sep 1	07 27	Ch'i-ying *et al.* to Pottinger. Shanghai merchants are unable to make up sum of five hundred thousand dollars because their ships full of goods are detained by Royal Navy. Request release of these and other ships so detained along coast of China.	7	114/30
/79	Sep 1	07 27	Ch'i-ying *et al.* to Pottinger. Elaborate on conditions of peace.	28	114/3
/80	Sep 3	07 29	Pottinger to Ch'i-ying *et al.* Has instructed Royal Navy to lift blockade of Wu-sung, Chen-hai and Amoy.	4	113/2
/81	Sep 3	07 29	Draft of previous entry.	5	253B/
/82	Sep 7	08 03	Ch'i-ying *et al.* to Pottinger. Have notified authorities of Liang-Kuang and Min-Che to release all prisoners of war. Any Briton captured in Taiwan will be delivered to Ku-lang-hsü. Request that British commander at Ku-lang-hsü be notified of this and that he	7	114/3

Date		Description	pp	Old Ref. F.O. 682/
1842	TK 22			

		give receipt for prisoners of war delivered to him.		
Sep 9	08 05	Ch'i-ying *et al.* to Pottinger. Are forwarding six hundred thousand taels from Anhwei. Request receipt for it.	5	114/33
n.d. [Sep -]	n.d.	Pottinger to Imperial Commissioners. Replies to elaborations on peace terms [by Ch'i-ying *et al.*]	19	113/292
n.d.	n.d.	Draft of previous entry.	24	253B/27
n.d. [Sep -]	[08 -]	Lieutenant-Colonel Man to Commander Shu of Chen-chiang. Orders Shu to proceed to Chen-chiang with minimum number of troops to help maintain order while the place is still under British occupation.	5	113/29b
Sep 12	08 08	Pottinger to Ch'i-ying *et al.* Eleven men-of-war had left England for China before news of peace reached England, but there is no need for alarm when they arrive.	6	113/30
Sep 12	08 08	Draft of previous entry.	5	253B/50
Sep 13	08 09	Ch'i-ying *et al.* to Pottinger. Jurisdiction over Chinese who are temporarily or permanently resident in Hong Kong should be the responsibility of Chinese officials. Customs duties are fixed by Ministry of Finance; exactions will be abolished. In treaty ports Britons will be governed by Consul and Chinese by Chinese officials.	21	114/34
Sep 14	08 10	Pottinger to Ch'i-ying *et al.* Congratulates Emperor Tao-kuang on his birthday.	5	113/31
Sep 14	08 10	Draft of previous entry.	4	253B/51
n.d. [Sep -]	n.d. [08 -]	Pottinger to [Ch'i-ying *et al.*] Has ordered Royal Navy to withdraw from Yangtze, consequent on Emperor's consent to accept terms of treaty.	3	113/32
n.d. [Sep -]	n.d. [08 -]	Draft of previous entry.	3	253B/48

F.O. 682/ 1975	Date 1842	TK 22	Description	pp	Old Re F.O. 682/
/94a	Sep -	08 -	Pottinger to [Ch'i-ying *et al*.] Requests the reinstatement of the Magistrate, who was dismissed during the hostilities on the grounds that a memorial addressed to the Emperor had been seized by Royal Navy while said memorial was travelling through the territory of his jurisdiction.	4	113/3:
/94b	Sep -	08 -	Draft of previous entry.	4	253B/
/95	Sep -	08 -	[Pottinger] to Bremer and Gough. As Emperor has agreed to terms of treaty and as six million dollars indemnity has been paid, British forces will leave Yangtze area for either Ting-hai or Hong Kong.	7	253B/
/96	Sep 16	08 12	Ch'i-ying *et al*. to Pottinger. Are pleased that naval units preparing to leave England for China have been stopped. Will transmit Pottinger's best wishes to Emperor on his birthday.	9	114/3
/97	Sep 16	08 12	Ch'i-ying *et al*. to Pottinger. Request receipts for five hundred and forty thousand taels delivered to British authorities at Kua-chou and for one million and five hundred thousand taels from Nanking.	5	114/3
/98	Sep 16	08 12	Ch'i-ying *et al*. to Pottinger. Are forwarding eight hundred thousand taels from Chekiang. Request receipt.	5	114/:
/99	Sep 17	08 13	Pottinger to Ch'i-ying *et al*. Suggests that Chinese, who are either temporary or permanent residents of Hong Kong, and who commit a criminal offence, should be handed over to Chinese author-ities in Kowloon; if they commit a civil offence, they will be dealt with locally. Exactions by Chinese customs officals must be prohibited.	16	113/:
/100	Sep 17	08 13	Draft of previous entry.	10	253B
/101	Sep 17	08 13	Ch'i-ying *et al*. to Pottinger. British man-of-war in Chekiang has been blackmailing local shipping and has detained a junk loaded	7	114/

. / 5	Date 1842	TK 22	Description	pp	Old Ref. F.O. 682/
			with copper. Request withdrawal of British man-of-war from Chekiang and an undertaking that Chinese shipping will not be troubled any longer.		
2	Sep 17	08 13	Ch'i-ying *et al.* to Pottinger. Request that the junk loaded with copper and detained at Chusan be released.	7	114/39
3	Sep 18	08 14	Ch'i-ying *et al.* to Pottinger. Five hundred thousand dollars is ready for delivery at Shanghai.	5	114/40
4	Sep 19	08 15	Ch'i-ying *et al.* to Pottinger. Concerning notice put up by British officer at Chen-chiang, request that British forces there be instructed not to disturb citizens.	7	114/41
5	Sep 19	08 15	Pottinger to [Ch'i-ying *et al.*] Forwards orders from Commodore Bremer for release of two Chinese junks loaded with copper, and any other Chinese merchant ship still detained by Royal Navy.	6	113/35
6	Sep 19	08 15	Draft of previous entry.	5	253B/44
7	Sep 20	08 16	Pottinger to Ch'i-ying *et al.* Five hundred thousand dollars from Nanking appear deficient in weight.	5	113/38
8	Sep 20	08 16	Draft of previous entry.	5	253B/34
9	Sep 20	08 16	Ch'i-ying *et al.* to Pottinger. Are forwarding four hundred thousand taels from Anhwei. Request receipt.	5	114/42
)	Sep 22	08 18	Pottinger to Intendant Wu I-hsi at Shanghai. Has sent HMS *Columbine* to Shanghai to fetch five hundred thousand dollars in his charge. Will be passing through Shanghai soon and will hear report about it.	6	113/36
1	Sep 22	08 18	Copy of previous entry.	4	253B/25
2	n.d.	n.d.	Draft of previous entry.	4	253B/39

F.O. 682/ 1975	Date 1842	TK 22	Description	pp	Old Re F.O. 682/
/113	Sep 22	08 18	Pottinger to Ch'i-ying *et al.* Has sent [Captain Ware in HMS *Columbine*] to Shanghai to fetch five hundred thousand dollars.	5	113/37
/114	Sep 22	08 18	Draft of previous entry.	4	253B/4
/115	Sep 23	08 19	Ch'i-ying *et al.* to Pottinger. Protest against Royal Navy plundering Ching-chiang [in Kiangsu] on 13 and 14 Aug 1842, and attacking Chinese forces on 15 Aug 1842.	7	114/43
/116	Sep 23	08 19	Ch'i-ying *et al.* to Pottinger. Are forwarding further sum of three hundred and ten thousand taels from Anhwei. Request receipt.	5	114/44
/117	Sep 24	08 20	Pottinger to Ch'i-ying *et al.* Five hundred and forty thousand silver dollars were received by Royal Navy at Kua-chou. Will issue official receipt after silver dollars have been fully examined and the weight found to be correct.	5	113/39
/118	Sep 24	08 20	Draft of previous entry.	4	253B/
/119			Number not used.		
/120	Sep 24	08 20	Ch'i-ying *et al.* to Pottinger. List sums of money so far delivered at various places and times, totalling six million dollars for year 1842.	8	114/4
/121	Sep 25	08 21	Pottinger to Ch'i-ying *et al.* Disturbance at Ching-chiang was caused by Royal Navy not knowing of conclusion of peace. Poster at Chen-chiang could not have been written by Royal Navy. Requests search for missing British and Indian soldiers.	6	114/5
/122	Sep 25	08 21	Draft of previous entry.	8	253B/
/123	Sep 26	08 22	Ch'i-ying *et al.* to Pottinger. Request that British commander at Ting-hai be notified of imminent delivery of British prisoners of war there.	7	114/4
/124	Sep 27	08 23	Pottinger to Ch'i-ying *et al.* Plans to leave for Canton within three days, inspecting treaty ports on way. Hopes to meet them before leaving.	6	113/4

O. 2/ 75	Date		Description	pp	Old Ref. F.O. 682/
	1842	TK 22			
25	Sep 27	08 23	Draft of previous entry.	5	253B/18
26	Sep 27	08 23	Ch'i-ying *et al.* to Pottinger. Are pleased to know that notice at Chen-chiang was not put up by British officer. Customs duties fixed by Ministry of Finance will be widely publicized to forestall exactions. Offences big or small committed by Chinese inhabitants of Hong Kong should be dealt with by Chinese official to be stationed at Kowloon, otherwise objections from Chinese courtiers may jeopardise negotiations for peaceful settlement.	17	114/47
27	Sep 27	08 23	Ch'i-ying *et al.* to Pottinger. Are delighted that British officer at Chen-chiang did not put up notice ordering Chinese escort to sea and removal of entire population from the city. Will investigate possibility of Chinese outlaws being responsible for this notice. Will also investigate disappearance of British and Indian soldiers.	7	114/48
28	Sep 28	08 24	Ch'i-ying *et al.* to Pottinger. Agree to meet Pottinger and name Cheng-Chüeh-ssu inside Nanking as meeting place. Will negotiate Supplementary Treaty with Pottinger on arrival at Canton.	7	114/49
29	Oct 8	09 05	Captain-General Wen-wei of Banner Forces to Pottinger. Returns three British and seven Indian prisoners of war.	6	114/51
30	Oct 11	09 08	Wu I-hsi to J.R. Morrison. Lists dates and sums of money totalling three hundred and fifty-five thousand taels delivered to British officers.	7	114/50
31	Oct 13	09 10	Prefect Hsiung of Taiwan to Chads. Was preparing to deliver remaining nine British soldiers to Chinese authorities in Amoy when Chads' deputies came to demand them on 10 October. Cannot hand them over for lack of Chinese authorization. Ship was in fact sunk in action and not wrecked by storm.	15	114/57

F.O. 682/ 1975	Date 1842	TK 22	Description	pp	Old Re F.O. 682/
/132	Oct 15	09 12	Pottinger to Niu Chien and Governor Ch'eng Yü-ts'ai of Kiangsu. Three hundred and fifty-five thousand taels of silver received from Intendant at Shanghai appear to be deficient in weight.	6	113/42
/133	Oct 15	09 12	Draft of previous entry.	5	253B/3
/134	Oct 18	09 15	Viceroy I-liang of Min-Che to Chads. Authorities in Taiwan have refused to hand over British sailors because obviously they have not received I-liang's order to do so.	7	114/58
/135	n.d. [Oct -]	n.d. [9 -]	Pottinger to Chinese authorities. Has prepared fast boat to fetch British [sailors] detained in Taiwan.	3	253B/2
/136	Nov 3	10 01	Pottinger to Governor Liu Yün-k'o of Chekiang. Requests that Emperor be asked to appoint Ch'i-ying to go to Canton to negotiate Supplementary Treaty, and to publish public pardon of Chinese who were in any way connected with British authorities.	7	113/43
/137a	Nov 3	10 01	Pottinger to Ch'i-ying. Suggests that Ch'i-ying should approach Emperor for re-appointment as Imperial Commissioner to enable him to go to Canton to negotiate Supplementary Treaty, and for publication of public pardon of Chinese who were in any way connected with British authorities.	9	113/44
/137b	Nov 3	10 01	Draft of previous entry.	9	253B/3
/138	Nov 5	10 03	Imperial Commissioner I-li-pu to Pottinger. British merchant ship has arrived at Shanghai to trade. As customs duties have yet to be agreed upon and Consuls yet to be appointed, requests that said ship be ordered to leave.	8	114/53
/139	Nov 5	10 03	Intendant Lu Tse-ch'ang of Ning-Shao-T'ai to Pottinger. Inhabitants of Ting-hai have petitioned for Chinese Magistrate to be sent there to keep peace as British occupying	6	114/52

). ?/ 75	Date 1842	TK 22	Description	pp	Old Ref. F.O. 682/
			forces are unfamiliar with local conditions. Suggest that such Magistrate be appointed to station at Kan-lan, twenty miles from city of Ting-hai.		
+0	Nov 6	10 04	Pottinger to Lu Tse-ch'ang. Appreciates Lu's request to station Magistrate at Ting-hai to keep order among populace but must consult Commander-in-Chief of occupying forces General Gough.	6	113/45
+1	Nov 6	10 04	Draft of previous entry.	5	253B/41
+2	Nov 8	10 06	Hsiung to Chads. On 19 Oct 1842 a British merchant ship was wrecked in storm. All twenty-six sailors were saved by local officials, but one died of illness afterwards. Will return all twenty-five survivors tomorrow. Encl. List of names of twenty-five survivors, n.d.	9 3	114/59 A+B
+3	Nov 11	10 09	Lu Tse-ch'ang to Pottinger. Requests release of Chinese civilians abducted by British forces. Encl. List of Chinese abducted, with time and place of abduction, n.d.	7 3	114/56
+4	Nov 11	10 09	Proclamation by Pottinger to inhabitants of Ting-hai. Peace has been concluded but British forces will continue to occupy Ting-hai until all indemnity has been paid. Meanwhile, Chinese Magistrate will be stationed in neighbouring island of Ta-hsieh, to whom inhabitants of Ting-hai may take their law suits.	10	253B/40
45	Nov 12	10 10	Pottinger to I-li-pu and Liu Yün-k'o. Apart from Canton, other treaty ports may not be opened for foreign trade until trade regulations are formulated and Consuls appointed. Agrees that Chinese serving in Royal Navy should not be taken to distant lands against their will, and that they be returned to their native lands if they so wish.	8	113/46
46	Nov 12	10 10	Draft of previous entry.	8	253B/37

F.O. 682/ 1975	Date 1842	TK 22	Description	pp	Old R F.O. 682/
/147	Nov 14	10 12	Proclamation by Pottinger. For time being British merchants are allowed to trade only in Canton, which is an established trading port, and in Ting-hai and Ku-lang-hsü, which are at present occupied by British forces.	4	253B/
/148	Nov 15	10 13	Pottinger to Lu Tse-ch'ang. Has consulted General Gough. As Chusan is garrisoned by British forces, it will be better for Chinese official to be posted not there but in neighbouring Ta-hsieh Island instead. Ningpo should not be opened for foreign trade until Consul is appointed. Passports should be issued to Chinese officials going to Ting-hai and to British officials visiting Ningpo.	7	113/4
/149	Nov 15	10 13	Draft of previous entry.	7	253B/
/150	Nov 15	10 13	Pottinger to Liu Yün-k'o. Acknowledges receipt of letter of 10 November, pointing out that word Plenipotentiary has been placed two spaces below words Imperial Commissioner. Letter is herewith returned for correction.	5	113/4
/151	Nov 15	10 13	Draft of previous entry.	5	253B/
/152	Nov 21	10 19	I-li-pu and Liu Yün-k'o to Pottinger. As all British and Indian prisoners of war have been returned, Chinese abducted by British forces and transported to Hong Kong or kept elsewhere ought to be repatriated.	8	114/5
/153	Nov 21	10 19	Liu Yün-k'o to Pottinger. Cannot request Emperor, as Pottinger desires, to send Ch'i-ying to Canton to negotiate Supplementary Treaty. It is unlikely that Emperor will change his mind, and Pottinger should not delay his departure for Canton any longer. Will order release of any British or Indian soldier still in captivity, but cannot use yellow paper to publicise such an order as yellow paper is reserved for exclusive use by Emperor.	17	114/5

. / 5	Date 1842	TK 22	Description	pp	Old Ref. F.O. 682/
4	Nov 21	10 19	I-li-pu to Pottinger. Is proceeding to Canton at full speed, hoping Pottinger will not keep him waiting for too long. Will transmit Pottinger's congratulations to the Empress Dowager on her birthday.	10	114/65
5	Nov 21	10 19	I-li-pu and Liu Yün-k'o to Pottinger. Will reply separately on matter of trade. Have issued strict orders to scribes to copy diplomatic correspondence in proper format.	5	114/62
6	Nov 23	10 21	Proclamation by Pottinger to Chinese populace. Authorities in Taiwan have massacred about two hundred British sailors shipwrecked there, pretending that they were captured in action. Such officials should be executed and their property confiscated.	7	253B/1
7	Nov 23	10 21	Copy of previous entry.	7	253B/32
8	Nov 24	10 22	Pottinger to I-li-pu. Chinese commanding officer in Taiwan massacred shipwrecked British sailors and told Emperor that he had killed them in action. Regrettably Emperor endorsed this misrepresentation. Requests I-li-pu to inform Emperor of the true story, or he will sail to Tientsin to communicate with Peking directly.	10	113/50
9	Nov 24	10 22	Draft of previous entry.	10	253B/4
0	Nov 24	10 22	Pottinger to Ch'i-ying. Same content as F.O. 682/1975/158.	10	113/49
1	Nov 24	10 22	Draft of previous entry.	10	253B/2
2	Nov 26	10 24	Pottinger to Liu Yün-k'o. Returns Liu's despatch for correction as characters for Plenipotentiary were not elevated two spaces as those for Imperial Commissioner were. Encloses two copies of proclamation condemning massacre of British sailors shipwrecked in Taiwan. [Enclosures wanting]	12	113/51
3	Nov 26	10 24	Draft of previous entry.	12	253B/58

F.O. 682/ 1975	Date 1842	TK 22	Description	pp	Old Ref F.O. 682/
/164	Nov 26	10 24	Pottinger to Lu Tse-ch'ang. Under-takes to return all Chinese kept on board British ships or in Hong Kong.	6	113/52
/165	Nov 26	10 24	Draft of previous entry.	4	253B/1
/166	Nov 27	10 25	Pottinger to I-liang. Encloses proclamation denouncing massacre of British sailors shipwrecked in Taiwan, and prohibiting British merchants from going to treaty ports of Min-Che until trade regulations are established jointly with Ch'i-ying and I-li-pu. Re-quests that two letters be forwarded to Intendant Lu Tse-ch'ang and that any letter from Ch'i-ying be forward-ed to him.	9	113/53
			Encl. Proclamation by Pottinger. Only nine of total of two hundred. and eighty-three sailors belonging to two British ships wrecked in Taiwan have escaped death by execution or starvation by Taiwan authorities. Is relying on Emperor to take appropriate action in order to forestall revenge by British forces. 27 Nov 1842.	6	253B/1
/167	Nov 27	10 25	Draft of previous entry.	8	253B/1
/168	Nov 30	10 28	I-liang to Pottinger. Acknowledges receipt of letter and five enclosures three of which have been forwarded to addressees and remaining two will be dealt with after Pottinger has come to agreement with Ch'i-ying and I-li-pu.	6	114/60
/169	Nov -	10 -	Ch'i-ying to Pottinger. Is confident that I-li-pu will be just as efficient at Canton without Ch'i-ying himself being there. General amnesty of Chinese who were in British service will be publicized, but not on yellow paper as it is reserved for exclusive use by Emperor.	13	114/66
/170	Dec 13	11 12	Pottinger to Ch'i Kung. Has arrived at Hong Kong on 2 December. Is shocked to learn that foreign factories in Canton were attacked,	8	113/5

. / 5	Date 1842	TK 22	Description	pp	Old Ref. F.O. 682/
			plundered and burnt on 7 December. Demands apprehension of offenders and offers to send troops to help. Also demands compensation for losses. Encloses two copies of proclamation about massacre of shipwrecked sailors in Taiwan.		
1	Dec 13	11 12	Draft of previous entry.	6	253B/3
2	Dec 14	11 13	Ch'i-ying to Pottinger. Massacre of shipwrecked British sailors in Taiwan occurred during [and because of] war. Nonetheless, has inform-ed Emperor of massacre, and officer responsible will no doubt be heavily punished. Sailors ship-wrecked since the war have been helped. [2 copies]	11	931
3	Dec 15	11 14	Ch'i Kung to Pottinger. Destruction of foreign factories in Canton began with Indian sailors creating trouble. Villains who plundered factories during the fire will be tracked down but Pottinger must also restrain Indian sailors. Declines Pottinger's offer of military assistance to keep peace.	10	114/64
4	Dec -	11 -	Interpreter R. Thom to Prefect I Ch'ang-hua of Canton. Pottinger is prepared to steam out of Canton if this should help Cantonese to quieten down, but Chinese author-ities must guarantee safety of all foreigners in Canton.	5	113/55
5	Dec -	11 -	Draft of previous entry.	4	253B/54
6	Dec 20	11 19	I Ch'ang-hua to R. Thom. Is pleased that Pottinger has ordered steamer out of Canton River. Requests that sampan be used instead of steamer to carry mail as sight of steamer causes consternation. Will do ut-most to protect British merchants in Canton.	5	114/61
7	Dec 21	11 20	R. Thom to I Ch'ang-hua. Has trans-lated I's letter for Pottinger; original is herewith returned for correction as words Ta-Ch'ing are placed two spaces above Ta-Ying.	5	113/56

F.O. 682/ 1975	Date 1842	TK 22	Description	pp	Old Re E.O. 682/
/178	Dec 21	11 20	Draft of previous entry.	4	253B/5
/179	Dec 22	11 21	I Ch'ang-hua to R. Thom. Has instruc- ted scribes to copy diplomatic correspondence correctly.	5	114/6.
/180	Dec 27	11 26	Liu Yün-k'o to Pottinger. Has dismissed scribe who wrote letter wrongly. Did not know of massacre of shipwrecked British sailors in Taiwan: has not reported it to Emperor.	10	927
/181	Dec 28	11 27	I-li-pu to Pottinger. Was on his way to Canton when he heard of massacre in Taiwan and reported it to Emperor.	9	930
/182	Dec 30	11 29	Ch'i-ying to Pottinger. Emperor has ordered Viceroy of Min-Che, I-liang, to go to Taiwan to investigate alleged massacre of shipwrecked British sailors. Hopes incident will not be allowed to jeopardise cordial relations.	9	994
/183	Dec 30	11 29	Ch'i-ying to Pottinger. Wonders if his letters of 12 November and 14 December have been received.	9	928

	Date		Description	pp	Old Ref. F.O. 682/
6	1843	TK 22			
1	Jan 4	12 04	Viceroy Ch'i Kung of Liang-Kuang to Pottinger. Forwards two letters, from Viceroy of Liang-Chiang, Ch'i-ying, and Imperial Commissioner I-li-pu.	5	987
2	Jan 6	12 06	Pottinger to Ch'i Kung. Acknowledges receipt of letters from Ch'i-ying and I-li-pu. Wonders whether he or Ch'i Kung should ascertain compensation for destruction of British factory.	6	932
3	Jan 6	12 06	Pottinger to I-li-pu. Acknowledges letter of 28 Dec 1842. Will be pleased to go to Canton to meet him on his arrival.	4	933
4	Jan 6	12 06	I-li-pu to Pottinger. Has arrived at Shao-chou; will reach Canton in a few days. Has confidential message from Emperor, which may be delivered only verbally. Requests arrangement for meeting as soon as possible.	5	990
5	Jan 9	12 09	Ch'i Kung to Pottinger. Forwards I-li-pu's letter; Pottinger's reply may be given to same courier.	5	989
6	Jan 9	12 09	Ch'i Kung to Pottinger. Will forward Pottinger's letter to I-li-pu immediately. Suspects loss of property as reported by foreign merchants is exaggerated. Asks Pottinger to investigate and give true figures.	11	988
7	Jan 9	12 12	Pottinger to Ch'i Kung. Is sending Mr R. Thom, the interpreter, to Canton to arrange meeting with I-li-pu.	5	934
8	Jan 12	12 12	Pottinger to I-li-pu. Is sending interpreter to Canton for preliminary arrangements. Will come inland when I-li-pu arrives.	5	935
9	Jan 12	12 12	I-li-pu and Ch'i Kung to Pottinger. I-li-pu has arrived at Canton on 9 January and assumed duties on 11 January. Wish to make appointment for meeting on board British ship at Whampoa.	6	991

F.O. 682/ 1976	Date 1843	TK 22	Description	pp	Old R F.O. 682/
/10	Jan 16	12 16	I-li-pu and Ch'i Kung to Pottinger. Acknowledge letter of 12 January. Repeat request for appointment to meet one another. Forward letter from Liu Yün-k'o.	7	992
/11	Jan 17	12 17	Pottinger to I-li-pu and Ch'i Kung. Will meet them at Whampoa on 19 January.	6	936
/12	Jan 17	12 17	Pottinger to Ch'i Kung. Proposes to compensate for loss of life and property consequent to British steamer sinking salt junk by accident.	5	937
/13	Jan 18	12 18	I-li-pu to Pottinger. Forwards letter from Ch'i-ying. Repeats request for appointment to meet each other.	7	993
/14	Jan 19	12 19	I-li-pu and Ch'i Kung to Pottinger. Are pleased that Pottinger will arrive at Whampoa today in the evening. Will proceed to Whampoa tomorrow morning and hope to meet at noon.	7	996A
/15	Jan 19	12 19	Ch'i Kung to Pottinger. Declines offer of compensation for losses consequent to British steamer sinking salt junk by accident. Has settled matter according to Chinese practice.	8	995
/16	Jan 19	12 19	Pottinger to Ch'i-ying. Had hoped that Ch'i-ying would be appointed to negotiate at Canton; but since I-li-pu is appointed instead, looks forward to meeting I-li-pu. Agrees that massacre of shipwrecked British sailors at Taiwan should not be allowed to jeopardise negotiations.	9	939
/17	Jan 19	12 19	Pottinger to Viceroy I-liang of Min-Che. Two British ships are going to survey coast of China for navigation. Requests cooperation.	6	938
/18	Jan 20	12 20	Pottinger to Governor Liu Yün-k'o of Cheking. Is pleased that scribe responsible for mistake in format of previous communication has been dismissed, and that the officer	6	940

. / 6	Date 1843	TK 22	Description	pp	Old Ref. F.O. 682/
			responsible for massacre in Taiwan will be punished. Agrees that letters from Chinese government need not be translated into English, because of lack of interpreter.		
9	Jan 21	12 21	Pottinger to I-li-pu. Encloses reply to Ch'i-ying's two letters and asks that they be forwarded by express mail. Is sending two interpreters, Mr J.R. Morrison and Mr R. Thom, to Canton to complete draft of Supplementary Treaty before returning to Britain.	7	941
0	Jan 21	12 21	Pottinger to Ch'i Kung. Demands compensation for burning and plundering of foreign factories in Canton on 7 Dec 1842. Regrets that sufficient protection was not provided by Chinese authorities.	8	942
1	Jan 22	12 22	Pottinger to I-li-pu et al. Lists nine points for Supplementary Treaty.	21	943
2	Jan 22	12 22	I-li-pu et al. to Pottinger. Propose new system of monopoly that has advantages of Co-hong but not its abuses.	14	997
3	Jan 23	12 23	I-li-pu et al. to Pottinger. Request list of fees charged under Co-hong system so that illegal ones may be abolished.	8	998
4	Jan 24	12 24	I-li-pu et al. to Pottinger. To prevent Chinese and British merchants from owing each other money, all future transactions should be conducted in cash or by barter.	10	999
5	Jan 27	12 27	I-li-pu et al. to Pottinger. Five hundred thousand dollars is hereby delivered as part of payment of three million dollars owed by hong merchants to British merchants.	6	1000
6	Jan 28	12 28	Pottinger to i-ii-pu et al. Declines to consider Co-hong style monopoly.	10	944
7	Jan 29	12 29	Pottinger to I-li-pu et al. Argues further against monopoly system.	8	945

F.O. 682/ 1976	Date 1843	TK 22	Description	pp	Old R F.O. 682/
/28	Jan 29	12 29	Ch'i Kung to Pottinger. It was extremely difficult to check plundering during great fire in small hours. Losses, even as reported by foreign merchants come to only $43,552 and cannot possibly be $240,000.	9	1001
		TK 23			
/29	Feb 1	01 03	Pottinger to I-li-pu *et al*. Was pleased to receive at Whampoa Imperial Edict conveying news of Viceroy of Min-Che having been ordered to investigate massacre of British sailors shipwrecked at Taiwan. Protests about phrase in edict 'the Celestial Court controls the outer *i*'.	8	946
/30	Feb 6	01 08	Memo on new taxes in view of abolition of Co-hong system and opening of new ports.	6	947
/31	Feb 9	01 11	Ch'i-ying to Pottinger. Complains about K. Gutzlaff's policies in British occupied Ting-hai.	11	1009
/32	Feb -	01 -	I-li-pu *et al*. to Pottinger. List reservations about some of Pottinger's proposed trade arrangements and about British jurisdiction over Chinese in Hong Kong. Propose to transfer Sheriff to Kowloon to settle disputes among Chinese in Hong Kong. (Rec'd 10 Feb 1843).	18	1002
/33	Feb -	01 -	I-li-pu *et al*. to Pottinger. Have reservations about Pottinger's suggestions concerning pirate suppression. (Rec'd 10 Feb 1843).	14	1003
/34	Feb -	01 -	I-li-pu to Pottinger. $250,000 taken from inhabitants of Ningpo should form part of instalment of indemnity to be paid in June/July. (Rec'd 10 Feb 1843).	7	1004
/35	Feb 18	01 20	Pottinger to I-li-pu *et al*. British merchants have not been able to supply list of old fees and dues levied on exports and imports as they were incorporated in cost of	9	948

. ./ '6	Date 1843	TK 23	Description	pp	Old Ref. F.O. 682/
			goods. Invites Cantonese authorities to fix new and reasonable fees and dues.		
'6	Feb 18	01 20	Pottinger to Ch'i Kung. Presents verified list of claims for losses as result of fire and plundering of foreign factories on 7 Dec 1842.	8	949
7	Feb 19	01 21	Pottinger to I-li-pu *et al*. Asks them to inform J.R. Morrison as to when steamer may go to Whampoa to fetch $500,000 owed by *hong* merchants to British merchants.	4	950
8	Feb 19	01 21	Pottinger to I-li-pu. Points out fallacy of objections to his proposals to deal with pirates.	14	951
9	Feb 19	01 21	Pottinger to Ch'i-ying. Acknowledges letters. Negotiations with I-li-pu are going well; final settlement will take some time.	8	953
0	Feb 20	01 22	Pottinger to I-li-pu *et al*. Defends his proposals about establishment of consulates, trade at Hong Kong and fixing transit dues. Agrees to have Sheriff posted to Kowloon to settle disputes among Chinese residents of Hong Kong.	14	952
	Feb 20	01 22	Pottinger to Ch'i-ying. Is surprised that Chinese gentry in Ting-hai have accused K. Gutzlaff and British occupying forces of causing armed conflicts with local people, as no such reports have reached him officially or unofficially from British soldiers. Proposes meeting of British officers and Chinese gentry to determine who were lying.	10	954
2	Feb 20	01 22	I-li-pu to Pottinger. Has received complaints from gentry and elders of Whampoa area about foreigners entering villages, shooting birds, surrounding women and staring at them and fighting with cowherds. Requests restraint.	7	1005
	Feb 20	01 22	I-li-pu to Pottinger. Two British ships are reported trying to obtain pilots to sail to Teng-chou which is not a treaty port.	8	1006

F.O. 682/ 1976	Date 1843	TK 23	Description	pp	Old Re F.O. 682/
/44	n.d. [Feb 21]	n.d. [01 23]	Pottinger to I-li-pu. Has never sent two ships to Teng-chou: has sent the ships only to survey the coast.	6	956
/45	n.d. [Feb 21]	n.d. [01 23]	Pottinger to I-li-pu. It is difficult to determine if foreigners who land-ed in Whampoa and intruded into nearby villages were Britons. Will issue notice prohibiting such intrusion and will post Vice-Consul to Whampoa. Requests market be established there to make it un-necessary for sailors to go to villages for shopping.	7	955
/46	n.d. [Feb 21]	n.d. [01 23]	Pottinger to I-li-pu. It is better to establish customs house on island to west of Ku-lang-hsü on condition that this does not interfere with normal supply to British garrisons.	7	957
/47	Feb 21	01 23	I-li-pu to Pottinger. Requests return of customs house at Ku-lang-hsü when Amoy is opened as treaty port. Otherwise, he plans to establish one on island to west of Ku-lang-hsü. British garrison in Ku-lang-hsü should know that Chinese customs police will begin patrolling the area once Amoy is opened.	8	1007
/48	Feb 22	01 24	Ch'i-ying to Pottinger. Agrees that surveying coastal waters is neces-sary but it would be much safer to sail further out to sea.	16	1016
/49	Feb 22	01 24	Colonel Lai En-chüeh to Pottinger. Gives details of his plans to suppress piracy along coast of Kwangtung; requests co-operation.	8	1008
/50	Feb 28	01 30	Liu Yün-k'o to Pottinger. Has receiv-ed two letters forwarded by I-li-pu: one in English which no one can read, and the other in Chinese. Agrees to issue proclamation to the coastal areas of the coming of two surveying ships *Plover* and *Stirling* and to exhort co-operation.	8	1018
/51	Mar 6	02 06	Ch'i Kung to Pottinger. I-li-pu has died. Is prepared to discuss matters of urgency while waiting for arrival of new Imperial Commissioner.	6	1010

). 2/ 76	Date 1843	TK 23	Description	pp	Old Ref. F.O. 682/
52	n.d. [Mar 7]	n.d. [02 07]	Pottinger to Ch'i-ying. Is grieved by I-li-pu's death. Hopes Ch'i-ying will be appointed successor; is prepared to go to Chekiang to meet him.	8	958
53	Mar 9	02 09	Ch'i Kung to Pottinger. Is pleased that Pottinger is sending steamer to Whampoa to fetch $500,000 instalment of indemnity.	4	1011
54	Mar 9	02 09	Ch'i Kung to Pottinger. Acknowledges letter of 20 February. Agrees with proposals therein concerning trade with Hong Kong and jurisdiction over Chinese in the colony.	7	1012
55	Mar 13	02 13	Ch'i Kung to Pottinger. Has ordered Colonel Lai En-chüeh to arrange with British authorities for co-operation in suppressing piracy.	5	1013
56	Mar 14	02 14	Ch'i Kung to Pottinger. Is pleased with Pottinger's proclamation prohibiting Britons entering villages in Whampoa area and with promise to post Vice-Consul there to control British sailors. Agrees to set up market in Whampoa to make it unnecessary for sailors to wander into villages on purchasing expeditions.	5	1014
57	Mar 17	02 17	Pottinger to Ch'i Kung. Is grieved that I-li-pu has died. Hopes Ch'i-ying will be appointed his successor.	7	959
58	Mar 17	02 17	Ch'i Kung to Pottinger. Inquires if Admiral Pa [Parker] who visited Foochow is same person as Mr Pa [Sir William Parker] now in Hong Kong.	6	1015
59	Mar 18	02 18	Pottinger to Ch'i Kung. Agrees to subtract $250,000 (taken by British occupying forces from inhabitants of Ningpo) from payment of indemnity for that year.	7	960
60	Mar 19	02 19	Ch'i Kung to Pottinger. In Ningpo and other ports, the repair of forts and the building of city walls and ships are aimed at pirates, not British forces.	4	1017

F.O. 682/ 1976	Date 1843	TK 23	Description	pp	Old R F.O. 682/
/61	Mar 20	02 20	Pottinger to Ch'i-ying. Major Malcolm has ret rned with treaty ratified. Hopes Emperor has ratified it too. Is anxious that Ch'i-ying should succeed I-li-pu.	7	961
/62	Mar 20	02 20	Pottinger to Ch'i Kung. Encloses letter for Ch'i-ying. [See 1976/61]	4	962
/63	Mar 25	02 25	Ch'i Kung to Pottinger. Agrees that Ch'i-ying is best person to succeed I-li-pu and has said so to Emperor.	9	1019
/64	Mar 30	02 30	Ch'i Kung to Pottinger. According to Chinese law, the plundered party may be compensated only by property subsequently recovered. But since victims in this case have come from distant lands, he has ordered *hong* merchants to pay for losses by mid-May.	6	1020
/65	Mar 30	02 30	Ch'i Kung to Pottinger. Has forwarded letter to Ch'i-ying. Is confident that Ch'i-ying will be appointed to succeed I-li-pu.	6	1021
/66	Mar 31	03 01	Ch'i-ying to Pottinger. If appointed to succeed I-li-pu, best place to continue negotiations is still Canton.	14	1024
/67	Apr 5	03 06	Viceroy I-liang of Min-Che to Pottinger. Has ordered coastal authorities to give every facility to help the surveying ships.	7	1028
/68	Apr -	03 -	Pottinger to Ch'i Kung. Asks for co-operation in investigating fate of *Dovecote*, believed to have sunk near Ch'iung-chou.	7	963
/69	Apr 12	03 13	Ch'i Kung to Pottinger. Encloses commands to Brigadier and Intendant of Ch'iung-chou to investigate fate of *Dovecote*.	7	1022/
			Encl. Ch'i Kung to Intendant and Brigadier of Ch'iung-chou. Investigate fate of *Dovecote*, search for survivors, feed them and transport them overland to Canton. 12 Apr 1843.	6	1022
/70	Apr 13	03 14	Pottinger to Ch'i Kung. Smuggling flourishes because Chinese customs	7	964

J. 2/ 76	Date 1843	TK 23	Description	pp	Old Ref. F.O. 682/
			officials have been bribed. Requests Ch'i Kung to do something about it.		
71	Apr 14	03 15	Ch'i Kung to Pottinger. Forwards letter from Ch'i-ying.	5	1023
72	Apr 16	03 17	Ch'i Kung to Pottinger. Inevitably there are corrupt customs underlings and dishonest British merchants. Should work out mutually acceptable means of checking evasion of customs duties.	6	1025
73	Apr 20	03 21	Pottinger to Ch'i Kung. Thanks for co-operation in investigating fate of *Dovecote*. Survivors should be delivered to British man-of-war directly, instead of being sent overland to Canton.	5	965
74	Apr 20	03 21	Pottinger to Brigadier and Intendant of Ch'iung-chou. Encloses instruct- ions from Ch'i Kung to investigate fate of *Dovecote*. Survivors should be delivered to British man-of-war which conveys this communication.	7	966
75	Apr 20	03 21	Pottinger to Ch'i Kung. Thanks for having forwarded letter from Ch'i-ying.	5	967
76	Apr 23	03 24	Ch'i Kung to Pottinger. Ch'i-ying has been appointed to succeed I-li-pu.	5	1026
77	Apr 27	03 28	Ch'i Kung to Pottinger. Forwards letter from I-liang.	5	1027
78	May 12	04 13	Ch'i Kung to Pottinger. Brigadier and Intendant of Ch'iung-chou have received no news of *Dovecote* nor reports of any survivors. Has alerted coastal authorities. Ch'i- ying is on his way to Canton.	6	1029
79	May 29	05 01	Ch'i Kung to Pottinger. *Hong* merchants have agreed to compensate for losses sustained by foreign factories because of fire and plundering on 7 Dec 1842. Sum of $314,077.75 has been delivered.	5	1030
80	n.d. [May -]	n.d. [05 -]	Regulations on registration of residents, permanent or temporary, in the colony of Hong Kong.	5	968

F.O. 682/ 1976	Date 1843	TK 23	Description	pp	Old R F.O. 682/
/81	Jun 1	05 04	Pottinger to Ch'i Kung. Thanks for compensation of $314, 077.75. Only $67,399.25 is due to British merchants; rest is due to U.S. merchants and should be claimed by them through their own officials. Encl. Receipt for $67,399.25. 1 Jun 1843.	7 4	969A 969B
/82	Jun 4	05 07	Ch'i-ying to Pottinger. Has arrived at Canton today, ready for resumption of negotiations.	8	1031
/83	Jun 7	05 10	Pottinger to Ch'i-ying. Is pleased that Ch'i-ying has arrived at Canton. Asks for meeting to exchange ratified treaties.	7	970
/84	Jun 13	05 16	Ch'i-ying to Pottinger. Proposes meeting in Hong Kong on 23 Jun 1843.	9	1032
/85	Jun 13	05 16	Ch'i-ying to Pottinger. Asks for explanation of Captain Hope's letter to Intendant at Shanghai, specially the term *i-shih* [emergency situation]. Encl. Copy of two letters from Captain Hope to Intendant at Shanghai: has posted man-of-war to mouth of Yangtze River to stop illegal trade in cities of the delta, 15 Apr 1843; has decided to withdraw man-of-war from Yangtze because of "emergency situation", 10 May 1843.	14 3	1033
/86	Jun 22	05 25	Ch'i-ying to Pottinger. Ship with four British and ten Chinese sailors was shipwrecked near Amoy. Chinese authorities have helped survivors to recover weapons on board: two brass cannon, two iron cannon and a few guns.	8	1034
/87	[Jun 26]	[05 29]	Draft of tariff regulations.	37	971
/88	[Jun 26]	[05 29]	First draft of port regulations.	26	972
/89	Jun 26	05 29	Joint declaration by Pottinger and Ch'i-ying. After import and export duties are agreed upon, transit dues on foreign goods passing through interior of China should always remain as light as possible.	5	973

# /6	Date 1843	TK23	Description	pp	Old Ref. F.O. 682/
0	Jun 26	05 29	Copy of previous entry.	5	974
1	Jun 26	05 29	Copy of previous entry.	4	70/1
2	Jun 26	n.d.	Joint declaration by Pottinger and Ch'i-ying. Have compared English and Chinese versions of ratified Treaty of Nanking and found no mistakes in either. Copies are hereby exchanged. Encl. 1. Ch'i-ying's reply to Pottinger's proposals of 25 June. Not unwilling to settle question of tariff regulations speedily. Chinese trade with Hong Kong should be taxed. Disagrees that Chinese in Hong Kong should be governed by British law. Has made arrangements to facilitate surveying of coastal waters. Has arrested Brigadier and Intendant of Taiwan. Agrees to joint effort to suppress piracy. Cannot fix a place specially for mooring of opium vessels. 9 Jul 1843. Encl. 2. Ch'i-ying's reply to Pottinger's draft proposals of 30 June. Cannot legalize opium. Will study Pottinger's memo to Emperor when delivered, and will forward it if appropriate. Thanks for promise of copy of map for coastal navigation when ready. Agrees with views on diplomatic letters. Cantonese are still violently opposed to foreigners entering their city. 9 Jul 1843.	5	975
33	Jun 26	05 29	Second draft of port regulations for the five treaty ports, with comments by Chinese authorities.	24	976
34	Jun 30	06 03	Pottinger to Ch'i-ying. Requests that contents of Treaty of Nanking, now ratified, and new agreements on tariff and port regulations, be publicized.	12	977
35	Jul 1	06 04	Pottinger to Ch'i-ying. Explains that Captain Hope has acted without authority and that only five of the ships at Chusan are men-of-war, the rest being mercantile and supply ships.	14	978

F.O. 682/ 1976	Date 1843	TK 23	Description	pp	Old Re F.O. 682/
/96	Jul 9	06 12	Ch'i-ying to Pottinger. Agrees to terms of regulations for trade and tariffs, but has reservations about their wording which is awkward and unclear due apparently to the translation from English.	6	1035
/97	Jul 9	06 12	Ch'i-ying to Pottinger. Regulations for trade and tariffs have to be approved and published by the Emperor.	10	1036
/98	Jul -	06 -	Ch'i-ying to Pottinger. Encloses amended and expanded port regulations. Encl. 1. Ch'i-ying's revised port regulations with Hoppo's comments on Pottinger's original draft, n.d. Encl. 2. Suggestions about exchange of drafts on tariff and port regulations, resumption of trade, renting of warehouses etc., n.d.	5 25 2	1037
/99	Jul 15	06 18	Pottinger to Ch'i-ying et al. Accepts fifteen of the sixteen entries in his draft port regulations. Pleased that Canton will be re-opened for trade on 27 July. Urges that other four ports be opened soon. Encl. Finalized and approved port regulations. [15 Jul 1843.]	13 27	979 980
/100	Jul 18	06 21	Ch'i-ying to Pottinger. Accepts Pottinger's revised port regulations. Will forward them to Emperor for approval and publication. Asks when and how Pottinger is going to withdraw men-of-war from Chusan and Hong Kong.	7	1038
/101	Jul 18	06 21	Ch'i-ying to Pottinger. Has report from Prefect of Ningpo investigating allegations of British soldiers disturbing occupied areas. British commanding officer has not encouraged soldiers to be unruly, and has promised to control them more vigorously in future.	9	1039
/102	Jul 20	06 23	Pottinger to Colonel Lai En-chüeh. Pirates have attacked Lorcha No. 11 and killed British passengers.	8	981

.	Date		Description	pp	Old Ref.
:/					F.O.
6	1843	TK 23			682/
			Suspects Chinese sailors on board are accomplices.		
3	Jul 20	06 23	Pottinger to Ch'i-ying. British merchants should be allowed to rent warehouses from Chinese merchants to the east of original foreign factories in Canton.	7	982
4	Jul 20	06 23	Captain Ts'ai to Pottinger. Is acting in place of Colonel Lai En-chüeh. Has mobilized marine forces to hunt down pirates who attacked Lorcha No. 11.	7	1040
5	Jul 21	06 24	Sub-Magistrate Hsieh Hsiao-chuang of Macao to Pottinger. Will do all he can to apprehend pirates who attacked Lorcha No. 11.	9	1041
6	Jul 22	06 25	Ch'i Kung and Ch'eng Yü-ts'ai to Pottinger. Have ordered Colonel Lai En-chüeh, Provincial Judge, Magistrates of Hsiang-shan and Hsin-an, and Sub-Magistrate of Macao to investigate attack on Lorcha No. 11.	9	1042
7a	Jul 24	06 27	Ch'i-ying *et al.* to Pottinger. Agree that British merchants might hire warehouses to east of factory area.	5	1043
7b	Jul 24	06 27	Ch'i-ying and Ch'eng Yü-ts'ai to Pottinger. According to treaty, $3,000,000 instalment of indemnity is to be paid in the twenty-third year of Tao-kuang's reign. As the silver ingots have come from different provinces with different standards, it is best to apply Kwangtung Provincial Treasury standard to them all. According to this standard, 0.7 tael contains more silver than one silver dollar and will be safe as rate of conversion. Using this rate, $3,000,000 is equivalent to 2,150,000 taels. It was agreed that the $250,000 (equivalent to 175,000 taels) paid at Ningpo should be deducted from present instalment of indemnity. Hence present payment amounts to 1,925,000 taels. Requests Pottinger to appoint place and time for delivery of the treasure.	4	352/1

F.O. 682/ 1976	Date 1843	TK 23	Description	pp	Old R F.O. 682/
/107c	Jul 24	06 27	Ch'i-ying to Pottinger. On 29 May 1843, a lorcha loaded with cloth went to trade at Cha-p'u [Chekiang]. As Cha-p'u is not treaty port, lorcha has contravened treaty.	3	352/2
/108	Jul 24	06 27	Ch'i-ying et al. to Pottinger. Since Canton will be re-opened for trade on 27 July, final version of port and tariff regulations should be published in English as well.	6	1044
			Encl.1. Finalized port regulations, n.d.	20	1045
			Encl. 2. Finalized tariff regulations: imports, n.d.	34	1046
			Encl. 3. Finalized tariff regulations: exports, n.d.	34	1047
/109a	Jul 25	06 28	Ch'i-ying to Pottinger. Supplementary Treaty should be signed before Canton is re-opened for trade.	24	1048
/109b	Jul 28	07 02	Sub-Magistrate Hsieh Hsiao-chuang of Macao to Pottinger. In response to Pottinger's request to instruct pilots to observe new port regulations, has asked his superiors for a copy of these regulations for guidance.	11	68/3
/110a	Jul 29	07 03	Ch'i-ying et al. to Pottinger. Again urge that port and tariff regulations be published in English. Hope that one amendment, agreed upon by both sides, be included in the publication.	6	1049
/110b	Aug 1	07 06	Ch'i-ying et al. to Pottinger. Agree that foreign ships no longer have to proceed to Macao for registration or hiring pilots there. From now on, all foreign ships should stop at Heng-tang Fort for registration, for hiring of pilots from among licenced fishermen or pilots formerly of Macao, and for the boarding of customs officers to accompany the ships to Whampoa in order to forestall smuggling.	10	68/3
/111	Aug 4	07 09	Ch'i-ying and Ch'i Kung to Pottinger. Instalment of three million dollars of indemnity plus four days' interest are ready for collection. Reiterate willingness to pay interest on any future delay.	6	1050

№.	Date	Description	pp	Old Ref. F.O. 682/
*/ ⁶6	1843	TK 23		

'E: *The symbol ᴊ in the third column stands for intercalary month.*

2	Aug 24	07 29 Ch'i-ying *et al.* to Pottinger. Acknowledge receipt of Pottinger's proclamation prohibiting British merchants from selling opium in Canton River area. Appropriate that British authorities deal with British smugglers and Chinese authorities with Chinese collaborators. India is the [main] source of opium and is a British colony; hope British author-ities will stop the trade. Decline to discuss legalisation of opium.	14	253A/4A/8
3	Aug 24	07 29 Ch'i-ying *et al.* to Pottinger. Pottinger should look after employ-ment of pilots himself. Agree that papers for entering Whampoa should be issued at Hong Kong or Macao and should be examined by Chinese officers at Heng-tang Fort. Also agree that one British man-of-war should stay in each port to keep sailors in order.	11	985
4a	Aug 24	07 29 Ch'i-ying *et al.* to Pottinger. Are pleased that Pottinger has received set of weights and measures they sent him. Would appreciate a note stating names and ranks of Consuls appointed to treaty ports.	5	1051
4b	Aug 25	ᴊ7 01 Ch'i Kung and Ch'eng Yü-ts'ai to Pottinger. Have arrested pirate-suspects in connection with the plundering and burning of Lorcha No. 11, of another boat near Macao, and of an opium clipper. Will punish them severely. Chinese law does not provide for government officials to act as witnesses against criminals, therefore Pottinger needs not send British officials to Canton as witnesses.	23	68/3B/2
5	Aug 28	ᴊ7 04 Ch'i-ying and Ch'i Kung to Pottinger. Gentry and elders of villages in Chiao-t'ang-ssu reported sailors from nineteen Hong Kong ships landing in the area, causing consternation. This is contrary to treaty stipulat-ions and must be stopped.	8	984

F.O. 682/ 1976	Date 1843	TK 23	Description	pp	Old Re F.O. 682/
/116	Sep 4	i7 11	Ch'i-ying *et al.* to Pottinger. Emperor has approved port and tariff regulations [terms for Supplementary Treaty].	6	983
/117	Sep 25	08 02	Ch'i-ying to Pottinger. British ship *Gevant Packet* was stranded near mouth of Yangtze River. Rescue work is completed. All ships must be made aware of this dangerous area. Recommends employment of pilots.	9	986
/118a	Sep 29	08 06	Ch'i-ying to Pottinger. Encloses two letters of introduction for Captains Balfour and Gribble to Intendants at Shanghai and Amoy, announcing their appointment as Consuls.	6	1052
/118b	Oct 5	08 12	Acting Colonel Shen Chen-pang of Ta- p'eng to Pottinger. Three men admit that they picked up sixteen bags of spices floating in the sea. A fourth man admits having bought all sixteen bags of spices from them. A [pirate- suspect] has been arrested near Macao. All five men will be interrogated together in connection with the plundering of Lorcha [No. 11] which was loaded with spices. The sixteen bags of spices recovered are delivered herewith.	10	68/3B
/119a	Oct 8	08 15	Ch'i-ying to Pottinger. Last month two foreign ships went illegally to Chihli and Shantung trying to sell woollens, opium and other goods. Requests information about these vessels, and that all foreigners be told to confine their trade to treaty ports.	11	1053
/119b	Oct 14	08 21	Ch'i Kung and Ch'eng Yü-ts'ai to Pottinger. Agree that pirates must be punished severely. Will spare no effort in extracting information from pirate-suspects and in hunting down their accomplices still at large.	7	68/3I
/120	Oct 15	08 22	Ch'i-ying and Ch'i Kung to Pottinger. Are pleased that Consuls have been posted to Canton, Shanghai and Amoy. Foreign vessels should be told not to visit Ningpo and Foochow until Consuls are sent there.	8	1054

	Date		Description	pp	Old Ref. F.O.
	1843	TK 23			682/

1	Oct 15	08 22	Ch'i-ying to Pottinger. Since terms of Supplementary Treaty have been agreed upon, question of how many British warships remain in Chinese waters should be settled.	6	1055
2	Nov 5	09 14	Ch'i-ying to Pottinger. Has referred Pottinger's request for expanding Canton factory area to Viceroy of Liang-Kuang and Governor of Kwangtung.	9	1056
3a	Nov 7	09 16	Ch'i-ying to Pottinger. There is a new uniform scale of duties charged on ginseng, made at request of U.S. Consul. Has informed Hoppo and authorities in other treaty ports.	5	1057
3b	Nov 14	09 23	Ch'i Kung and Ch'eng Yü-ts'ai to Pottinger. Gentry of Chiao-t'ang-ssu in P'an-yü have complained that groups of foreigners continue to wander into villages demanding to buy fruits and flowers and even intruding into private homes. Request restraint.	8	68/3B/6
3c	Dec 1	10 10	Intendant Kung Mu-chiu of Su-Sung-T'ai to Pottinger. Acknowledges receipt of Pottinger's despatch in which Pottinger requested assistance of Chinese troops under Kung's command in case Consul G. Balfour should fail to control rowdy British sailors. Regrets that he cannot mobilize his troops for such a purpose without previous authorization from Emperor and in any case such a provision was not written into the treaty. Considers the 160 bluejackets on board British battleship sufficient to keep peace and order, pledging support of his linguists to settle disputes. Shanghai was opened for trade on 17 Nov 1843.	10	68/3B/7
4	Dec 22	11 02	Provincial Treasurer Huang En-t'ung of Kwangtung to Pottinger. Encloses ratified Supplementary Treaty. [Encl. wanting]	6	1058
5	Dec 25	11 05	Ch'i Kung and Ch'eng Yü-ts'ai to Pottinger. Consul G.T. Lay's argument that villagers should first ascertain nationality of troublesome sailors before complaining cannot be sustained. Treaty stipulates that sailors	15	1059

F.O. 682/ 1976	Date 1843	TK 23	Description	pp	Old R F.O. 682/
			must not disturb villagers, who are entitled to round up such intruders and hand them over to authorities.		
/126	Dec 25	11 05	Ch'i Kung to Pottinger. Agrees to hand over to British Consul any deserter from British ships.	3	352/3

. / 7	Date 1844	TK 23	Description	pp	Old Ref. F.O. 682/
1	Jan 2	11 13	Ch'i Kung to Pottinger. Is surprised to read that British Consul at Amoy [H. Gribble] claims trade regulat- ions provide for imported goods to be taxed as they are sold. Rather, treaty stipulates that import duties should be paid in full as soon as goods enter port. Requests that Consul be instructed to observe regulations.	9	104/1
2	Jan 11	11 22	Pottinger to Ch'i-ying and Ch'eng Yü- ts'ai. Will send deputy to Canton around 20 January to fetch instal- ment of indemnity but reserves right to claim compensation should silver be found to be deficient.	7	104/2
3a	Jan 11	11 22	Pottinger to Ch'i Kung. English version of Art. 6 of trade agreement differs from Chinese. Subsequent meetings between Consul at Amoy and local authorities come to conclusion that all ships, on entering port, should pay tonnage dues and pilot fees; however, their cargo should be taxed according to quantity landed or sold to local shipping, but not that still on board. Encl. English version of Art 6 translated into Chinese, n.d.	12 1	104/3 A+B
3b	Jan 11	11 22	Huang En-t'ung to Pottinger. Another instalment of indemnity is ready for collection.	5	1252
4	Jan 15	11 26	Proclamation by Pottinger to inhabitants of Hong Kong. Concerning two British subjects murdered by Chinese fishermen, murderers have now been executed by order of Emperor and their heads hung up at scenes of crime.	6	104/4
5	Jan 17	11 28	Ch'i Kung and Ch'eng Yü-ts'ai to Pottinger. British shopping expedition to Chang-chou is breach of treaty. Chi-li-pu's [Consul H. Gribble's] request to build house in Ku-lang-hsü is unwise because island will be returned to China after full indemnity is paid and his house will have to be demolished. Foreign ships entering Amoy with intention to export tea must pay tonnage dues on arrival, even if empty.	14	426/6

F.O. 682/ 1977	Date 1844	TK 23	Description	pp	Old Ref F.O. 682/
/6	Jan 18	11 29	Pottinger to Ch'i-ying. Canton author- itites agree that it is good idea to make Ku-lang-hsü place of residence for foreigners. Wonders what Ch'i- ying thinks of proposal to charge tonnage dues and pilot fees for all ships entering port, and to tax imports according to quantity landed and sold to local shipping, but not that still on board.	8	104/5
/7a	Jan 21	12 02	Ch'i-ying to Pottinger. Proposal to let foreigners trade in Amoy but live in Ku-lang-hsü contradicts treaty. Is certain that Britons may find suitable places to live apart from sites where there are forts and graves.	9	104/22
/7b	Jan 24	12 05	Pottinger to Provincial Treasurer Huang En-t'ung of Kwangtung. While converting silver taels to silver dollars to pay indemnity, standard commonly used in Canton must be employed. If silver is found to be deficient in weight resulting in delay in payment, interest will be charged.	7	104/7
/8	Jan 24	12 05	Ch'i Kung to Pottinger. Inquires about Consul R. Thom's date of departure from Canton for Ningpo.	6	104/8
/9	Jan 30	12 11	Pottinger to Ch'i Kung and Ch'eng Yü- ts'ai. Britons in Amoy went to Chang-chou contrary to his own instructions. Has reprimanded them and will ensure no similar excursions will take place in future. Agrees that permanent residence should not be established in Ku-lang-hsü. If local authorities insist on any vessel entering Amoy paying tonnage dues even if only carrying goods or letters, will issue instructions to this effect. Attributes above confusion to lack of competent interpreter.	13	104/10
/10	Jan 31	12 12	Pottinger to Ch'i Kung. Consul R. Thom left Hong Kong on 4 Dec 1843 arriving at Ningpo on 19 Dec 1843, and opened the port for trade on 1 Jan 1844.	5	104/9

. / 7	Date 1844	TK 23	Description	pp	Old Ref. F.O. 682/
1	[Rec'd.] Feb 1	12 -	Huang En-t'ung to Pottinger. Has been instructed by Peking to pay instalments of indemnity according to standard fixed by Ministry of Finance. This standard is higher than silver delivered to Canton from rest of country and his department has to supplement this deficiency in weight to the order of 12,000 taels. Now Pottinger's demand to use commercial standard in Canton, which is still higher, will cost his department further 10,000 taels.	13	104/11
2	Feb 3	12 15	Pottinger to Ch'i Kung *et al.* Encloses receipt of instalment of indemnity for 23rd year of Tao-kuang's reign. Encl. Pottinger's note acknowledging receipt of 1,925,000 taels of silver which, when converted according to standard commonly used in commercial circles in Canton, amounts to 2,750,000 silver dollars, n.d.	5 3	104/12 A+B
3	Feb 4	12 16	Pottinger to Huang En-t'ung. Reminds Huang that while negotiating treaty at Nanking, it was made clear that with regard to payment of indemnity, silver taels were to be converted to silver dollars according to commercial standard at Canton, i.e. 710 taels to 1,000 dollars. Assures Huang that if overpaid, excess will be credited to Chinese government but if underpaid, Chinese will have to make up the sum.	14	104/13
4	Feb 12	12 24	Ch'i Kung to Pottinger. Has resigned on grounds of ill health and has handed over duties to Governor Ch'eng Yü-ts'ai today.	6	104/14
5	Feb 12	12 24	Ch'i-ying to Pottinger. Agrees that in Amoy, goods not unloaded from foreign vessels need not pay any tax; in Shanghai and Ningpo a similar rule is coming into operation. To inspire respect for the treaty, it is best that Britons do not begin living in Ku-lang-hsü as treaty does not provide for this. Excursion from Amoy to Chang-chou must not be repeated as this is breach of treaty.	11	104/28

F.O. 682/ 1977	Date 1844	TK 23	Description	pp	Old Re F.O. 682/
/16	Feb 15	12 27	Huang En-t'ung to Pottinger. Canton Customs Office and Kwangtung Provincial Treasury are separate departments with different standards set by Ministry of Finance more than 100 years ago and each paying into Ministry according to its own standard. Merchants pay taxes according to Customs Office standard and peasants according to Treasury Standard which is lower. If Pottinger insists, will pay indemnity according to Customs Office standard.	15	104/1!
/17	Feb 17	12 29	Pottinger to Ch'eng Yü-ts'ai. Royal Navy has saved fourteen of seventeen Chinese sailors whose ship was sinking in Straits of Taiwan. They have now boarded merchant ship sailing to Amoy from Hong Kong via Canton.	6	104/1
/18	Feb 17	12 29	Pottinger to Ch'eng Yü-ts'ai. Thanks Amoy authorities for having saved sailors and goods of *Eliza Stewart* which went aground nearby.	7	104/1
/19	Feb 17	12 29	Ch'eng Yü-ts'ai to Pottinger. Endorses Pottinger's handling of confusion in Amoy by: (1) reprimanding Britons who ventured to Chang-chou; (2) restraining Britons from building houses in Ku-lang-hsü; (3) leaving question of taxing mail boats to Chinese authorities. Agrees that confusion is caused by lack of competent interpreter.	14	104/2
/20	Feb 17	12 29	Ch'eng Yü-ts'ai to Pottinger. Colonel of Ta-p'eng reports that Royal Navy has built ten chimney-like stone structures on various hill-tops in P'u-t'ai-shan area, intending them to be landmarks for navigation. Royal Navy has no right to do this in Chinese territory.	6	104/:
/21	Feb 19	TK 24 01 02	Pottinger to Ch'eng Yü-ts'ai. Reply from Consul [H. Gribble] at Amoy confirms earlier suspicions that various instances of confusion there resulted from absence of competent interpreter.	12	104/

Date		Description	pp	Old Ref. F.O.
1844	TK 24			682/

Feb 19	01 02	Pottinger to Ch'i Kung. Wishes him speedy recovery from illness.	6	104/19
Feb 20	01 03	Pottinger to Ch'eng Yü-ts'ai. *Isabella*, loaded with 7,440 silver dollars and unarmed, was plundered by Chinese pirates between Hong Kong and Macao. Chinese cooks on board are accomplices and have now been arrested by Macao authorities.	7	104/20
Feb 21	01 04	Pottinger to Ch'eng Yü-ts'ai. Requests Ch'eng to confirm treaty provision according to which British vessels may import rice to China free of tonnage dues and taxes, and leave free of same if they carry no exports, or enjoy half tonnage dues if they carry exports.	7	104/21

Number not used.

Feb 21	01 04	Ch'eng Yü-ts'ai to Pottinger. Since 1841 Britons have been building houses, roads and bridges in Nan-ao. They also keep horses, and are visited periodically by foreign ships. Now that treaty has specified five ports for foreign trade and residence, Britons should be ordered to leave Nan-ao.	10	104/25
Feb 27	01 10	Ch'eng Yü-ts'ai to Pottinger. British authorities have planted flag on north side of entrance to Hong Kong harbour with intention of building forts there. As place is in Chinese territory, this contravenes treaty provisions.	11	104/31
Feb 28	01 11	Proclamation by Major Caine to inhabitants of Hong Kong, exhorting them to report on outlaws.	4	104/26
Feb 28	01 11	Major Caine to Colonel Shen Chen-pang of Ta-p'eng. Requests co-operation in completing legal cases referred to him last year.	4	104/27
Feb 28	01 11	Proclamation by Pottinger *et al.* prohibiting practice of keeping male or female slaves or bond servants, giving details of various forms of punishment to different kinds of	10	104/30

F.O. 682/ 1977	Date 1844	TK 24	Description	pp	Old R F.O. 682/
			offenders as well as assistance to victims.		
/31	Feb 28	01 11	Ch'eng Yü-ts'ai to Pottinger. Has forwarded to Amoy authorities Pottinger's appreciation of help given to *Eliza Stewart* which ran aground on 27 Jan 1844 near Amoy.	7	104/3
/32	Feb 28	01 11	Ch'eng Yü-ts'ai to Pottinger. Has forwarded to Fukien authorities Pottinger's message about Royal Navy having saved thirteen Chinese sailors near Taiwan.	7	104/3
/33	Feb 28	01 11	Ch'eng Yü-ts'ai to Pottinger. Has forwarded Pottinger's letter to Fukien authorities about confusion in Amoy.	12	104/3
/34	Feb 28	01 11	Ch'eng Yü-ts'ai to Pottinger. Has referred to Ch'i-ying the question of how foreign ships bringing rice to China should be taxed.	11	104/3
/35	Feb 28	01 11	Ch'eng Yü-ts'ai to Pottinger. Concerning plundering of *Isabella*, has ordered Sub-Magistrate of Macao to obtain from arrested thieves the names and addresses of accomplices still at large, and has commanded civil officials and military officers of Hsiang-shan to spare no effort in capturing them.	10	104/3
/36	Feb 29	01 12	Major Caine to Colonel Shen Chen-pang. Encloses list of thieves who burgled Mr White's house. [Encl. wanting]	6	104/2
/37	Mar 5	01 17	Major Caine to Colonel Shen Chen-pang. Hands over herewith thirty-one criminals captured in Hong Kong for trial in Kowloon. Wonders if Shen has arrested offenders according to information supplied to him on 29 Feb 1844.	9	104/
/38	Mar 7	01 19	Pottinger *et al.* proclaiming thirteen regulations governing Chinese junks visiting Hong Kong.	13	104/
/39	Mar 8	01 20	Ch'eng Yü-ts'ai to Pottinger. Requests Pottinger to confirm if British man-of-war has visited	8	104/

). 2/ 77	Date 1844	TK 24	Description	pp	Old Ref. F.O. 682/
			Hai-men in Chekiang to survey waters.		
40	Mar 9	01 21	Major Caine to Colonel Shen Chen-pang. Provides further information for apprehension of thieves.	8	104/39
41	Mar 11	01 23	Pottinger to Ch'eng Yü-ts'ai. Denies that Royal Navy has built chimney-like stone structures in P'u-t'ai-shan area.	5	104/40
42	Mar 11	01 23	Pottinger to Ch'eng Yü-ts'ai. Flags are erected for purpose of survey. Forts will be built on island of Hong Kong for self-defence.	10	104/41
43	Mar 12	01 24	Pottinger to Ch'eng Yü-ts'ai. Britons who have built houses, roads and bridges in Nan-ao have done so with connivance of local Chinese officials. Suggests that six months notice be given them to leave.	20	104/42
44	Mar 12	01 24	Pottinger to Ch'eng Yü-ts'ai. Encloses proclamation prohibiting practice of keeping slaves or bond servants in Hong Kong.	6	104/43
45	Mar 16	01 28	Pottinger to Ch'eng Yü-ts'ai. It is possible that British man-of-war has been to Hai-men to survey waters as he and Ch'i-ying have agreed that coastal waters should be surveyed. As to name of captain of vessel involved, does not know it personally, but if Ch'eng forwards card left by captain, Pottinger might be able to provide further information.	6	104/45
46	Mar 20	02 02	Ch'eng Yü-ts'ai to Pottinger. Agrees that Britons could have built houses, roads and bridges in Nan-ao only with connivance of Chinese officials. They will be duly punished. Also agrees that six months notice be given Britons to leave Nan-ao.	7	104/47
47	Mar 21	02 03	Pottinger to Ch'eng Yü-ts'ai. Requests that Chinese boats that traded between Hong Kong and Canton be allowed to have licences renewed.	5	104/46
48	Mar 25	02 07	Pottinger to Viceroy Ch'i-ying of Liang-Chiang. Requests him to write	8	1108

F.O. 682/ 1977	Date 1844	TK 24	Description	pp	Old Re F.O. 682/
			to Viceroy of Min-Che to assign land to foreigners to build houses in Amoy. Agrees to prohibit Britons going up Yangtze river.		
/49	Mar 30	02 12	Ch'eng Yü-ts'ai to Pottinger. Chinese merchants wishing to trade at Hong Kong will be required to apply to Chinese customs officials for licence according to treaty stipulation.	9	1136
/50	Apr 5	02 18	Ch'eng Yü-ts'ai to Pottinger. Has sent Prefect Ni Li with an interpreter to Nan-ao to supervise evacuation of Britons who have gone there illegally to live and trade.	7	1135
/51	Apr 19	03 02	Pottinger to Ch'eng Yü-ts'ai. Has ordered Britons living in Nan-ao to leave within six months.	7	1109
/52	Apr 20	03 03	Pottinger to Ch'eng Yü-ts'ai. A special Chinese official should be posted to Kowloon to co-operate with Hong Kong authorities in dealing with Chinese outlaws.	3	1110
/53	Apr 22	03 05	Pottinger to Ch'eng Yü-ts'ai. Requests copy of court proceedings concerning murder of Dr McLinley.	7	1111
/54	Apr 27	03 10	Ch'eng Yü-ts'ai to Pottinger. At behest of Pottinger, Cantonese authorities have decided to exempt foreign ships importing rice (and nothing else) to China from all taxes, and to exempt them from half of tonnage dues when exporting goods from China. Authorities in other treaty ports have been notified of decision.	18	1137
/55	May 5	03 18	Ch'eng Yü-ts'ai to Pottinger. British authorities must not build forts in Kowloon because only Hong Kong Island has been ceded.	13	1138
/56	May 5	03 18	Ch'eng Yü-ts'ai to Pottinger. Has permission from Emperor to transfer Sheriff of Kuan-fu and Colonel of Ta-p'eng to Kowloon, so that they may co-operate with K. Gutzlaff in apprehending Chinese outlaws.	11	1139

. / 7	Date 1844	TK 24	Description	pp	Old Ref. F.O. 682/
7	May 5	03 18	Ch'eng Yü-ts'ai to Pottinger. A ship from Hong Kong with four foreigners on board has visited village in Shun-te magistracy, contrary to treaty.	8	1140
8	May 8	03 21	Pottinger to Viceroy Ch'i-ying of Liang-Kuang. Announces appointment of Sir John Davis as his successor.	5	1112
9	May 8	03 21	Pottinger to Ch'eng Yü-ts'ai. His successor Sir John Davis takes up duties today.	5	1113
0	May 9	03 22	Davis to Ch'eng Yü-ts'ai. Has taken up office of H.M. Plenipotentiary. Requests interview.	5	1114
1	May 10	03 23	Davis to Ch'i-ying. Has assumed duties as H.M. Plenipotentiary. Is pleased that Ch'i-ying has been appointed Viceroy of Liang-Kuang [to hold office concurrently as Imperial Commissioner for Foreign Affairs]. Requests interview in Canton.	6	1115
2	May 12	03 25	Ch'eng Yü-ts'ai to Pottinger. Is sorry that Pottinger is leaving when Ch'i-ying is about to return to Canton. Hopes Davis will follow Pottinger's policy concerning evacuation of Britons from Nan-ao and building of forts in Kowloon.	9	1141
3	May 12	03 25	Ch'eng Yü-ts'ai to Davis. Is pleased that Davis has taken up office of H.M. Plenipotentiary. Commissioner Ch'i-ying has been appointed new Viceroy of Liang-Kuang, and will return to Canton soon to look after foreign affairs.	8	1142
4	May 14	03 27	Huang En-t'ung to Pottinger. Asks that Pottinger's successor be informed of method of paying indemnity so far.	9	1143
5	May 15	03 28	Davis to Ch'eng Yü-ts'ai. Will find out who were the foreigners who roamed around Shun-te. Regards matter not serious on the ground that there were no incidents. Chinese pirates have plundered a Hong	8	1116

F.O. 682/ 1977	Date 1844	TK 24	Description	pp	Old Re F.O. 682/
			Kong vessel carrying 12,000 silver dollars of colonial salary, killing four British soldiers on board.		
/66	May 18	04 02	Davis to Ch'eng Yü-ts'ai. F.C. Macgregor is to succeed G.T. Lay as Consul at Canton.	6	1117
/67	May 20	04 04	Pottinger to Ch'eng Yü-ts'ai. Has handed over all diplomatic correspondence to his successor Davis.	6	1118
/68	May 20	04 04	Pottinger to Huang En-t'ung. Has handed over all correspondence concerning payment of indemnity to his successor Davis.	5	1119
/69	May 22	04 06	Ch'eng Yü-ts'ai to Davis. Although foreigners who roamed about in Shun-te magistracy have not created any incidents, they have breached the treaty. Pledges to do all he can to capture pirates.	10	1144
/70	May 24	04 08	Ch'eng Yü-ts'ai to Pottinger. Acknowledges that Pottinger has handed over all diplomatic correspondence to Davis. Earnestly hopes that both sides will for ever abide by the treaty.	6	1146
/71	May 24	04 08	Ch'eng Yü-ts'ai to Davis. G.T. Lay has been successful Consul at Canton. Hopes his successor F.C. Macgregor will follow same policy. Wishes to know where Lay is being transferred.	8	1145
/72	May 31	04 15	Davis to Ch'eng Yü-ts'ai. Has captured Ch'en A-t'ai, one of the pirates suspected of having committed piracy on 15 May 1844. Deposition reveals accomplices living in Canton area.	6	1120
/73	May 31	04 15	Davis to Ch'eng Yü-ts'ai. F.C. Macgregor is suitable as British Consul at Canton. G.T. Lay is transferred to Foochow. Looks forward to meeting Imperial Commissioner Ch'i-ying when he returns [from Peking].	6	1121
/74	Jun 6	04 21	Ch'i-ying to Davis. Has just returned to Canton. Hopes to see Davis on 12	8	1147

.	Date		Description	pp	Old Ref.
:/					F.O.
7	1844	TK 24			682/

			June at Hu-men.		
5	Jun 6	04 21	Ch'i-ying to Davis. Has read Davis' despatch to Ch'eng Yü-ts'ai about pirate suspect Ch'en A-t'ai. Has urged Sheriff of Kowloon and Colonel of Ta-p'eng to capture accomplices quickly.	7	1148
6	Jun 6	04 21	Ch'i-ying to Davis. Has read Davis' letter to Ch'eng Yü-ts'ai about F.C. Macgregor's appointment as Consul at Canton, and G.T. Lay's transfer to Foochow. Evacuation of Britons from Nan-ao and British intention to build forts in Kowloon must be governed by terms of treaty.	7	1149
7	Jun 6	04 21	Ch'i-ying to Pottinger. Has just returned to Canton. Hopes to see Pottinger on 12 June at Hu-men before Pottinger returns to Britain.	8	1150
8	Jun 7	04 22	Ch'i-ying to Davis. Prefect Ni Li has reported that Britons in Nan-ao have asked for extension of deadline for evacuation from six to ten months. Is prepared to grant request out of special consideration but Davis must tell compatriots that they are breaching treaty.	11	1151
9	Jun 7	04 22	Ch'i-ying to Pottinger. Agrees to extend deadline for Britons to evacuate Nan-ao from six to ten months. Urges Pottinger to discipline Britons there.	11	1176
0	Jun 15	04 30	Davis to Ch'i-ying. Requests that new regulations governing rice imported by foreign vessels etc. be made known to officials at Amoy to stop them levying tonnage dues and refusing to accept *sycee* silver.	6	1122
1	Jun 15	04 30	Davis to Ch'i-ying. Guarantees return of Ku-lang-hsü on full payment of indemnities. Another instalment is due on 30 Jun 1844.	7	1123
2	Jun 20	05 05	Davis to Ch'i-ying. Requests return of pirate Ch'en A-t'ai [whom Davis has handed over to Chinese authorities	6	1124A

F.O. 682/ 1977	Date 1844	TK 24	Description	pp	Old R F.O. 682/
			to help to locate accomplices]. One hundred and fifty pirates attacked Hong Kong warehouses on 18 Jun 1844. Ch'ang-chou [an island between Hong Kong and Macao] should be searched.		
/83	Jun 20	05 05	Davis to Ch'i-ying. Requests more land for building purposes in Canton and Whampoa.	6	1125
/84	Jun 20	05 05	Davis to Ch'i-ying. Protests about recent disturbances affecting British Consulate at Canton.	7	1126
/85	Jun 21	05 06	Davis to Ch'i-ying. G.T. Lay has left for Foochow to take up post as Consul.	6	1127
/86	Jun 21	05 06	Davis to Viceroy Liu Yün-k'o of Min- Che. Announces arrival of G.T. Lay as Consul at Foochow.	6	1128
/87	Jun 21	05 06	Ch'i-ying to Davis. Declines to return pirate Ch'en A-t'ai because treaty stipulates that Chinese authorities deal with Chinese criminals while British with Britons. Has arrested five of Ch'en's accomplices with his help. Will hand them all over to Provincial Judge for trial.	9	1152
/88	Jun 22	05 07	Davis to Ch'i-ying. Opium should be legalized to benefit Chinese coffers and reduce number of addicts.	12	1129
/89	Jun 24	05 09	Davis to Ch'i-ying. Ch'en A-t'ai had been captured in Hong Kong, lent to Chinese authorities to help arrest accomplices, and should be returned to Hong Kong authorities.	8	1130
/90	Jun 25	05 10	Ch'i-ying to Davis. Has informed Amoy authorities of decisions at Canton: (1) foreign ships importing rice to China are required to pay only half of tonnage dues when exporting goods from China; (2) foreign merchants may pay taxes in *sycee* silver.	7	1153
/91	Jun 25	05 10	Ch'i-ying to Davis. According to [Chinese version of] treaty and pay- ment of previous three instalments	11	1154

). 2/ 77	Date 1844	TK 24	Description	pp	Old Ref. F.O. 682/
			of indemnity, Chinese calendar should be referred to for dates of payment of indemnity.		
92	Jun 25	05 10	Ch'i-ying to Davis. Another instalment of $2,500,000 of indemnity is ready for collection.	7	1155
93	Jun 26	05 11	Davis to Ch'i-ying. Since Chinese want to pay indemnity according to Chinese dates as they appear in Chinese version of treaty, will refer matter to London.	7	1131
94	Jun 28	05 13	Ch'i-ying to Davis. Chinese legal procedures do not allow summary execution of pirate Ch'en A-t'ai. Has ordered Commander-in-Chief Lai En-chüeh to apprehend pirates based at Ch'ang-chou.	10	1156
95	Jun 28	05 13	Ch'i-ying to Davis. Will consult gentry and elders about selecting new site for foreign building projects in Canton.	11	1157
96	Jun 28	05 13	Ch'i-ying to Davis. Is in Macao at present but has been informed of disturbance in Canton arising out of an American shooting dead a Chinese. Will return to Canton soon to settle matter.	7	1158
97	Jun 28	05 13	Ch'i-ying to Davis. Has informed authorities in Fukien of G.T. Lay's appointment as Consul at Foochow.	6	1159
98	Jul 2	05 17	Acting Colonel of Ta-p'eng Shen Chen-pang to Davis. Pirate suspect Huang Hsin-kuang should be handed over to Chinese authorities at Kowloon for trial.	11	1160
99	Jul 3	05 18	Ch'i-ying to Davis. Inquires if a British steamer has recently been to Chekiang to survey the coast.	7	1165
00	Jul 5	05 20	Ch'i-ying to Davis. Is sending K. Gutzlaff to Canton with ratified Supplementary Treaty to perform ceremony of exchanging treaties with Provincial Treasurer Huang En-t'ung.	6	1072

F.O. 682/ 1977	Date 1844	TK 24	Description	pp	Old Re F.O. 682/
/101	Jul 9	05 24	Ch'i-ying to Davis. Acknowledges receipt of Supplementary Treaty.	6	1190
/102	Jul 10	05 25	Davis to Ch'i-ying. Explains that main object of surveying ships is to chart routes for navigation.	7	1073
/103	Jul 11	05 26	Ch'i-ying to Davis. Viceroy Liu Yün-k'o of Min-Che wishes to know if British surveying ships have returned to Hong Kong.	6	1166
/104	Jul 13	05 28	Davis to Ch'i-ying. Argues for legalization of opium.	11	1074A
/105	Jul 13	05 28	Davis to Ch'i-ying. Is sending Mr Coffin to fetch instalment of $2,500,000 of indemnity.	4	1075
/106	Jul 16	06 02	Davis to Ch'i-ying. Because of difficulties of transport, he requests that Chinese authorities forward letters to and from Foochow via Amoy.	5	1074B
/107	Jul 16	06 02	Davis to Ch'i-ying. Explains circumstances in which surveying ships may have to abandon work temporarily; surveying is very tedious work.	7	1076
/108	Jul 16	06 02	Ch'i-ying to Davis. Cannon are not included in items of trade, and British merchants should be instructed not to import any to Shanghai.	8	1162
/109	Jul 18	06 04	Davis to Ch'i-ying. Two British officers have been robbed by Chinese pirates near Ch'ang-chou [between Hong Kong and Macao]. Threatens to take unilateral action.	6	1077
/110	Jul 18	06 04	Polished version of previous entry.	6	1078
/111	Jul 21	06 07	Davis to Ch'i-ying. British Consul [G. Balfour] at Shanghai has instructed British merchants not to bring cannon to China for sale.	6	1079
/112	Jul 23	06 09	Ch'i-ying to Davis. Has instructed Colonel of Ta-p'eng and Magistrate of Hsin-an to capture pirates who landed at Ch'ang-chou.	8	1161

. / 7	Date 1844	TK 24	Description	pp	Old Ref. F.O. 682/
3	Jul 24	06 10	Ch'i-ying to Davis. Insists that dispute about dates of payment of indemnity be settled by reference to Chinese version of treaty and that alone: British officials knew both languages and drafted Chinese version, while Chinese officials knew no English and signed treaty on basis only of Chinese version.	8	1167
4	Jul 24	06 10	Ch'i-ying to Davis. Requests acknowledgement of receipt of $2,500,000 instalment of indemnity.	6	1163
5	Jul 24	06 10	Ch'i-ying to Davis. Is willing to comply with request to instruct local authorities to forward for Davis British despatches to and from Amoy via Foochow, but is afraid that local authorities may object. Suggests that such despatches be sent to Ch'i-ying himself to be forwarded to Davis as a temporary measure, until ships begin to visit Foochow more regularly.	9	1164
6	Jul 27	06 13	Davis to Ch'i-ying. Acknowledges receipt of $2,500,000 instalment of indemnity.	5	1080
7	Aug 10	06 27	Davis to Ch'i-ying. Is going on tour of inspection of treaty ports for about forty days. Deputy will act in his place during absence.	5	1071
8	Aug 12	06 29	Ch'i-ying to Davis. British ships may survey routes between treaty ports, but must not survey Taiwan and other Chinese areas. Demands immediate withdrawal of survey ships from Taiwan.	11	1171
9	Aug 13	06 30	Davis to Ch'i-ying. Chusan will be returned to China when all indemnity is paid by end of 1845.	6	1081
0	Aug 13	06 30	Davis to Ch'i-ying. As no reply has been received to his despatch of 3 Jul 1844 listing his arguments for legalization of opium, is now enclosing another of these arguments. [Enclosure missing.]	4	1082

F.O. 682/ 1977	Date 1844	TK 24	Description	pp	Old R● F.O. 682/
/121	Aug 13	06 30	Ch'i-ying to Davis. Has informed officials in maritime provinces of Davis' pending visit to treaty ports.	6	1170
/122	Aug 17	07 04	Davis to Ch'i-ying. Protests about Cantonese interfering with re-building of foreign factories.	6	1083
/123	Aug 19	07 06	Ch'i-ying to Davis. Cannot ask Emperor to legalize opium for fear of incurring his displeasure and of possible punishment.	11	1172
/124	Aug 19	07 06	Ch'i-ying to Davis. Cantonese oppose erection of Western style buildings outside original site of foreign factories.	8	1133
/125	Aug 19	07 06	Ch'i-ying to Davis. Although China may benefit by having Chusan return-ed earlier if indemnity is paid according to Western calendar, will pay indemnity only according to Chinese calendar as stipulated in treaty [Chinese version].	14	1134
/126	Aug 20	07 07	Davis to Ch'i-ying. Americans have paid Chinese officials in Kowloon for permission to live and build houses there. Cannot agree to this.	5	1084
/127	Aug 24	07 11	Davis to Ch'i-ying. R. Alcock has been appointed Consul at Foochow, and G.T. Lay Consul at Amoy.	5	1085
/128a	Aug 26	07 13	Ch'i-ying to Davis. Chinese govern-ment cannot be held responsible for losses sustained by foreign factories in the event of a disturbance; offers to send more troops to patrol the area.	9	1169
/128b	Aug 28	07 15	[Acting Governor of Hong Kong] General D'Aguila to Ch'i-ying. Goods bought in Hong Kong by Chinese merchants for sale in Ch'ao-chou [Kwangtung] have been plundered by marines from Chinese patrol boats.	6	1086
/129	Aug 30	07 17	Ch'i-ying to Davis. Will investigate allegation that Chinese officials in Kowloon were bribed to allow Americans to build houses there. Has notified	8	1177

.	Date		Description	pp	Old Ref. F.O.
/					
7	1844	TK 24			682/

			U.S. Minister, Mr. C. Cushing, of this American violation of treaty. At Cushing's request, has given Americans four months to evacuate Kowloon. Asks Davis to evacuate any Briton who might have participated in same building programme.		
0	Sep 7	07 25	General D'Aguila to Ch'i-ying. Urges that Chinese pirates listed in previous communications [accomplices of Ch'en A-t'ai] be arrested.	6	1087
1	[Rec'd] Sep 14	07 -	Ch'i-ying to [D'Aguila]. Has arrested three pirates, who attacked British ship near Ch'ang-chou. Will quickly capture rest.	9	1173
2	Sep 19	08 08	Ch'i-ying to [D'Aguila]. Encloses copy of treaty with America for reference.	1	1184
3	n.d. [Sep 24]	n.d. [08 13]	D'Aguila to Ch'i-ying. Acknowledges receipt of copy of Chinese treaty with America.	4	1132
4	Sep 25	08 14	Ch'i-ying to [D'Aguila]. Customs authorities at Foochow and Amoy have agreed to follow Canton example of foreign vessels importing rice and exporting Chinese goods, and payment of duties in silver. Rate of premium to be applied on various silvers paid as taxes have also been agreed upon.	7	1178
			Encl. Rate of premium to be applied on various silvers paid as taxes, n.d.	4	1178 Incl.
5	Oct 21	09 10	Davis to Ch'i-ying. Consul G.T. Lay, (who is delayed at Foochow), should be allowed to occupy a more respectable house, a house suitable to be Consulate. R. Alcock is temporarily in charge of Consulate at Amoy.	6	1088
5	Oct 21	09 10	Davis to Ch'i-ying. What has happened to Chinese pirate Ch'en A-ta *et al.*?	6	1089
7	Oct 26	09 15	Davis to Ch'i-ying. Protests against blackmailing of Hong Kong stone dealer by Chinese marines.	8	1090
3	Oct 30	09 19	Ch'i-ying to Davis. Agrees to investigate two incidents in which Chinese officers blackmailed Chinese owner of a Hong Kong quarry and detained one of his boats.	7	1179

F.O. 682/ 1977	Date 1844	TK 24	Description	pp	Old Re F.O. 682/
/139	Oct 30	09 19	Ch'i-ying to Davis. More accomplices of pirate Ch'en A-ta have been captured and will be examined by Provincial Judge.	6	1191
/140	Oct 30	09 19	Ch'i-ying to Davis. Assures him that proper abode will be found for Consul G.T. Lay at Foochow.	9	1180
/141	Nov 4	09 24	Davis to Ch'i-ying. Protests about interference with free trade: some local authorities have tried to prevent tea from going to Shanghai; a Chinese merchant has tried to monopolise sale of cassia bark and iron; foreign textiles are taxed in north Kwangtung.	9	1091
/142	Nov 7	09 27	Davis to Ch'i-ying. Urges execution of pirate Ch'en A-ta who attacked British ship near Stanley [Hong Kong].	6	1092
/143	Nov 11	10 02	Ch'i-ying to Davis. Reports that local officials were preventing tea from going to Shanghai and channelling it to Canton as before, are unfounded. Will investigate allegations that certain Chinese merchants monopolis-ed sale of iron and cassia bark, and that foreign textiles are taxed in north Kwangtung.	19	1181
/144	Nov 11	10 02	Ch'i-ying to Davis. Viceroy Liu Yün-k'o of Min-Che is pleased that Davis is preparing for evacuation from Ku-lang-hsü once indemnity due in the last month of 24th year of Emperor Tao-kuang's reign is paid; suggests that evacuated foreigners lease temporary abode in Amoy.	9	1192
/145	Nov 13	10 04	Ch'i-ying to Davis. All captured pirates will be severely punished according to Chinese law.	7	1182
/146	Nov 15	10 06	Davis to Ch'i-ying. Insists that Britons be allowed to stay on in Ku-lang-hsü after withdrawal of occupy-ing forces while suitable dwellings are being built for them in Amoy.	7	1093
/147	Nov 15	10 06	Davis to Ch'i-ying. Further protests against interference with free trade in cassia bark; threatens to go to Peking. Again urges execution of	8	1094A

0. 2/ 77	Date 1844	TK 24	Description	pp	Old Ref. F.O. 682/
			pirate Ch'en A-ta.		
48	Nov 19	10 10	Davis to Ch'i-ying. A Briton, [Mr] Warren, has been murdered by Chinese pirates while travelling to Whampoa.	5	1094B
49	Nov 20	10 11	Davis to Huang En-t'ung. Chinese in Hong Kong should no longer be required to pay land tax to China.	5	1095
50a	Nov 22	10 13	Davis to Ch'i-ying. Clerk from Hsin-an, Cheng Tung, has been arrested while selling licences to fishermen in Hong Kong.	6	1187
50b	Nov 22	10 13	Copy of previous entry.	6	1781D
51	Nov 24	10 15	Ch'i-ying to Davis. Asks that Consul G. Balfour at Shanghai be told to follow arrangement regarding payment of duties as in Canton, Foochow and Amoy.	8	1183
52	Nov 24	10 15	Ch'i-ying to Davis. Prefers to stick to treaty whereby Ku-lang-hsü would be returned after all indemnity is paid, as Davis' proposal to evacuate troops and leave civilians behind poses difficult problems.	16	1185
53	Nov 24	10 15	Ch'i-ying to Davis. Has sent agents to investigate allegation that cassia bark from Kwangsi is being illegally taxed. Pirates Ch'en A-ta et al. are being examined by Provincial Judge.	9	1186
54	Nov 24	10 15	Ch'i-ying to Davis. Agrees to investigate matter of a clerk from Hsin-an having gone to Hong Kong to sell fishing licences.	7	1066
55	Nov 25	10 16	Huang En-t'ung to Davis. Agrees to investigate Mr Teng's plea for tax exemption for his land in Hong Kong.	8	1065
56	Dec 3	10 24	Davis to Ch'i-ying. Again insists that Britons should be allowed to continue to live in Ku-lang-hsü after withdrawal of occupying forces. Complains about difficulties in obtaining proper houses for Consuls at Amoy and Foochow.	10	1096
57	Dec 4	10 25	Davis to Ch'i-ying. Has authorized Consul G. Balfour at Shanghai to	4	1097

F.O. 682/ 1977	Date 1844	TK 24	Description	pp	Old Re F.O. 682/
			follow practice in Canton regarding payment of duties in silver.		
/158a	Dec 6	10 27	Davis to Ch'i-ying. Clerk from Hsin-an will be released if it can be proved that he acted without authority. Will not tolerate interference with British administration of Hong Kong.	6	1188
/158b	Dec 6	10 27	Copy of previous entry.	6	1781A
/159a	Dec 6	10 27	Davis to Ch'i-ying. Requests official notification of execution of pirate Ch'en A-ta. Again threatens to take unilateral action against pirates.	6	1098
/159b	n.d. [Dec 10]	n.d. [11 01]	[Ch'i-ying to Davis]. Clerk from Hsin-an is Chinese subject and, according to treaty, must be tried by Chinese government, whether or not he has acted with authority. Requests that said clerk be handed to Chinese officials in Kowloon.	4	1438/
/160a	Dec 14	11 05	Davis to Ch'i-ying. Will hand over to Chinese authorities the clerk from Hsin-an as he has acted without authority in selling licences to fishermen in Hong Kong.	5	1189
/160b	Dec 14	11 05	Copy of previous entry.	5	1781C
/161	Dec 17	11 08	Ch'i-ying to Davis. Pirate leader Ch'en Meng-niu has died in prison: his body will be flogged as punishment and Tu A-te will be executed. Their heads will be hung up for exhibition. Will suggest to Ministry of Justice that accomplices Ch'en A-erh and Lin Fu-tsai be executed.	9	1061
/162	Dec 18	11 09	Ch'i-ying to Davis. Consul should reside at Amoy and not Ku-lang-hsü as former is treaty port and latter is not. Will instruct Amoy authorities to facilitate building of Consulate. Will also instruct Foochow authorities to find better place to house Consul.	13	1060
/163a	Dec 18	11 09	Ch'i-ying to Davis. Has arrested for trial the clerk from Hsin-an, who went to Hong Kong to sell fishing	7	1062

). 2/ 77	Date 1844	TK 24	Description	pp	Old Ref. F.O. 682/
			licences.		
53b	n.d.	n.d.	Draft of previous entry.	4	1781B
64	Dec 19	11 10	Davis to Ch'i-ying. Argues that treaty contains no stipulation forbidding British residence in Ku-lang-hsü. Complains that Consul R. Alcock cannot find decent residence in Amoy.	9	1099
65	Dec 19	11 10	Davis to Ch'i-ying. The *Stirling* has been attacked by pirates, three sailors have been killed. Threatens to take unilateral action against pirates. Has outlawed secret societies in Hong Kong.	7	1100
66	Dec 20	11 11	Ch'i-ying to Davis. Another instalment of indemnity, $2,500,000, is ready for collection.	5	1063
67	Dec 21	11 12	Davis to Ch'i-ying. Is satisfied with execution of pirates Ch'en Meng-niu *et al*.	7	1101
68	Dec 21	11 12	Davis to Ch'i-ying. Chinese employed by British forces in Ku-lang-hsü have been attacked [by fellow Chinese].	7	1102
69	Dec 24	11 15	Ch'i-ying to Davis. Treaty distinctly stipulates return of Ku-lang-hsü and Chusan together with all buildings therein after last instalment of indemnity is paid; therefore Davis' claim of access to Ku-lang-hsü after its return is unfounded.	17	1069
70	Dec 24	11 15	Davis to Ch'i-ying. Is waiting for suitable vessel to be despatched to Canton to collect the $2,500,000 instalment of indemnity.	5	1103
71	Dec 24	11 15	Huang En-t'ung to Davis. Mr Teng [of the New Territories] should no longer pay tax for land he possesses in island colony of Hong Kong.	8	1064
72	Dec 24	11 15	Ch'i-ying to Davis. Will do all he can to capture pirates who attacked the *Stirling*; requests further information about date and place of incident.	7	1068

F.O. 682/ 1977	Date 1844	TK 24	Description	pp	Old Re F.O. 682/
/173	Dec 24	11 15	Ch'i-ying to Davis. A suitable abode for Consul G.T. Lay will be found in commercial area in Foochow.	14	1070
/174	Dec 26	11 17	Davis to Huang En-t'ung. Is pleased that Chinese in Hong Kong are no longer required to pay land tax to Chinese government. Will send a vessel to collect instalment of indemnity on arrival of the Admiral [Rear-Admiral Sir Thomas Cochrane].	6	1104
/175	Dec 28	11 19	Davis to Ch'i-ying. Earlier report that the *Stirling* had been attacked by pirates was unfounded. Is pleased that execution of some pirates apparently has produced deterrent effect.	5	1105
/176a	Dec 28	11 19	Davis to Ch'i-ying. Reiterates necessity for Consul G.T. Lay to be provided with respectable residence in Foochow.	8	1106
/176b	n.d.	n.d.	Draft of previous entry [incomplete].	1	1781E
/177	Dec 29	11 20	Davis to Ch'i-ying. Reiterates necessity for Consul R. Alcock to be provided with respectable residence at Amoy.	6	1107A
/178	Dec 30	11 21	Davis to Ch'i-ying. Chinese authorities must not use character *cha* [command] when writing to British Consuls; instead, *cha* [memo] should be used.	6	1107B
/179	Dec 30	11 21	Ch'i-ying to Davis. Has asked local authorities to investigate attack on Chinese employed by British author- ities in Ku-lang-hsü.	7	1222
/180	Dec 30	11 21	Ch'i-ying to Davis. Is pleased with Davis' efforts to suppress secret societies in Hong Kong. Intimates that members of these outlawed societies should be handed over to Chinese authorities in Kowloon for trial.	7	1223
/181	Dec 31	11 22	Huang En-t'ung to Davis. Next instal- ment of indemnity is ready for collection.	5	1252

. / 8	Date 1845	TK 24	Description	pp	Old Ref. F.O. 682/
1	Jan 1	11 23	Davis to Ch'i-ying. Will despatch HMS *Proserpine* to collect instalment of indemnity.	5	1193
2	Jan 5	11 27	Ch'i-ying to Davis. In accordance with most-favoured-nation principle, privileges granted to France may be shared by Great Britain.	9	1224
		TK 25			
3	Mar 2	01 24	Davis to Ch'i-ying. Has despatched steamer to evacuate British troops occupying Ku-lang-hsü.	4	1194
4	Mar 3	01 25	Davis to Ch'i-ying. R. Alcock has been delayed in taking up appointment as Consul at Foochow, but will proceed there after evacuation of Ku-lang-hsü. G.T. Lay will then sail to Amoy as Consul.	5	1195
5	Mar 6	01 28	Ch'i-ying to Davis. Is pleased that British troops are evacuating Ku-lang-hsü. Will notify Viceroy of Min-Che and order authorities in Amoy to find accommodation promptly for British Consul.	5	1225
6	Mar 7	01 29	Davis to Ch'i-ying. Demands explanation of confrontation of British shipping by Chinese patrol boats.	4	1196
7	Mar 9	02 02	Ch'i-ying to Davis. Is pleased that R. Alcock is at last proceeding to Foochow and G.T. Lay to Amoy. Will notify provincial authorities of Fukien.	4	1226
8	Mar 9	02 02	Ch'i-ying to Davis. Some government patrol boats have been seized by pirates and used to confront British ships. Chinese marines are innocent.	8	1227
9	Mar 16	02 09	Ch'i-ying to Davis. Has received report concerning attack on Chinese employed by British authorities in Ku-lang-hsü. The attacked were victims of a feud, not of their employment. Feud is now settled.	8	1228
0	Mar 19	02 12	Davis to Ch'i-ying. Wonders why there is no reply to his letter of 13 Jan 1845.	5	1197

F.O. 682/ 1978	Date 1845	TK 25	Description	pp	Old R∢ F.O. 682/
/11	Mar 22	02 15	Davis to Ch'i-ying. Protests about Cantonese attack on Vice-Consul and two consular officials. Attributes attack to contempt of Cantonese for Britons as a result of their success-ful refusal to allow Britons to enter walled city. Demands entrance into walled city.	8	1198
/12	Mar 24	02 17	Ch'i-ying and Huang En-t'ung to Davis. Have received no communication from Davis dated 13 Jan 1845 and there-fore could not reply. Wonder if it has gone astray.	8	1229
			Encl. Davis to Ch'i-ying. Pirates bearing government marine identities have been found. Asks him to invest-igate. 6 Feb 1845.	2	1229
/13	Mar 29	02 22	Davis to Ch'i-ying. Encloses copy of his letter of 13 Jan 1845. [Encl. wanting]	4	1199
/14	Mar 29	02 22	Ch'i-ying and Huang En-t'ung to Davis. Have arrested Ch'en A-an who attack-ed British Vice-Consul et al. Gold watch has been recovered. Personally they do not object to Britons entering city, but Cantonese will not agree.	9	1230
/15	Apr 2	02 26	Ch'i-ying and Huang En-t'ung to Davis. Reply to Davis' of 13 Jan 1845. Will investigate claim by Chinese pirate-suspects captured by Royal Navy that they had been authorized to capture pirates.	6	1231
/16	Apr 8	03 02	Copy of next entry.	12	1200
/17	Apr 8	03 02	Davis to Ch'i-ying and Huang En-t'ung. Is pleased that [Ch'en A-an] is captured. Urges prompt action to apprehend accomplices. Regards it most unreasonable that foreigners should still be refused entry into walled city of Canton; they are allowed in all other treaty ports. Chinese authorities must bring Cantonese to reason.	8	1201
/18	Apr 12	03 06	Davis to Ch'i-ying. Requests: (1) reduction of export duties on pottery at Amoy; (2) refund of duties paid for pottery which have	6	1202

). / 78	Date 1845	TK 25	Description	pp	Old Ref. F.O. 682/
			been damaged or stolen prior to going through customs at Amoy.		
9	Apr 17	03 11	Davis to Ch'i-ying. Has ordered HMS *Driver* to take up station at Whampoa, in accordance with treaty stipulation that all treaty ports should have one warship to keep foreign shipping in order.	4	1203
0	Apr 18	03 12	Ch'i-ying and Huang En-t'ung to Davis. Five accomplices of Ch'en A-an are captured. Two are still at large. All stolen goods except silver watch have been recovered. All Cantonese gentry have warned against opening city gates to foreigners. Have referred Davis' two requests concerning export duties in Amoy to Hoppo.	12	1232
1	Apr 21	03 15	Ch'i-ying and Huang En-t'ung to Davis. As regards customs duties at Amoy, the practice at Canton should be followed: 5% on value of all goods, and levied after containers are opened, not before.	11	1233
2	Apr 24	03 18	Davis to Ch'i-ying and Huang En-t'ung. Is pleased that Ch'en A-an *et al.* are apprehended. The two still at large should be arrested promptly. Has reported to London on Cantonese refusal to open city gates to foreigners. Protests about a proclamation by Magistrate of P'an-yü declaring that Vice-Consul *et al.* are traders as greedy as anyone else.	7	1204
3	Apr 26	03 20	Davis to Ch'i-ying. Consul F.C. Macgregor of Canton has imposed a fine of $500 on a British ship engaged in smuggling sulphur and confiscated her goods. Many foreign ships at Whampoa are engaged in smuggling opium and Chinese authorities must do something about them.	8	1205
4	Apr 28	03 22	Davis to Ch'i-ying and Huang En-t'ung. Agrees that opening of all containers before levying taxes is the answer to problems in Amoy.	4	1206

F.O. 682/ 1978	Date 1845	TK 25	Description	pp	Old R F.O. 682/
/25	May 6 [Rec'd]	03 -	Ch'i-ying and Huang En-tung to Davis. Have memo from Viceroy of Min-Che. Site has been found for building Consulate at Amoy. Consul R. Alcock will build it. If building expenses amount to $10,000, annual rent will be $1,000. When completed, Consul and all British merchants must leave Ku-lang-hsü and proceed to Amoy according to treaty.	7	1234
/26	May 3	03 27	Ch'i-ying to Davis. Thanks for action against British ship engaged in smuggling sulphur. Agrees that measures should be taken against foreign shipping engaged in smuggl- ing opium.	10	1235
/27	May 3	03 27	Ch'i-ying and Huang En-t'ung to Davis. Will hunt down remaining two villains who plundered Vice-Consul *et al.* Have ordered Magistrate of P'an-yü to correct wording of notice and show it to Consul F.C. Macgregor	7	1236
/28	May 8 [Rec'd]	03 -	Ch'i-ying and Huang En-t'ung to Davis. Have memo from Viceroy of Min-Che: Consuls G.T. Lay at Foochow and R. Alcock at Amoy are to exchange posts. Alcock has just designed building of Consulate at Amoy and Lay has been at Foochow for only eight months. Would it be better if transfer is postponed until building is completed?	10	1237
/29	May 8	04 03	Davis to Ch'i-ying and Huang En-t'ung. G.T. Lay must go to Amoy and R. Alcock to Foochow without delay, as this has been decided in London. Lay will have no difficulty super- vising building of Consulate according to design.	7	1221
/30	May 8	04 03	Davis to Ch'i-ying and Huang En-t'ung. Is pleased that: (1) action will be taken against foreign shipping engaged in smuggling at Whampoa anchorage; (2) no effort will be spared in arresting two villains still at large; (3) proclamation by Magistrate of P'an-yü has been rectified.	6	1207

. / 8	Date 1845	TK 25	Description	pp	Old Ref. F.O. 682/
1	May 16 [Rec'd]	04 -	Ch'i-ying and Huang En-t'ung to Davis. Are satisfied with wisdom of trans- ferring R. Alcock and G.T. Lay. Foreign shipping engaged in smuggl- ing has heard that action is pend- ing and has disappeared from Whampoa; stringent measures will be devised to stamp out any smuggling in future.	8	1238
2	Jun 11	05 07	Davis to Ch'i-ying. Protests that movement of British merchants in Canton is as restricted as before the war and that city gates of Canton are still closed to foreigners.	7	1208
3	Jun 11	05 07	Copy of previous entry.	10	1209
4	Jun 15	05 11	Ch'i-ying and Huang En-t'ung to Davis. Movement of Britons at Canton is still restricted because the extent to which they may move into the countryside has not been agreed upon. Feeling of Cantonese must be taken into account too, not just that of Britons.	10	1239
5	Jun 21	05 17	Ch'i-ying and Huang En-t'ung to Davis. Another instalment of indemnity is ready for collection.	6	1240
6	Jun 21	05 17	Ch'i-ying and Huang En-t'ung to Davis. Have devised eight regulations to minimise chances for smuggling. Encl. Eight regulations, *op. cit.*, n.d.	7 12	1241
7	Jun 26	05 22	Davis to Ch'i-ying and Huang En-t'ung. Will despatch official to collect instalment of indemnity.	4	1210
8	Jun 27	05 23	Davis to Ch'i-ying and Huang En-t'ung. Acknowledges receipt of eight regulations, and lists both his objections to and agreement with some of them.	10	1211
9	Jul 4	05 30	Davis to Ch'i-ying and Huang En-t'ung. Has despatched two officers to Canton to collect instalment of indemnity.	4	1212
10	Jul 4	05 30	[Acting] Provincial Treasurer of Kwangtung [K'ung Chi-yin] to Davis. Has handed over instalment of indemnity to two British officers	6	1213

F.O. 682/ 1978	Date 1845	TK 25	Description	pp	Old R F.O. 682/
			and sent soldiers to escort them.		
/41	Jul 8	06 04	Davis to Ch'i-ying. Returns letter from [Acting] Provincial Treasurer [K'ung Chi-yin] of Kwangtung [see previous entry] as language employed therein is most unsuitable.	6	1214
/42	Jul 13	06 09	Ch'i-ying and Huang En-t'ung to Davis. Provincial Treasurer K'ung [Chi-yin] is new to post and unaware of new arrangements. Have returned letter to him to be cancelled.	7	1242
/43	Jul 17	06 13	Davis to Ch'i-ying. Acknowledges receipt of instalment of indemnity.	4	1215
/44	Aug 4	07 02	Davis to Viceroy Liu Yün-k'o of Min-Che. Protests about ill-treatment of Britons by people of Foochow. As matter is urgent, has despatched steamer to deliver protest instead of asking Ch'i-ying to transmit it by land.	10	1255A
/45	Aug 4	07 02	Davis to Ch'i-ying. Encloses copy of letter to Liu Yün-k'o [see previous entry].	4	1255B
/46a	Aug 27	07 25	Davis to Ch'i-ying. Invention of steam engine is great technological break-through. Wonders if Chinese are interested in employing British engineers to construct steamships, railways and to keep Yellow River and Grand Canal in good repair.	8	1255C
/46b	Sep 10	08 09	Ch'i-ying and Huang En-t'ung to Consul F.C. Macgregor. Have ordered invest-igation into allegations of British-hired boats having been stopped un-necessarily by Chinese customs officials.	6	327/5
/47	Sep 13	08 12	Davis to Ch'i-ying. Royal Navy fleet has just finished suppressing piracy in South China Sea and will be stationed in five treaty ports according to treaty.	5	1255E
/48a	Sep 16	08 15	Davis to Ch'i-ying. Has been knighted.	4	1255

). 2/ 78	Date 1845	TK 25	Description	pp	Old Ref. F.O. 682/
48b	Sep 17	08 16	Ch'i-ying and Huang En-t'ung to Davis. Thank Davis for notification of arrival of Royal Navy fleet and of despatch of individual warships to be stationed at five treaty ports.	6	327/5/66
48c	Sep 20	08 19	Ch'i-ying and Huang En-t'ung to Davis. Thank British steamer for having saved six Chinese shipwrecked on Fukien coast, taken them to Hong Kong, and paid their fares to return to Fukien on ship from Macao.	6	327/5/71
48d	Sep 20	08 19	Ch'i-ying and Huang En-t'ung to Davis. Endorse measures taken by Viceroy of Min-Che to protect British merchants at Nan-t'ai [Foochow].	6	327/5/73
48e	Sep 22	08 21	Ch'i-ying and Huang En-t'ung to Consul F.C. Macgregor. Will investigate allegation that a Briton resident in Canton has been twice disturbed by mobs.	4	327/5/75
49	Sep 30	08 29	Davis to Ch'i-ying. A Chinese official at Amoy has admitted to Consul [G.T. Lay] that he has to accept bribes. Requests his removal.	6	1255F
50a	Oct 15	09 15	Ch'i-ying to Davis. Proposes to leave Canton for Hong Kong on 20 Nov 1845. Requests steamer to meet him at Whampoa.	7	1243
50b	Oct 31	10 01	Ch'i-ying and Huang En-t'ung to Consul F.C. Macgregor. Five Chinese who helped themselves to furniture of British tenant during argument will be caned eighty times and cangued for half a month.	6	327/5/59
50c	Nov 6	10 07	Ch'i-ying to Davis. Thanks Davis for his congratulations to Empress Dowager on her 70th birthday.	4	327/5/63
51	Nov 19	n.d. [10 20]	Ch'i-ying to Davis. Foreign shipping must not visit any place other than five treaty ports. British ship surveying in Taiwan must be withdrawn. Is pleased that survey of coastal waters is complete as all ships will benefit.	10	1244

F.O. 682/ 1978	Date 1845	TK 25	Description	pp	Old R◄ F.O. 682/
/52	Nov 19	10 20	Ch'i-ying to Davis. Has memo from authorities at Foochow. Consul G.T. Lay must have misunderstood message. Export duty on Chinese pottery is 5% *ad valorem* and that on porcelain is 5 taels per 100 catties.	9	1245
/53	Nov 29	11 01	[Rear-] Admiral [Sir Thomas Cochrane] to Ch'i-ying. Thanks for generous gift to bluejackets but cannot distribute it because of Royal Navy regulations. Requests permission to present it as donation to seamen's hospital.	7	1216
/54	Dec 3	11 05	Ch'i-ying to Davis. Thanks for hospitality in Hong Kong. Last instalment of indemnity will be paid in about ten days, after which Chusan should be evacuated. Has instructed two Circuit Intendants to supervise evacuation. Encloses proclamation to inhabitants of Chusan. Entry into walled city of Canton must be deferred. Encl. Proclamation to inhabitants of Chusan, *op. cit.*, n.d.	8 3	1246
/55	Dec 5	11 07	Davis to Ch'i-ying. Consul G.T. Lay at Amoy has died. T.H. Layton is Acting Consul. Silver inspectors at Amoy also engage in trading with foreigners and abuse their power. They should be forbidden to trade.	5	1217
/56	Dec 8	11 10	Davis to Ch'i-ying. Chusan will be returned after last instalment of indemnity is paid. Suggests some minor changes to Ch'i-ying's proclamation to inhabitants of Chusan. Entry into city of Canton must not be deferred any longer.	8	1218
/57	Dec 11	11 13	Davis to Ch'i-ying. There is a proclamation in Shanghai saying that Ch'i-ying and Huang En-t'ung are about to become Catholics. Requests another proclamation to be issued declaring that Church of England is also protected.	9	1219
/58	Dec 12	11 14	Ch'i-ying to Davis. Is sorry to hear of the death of Consul G.T. Lay and	8	1247

Date		Description	pp	Old Ref. F.O. 682/
1845	TK 25			

is confident that T.H. Layton is
the right choice. Has notified
Viceroy of Min-Che to take action
against silver inspectors who
engage in foreign trade and abuse
their power.

[Dec 16] [11 18] Ch'i-ying to Davis. Agrees to have   5   1248
[Rec'd]   gift to bluejackets presented to
seamen's hospital in London.

Dec 15   11 17   Ch'i-ying to Davis. Another instal-   6   1249
ment of indemnity is ready for
collection.

Dec 15   11 17   Ch'i-ying to Davis. Accepts Davis'   19   1250
suggested alterations to his
proclamation to inhabitants of
Chusan. Treaty stipulates return
of Chusan and Ku-lang-hsü on the
day the last instalment of indemnity
is paid, not an unspecified date
afterwards. Chinese government has
no objection to foreigners entering
walled city of Canton but citizens
are violently opposed to it. Has
summoned gentry several times ask-
in them to bring citizens to
reason. Has also referred matter
to Emperor. Davis should remember
that treaty gives Britons no right
to enter city. They are allowed
into walled cities of other treaty
ports only as gesture of friendship,
not as matter of right.

Dec 18   11 20   Ch'i-ying to Davis. Has sent official   8   1251
to Amoy to investigate allegations
of Acting Sub-Magistrate Huo of Amoy
having accepted bribes. Consul G.T.
Lay is dead and there is no way of
knowing evidence on which he based
his allegations. Vice Consul T.H.
Layton, who is Acting Consul,
together with his staff and all
British merchants questioned have
professed no knowledge of such bribes.

Dec 19   11 21   Davis to Ch'i-ying. Cannot identify   7   1220
ship which ran over a junk, sank it,
and left without stopping to save
the drowning, resulting in fifty-
two deaths. Thanks for help afford-
ed *Huntley* which sank to the south

F.O. 682/ 1978	Date 1845	TK 25	Description	pp	Old R F.O. 682/
			of Ch'iung-chou.		
/64	Dec 20	11 22	Davis to Ch'i-ying. Is not unwilling to return Chusan but according to treaty all five treaty ports must be opened to trade before Chusan can be returned; Canton is not opened to the same degree as other treaty ports. Has been instructed by London to gain entry into walled city of Canton before returning Chusan.	12	1253
/65	Dec 21	11 23	Davis to Huang En-t'ung. Has been instructed by London to obtain entry into Canton before returning Chusan. If foreigners are allowed into walled cities of other treaty ports, he cannot see why not in Canton.	8	1254
/66	Dec 27	11 29	Ch'i-ying to Davis. According to treaty, Chusan must be returned to China upon full payment of indemnity. Is surprised that Davis has not acknowledged notification that last instalment of indemnity is ready for collection. If transfer of this money takes place after the date it is due, the fault does not lie with China and no interest should be charged. Entry into Canton city is not provided for in the treaty and Davis cannot demand it on the ground that he has been instructed by London to do so. A treaty will be meaningless if terms may be added to it or taken out of it according to one's instructions. On 28 Nov 1845 and again on 15 and 16 Dec 1845, groups of Britons, brandishing pistols, tried to force their way into the city; they must be restrained.	16	327/!

	Date		Description	pp	Old Ref. F.O. 682/
	1846	TK 25			
	Jan 8	12 11	Ch'i-ying to Davis. Undertakes not to cede Chusan to any Power after British evacuation. Is prepared to come to secret agreement to this effect. Has ordered local officials, as requested by Davis, to have troublemakers paraded through streets of Canton.	8	1256
2	Jan 11	12 14	Ch'i-ying to Davis. Has issued proclamation exhorting Cantonese to be reasonable about foreigners entering their city. Is now waiting anxiously for reaction.	9	1257
3	Jan 15	12 18	Ch'i-ying to Davis. Acknowledges receipt of draft agreement stipulating that Chusan shall not be ceded to another power after its return.	6	1258
a	Jan 18	12 21	Ch'i-ying and Huang En-t'ung to Davis. Proclamation exhorting Cantonese to be reasonable about entry question, issued at behest of Davis, has been torn to pieces by Cantonese. Prefect of Canton has been attacked and his *yamen* ransacked and burnt down because of rumour that he had British guests in his *yamen*. If Britons enter city there is no guarantee for their safety, nor indeed that of Chinese officials.	8	1259
b	Jan 18	12 21	Copy of previous entry.	1	1468A/9/1
	Jan 21	12 24	Ch'i-ying to Davis. Will investigate allegation that Chinese marines detained Ma Chi-hsing and his wife in a boat moored to the west of Hong Kong.	7	1260
	Jan 21	12 24	Ch'i-ying to Davis. Acknowledges receipt of copy of his own proclamation to inhabitants of Chusan, forwarded to Davis by British commander in Chusan. Has also sent second proclamation, drafted by Davis, to Chusan to be issued in Ch'i-ying's name. Does not think it necessary to forward third proclamation drafted by Davis, to be issued in Ch'i-ying's name at Chusan, as it is repetition of second.	6	1261
a	Jan 22	12 25	Davis to Ch'i-ying. Will persuade	2	1468/9/2

F.O. 682/ 1979	Date 1846	TK 25	Description	pp	Old F.O. 682/
			Britons to wait for more opportune time to enter city but Cantonese hostility must be dealt with.		
/7b	Jan 22	12 25	Ch'i-ying and Huang En-t'ung to Davis. Have handed over last instalment of indemnity. Expect Davis to observe treaty stipulation that Chusan will be returned on day last instalment of indemnity is paid.	8	1262
/8a	Jan 22	12 25	Ch'i-ying to Davis. Will protect foreigners as requested. Will have no difficulty in doing so if all foreigners observe treaty. Additional demand, not included in treaty, to enter city has resulted in rioting and burning down of Canton Prefect's *yamen*. If Britons actually set foot in city, Ch'i-ying will not be able to protect himself, let alone foreigners. Declines Davis' offer of help to control Cantonese.	10	1263
/8b	Jan 25	12 28	Ch'i-ying to Davis. Declines to release two Chinese criminals captured at sea outside Hong Kong. Requests that similar representations made to British officials be firmly rejected in order to deter crimes.	6	327/
/9	Jan 25	12 28	Ch'i-ying to Davis. Has report about detention of Ma Chi-hsing *et al.* They are all robber suspects and should not be lightly released. In future, Davis should make sure people who petition him are not connected with criminals before protesting to Chinese government. Besides, arrests were made at sea and not in Hong Kong.	8	126L
/10	Jan 25	12 28	Ch'i-ying to Davis. At Pei-hsin-kuan [a local customs house] imported cloth of 4 ft width is taxed according to old scale, and that of lesser width taxed less than before. This is no breach of treaty stipulation that imported goods must not be taxed excessively in interior.	7	126
/11	Jan 26	12 29	Ch'i-ying to Davis. It is difficult for Cantonese to forget Opium War.	10	126

Date		Description	pp	Old Ref. F.O. 682/
1846	TK 26			

I-li-pu and then Ch'i-ying himself
have tried hard to placate them and
they appear more settled in recent
years. Davis' demand to enter city
put salt in the wound resulting in
a riot on 15 Jan 1846. Next day
mob surrounded foreign factories,
and was dispersed by troops with
great difficulty. Populace is still
restless. Welcomes Davis' suggest-
ion to station steamer at Whampoa so
that Britons may take refuge on
board if need be.
Encl. Ch'i-ying's proclamation to
placate Cantonese, n.d.

	Jan 28	01 02	Davis to Ch'i-ying. Has issued notice forbidding Britons to try to force their way into Canton city. Suggests that respectable Britons be issued passes to enter city. [Incomplete]	10	1346A
	Feb 2	01 07	Ch'i-ying to Davis. Treaty states that Britons may trade in Canton without restrictions, but trade has always been conducted in factory area outside walled city. Entry into city is in no way related to trade or treaty. Requests Davis to issue notice forbidding Britons from trying to enter city, at least for time being.	19	1267
	Feb 2	01 07	Ch'i-ying to Davis. Has received Davis' receipt for final instalment of indemnity. Chusan should now be returned in accordance with treaty. Cantonese have been more settled; only people of interior are still restless. To request edict from Emperor ordering Cantonese to open gates of Canton will prove useless.	13	1332
a	Feb 5	01 10	Ch'i-ying to Davis. Is pleased that Davis has issued notice forbidding Britons from forcing their way into Canton city. Will restrain Cantonese.	6	389/41
b	Feb 5	01 10	Ch'i-ying to Davis. Is pleased that Davis has issued notice forbidding Britons from trying to force their way into the city. Suggestion that respectable Britons be issued official passes to enter city is impracticable. Official papers have	12	1268

F.O. 682/ 1979	Date 1846	TK 26	Description	pp	Old R F.O. 682/
			little effect on Cantonese, witness tearing to pieces of Ch'i-ying's proclamation. Expects Davis to keep his word and observe treaty concerning the return of Chusan.		
/16	Feb 7	01 12	Davis to Ch'i-ying. To trade in Canton without restrictions means Britons can trade wherever they like, including walled city of Canton. If entry into city is delayed, return of Chusan can also wait.	17	1284
/17	Feb 8	01 13	Davis to Ch'i-ying. Is surprised to read that Ch'i-ying thinks Cantonese are more settled in recent years. Incidents of Britons being attacked in countryside around Canton have increased. If this development cannot be halted before return of Chusan, little can be done after its return.	10	1285
/18	Feb 9	01 14	Davis to Ch'i-ying. Naval officer of steamer which took Ch'i-ying to Hong Kong has been attacked by villagers while shooting birds near Whampoa. Demands physical punishment of ringleaders in presence of said officer, or bluejackets will destroy village.	6	1286
/19	Feb 9	01 14	Davis to Ch'i-ying. Suggests that Ch'i-ying issues proclamation to following effect: because of Cantonese refusal to allow Britons into their city, Great Britain has decided to postpone return of Chusan. Such proclamation may change attitude of Cantonese.	8	1287
/20	Feb 9	01 14	Davis to Ch'i-ying. Suggests that, like sulphur and saltpetre, salt imported by British merchants, should be required to be sold to government appointed agents so as to forestall salt being smuggled like opium.	5	1288
/21	Feb 9	01 14	Provincial Treasurer Hsü [Chi-yü] of Fukien to Consul R. Alcock at Foochow. Agrees to issue proclamation of religious toleration.	6	1273
/22	Feb 12	01 17	Ch'i-ying to Davis. Has report from Tartar-General of Foochow. Acting	10	1269

). 2/ 79	Date 1846	TK 26	Description	pp	Old Ref. F.O. 682/
			Consul T.H. Layton at Amoy insists that customs duties on porcelain should be 5% *ad valorem* instead of 5 taels per 100 catties. This is in contravention of trade agreement. Would Davis instruct Layton to observe treaty?		
23	Feb 14	01 19	Ch'i-ying to Davis. Has sent officials to investigate attack on Royal Navy officer by villagers near Whampoa.	6	1270
24	n.d. [Feb 14]	n.d. [01 19]	Ch'i-ying to Davis. Neither Treaty of Nanking nor Supplementary Treaty contains provision for entry into city of Canton. If force and torture should be used to cow Cantonese, rebellion is bound to follow. Chusan was kept as guarantee for payment of indemnity. Indemnity has been paid and additional demand to enter city of Canton is flimsy excuse for prolonged occupation of Chusan. [Incomplete.]	15	1271
25	Feb 15	01 20	Davis to Ch'i-ying. Will instruct Consul T.H. Layton at Amoy to tax porcelain according to trade agreement.	4	1289
26	Feb 18	01 23	Davis to Ch'i-ying. Ch'i-ying promised Pottinger that Britons would be allowed into Canton city. Observance of treaty is not complete until Britons are allowed into city. Trouble makers at Feng-hua have been punished; why not Cantonese?	15	1346B
27a	Feb 19	01 24	Ch'i-ying to Davis. Salt is state monopoly. Rejects request that foreign salt be allowed into Shanghai.	8	253A/4B/3
27b	Feb 19	01 24	Ch'i-ying to Davis. According to trade agreement, imported cloth should be taxed at about 0.5 tael per roll. Transit dues at Pei-hsin-kuan are now only 0.15 tael per roll.	8	1330
28	Feb 21	01 26	Ch'i-ying to Davis. Has report from officials investigating attack on Royal Navy officer near Whampoa. On 4 Feb 1846 Royal Navy officer with	12	1272

F.O. 682/ 1979	Date 1846	TK 26	Description	pp	Old Re F.O. 682/
			about ten bluejackets penetrated ten *li* inland into densely populated villages. Their presence with muskets and pistols caused consternation, especially among women. Villagers gathered and threw stones at them to prevent them from going any further, not with intention to hurt or plunder. No one was injured. Gentry have been told to restrain villagers. Davis must restrain Britons roaming in countryside.		
/29	Feb 25	01 30	Davis to Ch'i-ying. Is disturbed that Ch'i-ying has not punished ringleader of villagers who attacked Royal Navy officer. If Ch'i-ying is unwilling or unable to protect Britons, Britons will take steps to protect themselves. Corrupt Chinese officials turn blind eye to opium smuggling; opium trade should be legalised.	8	1290
/30	Mar 1	02 04	Ch'i-ying to Davis. Has reply from Emperor: since entry into Canton city is not prescribed by treaty and is objected to by citizens, Ch'i-ying *et al.* must go about it very carefully. Chusan is in no way related to Canton city question and must be returned. [This despatch was rejected and returned to Ch'i-ying on the ground that its language was improper - see F.O. 682/1979/34.]	5	1331
/31	Mar 1	02 04	Copy of previous entry, made by British authorities before rejecting original.	6	1274
/32	Mar 1	02 04	Ch'i-ying to Davis. Promised Pottinger only to discuss entry question after Canton has settled down. Has repeated this point in all subsequent correspondence with Davis and during their meeting in Hong Kong. Recently issued proclamation at Davis' behest concerning entry and that led only to riots. Davis cannot accuse Cantonese of breach of treaty as entry into city is not in treaty. Davis cannot insist that stubborn Cantonese be executed: 'villains' at Feng-hua were executed because they plotted	17	1276

). 2/ 79	Date 1846	TK 26	Description	pp	Old Ref. F.O. 682/
			to rebel. [This despatch was reject- ed by Davis and returned to Ch'i-ying on the ground that its language was improper - see F.O. 682/1979/34.]		
33	Mar 1	02 04	Copy of previous entry, made by British authorities before rejection of original.	16	1275
34	Mar 3	02 06	Davis to Ch'i-ying. Returns two of Ch'i-ying's despatches on the ground that their language is improper.	8	1291
35	Mar 6	02 09	Ch'i-ying to Davis. Cannot punish villagers as they have not committed any crime. If Davis prevents blue- jackets from venturing into villages, Ch'i-ying himself will instruct local officials to restrain villagers. Will investigate allegation that corrupt Chinese officials turn blind eye to opium smuggling.	8	1337
36	Mar 7	02 10	Davis to Ch'i-ying. Again argues for legalisation of opium.	7	1292
37	Mar 9	02 12	Davis to Ch'i-ying. Has made it clear to British opium smugglers that he will not protect them, but only China can take action against them. If villagers around Canton continue to be hostile, foreign merchants will be driven to other treaty ports.	9	1293
38	Mar 13	02 16	Ch'i-ying to Davis. Since treaty has not been observed [i.e. British authorities have not returned Chusan], Emperor is bound to be greatly annoyed. Therefore, it would be unwise at this stage to approach him about legalisation of opium, which is not included in treaty. As regards alleged attack on Royal Navy officer *et al.*, they should not have gone to the villages to begin with. Since nobody was hurt, the subject should be dropped.	11	1277
39	Mar 14	02 17	Davis to Ch'i-ying. Encloses copy of five-point convention four of which Ch'i-ying suggested previously; the fifth provides for ratification by Emperor. As soon as it is ratified and exchanged,	10	1294

F.O. 682/ 1979	Date 1846	TK 26	Description	pp	Old Re F.O. 682/
			Chusan will be returned. Encl. Anglo-Chinese Convention, n.d.	3	116/5
/40	Mar 26	02 29	Davis to Ch'i-ying. Hopes to see Ch'i-ying at Hu-men on 3 April to sign convention.	6	1295
/41	Mar 28	03 02	Davis to Ch'i-ying. Commenting on Ch'i-ying's recent proclamation to Cantonese: (1) protests about Ch'i-ying's declaration that matter of British entry into city has been terminated; (2) endorses Ch'i-ying's threat to execute 'villains' who stir up trouble.	6	1296
/42	Mar 31	03 05	Ch'i-ying to Davis. Has not declared that matter of British entry into city is terminated. Has merely said that it has 'stopped for time being', not 'stopped forever'.	7	1340
/43	Apr 1	03 06	Joint proclamation by Viceroy Liu Yün-k'o of Min-Che and Acting Governor Hsü Chi-yü of Fukien. Mob should disperse and let Chinese and British officials settle dispute [in Foochow].	5	1338
/44	Apr -	03 -	Joint proclamation by Liu Yün-k'o and Hsü Chi-yü. Consul R. Alcock has established that certain Britons and their followers caused the incident and he will be fair in settling dispute. Neither side should harbour grievances against the other.	11	1339
/45a	Apr 4	03 09	Amoy Customs Officer Hsing to Acting Vice-Consul G.G. Sullivan at Amoy. Has reply from Ch'i-ying. Porcelain should be taxed according to its weight in accordance with treaty. Pottery may be taxed according to its value. Encl. List of seven British ships and sums they should have paid as taxes, n.d.	11 3	1346E
/45b	Apr 9	03 14	Hoppo to Consul F.C. Macgregor. Treaty does not prohibit steamers from carrying exports nor does it permit it. Goods for Hong Kong are usually carried by lorchas. If Macgregor insists on starting to use steamer, only Imperial Commissioner can decide if this may be done.	4	253A/

O. 2/ 79	Date 1846	TK 26	Description	pp	Old Ref. F.O. 682/
45c	Apr 11	03 16	Ch'i-ying to F.C. Macgregor. British steamer has always been used for carrying letters, not goods, between Canton and Hong Kong. Art. 17 of Supplementary Treaty refers only to lorchas for carrying goods; hence use of steamers for such purpose means breach of treaty and is therefor not permitted.	4	253A/4B/12
45d	Apr 16	03 21	Ch'i-ying to F.C. Macgregor. American steamer had undertaken to carry only letters and passengers before it was allowed to ply between Canton and Hong Kong. It subsequently carried miscellaneous items twice but stopped on discovering that it was too much trouble doing so.	8	253A/4B/13
46	Apr 23	03 28	Amoy Customs Officer Ko to Consul T.H. Layton. A ship from Luzon importing cotton and sugar insists that her sugar be taxed according to its value. Could Layton please notify the ship that trade agreement requires tax of 0.25 tael per 100 catties of sugar.	7	1278
47	Apr 27	[4] 02	Ch'i-ying to Davis. Although Treaty of Nanking does not forbid cargo steamers going up Pearl River, it does not authorise this either. Art. 17 of Supplementary Treaty provides for sailing boats only. Pearl River is too narrow and too congested for cargo steamers. Witness recent accidents in which steamers ran over junks and sank them, causing about sixty deaths. U.S. steamers visiting Canton carry letters only, having agreed not to accept any cargo. Encl. Ch'i-ying to F.C. Macgregor, n.d.	18 4	1333
48	May 5	04 10	Ch'i-ying to Davis. Had not intended to refer to treaty but felt obliged to when F.C. Macgregor started subject. Boats with three sails are allowed into Pearl River, though not authorised by treaty, because they are not as fast as steamers and not likely to run over local ships.	8	1334
49	May 10	04 15	Provincial Treasurer Hsü Chi-yü of Fukien to Consul R. Alcock at Foochow.	8	1346F

F.O. 682/ 1979	Date 1846	TK 26	Description	pp	Old Ref F.O. 682/
			Losses claimed by British merchants as result of attack on their firms are greatly exaggerated.		
/50a	May 10	04 15	Ch'i-ying to Davis. Has received ratified five-point convention from Emperor. Hopes that Davis will instruct commander of garrison in Chusan to evacuate the island, and that Davis will inform Ch'i-ying of such instructions so that Ch'i-ying in turn may instruct Intendant [Hsien-ling] at Shanghai to act in consort with said commander.	4	352/4
/50b	May 15	04 20	Ch'i-ying to Davis. Repeats that he has received ratified five-point convention from Emperor. Looks forward to Chusan being returned.	6	1279
/51	May 16	04 21	Davis to General D'Aguila. Asks him to order commander of Chusan garrison to return island to China.	4	1297
/52	May 18	04 23	Davis to Ch'i-ying. Is determined to punish steamers severely should they damage Chinese junks either deliberately or through negligence. Has despatched ships to evacuate 1,500 or so British soldiers in Chusan.	7	1299
/53	May 21	04 26	Ch'i-ying to Davis. There is no such thing as tax manual for the interior customs house at Pei-hsin-kuan. But will ask authorities there to prepare statement about tax on imported cloth and forward it to British Consul at Shanghai.	6	1280
/54	May 21	04 26	Ch'i-ying to Davis. Is pleased that Davis is determined to punish cargo steamers that damage Chinese shipping, and that Chusan is being evacuated.	8	1281
/55	Jun 12	05 19	Hsü Chi-yü to R. Alcock. It was decided in a meeting with Alcock that Chinese government would lend $46,163.77 to British merchants who had been robbed by Chinese mob. This sum will be handed over on 15 June.	7	1346D
/56	Jun 23	05 30	Davis to Ch'i-ying. Is pleased that British merchants plundered at	6	1347

0. 2/ 79	Date 1846	TK 26	Description	pp	Old Ref. F.O. 682/

TE: *The symbol* i *in the third column stands for intercalary month.*

			Foochow have been indemnified. Has hired enough ships to evacuate troops from Chusan. Will proceed thence eight days later.		
57a	Jun 25	i5 02	Davis to Ch'i-ying. Chusan has been returned to Chinese representatives [Hsien-ling *et al.*].	5	1298
57b	Jun 26	i5 03	Ch'i-ying and Huang En-t'ung to Davis. Are pleased with Davis' proclamation that Britons who start trouble will not be compensated for losses in subsequent disturbance. *Bon voyage.*	3	68/3B/9
57c	Jul 9	i5 16	Ch'i-ying and Huang En-t'ung to F.C. McGregor. Command Macgregor to investigate how disturbance was started last night, in which three Chinese were shot dead and many others wounded.	2	68/3B/8
58	Jul 14	i5 21	Davis to Intendant [Hsien-ling at Shanghai]. Inhabitants of Chusan who entered into British service must be free from molestation after return of island.	6	1301
59	Jul 16	i5 23	[Hsien-ling] to Davis. Emperor has pardoned Chinese in British service and numerous proclamations have been issued to this effect.	9	1341
60	Jul 16	i5 23	[Hsien-ling] *et al.* to Brigadier Campbell. Are grateful to Campbell for having so successfully restrained occupying forces that no incidents have occurred.	7	1345
61	Jul 17	i5 24	Consul G. Balfour at Shanghai to Intendant Kung Mu-chiu of Su-Sung-T'ai. Although tax on imported cloth at Pei-hsin-kuan is same as before, quality and hence value of imported cloth has fallen considerably. Therefore to tax it according to quantity has become grossly unfair.	8	1309B
62	Jul 17	i5 24	Davis to [Hsien-ling]. Is pleased to read [Hsien-ling's] guarantee for safety of Chinese formerly employed by British forces in Chusan. Will warn two British merchants remaining in Chusan that they are staying on	4	1302

F.O. 682/ 1979	Date 1846	TK 26	Description	pp	Old Re F.O. 682/
			at their own risk.		
/63	Jul 22	𝘪5 29	[Hsien-ling] to Davis. Acknowledges receipt of barracks and hospital from Brigadier Campbell.	8	1282
/64	Aug 2	06 11	Davis to Ch'i-ying. Has returned from Chusan, where he saw the last soldier embark, handed over all ·buildings to Intendant [Hsien-ling], obtained [Hsien-ling's] guarantee of protection for Chinese previously employed by British forces, and ordered two remaining British merchants to leave.	6	1300
/65	Aug 4	06 13	Davis to Ch'i-ying. Protests against use of word *cha* (command) instead of *cha* (memorandum) in Ch'i-ying's letter to Consul F.C. Macgregor. As regards recent fighting between British merchants and Cantonese which led to attack on foreign factories, has drawn up regulations for protection of foreign factories.	8	1303
/66a	Aug 5	06 [14]	Davis to Ch'i-ying. Unlike merchant shipping, Royal Navy must have access to all Chinese ports to facilitate suppression of British and American pirates.	8	1304
/66b	Aug 7	06 16	Ch'i-ying and Huang En-t'ung to Davis. Thank Davis for supervising personally evacuation of Chusan. Agree to protect all Chinese who have given service to British forces in Chusan and to protect graves of Britons.	10	253/4B
/66c	Aug 9	06 18	Ch'i-ying and Huang En-t'ung to Davis. Mr. C. Compton is responsible for both riots, which were caused by Compton beating up Chinese. Britons would not listen to Consul F.C. Macgregor and fired into dispersing crowd. Three Chinese were shot dead far away from scene of riot; demand compensation.	13	253A/L
/66d	Aug 9	06 18	Ch'i-ying and Huang En-t'ung to Davis. Authorities in Kiangsu have notified return of British man-of-war to Shanghai. Have asked them to intensify search for pirates.	6	253A/

. :/ '9	Date 1846	TK 26	Description	pp	Old Ref. F.O. 682/
6e	Aug 13	06 22	Ch'i-ying to Davis. Treaty allows British men-of-war to be stationed at five treaty ports to protect trade. As foreign trade is confined to these ports, so must Royal Navy be.	8	253A/4B/7
7	Aug 14	06 23	Davis to Ch'i-ying. C. Compton was not drunk when he started incident. Protests about lack of protection for foreign factories during subsequent attack on it.	9	1305
			Encl. Testimony by Americans that they and Britons jointly defended foreign factories.	7	1780
8a	Aug 18	06 27	Davis to Ch'i-ying. G. Balfour is returning to England. He will be replaced as Consul at Shanghai by R. Alcock. T.H. Layton will replace R. Thom as Consul at Ningpo, R.B. Jackson will replace Alcock as Consul at Foochow.	5	1306
8b	Aug 23	07 02	Ch'i-ying and Huang En-t'ung to F.C. Macgregor. All witnesses available testify unanimously to improper conduct of C. Compton and other Britons.	6	253A/4B/9
8c	Aug 24	07 03	Ch'i-ying and Hung En-t'ung to Davis. Note G. Balfour's return to England and his replacement by R. Alcock at Shanghai, replacement of R. Thom by T.H. Layton at Ningpo, and of R. Alcock by R.B. Jackson at Foochow.	6	68/3B/10
9	Aug 26	07 05	Davis to Ch'i-ying. C. Compton will be fined for smashing roadside fruit stall, and compensation will be paid to relatives of Chinese shot dead. But foreign factories must be protected.	7	1307
0a	Aug 30	07 09	Ch'i-ying and Huang En-t'ung to Davis. Thank Davis for ordering two British merchants to remove stock from Chusan and to notify British merchants in Shanghai never to go to Chusan again.	6	253A/4B/10
0b	Sep 6	07 16	Ch'i-ying and Huang En-t'ung to Davis. Fining C. Compton for smashing fruit stall is beside the point; he should be punished for having bound and beaten up Chinese. Magistrate of Nan-hai, Prefect of Canton, Grain Intendant, Provincial Judge and	14	1343

F.O. 682/ 1979	Date 1846	TK 26	Description	pp	Old Re F.O. 682/
			numerous senior army officers have personally led troops to scene from all directions. How can Davis possibly accuse Chinese government of not having given foreigners sufficient protection?		
/71	Sep 11	07 21	Davis to Ch'i-ying. Insists that Chinese army officer refused to respond to requests for help when mob was attacking foreign factories, and finds it difficult to believe that C. Compton assaulted Chinese army officer.	10	1308
/72	Sep 18	07 28	Davis to Ch'i-ying. Transit dues at Pei-hsin-kuan must be lowered.	5	1309A
/73	Sep 19	07 29	Ch'i-ying and Huang En-t'ung to Davis. C. Compton had assaulted Chinese officer four days before incident. If Davis does not settle account of three Chinese deaths according to treaty, Chinese soldiers guarding factories may not be able to hold back angry Cantonese much longer. Encl. U.S. Consul Forbes at Canton to [Ch'i-ying]. American who shot dead Chinese will be handed to U.S. Minister C. Cushing for punishment.	11 1	1336
/74	Sep 19	07 29	Davis to Ch'i-ying. Will report to London that Chinese authorities are not giving sufficient protection to Britons in Canton.	8	1310
/75	Sep 23	08 04	Ch'i-ying to Davis. According to treaty, Chinese internal customs houses may not levy transit dues heavier than existing ones on imported goods. It does not provide for reduction of existing dues. Transit dues at Pei-hsin-kuan may not be reduced. Agrees to investigate allegations of corruption at Pei-hsin-kuan.	8	1329
/76	Sep 23	08 04	Ch'i-ying and Huang En-t'ung to Davis. Best way to protect Britons is to observe treaty by punishing those responsible for death of three Chinese. Otherwise additional guards to patrol factory area will only antagonise Cantonese further.	11	1335

.	Date		Description	pp	Old Ref. F.O.
/ 9	1846	TK 26			682/

7	Sep 26	08 07	Davis to Ch'i-ying. C. Compton has been fined $200. Britons killed three Chinese in self-defence. U.S.A. and other countries were also involved in battle to defend foreign factories; therefore Great Britain cannot shoulder all responsibilities. Chinese authorities must protect foreign community.	9	1311
8	Oct 3	08 14	Ch'i-ying to Davis. Chinese soldiers have not been slow to protect foreign factories. Is willing to accept Davis' legal concept that Britons may not be punished for having killed three Chinese in self-defence, although the three killed were innocent bystanders. But Davis must promptly materialise offer to compensate relatives of the dead, so as to placate populace, and forestall vengeance. Will also issue proclamation to placate Cantonese, and will see to enforcement of regulations for protection of foreign factories.	8	1328
9	Oct 7	08 18	Consul G. Balfour at Shanghai to Intendant Kung Mu-chiu. R. Alcock has come to take over British consulate in Shanghai. Thanks Chinese authorities for co-operation in past three years.	4	1319
0	Oct 9	08 20	Davis to Ch'i-ying. It is unfair to blame Britons alone for killing three Chinese. All foreigners present were involved in battle. If Britons had killed Chinese for any reason other than self-defence, they would have been punished.	8	1312
1	Oct 19	08 30	Davis to Ch'i-ying. Has sent officer to Canton to find out people responsible for killing of Chinese.	5	1313
2	Oct 20	09 01	Davis to Ch'i-ying. Has received ratified convention from London. Is sending two officers to forward it to Canton. Encl. Receipt from Ch'i-ying for ratified convention. [re Chusan].	5 4	1314
3	Oct 23	09 04	Davis to Ch'i-ying. Chinese officer Tai Kuan-pao and ten or so	5	1315

F.O. 682/ 1979	Date 1846	TK 26	Description	pp	Old R F.O. 682/
			constables came to a shop in Hong Kong, put four men in chains and took away some money; they are still detaining one man. Encl. Evidence by Li A-ch'uan, owner of shop, n.d.	3	1316
/84a	Oct 24	09 05	Ch'i-ying to Macgregor. The two foreigners were attacked because they had attempted to enter walled city of Canton. Those responsible for luring foreigners into city, knowing very well that these foreigners would be attacked, will be severely punished; but foreigners must not allow themselves to be lured into the city.	2	1468/
/84b	Oct 28	09 09	Ch'i-ying to Davis. Has ordered Colonel of Ta-p'eng to investigate allegations by Li A-ch'uan.	6	1283
/85	Oct 31	09 12	Davis to Ch'i-ying. Has report on killing of three Chinese. All foreigners present admitted having fired at mob to protect foreign factories, but none claimed responsibility for killing the three Chinese. If only Chinese soldiers were there when the incident occurred all this could have been avoided.	8	1317
/86	Oct 31	09 12	Davis to Ch'i-ying. Forwards copy of letter from G. Balfour to Kung Mu-chiu. Is satisfied to know that Balfour and Kung co-operated so well and hopes Ch'i-ying will report Kung's achievement to Emperor.	5	1318
/87	Nov 6	09 18	Davis to Ch'i-ying. Has letter from Colonel [of Ta-p'eng] stationed at Kowloon: the Colonel was aware of what was happening and had in fact authorised action. Strongly protests about intrusion into Hong Kong. Demands punishment of officer Tai Kuan-pao and release of detainee within ten days.	6	1320
/88	Nov 7	09 19	Ch'i-ying and Huang En-t'ung to Davis. It is too much to ask Chinese soldiers to be on the spot when incident occurred as they could not have known in advance that C. Compton was about to molest Chinese. All	12	134

Date		Description	pp	Old Ref. F.O.
1846	TK 26			682/

three Chinese were killed in streets far beyond troubled area. Davis cannot claim that they were shot while attacking factories. Nor could he claim that they were ruffians as all three were well-established business-men. Foreigners' best protection may be obtained not by bullying Cantonese but by observing treaty and by treating Cantonese fairly. Has reinforced guards patrolling factory area.

Nov 10	09 22	Davis to Ch'i-ying. Reiterates that Britons cannot be held solely responsible for killing of Chinese. Promises to restrain Britons but Ch'i-ying must restrain Cantonese also.	7	1321
Nov 13	09 25	Davis to Ch'i-ying. Is satisfied with Ch'i-ying's management of case of [Tai Kuan-pao]. Will extradite Chinese criminals in Hong Kong when requested through diplomatic channels.	5	1322
Nov 18	[09 30]	Davis to Ch'i-ying. Has letter from Governor-General of India about mission to Tibet to negotiate trade arrangements and to demarcate frontiers.	10	1323
		Encl. Lord Henry Hardinge to Ch'i-shan, [1846].	6	1324
Nov 23	10 05	Davis to Ch'i-ying. Protests about language employed in proclamation by Magistrate of Nan-hai. Has printed 500 copies of Treaty of Nanking for distribution by and edification of [Cantonese officials].	5	1325
Nov 27	10 09	Ch'i-ying and Huang En-t'ung to Davis. Magistrate of Nan-hai had merely up-dated old proclamation about provincial military examination without being aware that some clauses therein were obsolete. Has instructed him to delete such clauses.	9	1342
Nov 29	10 11	Ch'i-ying and Huang En-t'ung to Davis. Both Davis and Consul F.C. Macgregor have persistently stated that Britons and Americans jointly defended foreign factories. As U.S. Consul Forbes has declared that Americans stayed indoors guarding their own	15	1346C

F.O. 682/ 1979	Date 1846	TK 26	Description	pp	Old R F.O. 682/

firms and did not go out to join
Britons in fighting, it is obvious
that Britons were responsible for
shooting. Even if other foreigners
were involved, they were only
accomplices while Britons were ring-
leaders. It is useless to defend
Britons by saying that they killed
in self-defence as three Chinese
were shot in streets far beyond
troubled area. Unless murderer(s)
are punished according to treaty,
Chinese soldiers may not have
deterrent effect on crowd much
longer. Davis cannot demand
compensation for losses in disturb-
ances as treaty provides for arrest
of criminals and recovery of lost
property only.

Encl. Forbes to Ch'i-ying. Americans 4
stayed indoors guarding own firms
and did not go out to join British
crowd, 11 Aug 1845 [Rec'd].

/95	Dec 1	10 13	Davis to Ch'i-ying. It is foolish of Magistrate of Nan-hai to try to stop steamers coming to Canton by pestering Chinese passengers.	5	1326
/96	Dec 3	10 15	Davis to Huang En-t'ung. Since Ch'i-ying is away in Kwangsi, letter about mission to Tibet should wait till his return.	5	1327
/97	Dec 26	11[09]	Consul R. Alcock at Shanghai to Kung Mu-chiu. It is much fairer to tax cloth imports and silk exports according to value. Requests him to ask new tax officer at Pei-hsin-kuan to abolish old and unfair tax rules.	21	1355
/98	Dec 30	11 13	Ch'i-ying and Huang En-t'ung to Davis. Request arrest and extradition of several secret society leaders with criminal records who are taking refuge in Hong Kong.	10	1348

. √ 0	Date 1847	TK 26	Description	pp	Old Ref. F.O. 682/
1	Jan 13	11 27	Ch'i-ying to Davis. Treaty allows Britons to trade in five treaty ports only. Hence they must not attempt to go to Tibet. Old boundaries had been agreed upon between China and Indian states; why should Britons want new demarcations?	10	1349
2	Jan 16	11 30	Ch'i-ying to Davis. As peace has been concluded, Britain should no longer disturb territories of China or those of her vassal states. Protests about several visits by British man-of-war to Liu-ch'iu and about physician having gone there to stay.	8	1350
3	Jan 20	12 04	Draft of next entry.	10	1357B
4	Jan 20	12 04	Davis to Ch'i-ying. Governor-General of India merely wanted to find out existing boundaries, not to demarcate new ones. Trade already exists between Indian states and Tibet and it is not a matter of starting new trade. In any case, he is not asking for permission to send mission to Tibet; mission has been sent and Ch'i-ying was notified as a matter of courtesy.	10	1351
5	Jan 21	12 05	Davis to Ch'i-ying. China has no say over movement of Royal Navy. The physician is providing medical service for Liu-ch'iu and China should not have any objection.	6	1352
6	Jan 26	12 10	Ch'i-ying to Davis. If it were only matter of existing boundaries and existing trade, he does not wish to say anything as he knows nothing about Tibet. Will mention matter to Emperor.	8	1353
7a	Jan 30	12 14	Davis to Ch'i-ying. Has letter from Prime Minister: regrets death of three Cantonese but Britons must protect themselves if Chinese government cannot restrain Cantonese; has instructed man-of-war to anchor opposite foreign factories to ensure safety of Britons and their property.	7	1354

F.O. 682/ 1980	Date 1847	TK 26	Description	pp	Old R F.O. 682/
/7b	Feb 3	12 18	Davis to Ch'i-ying. Protests against increase of tax on imported cloth at Pei-hsin-kuan.	7	112/4
/8a	Feb 8	12 23	Ch'i-ying to Davis. Is greatly puzzled that British Prime Minister also used 'self-defence' as excuse not to punish Britons who shot dead three Cantonese and wounded six others. It is not a matter of restraining Cantonese but of restraining Britons as Mr C. Compton had provoked Cantonese. Cantonese will submit to reason only: to anchor man-of-war opposite foreign factories with the intention to cow Cantonese is a bad move.	10	1356

TK 27

/8b	Apr 4	02 19	Davis to Ch'i-ying. Details record of meeting of today: (1) date should be fixed for Davis to return visit to Ch'i-ying in Ch'i-ying's *yamen* inside city of Canton; (2) Britons should be allowed to visit places within one day's return journey from Canton; (3) Cantonese who attacked Britons in Sep/Oct last year and Feb/Mar this year must be punished immediately and their punishments be communicated to Davis; (4) Britons should be allowed to lease land in Ho-nan for building houses; (5) Britons should be allowed to lease land at Canton to build churches, and land at Whampoa to establish a cemetery; (6) footbridge and kitchen should be built over strip of land between two gardens [in factory area]; sheds should not be allowed to be built against walls [of the factories]; (7) [Chinese] boats must not be allowed to moor in front of factory area. Davis himself will return to Hong Kong when these conditions are agreed upon.	2	1468f
/9a	Apr 5	02 20	Ch'i-ying to Davis. Replies to demands: (1) to return Davis' hospitality by entertaining him inside Canton city is gesture of good-will and therefore must comply with wishes of citizens; fixing date of entry within two years is too soon; perhaps four or five years; (2)	14	1357

). 2/ 30	Date 1847	TK 27	Description	pp	Old Ref. F.O. 682/
			Britons may visit places within one day's return journey from Canton; (3) has spared no effort in apprehending those who attacked Britons; (4) Britons may lease land to build houses in Ho-nan; (5) Britons may build churches in factory area and establish cemetery in Whampoa; (6) will urge ex-*hong* merchants to remove shanty town around foreign factories and to build footbridge joining gardens in the area; (7) will forbid sampans mooring outside foreign factories.		
/9b	Apr 9	02 24	Ch'i-ying to Davis. Has ordered investigation into proposal to purchase forty shops at southern end of Hog Lane for land to build church, and to block northern end of Hog Lane.	4	327/5/8
/9c	[Apr 9]	02 24	Draft of previous entry.	2	327/5/5
10	Apr 28	03 14	Davis to Ch'i-ying. Is pleased to read that Chinese who attacked British sailor has been captured and tortured to extract information about accomplices. Wishes to know their ultimate punishment as well. French navy has attacked Annam in retaliation for ill-treatment of French teacher.	6	1358
11	Apr 29	03 15	Davis to Ch'i-ying. Recovered property should be handed over to Consul F.C. Macgregor to be sent to Hong Kong [see previous entry].	4	1359
12	Apr 29	03 15	Davis to Ch'i-ying. Best way to deal with British opium smugglers is to legalise the drug. Plans to write to Emperor about legalising opium and hopes Ch'i-ying will help him with format of letter.	8	1360
13	May 4	03 20	Davis to Ch'i-ying. Urges that questions of building churches in factory area and houses in Ho-nan be quickly settled.	7	1361
14	May 11	03 27	Colonel Wang P'eng-nien of Ta-p'eng to Hong Kong authorities. Has asked civil authorities of Hsiang-shan, Hsin-an and Kowloon to apprehend three Chinese servants who burgled	6	1357C

F.O. 682/ 1980	Date 1847	 TK 27	Description	pp	Old R F.O. 682/
			their British employer's house in Hong Kong.		
/15	May 18	04 05	Ch'i-ying to Davis. Chinese merchants do not feel secure in Canton because Davis has put salt in wounds of Opium War by his actions on 3 April. [Davis led gunboats up Pearl River, dismantling Chinese forts on his way and forced Ch'i-ying to promise, among other things, to open gates of Canton within two years.]	10	1362
/16	May 18	04 05	Ch'i-ying to Davis. Agrees that legalisation of opium is best solution to opium smuggling and to outflow of silver, but it is bad time to raise matter with Emperor. Will speak to Emperor personally about this on next visit to Peking.	6	1363
/17	May 19	04 06	Ch'i-ying to Davis. Has wasted enough time on question of Pei-hsin-kuan without settlement. As British merchants seem to have no complaints about neighbouring customs house at Hu-shu, he proposes that tax regulations of Pei-hsin-kuan follow those of Hu-shu-kuan.	8	1364
/18	May 20	04 07	Ch'i-ying to Davis. Wu A-liu is same person as that referred to by Davis and has been punished.	6	1365
/19	May 22	04 09	Ch'i-ying to Davis. Some landlords in Ho-nan seem willing to lease out land to Britons but none has appeared before Chinese officials to sign lease. Has urged Consul F.C. Macgregor to prepare list of willing landlords who might be summoned to sign leases.	7	1366
/20a	May 24	04 11	Ch'i-ying to Davis. Has spared no effort in protecting Britons and in apprehending ruffians who attacked them.	6	1367
/20b	May 28	04 15	Consul F.C. Macgregor to Ch'i-ying. Requests co-operation in effecting purchase of eight shops at southern end of Hog Lane as site for building church. Both Hog Lane and Erh-hua-yüan should be blocked to prevent	6	327/5

). 2/ 30	Date 1847	TK 27	Description	pp	Old Ref. F.O. 682/
			gangsters entering factory area.		
21	Jun 17	05 05	Magistrate Lu Sun-ting of Hsiang-shan to Hong Kong authorities. Has sent police constables to arrest three Chinese who burgled their employer's house in Hong Kong, but cannot find them in their native village.	5	1357D
22	Jun 22	05 10	Ch'i-ying to Davis. Mr Ch'en of Ho-nan is willing to let five ware-houses. Work has started on site at Hog Lane; soldiers have continued to guard it. No incidents have been reported so far.	9	1368
3	Jun 27	05 15	Ch'i-ying to Davis. Has instructed civil and military authorities of Hsiang-shan to arrest three Chinese who burgled their British employer's house in Hong Kong. Has also order-ed village elders to hand them over.	7	1369
4	Jul 2	05 20	Ch'i-ying to Davis. Mr Ch'en and Mr Wu have both withdrawn offers to let houses in Ho-nan because Britons wish to dismantle houses to build western houses. Owners of warehouses to east of foreign factories have submitted to Consul F.C. Macgregor a list of rents they ask for. Owner of Shih-wei-t'ang area is willing to lease out land but tenant farmers there will not agree.	8	1370
5	Jul 7	05 25	Ch'i-ying to Davis. One Briton has rented Mr Wu's warehouse in Ho-nan. No Briton seems interested in those to east of foreign factories. Elders and gentry of Shih-wei-t'ang area have petitioned that their livelihood should not be denied by Britons taking over the land for commercial use.	10	1371
6	Jul 7	05 25	Ch'i-ying to Davis. Asks Davis to name official of Hsiang-shan who blackmailed fisherman from Hong Kong for $30.	7	1413
7	Jul 7	05 25	Ch'i-ying to Davis. Endorses Consul F.C. Macgregor's proposal to build wall to west of foreign factories	8	1372

F.O. 682/ 1980	Date 1847	TK 27	Description	pp	Old R F.O. 682/
			to protect shipyard nearby, so that plans by ruffians to set fire to shipyard [in the hope that the fire will spread to the foreign factories] may be foiled. However, the building of the wall involves dismantling bridge erected at expense of inhabitants and shopkeepers of six streets, who may raise violent objections. Therefore, he will send troops to patrol the six streets to forestall any disturbance. He will also instruct Magistrate of Nan-hai to reinforce guards patrolling shipyard. He will write again when he is certain that the building of the wall may proceed without serious incidents.		
/28	Jul 16	06 05	Ch'i-ying to Davis. Is pleased that Davis agrees not to have wall to west of foreign factories erected at once [so as to give time to assess reaction of local inhabitants] and that Davis has informed Consul Macgregor to this effect. Endorses Davis' decision to withdraw British troops from foreign factories, now that Chinese government is providing sufficient protection to the area.	8	1373
/29	Jul 16	06 05	Ch'i-ying to Davis. Is surprised to read that name of official alleged to have blackmailed Hong Kong fisherman for $30 is Lu Sun-ting, who enjoys a very good reputation as an upright and hardworking official, and who has served for a long time as Magistrate of Hsiang-shan.	6	1374
/30	Jul 16	06 05	Ch'i-ying to Davis. Tenants at Shih-wei-t'ang have submitted to Consul F.C. Macgregor two days ago a list of annual incomes from flowers, fruits, fish ponds, etc. for settlement. He understands that so far only one proprietor, a Mr Wu, has offered his house for lease to a British merchant. He will send his deputies to find out more proprietors who may be	8	1375

0. 2/ 80	Date 1847	TK 27	Description	pp	Old Ref. F.O. 682/
			willing to offer their warehouses for lease to British merchants. Encl. List submitted by tenants of Shih-wei-t'ang, n.d.	6	
31	Jul 25	06 14	Ch'i-ying to Davis. Has sent deputy together with Magistrate of P'an-yü to go to Whampoa and inspect site for cemetery with British Vice-Consul. It is impossible to have separate burial ground for foreigners surrounded by walls, as the place is dotted with graves. Proprietor of land is willing to let burial plots individually; rent will be charged according to social position of dead, ranging from $20 for the upper class and $2 for a sailor.	11	1376
32	Jul 26	06 15	Ch'i-ying to Davis. Has investigated Davis' accusation that rent reques- ted by tenants of Shih-wei-t'ang is too high. They have built houses, dug fish ponds, planted flowers and fruit trees etc. which support their living. They must be compensated accordingly in terms of rent.	9	1377
33	Jul 29	06 18	Ch'i-ying to Davis. Has instructed Magistrate of Nan-hai to make P'an Shih-ch'eng and P'an Shih-ping pay their debts of $17,452.88 and $36,565.31 respectively, which they owe British firms.	6	1378
34	Aug 1	06 21	Davis to Ch'i-ying. Wonders if Ch'i- ying has reported to Emperor about British mission to Tibet. Governor- General of India has sent three officers to ascertain frontier with Tibet but no offical from China appeared to join in project.	7	1379
35	Aug 1	06 21	Ch'i-ying to Davis. Denies that leas- ing out burial plots individually is breach of treaty. If foreigners [Indians] insist on building walls to form cemetery of their own in Whampoa, many Chinese graves will either have to be removed or lie under bricks.	9	1380

F.O. 682/ 1980	Date 1847	TK 27	Description	pp	Old Re F.O. 682/
/36	Aug 5	06 25	Davis to Ch'i-ying. Protests about the gathering in Shih-wei-t'ang of a crowd carrying arms after withdrawal of British troops from foreign factories.	5	1381
/37	Aug 5	06 25	Davis to Ch'i-ying. Insists that walls must be built round cemetery; if this cannot be done in Whampoa another place should be found.	7	1382
/38	Aug 18	07 08	Ch'i-ying to Davis. Disagrees that Chinese pirates captured by Royal Navy should henceforth be tried in Hong Kong on the ground that most of twelve pirates handed over to authorities in Amoy had been sentenced to death. Usually severe punishments are meted out to pirates in order to produce deterrent effect. Requests Royal Navy to continue to hand over pirates to Chinese authorities.	10	1383
/39	Aug 22	07 12	Ch'i-ying to Davis. Rejects claim by British Consul at Amoy that it is breach of treaty to forbid Chinese to employ foreign vessels to carry cargo: treaties prescribe such prohibition.	20	1384
/40	Aug 24	07 14	Ch'i-ying to Davis. Re Davis' request that Magistrate Chou of Shanghai be dismissed, Ch'i-ying himself has no power over official of another province but has referred matter to Magistrate Chou's superior Intendant [Hsien-ling].	7	1385
/41	Aug 24	07 14	Ch'i-ying to Davis. Has instructed Intendant [Hsien-ling] to find out tax scale at Hu-shu-kuan and to investigate allegation that difficulties have been put in way of tea going to Shanghai.	8	1386
/42	Aug 24	07 14	Ch'i-ying to Davis. Has arrested two villagers of Huang-chu-ch'i, who admitted having fired cannon but denied knowledge that a boat with foreigners on board was passing by, let alone aiming at it. Has spared no effort in protecting foreigners:	10	1387

). 2/ 80	Date 1847	TK 27	Description	pp	Old Ref. F.O. 682/
			it is unnecessary for Davis to despatch troops to Canton. Denies rumours that peasants refuse to pay taxes.		
43	Aug 25	7 15	Ch'i-ying to Davis. Both British consular officials and local Chinese authorities have worked hard on project for establishing cemetery in Whampoa. Indians now agree to accept area where there are no graves and to plant bamboos round it instead of building brick walls. Again denies reports that peasants refuse to pay taxes.	13	1338
44a	Aug 28	07 18	Ch'i-ying to Davis. Has arrested one more villager of Huang-chu-ch'i. All three admitted to having exercised one small old cannon but insisted that no cannon ball was used. Has decided that although no cannon ball had been used and no one was hurt, all three should be lashed thirty times each and paraded in factory area for one month.	11	1389
44b	Aug 29	07 19	Ch'i-ying to Davis. Requests that enclosed letter to Pottinger be forwarded.	2	327/5/16
45	Aug 31	07 21	Ch'i-ying to Davis. Thanks for offer to compensate Chinese merchant whose salt junk was sunk by steamer in collision.	6	1390
46	Sep 1	07 22	Ch'i-ying to Davis. Thanks for enclosing tax scale at Hu-shu-kuan. Will forward it to Pei-hsin-kuan. Internal customs offices do not concern Ch'i-ying himself in his capacity as Imperial Commissioner for Foreign Affairs; they are directly under Ministry of Revenue.	8	1391
47	Sep 1	07 22	Ch'i-ying to Davis. Is pleased to report that Magistrate Chou of Shanghai has been removed.	6	1392
48	Sep 1	07 22	Ch'i-ying to Davis. Local Chinese authorities and British consular officials have marked off site in Whampoa for cemetery.	8	1393

F.O. 682/ 1980	Date 1847	TK 27	Description	pp	Old Re F.O. 682/
/49	Sep 4	07 25	Ch'i-ying to Davis. Only annual rent for land to be used as cemetery remains to be settled.	8	1394
/50	Sep 6	07 27	Ch'i-ying to Davis. Agrees to allow Chinese merchants to hire British ships for carrying cargo, but Chinese must report for customs themselves and Britons must not pretend such cargo is their own.	6	1395
/51	Sep 6	07 27	Ch'i-ying to Davis. Is pleased that Davis is satisfied with punishment meted out to three villagers of Huang-chu-ch'i.	6	1396
/52	Sep 18	08 10	Ch'i-ying to Davis. As regards legal-isation of opium, again promises to mention matter to Emperor when next in Peking.	8	1397
/53	Sep 18	08 10	Ch'i-ying to Davis. Cemetery at Whampoa for Indians will be leased out for one hundred years at 25 taels per annum.	9	1398
/54	Sep 21	08 13	Ch'i-ying to Davis. Is pleased that Lord Palmerston is satisfied with his handling of Cantonese who attacked Britons.	7	1399
/55	Oct 3	08 25	Ch'i-ying to Davis. Buying and leas-ing of land in Hog Lane for British merchants are now settled.	10	1400
/56	Oct 3	08 25	Ch'i-ying to Davis. Will command local officials to speed up arrest of three Chinese who burgled their employer's house in Hong Kong.	8	1401
/57	Oct 8	08 30	Ch'i-ying to Davis. *Bon voyage.*	6	1402
/58	Oct 16	09 08	Ch'i-ying to Acting Governor of Hong Kong General D'Aguila . Has arrested Wu A-liu and eight accomplices who plundered British boats in Pearl River. Box full of cloth has been recovered.	8	1403
/59	Oct 31	09 23	Ch'i-ying to D'Aguila . Agrees that exportation of copper cash from China by tens of thousands will deplete the local money supply. It	8	1404

0. 2/ 80	Date 1847	TK 27	Description	pp	Old Ref. F.O. 682/
			is a good idea to set date after which copper cash may not be exported in large quantities.		
0	Nov 5	09 28	Ch'i-ying to Davis. Is pleased that Davis has returned safely. Will arrest ringleader at Ch'a-t'ou and issue proclamation to that village prohibiting further threatening behaviour towards foreigners.	7	1405
1	Nov 10	10 03	Ch'i-ying to Davis. Is pleased that $900 has been paid to owner of salt junk sunk by steamer during collision. Has ordered Magistrate of Hsiang-shan to issue summons to Huang gentry who have so far refused to hand over three of their clansmen charged with burglary in Hong Kong.	9	1406
2	Nov 10	10 03	Ch'i-ying to Davis. Has ordered gentry and elders of Ch'a-t'ou village to hand over two villagers who stopped boat carrying Britons and threatened them with violence. Has also ordered investigation into allegation that on evening of 4 November crowd on land behaved threateningly towards Briton passing by in boat. Encl. Copy of his despatch of 5 Nov 1847. 2	8	1407
3	Dec 13	11 06	Ch'i-ying to Davis. Britons had shot dead one villager and fatally wounded another before they were overwhelmed and killed by crowd in Huang-chu-ch'i. Only gentry and elders of Huang-chu-ch'i are capable of finding out murderers and they have agreed to do so.	11	1408
4a	Dec 17	11 10	Ch'i-ying to Davis. Has meted out punishment to villagers of Huang-chu-ch'i many times more severe than warranted by their crimes, including summary execution of four ring-leaders: Britons who killed Chinese recently have not been executed. Denies that criminals waiting to be executed are not real ringleaders. Refuses to raze village to ground.	15	1409
4b	Dec 18	11 11	Cantonese gentry to Davis. Chinese authorities have punished villagers	14	1415B

F.O. 682/ 1980	Date 1847	 TK 27	Description	pp	Old Re F.O. 682/
			of Huang-chu-ch'i so severely that entire families have deserted their homes for fear of their lives. This is in stark contrast to the extraordinarily lenient treatment of Britons who had killed Chinese citizens before. If Davis continues to press for severe punishment of more villagers, Cantonese will be even more embittered and Britons may expect more difficult times ahead.		
/65	Dec 20	11 13	Ch'i-ying to Davis. Punishment of villagers is many times heavier than crimes warrant and it is therefore irrational to argue any further as to who started the fight. Four will be summarily executed next morning at scene of fighting, rest will be referred to Ministry of Justice for beheading, death by strangling or exile.	8	1410
/66	Dec 20	11 13	Ch'i-ying to Davis. Gives names of fifteen villagers who were involved in various degrees in Huang-chu-ch'i incident, and punishments meted out to them.	18	1411
/67	n.d.	n.d.	Return of local trade in Hong Kong for 1847 as reported monthly by K. Gutzlaff, Chinese Secretary [documents in English].	20	1412

. / ·1	Date 1848 TK 27	Description	pp	Old Ref. F.O. 682/

'E: *It appears that 1848 was the year when the Chinese Secretary began to*
     have the in-coming and out-going despatches copied into an entry-book,
     which is now preserved in the Public Record Office of London and
     classified as F.O. 677/26. By comparing the documents of 1848 with
     these entries, it seems that all those that were copied have survived.

1	Jan 3	11 [27]	Davis to Ch'i-ying. Is pleased that apart from punishing villagers of Huang-chu-ch'i, Ch'i-ying is also sending deputies to placate them, and that every effort will be made to protect foreigners.	16	1414
			Encl. Proclamation by Canton gentry exhorting populace to keep peace with foreigners. 18 Dec 1847.	14	1415B
2	Jan 3	11 27	Davis to Ch'i-ying. Governor-General of India has again urged that Chinese representative be sent to demarcate frontier.	5	1415A
3	Jan 6	12 01	Ch'i-ying to Davis. Will hear verdict by Ministry of Justice on Huang-chu-ch'i incident in a few months.	1	1468B
4	Jan 7	12 02	Davis to Ch'i-ying. Again urges compensation for Mr Wilson, whose Chinese servants stole valuables from his house in Hong Kong and ran away.	6	1416A
			Encl. 1. Petition for leniency by father of one of the thieves.	3	1416B
			Encl. 2. Statement of lost property, 8 Jan 1848 [*sic*].	6	1416C
5	Jan 7	12 02	Ch'i-ying to Davis. Chinese Commissioner in Tibet reported that he had not seen any British representative.	7	1869
6	Jan 7	12 02	Ch'i-ying to Davis. Has decided to impose customs duty of 5% *ad valorem* on imported timber.	8	1470
7	Jan 8	12 03	Ch'i-ying to Davis. Has instructed Magistrates of Nan-hai and P'an-yü each to provide ten police constables to accompany foreigners whenever they want to visit the countryside.	7	1471
8	Jan 10	12 05	Davis to Ch'i-ying. Appreciates gentry's efforts to restrain	10	1417

F.O. 682/ 1981	Date 1848	TK 27	Description	pp	Old R• F.O. 682/
			Cantonese but cannot accept their letter as he will deal only with Chinese authorities. Again urges speedy punishment of remaining eleven villagers of Huang-chu-ch'i.		
/9	Jan 10	12 05	Davis to Ch'i-ying. Requests that porcelain exports, like timber imports, be taxed at rate of 5% *ad valorem.*	5	1418
/10	Jan 12	12 07	Ch'i-ying to Davis. Has sent four Magistrates and Sub-Magistrates to tour villages in Canton Delta area; has ordered distribution of pamphlets exhorting peaceful co-existence with foreigners; and has ordered formation of special police unit of twenty to accompany foreigners when visiting country-side - in short has done everything he can to protect foreigners.	12	1472
/11	Jan 12	12 07	Ch'i-ying to Davis. Has ordered clansmen of one of the thieves to compensate Mr Wilson within twenty days.	8	1473
/12	Jan 13	12 08	Davis to Ch'i-ying. Asks that names of the twenty police constables designated to escort foreigners be submitted to British Consul for safe-keeping. These constables must not have substitutes. Again urges speedy punishment of eleven villagers of Huang-chu-ch'i.	6	1419
/13	Jan 13	12 08	Ch'i-ying to Davis. Endorses a suggestion that Chinese and foreign merchants should jointly devise measures to protect foreigners. Has not yet heard verdict by Ministry of Justice on eleven villagers of Huang-chu-ch'i.	10	1474
/14	Jan 14	12 09	Davis to Ch'i-ying. Has no objection to Chinese and British merchants working together to devise measures to protect foreigners as long as such measures do not contradict treaty.	5	1420
/15	Jan 15	12 10	Davis to Ch'i-ying. British merchants who left Canton because	9	1421

. :/ :1	Date 1848	TK 27	Description	pp	Old Ref. F.O. 682/
			of Huang-chu-ch'i incident will not return unless their houses and goods are protected. If Ch'i-ying does not enforce Art. 1 of Treaty of Nanking, which provides for protection of British subjects, Davis himself will instruct Consul F.C. Macgregor to stop payment of customs duties. Again urges speedy punishment of eleven villagers of Huang-chu-ch'i.		
6	Jan 16	12 11	Ch'i-ying to Davis. Rates of customs duties must not be changed too often. Maintains that porcelain should be taxed according to its weight as before.	9	1475
7	Jan 16	12 11	Ch'i-ying to Davis. Special police unit to escort foreigners has been formed, incorporating all of Davis' suggestions. Agrees that measures worked out jointly by Chinese and British merchants should not contradict treaty. Is still waiting for verdict by Ministry of Justice on eleven villagers of Huang-chu-ch'i.	8	1476
8	Jan 18	12 13	Davis to Ch'i-ying. Deadline of twenty days to compensate Mr Wilson is about to expire. Wonders if compensation is going to be paid to Consul at Canton or taken to Hong Kong.	5	1477
9	Jan 18	12 13	Ch'i-ying to Davis. Agrees with Davis' views on special police unit to escort foreigners and has in fact translated them into action.	6	1478
0	Jan 20	12 15	Ch'i-ying to Davis. Has done all he can to protect Britons in Canton. Rejects idea that British Consul should be instructed to stop payment of customs duties. Has written to urge Ministry of Justice to arrive at a verdict speedily on eleven Huang-chu-ch'i villagers. Encl. Measures to protect Britons, n.d.	10 2	1479
1	Jan 22	12 17	Davis to Ch'i-ying. Hong Kong resident T'an Ts'ai has complained that his vessel and crew have been detained by Magistrate of Ho-p'u.	4	1422

F.O. 682/ 1981	Date 1848	TK 27	Description	pp	Old R F.O. 682/
			Requests their release. Encl. T'an Ts'ai's petition and list of names of sailors detained, -Dec 1947	3	
/22	Jan 24	12 19	Davis to Ch'i-ying. Again urges speedy punishment of eleven Huang-chu-ch'i villagers.	7	1423
/23	Jan 25	12 20	Ch'i-ying to Davis. Has remitted to British Consul $1,630 as compensation for Mr Wilson.	6	1480
/24	Jan 28	12 23	Davis to Ch'i-ying. Hong Kong resident Lo A-chin has petitioned for release of his son who had been kidnapped by pirates and was subsequently taken prisoner together with pirates by Chinese authorities. Encl. Lo A-chin's petition to Davis.	4 3	1424
/25	Jan 28	12 23	Ch'i-ying to Davis. Has ordered Magistrate of Ho-p'u to release T'an Ts'ai's boat and crew.	6	1481
/26	Jan 31	12 26	Ch'i-ying to Davis. Lo A-chin's son is hereby released after establishing his innocence.	6	1482
/27	Feb 1	12 27	Davis to Ch'i-ying. Is pleased that compensation for Mr Wilson has been paid. Forty days have lapsed and Chinese Ministry of Justice has still not arrived at verdict on eleven Huang-chu-ch'i villagers.	6	1425
		TK 28			
/28	Feb 8	01 04	Davis to Ch'i-ying. Urges speedy settlement of debt owed to Mr Turner by Chinese firm Pao-ch'ang. Encl. 1. Magistrate of Nan-hai to Consul F.C. Macgregor, 30 Jan 1848. Encl. 2. Magistrate of Nan-hai to Consul F.C. Macgregor, 1 Feb 1848.	5 5 5	1426
/29	Feb 8	01 04	Davis to Ch'i-ying. As Ch'i-ying has suggested that transit dues at Pei-hsin-kuan follow those of Hu-shu-kuan, he must give details of transit dues levied at Hu-shu-kuan.	5	1427
/30	Feb 17	01 13	Ch'i-ying to Davis. Chinese firm Pao-ch'ang has submitted 3,000 taels as partial payment of debt to	5	1483

. ./ 1	Date		Description	pp	Old Ref. F.O.
	1848	TK 27			682/

			Mr Turner, insisting that final settlement of dispute has to await Mr McQueen's return to Canton.		
1	Feb 17	01 13	Ch'i-ying to Davis. Has asked Emperor to order authorities at Pei-hsin-kuan to reply promptly.	8	1484
2	Feb 26	01 22	Davis to Ch'i-ying. Consul F.C. Macgregor has reported that Ch'i-ying is about to leave for Peking. Again urges speedy punishment of eleven Huang-chu-ch'i villagers.	5	1428
3a	Feb 28	01 24	Ch'i-ying to Davis. Intendant [Hsien-ling] of Shanghai has reported that Consul R. Alcock has refused to obey Chinese law prohibiting export of Chinese copper cash on the ground that he has received no instruct-ions from Davis to that effect.	10	1485
3b	Feb 28	01 24	Ch'i-ying to British, French and U.S. Plenipotentiaries, and British, U.S. and Dutch Consuls at Canton. Has been summoned to Peking. Governor Hsü Kuang-chin will be Acting Imperial Commissioner.	6	327/5/57
3c	Feb 28	01 24	Ch'i-ying to Davis. Praises Consul R.B. Jackson for success in restrain-ing Britons from venturing outside permitted areas.	4	327/5/55
4	Feb 28	01 24	Ch'i-ying to Davis. Has been summon-ed to Peking for audience with Emperor. Hsü Kuang-chin will be Acting Imperial Commissioner as from 1 Mar 1848.	6	1486
5	Feb 28	01 24	Ch'i-ying to Davis. Viceroy of Min-Che has written to praise British Consul at Foochow for having successfully restrained Britons from wandering into the countryside.	5	1487
6	Feb 29	01 25	Ch'i-ying to Davis. Remaining eleven villagers of Huang-chu-ch'i still under detention will be dealt with as soon as reply from Ministry of Justice is received.	9	1488
7	Feb 29	01 25	Ch'i-ying to Davis. Viceroy of Liang-Chiang has transmitted report from	8	1489

F.O. 682/ 1981	Date 1848		Description	pp	Old Re F.O. 682/
		TK 28			
			Intendant at Shanghai. A Chinese, Hsü Chang-pao, was stabbed to death by a drunken sailor. British Vice-Consul investigated one ship and claimed he could not find the murderer. Requests that other ships in Shanghai harbour be investigated as well.		
/38	Feb 29	01 25	Ch'i-ying to Davis. After Shanghai, British merchants have tried to sell salt at Ningpo. This contravenes treaty.	6	1490
/39	Mar 3	01 28	Davis to Ch'i-ying. Hsü Chang-pao was murdered at Wu-sung which is outside jurisdiction of British Consul at Shanghai.	7	1429
/40	Mar 3	01 28	Davis to Ch'i-ying. Will instruct Consul R. Alcock at Shanghai to publicise Chinese prohibition on export of copper cash.	4	1430
/41	Mar 3	01 28	Davis to Ch'i-ying. Will instruct Consul R. Alcock to respect salt monopoly of Chinese government.	5	1431
/42	Mar 8	02 04	Davis to Acting Imperial Commissioner Hsü Kuang-chin. Is leaving for England at end of month. Hopes fate of eleven Huang-chu-ch'i villagers will be decided before he leaves.	5	1432
/43	Mar 10	02 06	Davis to Hsü Kuang-chin. Hong Kong resident Liu Ssu has had his boat detained by Chinese marines and its cargo of stones thrown overboard. Boat was then used by the marines to carry timber to Ta-p'eng. Requests compensation.	7	1433
/44	Mar 13	02 09	Hsü Kuang-chin to Davis. Ministry of Justice has instructed that of the eleven villagers of Huang-chu-ch'i under detention, four should be executed and the rest exiled.	16	1491
/45	Mar 16	02 12	Hsü Kuang-chin to Davis. Has ordered investigation into allegation by Liu Ssu that Chinese marines detained junk from Hong Kong, emptied its cargo of 173 pieces of stone into river, and used it to carry timber	9	1492

. :/ 31	Date 1848	TK 28	Description	pp	Old Ref. F.O. 682/
			to Ta-p'eng.		
46	Mar 18	02 14	Davis to Hsü Kuang-chin. Report from British Consul at Canton confirms Liu Ssu's allegations.	6	1434
47	Mar 20	02 16	Davis to Hsü Kuang-chin. Is succeeded today by Sir George Bonham as H.M. Plenipotentiary and has handed to him Hsü's despatch about punishment of eleven Huang-chu-ch'i villagers.	6	1435
48	Mar 21	02 17	Sir George Bonham to Hsü Kuang-chin. Has succeeded Davis as H.M. Plenipotentiary. Requests interview.	6	1436
49	Mar 23	02 19	Hsü Kuang-chin to Davis. Is still waiting for results of investigation into seizure of junk carrying stones from Hong Kong.	7	1494
50	Mar 23	02 19	Hsü Kuang-chin to Davis. Viceroy of Min-Che has replied. Li Shun-fa, Chinese born in Penang, has not been robbed in local feud. If Li is British, he should not have been living outside treaty ports. If he is Chinese, British Consul should not have interfered in local feuds.	25	1495
51	Mar 24	02 20	Hsü Kuang-chin to Davis. Is pleased that Davis' successor Sir George Bonham has arrived and wishes Davis a happy journey home.	6	1493
52	Mar 28	02 24	Hsü Kuang-chin to Bonham. Agrees to meet Davis and proposes to receive him at Hu-men on 29 Apr 1848.	6	1496
53	Apr 5	03 02	Bonham to Hsü Kuang-chin. Protests about stoning of two Britons in Ho-nan.	10	1439
54	Apr 6	03 03	Bonham to Hsü Kuang-chin. Agrees to meet at Hu-men on 29 Apr 1848.	5	1440
55	Apr 8	03 05	Hsü Kuang-chin to Bonham. Has punished Chinese who accidentally injured Britons in a stone-throwing brawl. Britons going on excursions outside Canton will be accompanied by Chinese police constables, but not when they go about their daily business in the streets.	8	1497

F.O. 682/ 1981	Date 1848	TK 28	Description	pp	Old Re F.O. 682/
/56	Apr 19	03 16	Bonham to Hsü Kuang-chin. Mr McQueen has returned to Canton but Pao-ch'ang has still not paid debt to Mr Turner.	8	1441
/57	Apr 22	03 19	Bonham to Hsü Kuang-chin. Lists other cases of debt owed by Chinese to British firms.	10	1442
/58	Apr 24	03 21	Hsü Kuang-chin to Bonham. Wonders if 4,150 taels of silver recovered from Chinese debtor should be delivered to British Consul for Mr Turner. Will endeavour to secure payment of rest of debt.	6	1498
/59	Apr 26	03 23	Hsü Kuang-chin to Bonham. Will instruct local officials to facilitate settlement of debts.	8	1499
/60	Apr 27	03 24	Bonham to Hsü Kuang-chin. Pao-ch'ang must pay debt to Mr Turner in full.	8	1443
/61	Apr 29	03 26	Hsü Kuang-chin to Bonham. Has permission from Emperor to instruct Pei-hsin-kuan to levy transit dues on foreign cloth at same rate as Hu-shu-kuan, namely 0.22 tael per 100 catties.	7	1523
/62	May 4	04 02	Hsü Kuang-chin to Bonham. Viceroy of Liang-Chiang has written: Junior Assistant Robertson of Shanghai has travelled inland to provincial seat to lodge complaint about Britons having been hurt in brawl in the interior of China. Both Robertson and Britons have breached treaty by going to places beyond a day's return journey from a treaty port.	9	1500
/63	May 11	04 09	Bonham to Hsü Kuang-chin. Denies that there had been a brawl in the hinterland of Shanghai; Britons were attacked and robbed.	18	1444
/64	May 13	04 11	Hsü Kuang-chin to Bonham. The trade in cassia bark, like salt and iron, are domestic matters of China with which foreigners have no right to interfere.	13	1501
			Encl. Correspondence between Hsü Kuang-chin and Consul A.W. Elmslie. n.d.	11	

No. 2/81	Date 1848	TK 28	Description	pp	Old Ref. F.O. 682/
65	May 17	04 15	Bonham to Hsü Kuang-chin. Accepts new rate of transit dues at Pei-hsin-kuan.	5	1445
66	May 17	04 15	Bonham to Hsü Kuang-chin. Again urges speedy settlement of debt owed by Pao-ch'ang to Mr Turner.	6	1446
67	May 19	04 17	Bonham to Hsü Kuang-chin. Urges abolition of cassia bark monopoly. From 1844 to 1847 there has been drop in trade of cassia bark because of excessive taxes.	18	1447
68	May 21	04 19	Hsü Kuang-chin to Bonham. Capital of 8,066.47944 taels is now paid by firm of Pao-ch'ang to Mr Turner, but not the interest.	7	1502
69	May 24	04 22	Bonham to Hsü Kuang-chin. Urges prompt payment of interest on debt owed by Pao-ch'ang to Mr Turner.	6	1448
70	May 30	04 28	Hsü Kuang-chin to Bonham. Has instructed Magistrate of Nan-hai to make sure that Chinese merchants pay all their debts to British merchants, including interest.	5	1503
71	May 30	04 28	Hsü Kuang-chin to Bonham. Has checked trade agreement signed on 6 Mar 1845. Chinese merchants wishing to deal in cassia bark have to have fellow merchants as guarantors and to state amount of cassia bark they wish to deal in before licences may be issued. These measures are designed to prevent unscrupulous persons from hoarding cassia bark and thus forcing up its export price, and from cheating foreign merchants by giving false names and addresses.	13	1504
2	Jun 7	05 07	Bonham to Hsü Kuang-chin. Lists subjects for discussion in future meetings: entry into city of Canton, restrictions on movements of foreigners, leasing of land, suppression of pirates, customs duties, legalisation of opium.	22	1449
3	Jun 10	05 10	Bonham to Hsü Kuang-chin. Requests further details on trade in cassia bark. Again urges abolition of	8	1450

F.O. 682/ 1981	Date 1848	TK 28	Description	pp	Old Re F.O. 682/
			cassia bark monopoly.		
/74	Jun 17	05 17	Bonham to Hsü Kuang-chin. Pei-hsin-kuan does not seem to know new rate of transit dues.	7	1451
/75	Jun 17	05 17	Hsü Kuang-chin to Bonham. Recent events have proved that demand to enter Canton city has greatly jeopardised trade. All possible measures have been taken for protection of foreigners going on excursions outside Canton. Britons cannot force Cantonese to lease out houses or land to them. Has sent marines against pirates. Will investigate any allegation of corruption by customs officials. Chinese hiring British vessels to carry cargo are required to pay rates according to Chinese law. Will write again when he has news of outcome of Ch'i-ying's discussion with Emperor concerning legalisation of opium.	20	1505
/76	Jun 21	05 21	Bonham to Hsü Kuang-chin. Regards Hsü's answers [as contained in previous entry] as unsatisfactory.	14	1452
/77	Jun 21	05 21	Hsü Kuang-chin to Bonham. Pei-hsin-kuan has not yet taxed imported cloth according to rate levied at Hu-shu-kuan obviously because it has not received instructions owing to postal delay.	6	1506
/78	Jun 21	05 21	Hsü Kuang-chin to Bonham. Cassia bark goes through three inland customs offices before reaching Hoppo: Wu-chou in Kwangsi, Chao-ch'ing and Fo-shan in Kwangtung. Transit dues vary from place to place. Will investigate any allegation of extortion. New firms are allowed to join the thirty already engaged in trade provided they can find guarantors among the thirty.	10	1507
/79	Jun 23	05 23	Bonham to Hsü Kuang-chin. Is going to inspect other four treaty ports. Will return in about twenty days.	4	1453
/80	Jun 27	05 27	Hsü Kuang-chin to Bonham. Forced	13	1508

). 2/ 31	Date 1848	TK 28	Description	pp	Old Ref. F.O. 682/
			entry into city of Canton can only harm trade. Cannot order Cantonese of Ch'ang-chou to lease out houses and land to Britons. Supplementary Treaty specifies that Chinese merchants trading with Hong Kong must do so in Chinese vessels. Transit dues vary from place to place: it is not possible to know them all or make them uniform.		
31	Jun 27	05 27	Hsü Kuang-chin to Bonham. Wishes Bonham *bon voyage* during visit to other four treaty ports.	5	1509
32	Jul 15	06 15	Bonham to Hsü Kuang-chin. Has returned from trip to inspect other four treaty ports.	4	1454
33	Aug 2	07 04	Hsü Kuang-chin to Bonham. Consul R. Alcock has breached treaty by keeping 2,082.15 taels of tonnage dues in retaliation for failure of deceased Shanghai merchant to settle accounts with British firm.	9	1510
34	Aug 5	07 07	Bonham to Hsü Kuang-chin. 2,082.15 taels of tonnage dues is value of cloth Consul R. Alcock has given former Intendant [Hsien-ling] as security. [Hsien-ling] has since left Shanghai without returning cloth. Encl. Alcock's statement, n.d.	9 4	1455
35	Aug 19	07 21	Hsü Kuang-chin to Bonham. Is shocked to learn that British Consul at Amoy has demanded refund of import duties paid for goods unsold.	10	1511
36	Sep 2	08 05	Bonham to Hsü Kuang-chin. At price of several wounded and one dead, Royal Navy captured sixty-two pirates and handed them over, together with their boats, to Chinese authorities at Amoy.	6	1456
37	Sep 8	08 11	Bonham to Hsü Kuang-chin. Villagers who plundered British lorchas which ran aground near Hu-men should be made to pay full compensation.	9	1457
38	Sep 8	08 11	Bonham to Hsü Kuang-chin. British Consul at Amoy has acted against	8	1458

F.O. 682/ 1981	Date		Description	pp	Old Re F.O. 682/
	1848	TK 28			
			treaty and has been instructed to withdraw demand for refund. Protests about wrong format of Hsü's last despatch.		
/89	Sep 10	08 13	Hsü Kuang-chin to Bonham. Is pleased that Royal Navy has captured sixty-two pirates along coast of Fukien and handed them over to local authorities. Will notify Viceroy of Min-Che of this.	6	1512
/90	Sep 14	08 17	Hsü Kuang-chin to Bonham. Is pleased that British Consul at Amoy will be instructed to abide by treaty provisions [with reference to demand for refund of import duties for goods unsold].	6	1524
/91	Sep 14	08 17	Hsü Kuang-chin to Bonham. Refuses to make whole village liable just because some of its villagers have plundered British lorcha.	8	1513
/92	Sep 26	08 29	Bonham to Hsü Kuang-chin. Protests about expulsion of British merchant Mr Cleland from his rented house and about a Chinese officer beating up the son, Teng Chih-p'ing, of Chinese landlord who let his house to another Briton.	7	1459
/93	Sep 29	09 03	Hsü Kuang-chin to Bonham. As regards dispute over renting of house in Canton, encloses copies of letters to British Consul. Encl. 1. Hsü to Consul A.W. Emslie, 25 Sep 1848. Encl. 2. Hsü to Consul A.W. Emslie, 29 Sep 1848.	6 2 2	1514
/94	Nov 4	10 09	Bonham to Hsü Kuang-chin. Has received order from Lord Palmerston to urge abolition of cassia bark monopoly.	16	1460
/95	Nov 10	10 15	Hsü Kuang-chin to Bonham. Number of firms licensed to deal in cassia bark may be increased from thirty to forty or more but system of licensing and guarantors cannot be abolished because it forestalls hoarding of goods and cheating of foreign merchants.	8	1515

0. 32/ 981	Date 1848	TK 28	Description	pp	Old Ref. F.O. 682/
'96	Nov [18]	10 23	Hsü Kuang-chin to Bonham. Requests action against Britons Hassain and partner [Abdullah] who absconded with over 54,000 silver dollars' worth of Chinese goods.	9	1516
			Encl. List of fifty-one firms with claims against Hassain and partner, n.d.	5	
'97	Nov 23	10 28	Bonham to Hsü Kuang-chin. Hassain is not British but Indian national and probably has fled back to India. Abdullah will be held responsible if he has been his partner, but not if he has been employee only. Protests against inappropriate language used in enclosure of Hsü's previous despatch.	10	1461
'98	Dec 1	11 06	Bonham to Hsü Kuang-chin. Interpreter T.T. Meadows has been robbed by pirates near Whampoa.	8	1462
99	Dec 1	11 06	Hsü Kuang-chin to Bonham. Three more firms have lodged claims of over $3,400 against Hassain and partner [Abdullah].	6	1517
			Encl. List of three firms with claims, n.d.	1	
00	Dec 2	11 07	Bonham to Hsü Kuang-chin. Again urges abolition of cassia bark monopoly in accordance with spirit of treaty; increasing number of firms dealing in cassia bark is irrelevant.	14	1463
01	Dec 4	11 09	Bonham to Hsü Kuang-chin. China must fulfil all treaty obligations.	10	1464
02	Dec 6	11 11	Hsü Kuang-chin to Bonham. Neither treaty nor Chinese law supports claim that local authorities compensate Interpreter T.T. Meadows for losses suffered during robbery near Whampoa. Has again instructed Magistrate of Nan-hai to intensify hunt for robbers.	6	1518
03	Dec 10	11 15	Hsü Kuang-chin to Bonham. Art. 5 of Treaty of Nanking specifies that British merchants may trade with whichever Chinese merchant (shang) they choose. By definition a	12	1519

F.O. 682/ 1981	Date 1848	TK 28	Description	pp	Old Re F.O. 682/
			Chinese *shang* is a rich person with plenty of property and government licence to trade, such as pawnshop merchant, salt merchant or iron merchant. If Britons are not happy with thirty firms already dealing in cassia bark, other firms may be allowed to engage in trade provided they obtain licences from government to do so.		
/104	Dec 12	11 17	Bonham to Hsü Kuang-chin. Rejects Hsü's argument that neither treaty nor Chinese law provides for compensation for T.T. Meadows:- according to British law Meadows must be compensated because he was robbed while on official business.	8	1465
/105	Dec 14	11 19	Bonham to Hsü Kuang-chin. Will appeal to Peking if cassia bark monopoly is not abolished.	12	1466
/106	Dec 20	11 25	Hsü Kuang-chin to Bonham. As regards T.T. Meadows' case, reiterates that it has never been the law in China to make local officials compensate victims of robberies.	8	1520
/107	Dec 20	11 25	Hsü Kuang-chin to Bonham. Has received reports from hinterland that thirty firms dealing in cassia bark have abused their privilege. Will investigate; and if confirmed, whole system will be abolished.	6	1521
/108	Dec 22	11 27	Bonham to Hsü Kuang-chin. Expects cassia bark monopoly to be abolished soon. T.T. Meadows must be compensated, otherwise he will not be able to do his duty efficiently. Expects Hsü to honour Ch'i-ying's promise of 1847 to open gates of Canton in 1849.	8	1467
/109	Dec 29	12 04	Hsü Kuang-chin to Bonham. Cantonese are unanimous in opposition to foreigners entering their city and it is not worth forcing issue at risk of disrupting trade. There is sufficient protection for foreigners; civilians can let and rent land as they please; piracy will be suppressed; customs duties	15	1595A

). 2/	Date		Description	pp	Old Ref. F.O.
31	1848	TK 28			682/

are officially fixed but transit
dues are beyond his control; it
contravenes treaty to let Chinese
employ British boats to trade with
Hong Kong; has not heard from Ch'i-
ying about legalisation of opium;
in addition to original four, one
more person has now been detained
in connection with case in which
T.T. Meadows was robbed;
commissioner investigating cassia
bark monopoly has reported that
inhabitants of P'ing-nan [Kwangsi]
also complain about monopoly, which
is herewith abolished.

| 0 | Dec 29 | 12 04 | Hsü Kuang-chin to Bonham. Requests co-operation in securing payment of moneys owed by British and Indian merchants to Chinese merchants. | 10 | 1596 |

F.O. 682/ 1982	Date 1849 TK 28	Description	pp	Old R• F.O. 682/

NOTE: *All the out-going despatches and three in-coming despatches of 1849 ap*
to be missing. Fortunately, their contents were copied at the time in
an entry-book now classified as F.O. 677/26. They are summarised here
with the existing documents in order to present a balanced picture.
Naturally, they are not given a new reference number in the first colu
which is left blank. The reference number F.O. 677/26, as provided in
the last column in square brackets, is still valid.

| /1 | Jan 1 | 12 07 | Acting Imperial Commissióner Hsü Kuang-chin to Bonham. One more firm has reported having been cheated of tea worth $1,225 by Hassain and partner [Abdullah]. Encl. Details of fraud, n.d. | 8

1 | 1525 |
	Jan 3	12 09	Bonham to Hsü Kuang-chin. Four who robbed T.T. Meadows are pirates and therefore must be executed.	2	[F.O. 677/2
	Jan 5	12 11	Bonham to Hsü Kuang-chin. Agrees that negotiation through correspondence is unsatisfactory and that deputies should be appointed to settle all matters except Canton city question which must be decided by Hsü and Bonham himself. Looks forward to being received by Hsü in his *yamen* within the city.	2	[F.O. 677/
	Jan 8	12 14	Bonham to Hsü Kuang-chin. Expects Hsü has publicised decision to abolish cassia bark monopoly. Requests copy of such public notice.	1	[F.O. 677/
	Jan 8	12 14	Bonham to Hsü Kuang-chin. New British Admiral [Rear-Admiral Sir Francis Collier] has arrived. Looks forward to pleasure of introducing him personally to Hsü when they meet in Canton.	2	[F.O. 677/
	Jan 8	12 14	Bonham to Hsü Kuang-chin. Hassain has fled to India which is beyond his jurisdiction. Abdullah is in prison in Hong Kong for other offences but will be made to pay debt only if he is proved to have been Hassain's partner. Other debtors to Chinese merchants have either disappeared without trace or fled to places where again nothing can be done.	1	[F.O. 677/

). 2/ 32	Date 1849	TK 28	Description	pp	Old Ref. F.O. 682/
'2	Jan 10	12 16	Hsü Kuang-chin to Bonham. Proposes to meet Bonham at Hu-men on 17 Feb 1849.	5	1526
'3	Jan 11	12 17	Hsü Kuang-chin to Bonham. Conveys request by debtors that Hassain's goods consigned to two Parsees at Canton be seized to repay part of debts.	8	1527
'4	Jan 15	12 21	Hsü Kuang-chin to Bonham. As regards case of attack on T.T. Meadows, eight who have committed piracy previously will be executed, others who are accomplices and who have committed offence for first time will be exiled.	8	1528
'5	Jan 15	12 21	Hsü Kuang-chin to Bonham. Has abolished system in which thirty firms were licenced to deal in cassia bark. Henceforth any firm may deal in it. Has instructed Hoppo to proclaim this. Encloses copy of Hoppo's proclamation [missing]. Will be pleased to see British Admiral during proposed meeting with Bonham on 17 Feb 1849.	6	1529
	Jan 19	12 15	Bonham to Hsü Kuang-chin. Is pleased that cassia bark monopoly is abolished; acknowledges copy of proclamation to this effect but protests about absence of prefix *Ch'in-ch'ai* to his title when referred to in proclamation.	1	[F.O. 677/26]
	Jan 20	12 26	Bonham to Hsü Kuang-chin. Insists that all those who robbed T.T. Meadows be executed. Requests that British officer be allowed to witness executions in an official capacity.	1	[F.O. 677/26]
	Jan 20	12 26	Bonham to Hsü Kuang-chin. It will take days of preparation for meeting at Hu-men, all of which will be unnecessary if they meet at Hsü's *yamen* at Canton. Proposes to send steamer to Canton to fetch Hsü to a meeting on board British Admiral's flag ship near Hu-men.	1	[F.O. 677/26]
	Jan 23	12 29	Bonham to Hsü Kuang-chin. British sailors shipwrecked in East	2	[F.O. 677/26]

F.O. 682/ 1982	Date 1849	TK 29	Description	pp	Old Re F.O. 682/
			Kwangtung were robbed by local people on 5 Jan 1849.		
	Jan 24	01 01	Bonham to Hsü Kuang-chin. [The *Kelpie*] has disappeared in South China Sea. Requests assistance.	2	[F.O. 677/2
	Jan 24	01 01	Bonham to Commander of Chinese forces at Lei-chou and Ch'iung-chou. The *Kelpie* has disappeared in South China Sea. Royal Navy has searched for it in vain. Will be grateful for assistance.	2	[F.O. 677/2
/6	Jan 27	01 04	Hsü Kuang-chin to Bonham. Has suggested meeting at Hu-men because residence of Commander-in-Chief of Kwangtung marines there is spacious and majestic. Has no objection to meeting on board naval ship if Bonham, the guest, so desires. Prefers to see to all matters personally, and deputies are therefore unnecessary; nonetheless will bring some assistants to the meeting.	7	1563A
/7	Jan 27	01 04	Hsü Kuang-chin to Bonham. Transit dues vary from one customs office to another and also from province to province; it is impossible to find out all about them. But as Hoppo is stationed in the same city as Hsü himself, it is easy enough to find out the rate he charges. A customs office taxes all goods passing through it; no such thing as a special customs office for cassia bark alone. No fixed routes for transportation of cassia bark, hence no way of knowing what customs offices a certain consignment has gone through. As regards T.T. Meadows' case, ringleader was shot and drowned on spot. Accomplices were exiled.	8	1530
/8	Feb 2	[01 10]	Hsü Kuang-chin to Bonham. Consul A.W. Elmslie has expressed appreciation that sailors shipwrecked off coast of East Kwangtung had been well-treated by local authorities. Among sailors, three Chinese have testified that all goods were lost in storm. Cannot understand why	9	1531

O. 2/ 82	Date 1849	TK 29	Description	pp	Old Ref. F.O. 682/
			Bonham should suddenly accuse local inhabitants of having plundered goods. Encl. Testimonies of three Chinese sailors, n.d.	3	
	Feb 7	01 15	Bonham to Hsü Kuang-chin. True, sailors shipwrecked in East Kwangtung were well-treated by Chinese local authorities, but they had been robbed by local inhabitants before authorities arrived.	1	[F.O. 677/26]
	Feb 8	01 16	Bonham to Hsü Kuang-chin. Steamer will take Hsü from Whampoa to Hu-men, whence he will be fetched by small steamer for meeting on board Admiral's flag ship.	1	[F.O. 677/26]
'9	Feb 9	01 17	Bonham to Hsü Kuang-chin. Encloses agenda for meeting. Encl. Agenda *op. cit.*, n.d.	6 36	1597
0	Feb 11	01 19	Hsü Kuang-chin to Bonham. Thanks for sending steamer to meet him at Whampoa. As host, he is having banquet prepared, ready for Bonham at 10 am on 17 February at Hu-men. Will return visit next day to Bonham's steamer.	7	1532
	Feb 14	01 22	Bonham to Hsü Kuang-chin. Suggests that original appointment on board Admiral's flag ship on 17 February be kept and then he and Admiral can visit Hsü at Hu-men the following day.	1	[F.O. 677/26]
	Feb 21	01 29	Bonham to Hsü Kuang-chin. The most important topic that emerged during discussions on 17 February was Canton city question, which Hsü proposed to refer to Emperor. Expects Hsü to reply by 1 April.	1	[F.O. 677/26]
	Feb 23	02 01	Bonham to Hsü Kuang-chin. Chinese servant Hsü A-chin who stole valuables from house of British employer [Robinson] and then set fire to it must be promptly punished.	1	[F.O. 677/26]
1	Feb 25	02 03	Hsü Kuang-chin to Bonham. During their meeting on 17 February, [Dr Bettelheim's] vessel anchored at	5	1533

F.O. 682/ 1982	Date 1849	TK 29	Description	pp	Old Re† F.O. 682/
			Liu-ch'iu was mentioned. Has now received request from Liu-ch'iu to effect departure of vessel.		
/12	Feb 27	02 05	Hsü Kuang-chin to Bonham. Personally, has no objections to British entry into city but Cantonese are united in opposition because ill-feeling engendered by San-yüan-li incident of 1841 is still raging. Has written to Emperor for advice. Expects reply by 2 April.	8	1534
/13	Feb 27	02 05	Hsü Kuang-chin to Bonham. Hsü A-chin has not yet received final punishment because he is only an accomplice. When ringleader is captured, final punishment will be meted out.	7	1535
	Feb 28	02 06	Bonham to Hsü Kuang-chin. Whalers go to Liu-ch'iu only for provisions. Is certain that [Dr Bettelheim's] boat has left.	1	[F.O. 677/2
	Mar 7	02 13	Bonham to Hsü Kuang-chin. Requests extradition of Hsü A-pao *et al.* who murdered two British officers in Hong Kong.	1	[F.O. 677/2
/14	Mar 11	02 17	Hsü Kuang-chin to Bonham. Has instructed local officials to hunt down Hsü A-pao *et al.*	5	1536
	Mar 12	02 18	Bonham to Hsü Kuang-chin. The [*Elizabeth*] and [*Thency*] have run aground at Liu-ch'iu and Royal Navy has gone to help.	2	[F.O. 677/
/15	Mar 13	02 19	Bonham to Hsü Kuang-chin. Protests against Chinese merchants' stopping cotton trade with British merchants as means of foiling British attempt to enter city.	18	1598
	Mar 18	02 24	Bonham to Hsü Kuang-chin. Notice is hereby given that more troops will be sent to defend factory area in Canton.	2	[F.O. 677/
/16	Mar 18	02 24	Hsü Kuang-chin to Bonham. Declines to prohibit formation of militia units in Canton as they are designed to keep banditry in check and to preserve peaceful trade.	8	1564

O.	Date		Description	pp	Old Ref.
2/					F.O.
82	1849	TK 29			682/

			Encl. Hsü to British Consul to same effect, n.d.	1	
	Mar 20	02 26	Bonham to Hsü Kuang-chin. Dr John Bowring, new British Consul for Canton, has arrived at Hong Kong from England.	1	[F.O. 677/26]
	Mar 21	02 27	Hsü Kuang-chin to Bonham. Sending more troops to Canton will only unsettle Cantonese further.	2	[F.O. 677/26]
17	Apr 1	03 09	Hsü Kuang-chin to Bonham. Emperor has decided that since Cantonese are opposed to foreigners' entering their city, he cannot contradict their wishes; otherwise, disturbances will erupt, citizens will be injured and foreign trade disrupted.	8	1537
18	Apr 2	03 [10]	Bonham to Hsü Kuang-chin. Asks if Emperor's Edict means definite refusal to honour Ch'i-ying's promise to let Britons into city; if so, Great Britain could have disregarded treaty and kept Chusan. Is shocked that Hsü does not seem to have legal power over Cantonese. Proposes to introduce the new Consul for Canton, Dr Bowring, to Hsü at Hsü's *yamen*.	22	1540
19	Apr 6	03 14	Hsü Kuang-chin to Bonham. Law has no effect on Cantonese as far as British entry into city is concerned. British evacuation of Chusan was not in any way related to entry question. Is prepared to meet new Consul but not in his viceregal *yamen* which is inside walled city. Proposes Howqua's Jen-hsin-lou as meeting place.	9	1538
	Apr 9	03 17	Bonham to Hsü Kuang-chin. Protests about the arrest, without prior notice to British Consul, of two linguists employed by the British Consulate at Canton.	2	[F.O. 677/26]
20	Apr 9	03 17	Bonham to Hsü Kuang-chin. Regrets that he cannot hold further discussions with Hsü on city question. Expects Hsü does not wish to see	12	1539

F.O. 682/ 1982	Date 1849	TK 29	Description	pp	Old Re F.O. 682/
			him at the foreign factories and therefore proposes that Hsü sees new Consul, Dr J. Bowring, at Hsü's own convenience, at Howqua's Jen-hsin-lou.		
/21	Apr 14	03 22	Hsü Kuang-chin to Bonham. Will not see Consul J. Bowring alone if Bonham is not there to introduce him, but will despatch official of appropriate rank to receive him. Linguists were arrested without knowing that they were consular employees. Will notify Consul first if similar action against consular employees is to be taken in future.	7	1541
	Apr 20	03 28	Bonham to Hsü Kuang-chin. Consul J. Bowring takes the view that the deputy whom Hsü is going to despatch to the meeting must hold rank as high as Bowring's own. Suggests that Grain Intendant or Prefect in civil hierarchy, or Colonel in military hierarchy, be deputed.	2	[F.O. 677/2
	Apr 23	04 01	Bonham to Hsü Kuang-chin. Dr J. Bowring is different from all other Consuls because he has been appointed by Crown. When A.W. Elmslie was only Acting Consul, he was met by Provincial Treasurer. Therefore Dr Bowring must be met by even more senior official.	1	[F.O. 677/:
/22	Apr 30	04 08	Hsü Kuang-chin to Bonham. Provincial Treasurer Huang En-t'ung, who met Acting Consul A.W. Elmslie, held additional appointment to deal with foreign affairs. Present Provincial Treasurer does not hold this additional appointment. A Colonel does not hold second rank in Imperial hierarchy of nine. The fact that the two most senior Magistrates of Kwangtung have been deputed and feast prepared at Jen-hsin-lou to receive Bowring, indicates the importance which the Chinese government attaches to the occasion.	6	1542

). 2/ 32	Date 1849		Description	pp	Old Ref. F.O. 682/
		TK 29			

	May 2	04 [10]	Bonham to Hsü Kuang-chin. Tax scale at Shanghai is higher than that at Canton. Requests adjustment.	2	[F.O. 677/26]
23	May 10	04 18	Hsü Kuang-chin to Bonham. Will instruct Intendant at Shanghai to tax raw silk at 2.5 taels per 100 catties in accordance with trade agreement. Rejects Bonham's proposal to tax porcelain at 5% *ad valorem* on the ground that trade agreement specifies that porcelain should be taxed at 5 taels per 100 catties.	7	1543
	May 14	04 22	Bonham to Hsü Kuang-chin. Again asks that porcelain be taxed at 5% *ad valorem* like other goods.	1	[F.O. 677/26]
24	May 20	04 28	Hsü Kuang-chin to Bonham. Again rejects Bonham's proposal to tax porcelain at 5% *ad valorem* as this contravenes treaty agreement. Will instruct Intendant at Shanghai to same effect.	6	1544
25	May 27	i4 06	Hsü Kuang-chin to Bonham. Is shocked that British Consul at Canton has used proceeds from sale of Hassain's goods to pay creditors other than Chinese. Insists that Abdullah's property be sold to pay the countless Chinese artisan creditors.	8	1545
	Jun 6	i4 16	Bonham to Liu Yün-k'o. Has letter from Lord Palmerston thanking for the help Fukien authorities gave to steamer(s) that ran aground.	1	[F.O. 677/26]
	Jun 11	i4 21	Bonham to Hsü Kuang-chin. The few belongings Abdullah possesses have already been handed over to his creditors in Hong Kong. Protests that Hsü's despatch ended with impolite note.	2	[F.O. 677/27]
26	Jun 15	i4 25	Hsü Kuang-chin to Bonham. Is surprised at accusation that previous despatch ended with impolite note. Has checked original draft and cannot find anything wrong with it.	5	1546

F.O. 682/ 1982	Date 1849	TK 29	Description	pp	Old Re F.O. 682/
			Perhaps interpreter's knowledge of Chinese is too poor. Would appreciate it if an educated man were found to point out where the despatch was improper.		
	Jun 25	05 06	Bonham to Hsü Kuang-chin. "Do not again let delay" is impolite note in question.	1	[F.O. 677/2
/27	Jun 25	05 06	Liu Yün-k'o to Bonham. Appreciates Lord Palmerston's note of thanks to assistance given to Royal Navy ships which ran aground near Min River.	6	1547
/28	Jul 2	05 13	Hsü Kuang-chin to Bonham. The allegedly impolite note in previous despatch was preceded by his request for Bonham's co-operation in expediting payment of debts by Britons to Chinese merchants, and sentence "do not again let delay" means "do not let British merchants further delay payment of debts". This kind of sentence is well-known in China to be used to address equals and the complaint about it shows how ignorant interpreter is.	6	1563B
	Aug 1	06 13	Bonham to Hsü Kuang-chin. British merchants will not be able to buy Chinese porcelain unless it is taxed at 5% *ad valorem*.	1	[F.O. 677/2
	Aug 2	06 14	Bonham to Hsü Kuang-chin. Royal Navy has captured pirates and handed them over to Amoy authorities. Requests co-operation in suppressing piracy. Urges speedy apprehension of Hsü A-pao *et al*.	2	[F.O. 677/2
/29	Aug 4	06 16	Hsü Kuang-chin to Bonham. Porcelain must be taxed according to treaty agreement. Will write again after reply from Intendant at Shanghai is received.	6	1548
/30	Aug 9	06 21	Bonham to Hsü Kuang-chin. Rogues interrupted burial of Parsee at Ch'ang-chou demanding money, and had to be dispersed by Royal Navy.	8	1549
	Aug 11	06 23	Bonham to Hsü Kuang-chin. Parsee on his way to Whampoa has been detained	1	[F.O. 677/2

. ·/ ·2	Date		Description	pp	Old Ref. F.O.
	1849	TK 29			682/

by Chinese civilians.

Aug 11	06 23	Bonham to Hsü Kuang-chin. Complains about Hoppo who, without prior notice to British Consul, seized warehouse of British merchant on ground that it had sheltered consignments of smuggled goods.	1	[F.O. 677/2]
1	Aug 12	06 24	Hsü Kuang-chin to Bonham. Appreciates handing over of pirates captured by Royal Navy near Amoy. Has executed criminal involved in case of robbery in Macao on 19 Mar 1849. Has intensified search for Hsü A-chin *et al.* These murderers, when captured, ought to be tried by Chinese government, not British, because they are Chinese subjects and because they have been involved in other criminal cases inside China as well.	8	1551
2	Aug 13	06 25	Hsü Kuang-chin to Bonham. Poor villagers of Ch'ang-chou have a custom of demanding money from anybody who buries the dead there and their action during burial of said Parsee was not directed at foreigners in particular. A few police constables will be sufficient to disperse the crowd and there is no need to mobilise 1,200 bluejackets. Has instructed Magistrate of P'an-yü to prohibit future disruptions to burials in Ch'ang-chou. The threat to involve Royal Navy is unnecessary.	8	1550
3	Aug 16	06 28	Hsü Kuang-chin to Bonham. On hearing that Parsee was detained by Chinese creditors, immediately ordered that he be handed over to British Consul. No sooner had this order been issued than Parsee was rescued forcibly by compatriots. Chinese soldiers dispersed crowd and averted incident. Has instructed Chinese merchants to refer similar cases to British Consul in future.	7	1565
4	Aug 16	06 28	Hsü Kuang-chin to Bonham. As regards seizure of Briton's warehouse, has established that two Chinese compradors were guilty of smuggling.	7	1552

F.O. 682/ 1982	Date 1849	TK 29	Description	pp	Old R F.O. 682/
			As no foreigners were involved, case should be tried by Chinese authorities alone and not jointly with British. Has notified Vice-Consul A.W. Elmslie to same effect. Encl. Hsü to Elmslie, n.d.	1	
/35	Aug 21	07 04	Bonham to Hsü Kuang-chin. British government is greatly displeased to learn that Chinese have refused to let Britons enter city of Canton and regards this as breach of treaty for which China must bear full responsibility.	19	1553
	Aug 23	07 06	Bonham to Hsü Kuang-chin. Is shocked by murder of Governor [Amaral] of Macao. Has despatched Royal Navy to Macao to meet any emergency. Demands speedy apprehension of murderer(s).	2	[F.O. 677/
/36	Aug 27	07 10	Hsü Kuang-chin to Bonham. Is surprised that Bonham raises city question again after his statement of 9 Apr 1849 that the question could not be discussed any further.	8	1554
/37	Aug 27	07 10	Hsü Kuang-chin to Bonham. Is shocked to learn that [Amaral, Governor of Macao] has been assassinated. Has heard much about [Amaral's] quick temper and will not be surprised if assassin is fellow Portuguese. Still, will instruct officials and officers of Hsiang-shan to investigate.	9	1555
	Aug 30	07 13	Bonham to Hsü Kuang-chin. Has said in letter of 9 Apr 1849 that, *for time being*, question could not be discussed any further. It is breach of treaty to deny British entry into city of Canton.	1	[F.O 677.
/38	Aug 31	07 14	Hsü Kuang-chin to Bonham. Authorities of Fukien complain that British merchants trading at Amoy have used all sorts of extraordinary excuses to avoid paying import duties and British Consul appears to be acting in consort with them.	14	1556

Date			Description	pp	Old Ref. F.O. 682/
1849		TK 29			

Sep 3	07 17		Bonham to Hsü Kuang-chin. Has asked Consul at Amoy to report on allegations of tax evasion by British merchants there.	1	[F.O. 677/26]
Sep 4	07 18		Hsü Kuang-chin to Bonham. Intendant at Shanghai has replied. For a long time Shanghai exported only fine silk. Recently some British merchants have mixed coarse silk with fine silk claiming consignments to be entirely coarse silk, and consequently should be taxed as such. Will henceforth open all consignments for inspection and separate "chaff from grain" for tax purposes. As regards porcelain, it should be taxed according to treaty agreement.	9	1557
Sep 4	07 18		Hsü Kuang-chin to Bonham. Rejects Bonham's claim as contained in letter of 30 Aug 1849 that shelving city question is breach of treaty. Cannot trouble Emperor with another letter on same issue as Emperor has made his position very clear.	8	1558
Sep 10	07 24		Bonham to Hsü Kuang-chin. Hsü will be held responsible for all consequences if he does not transmit to Peking the remonstrance from London about Britons being denied entry into city of Canton.	1	[F.O. 677/26]
Sep 13	07 27		Hsü Kuang-chin to Bonham. Understands that Bonham cannot reply to London until British remonstrance is transmitted to Peking; will do so next month when it will be time to send in routine report.	5	1559
Sep 17	08 01		Bonham to Hsü Kuang-chin. Will appreciate prompt reply from Hsü as soon as he has heard from Peking about British government's remonstrance against denial of British entry into city of Canton.	1	[F.O. 677/26]
Sep 17	08 01		Hsü Kuang-chin to Bonham. Has arrested and executed murderer of Amaral and recovered Amaral's hand and head which have been delivered to Portuguese authorities in Macao.	6	1594

F.O. 682/ 1982	Date 1849	TK 29	Description	pp	Old R. F.O. 682/
			Encl. Deposition by Shen Chih-liang: he assassinated Amaral because Amaral had levelled six of his ancestral graves, n.d.	1	
	Sep 20	08 04	Bonham to Hsü Kuang-chin. Murderer of Amaral had six to seven accomplices who must all be arrested quickly.	1	[F.O. 677/
	Sep 20	08 04	Bonham to Hsü Kuang-chin. Royal Navy has dispersed another pirate fleet off Tien-pai. Complains that Hsü has not been energetic enough in suppressing piracy.	2	[F.O. 677/
	Sep 24	08 08	Hsü Kuang-chin to Bonham. Will spare no effort in hunting down others involved in murder of Amaral.	1	[F.O. 677/
	Sep 24	08 08	Hsü Kuang-chin to Bonham. Lists over twenty recent cases of successful action against pirates, of whom total of nine hundred and one have been captured.	2	[F.O. 677/
	Sep 27	08 11	Bonham to Hsü Kuang-chin. Some Chinese captured with pirates by Royal Navy off Tien-pai have claimed to be captives of pirates. They have been handed over to local Chinese authorities for clarification.	2	[F.O. 677/
	Oct 2	08 16	Bonham to Hsü Kuang-chin. Royal Navy has captured Chinese near Chin-hsing-men [at mouth of Pearl River] and has found them in possession of foreign cloth. There is not sufficient circumstantial evidence to convict them. Will hand them over to Hsü.	2	[F.O. 677/
	Oct 2	08 16	Bonham to Hsü Kuang-chin. Although nine hundred and one pirates have been captured by Chinese marines, piracy is still rampant. Again requests co-operation in pirate suppression. Hsü A-pao, if captured, must be extradited to Hong Kong as he has committed murder in the colony.	2	[F.O. 677.
/43	Oct 3	08 17	Hsü Kuang-chin to Bonham. Has despatched agent to Tien-pai to find out if Chinese handed over by	5	1566

	Date		Description	pp	Old Ref. F.O. 682/
/ 2	1849	TK 29			

Royal Navy are innocent.

4	Oct 5	08 19	Bonham to Hsü Kuang-chin. Has learnt with surprise from Macao that Hsü is keeping head and hand of Amaral until three Chinese detained by Portuguese authorities are extradited.	2	[F.O. 677/26]
4	Oct 6	08 20	Hsü Kuang-chin to Bonham. Rejects request that Hsü A-pao, if captured, be handed over to Hong Kong on ground that Hsü A-pao is Chinese and if inside China should, according to treaty, be tried by Chinese authorities.	8	1567
	Oct 8	08 22	Bonham to Hsü Kuang-chin. Royal Navy has dispersed Hsü A-pao's fleet of twenty-three vessels and 1,400 pirates, killing over four hundred. Hsü A-pao is reported to be wounded but managed to escape. Royal Navy suffered four dead and seven wounded.	2	[F.O. 677/26]
	Oct 9	08 23	Bonham to Hsü Kuang-chin. Crew of Hong Kong merchant ship heading for Shanghai has been detained by Chinese fishing junk and handed over to Chinese authorities. Requests its release.	2	[F.O. 677/26]
	Oct 11	08[25]	Bonham to Hsü Kuang-chin. Hsü A-pao, if captured in China, must be extradited to Hong Kong where he had committed murder, in accordance with treaty.	2	[F.O. 677/26]
5	Oct 11	08 25	Hsü Kuang-chin to Bonham. Expresses concern over Royal Navy personnel injured during encounter with pirates. Remnants of pirates who fled ashore have been arrested.	8	1569
6	Oct 11	08 25	Hsü Kuang-chin to Bonham. His deputy had instructions to deliver Amaral's remains and to receive three Chinese soldiers detained by Portuguese. The deputy could not deliver remains when Portuguese refused to release Chinese soldiers. Encl. 1. Hsü to Portuguese authorities in Macao, 30 Sep 1849.	8 1	1570

F.O. 682/ 1982	Date 1849	TK 29	Description	pp	Old R F.O. 682/
			Encl. 2. Hsü to U.S. Minister, 6 Oct 1849.	1	
			Encl. 3. Hsü to French Minister, 8 Oct 1849.	1	
	Oct 13	08 27	Bonham to Hsü Kuang-chin. Again urges speedy return of Amaral's remains. Has written voluntarily about Amaral and not as result of prompting from U.S. or French Ministers.	2	[F.O. 677/
	Oct 15	08 29	Bonham to Hsü Kuang-chin. British vessel has been plundered and set on fire in Canton River by what appeared to be Chinese patrol boat. Indications are that Chinese patrol boat has avenged refusal by British opium smuggler to pay bribes. Requests compensation.	3	[F.O. 677/
/47	Oct 15	08 29	Hsü Kuang-chin to Bonham. As regards Amaral's case, Kuo A-an has been wounded, and Li A-pao killed, while resisting arrest.	6	1571
			Encl. Deposition by Kuo A-an: has killed Amaral in retaliation for Amaral's destruction of ancestral graves, n.d.	1	
/48a	Oct 17	09 02	Hsü Kuang-chin to Bonham. Wonders if vessel which fired on fishing junk first and was then sunk in ensuing battle was the one Bonham referred to. Will instruct Magistrate of Hsiang-shan to interrogate detained crew thoroughly.	14	1572
/48b	Oct 17	09 02	Hsü Kuang-chin to Bonham. Accepts Bonham's argument that Hsü A-pao, if captured, should be extradited to Hong Kong.	5	1573
/49	Oct 21	09 06	Hsü Kuang-chin to Bonham. Has asked Magistrate of P'an-yü to go in person to investigate if British merchant ship had been plundered by Chinese marines on patrol or by pirates posing as marines.	7	1574
	Oct 24	09 09	Bonham to Hsü Kuang-chin. Crew of Hong Kong merchant ship detained on its way to Shanghai has been released; they must be paid compensation	1	[F.O 677

). ·/ ·2	Date 1849	TK 29	Description	pp	Old Ref. F.O. 682/
			promptly.		
·0	Oct 26	09 11	Brigadier General Ho of Ch'iung-chou to Bonham. With co-operation of Royal Navy, Chinese marines have scored a great victory against a pirate fleet.	6	1600
	Oct 29	09 14	Bonham to Hsü Kuang-chin. Chinese Magistrates must not send police constables to Hong Kong to arrest suspects. Encl. Two arrest warrants issued by Magistrate of Hsiang-shan, n.d.	2

1 | [F.O. 677/26] |
| ·1 | Oct 29 | 09 14 | Hsü Kuang-chin to Bonham. Encloses report by Magistrate of P'an-yü. Encl. Magistrate's report: pirates Ch'en Hua-t'ou-men et al. have plundered British ships smuggling opium into China. Pirates have no connection with Chinese marines, n.d. | 6

1 | 1575 |
·2	Oct 29	09 14	Hsü Kuang-chin to Bonham. Fishermen who sank Hong Kong vessel swore they had not plundered it. Will have matter investigated further.	6	1576
	Oct 31	09 16	Bonham to Hsü Kuang-chin. London has raised strong objections to Cantonese erecting arches to commemorate so-called achievements of Hsü Kuang-chin and Yeh Ming-ch'en for having refused British entry into Canton city.	1	[F.O. 677/26]
	Oct 31	09 16	Bonham to Hsü Kuang-chin. London insists that Dr J. Bowring, Consul at Canton, must be received by official as senior as Provincial Treasurer.	2	[F.O. 677/27]
	Nov 2	09 18	Bonham to Hsü Kuang-chin. Requests speedy apprehension of pirates who posed as marines and plundered British ship in Canton River.	2	[F.O. 677/26]
·3	Nov 3	09 19	Hsü Kuang-chin to Bonham. Acknowledges treaty provision for extradition and explains that Chinese detectives have gone to Hong Kong to investigate as matter of secrecy.	6	1577
	Nov 5	09 21	Bonham to Hsü Kuang-chin. Objects to use of character ¿ in Hsü's enclosure	2	[F.O. 677/26]

F.O. 682/ 1982	Date 1849	TK 29	Description	pp	Old R F.O. 682/
			to despatch of 29 Oct 1849.		
	Nov 5	09 21	Bonham to Hsü Kuang-chin. Chinese detectives have come to Hong Kong not only to investigate but with warrants to arrest. This must not happen again.	2	[F.O. 677/
	Nov 6	09 22	Bonham to Hsü Kuang-chin. Gives details of sea battles in which Royal Navy dispersed Chang Shih-wu-tsai's pirate fleet near Ch'iung-chou.	2	[F.O. 677/
	Nov 6	09 22	Bonham to Hsü Kuang-chin. Expresses thanks for help given by Chinese authorities to British sailors and passengers shipwrecked near P'eng-hu.	2	[F.O. 677/
/54	Nov 6	09 22	Hsü Kuang-chin to Bonham. Endorses Bonham's desire for cordial Anglo-Chinese relations. Erection of monuments to commemorate settlement of Canton city question has been proposed by gentry. Has not seen copy of such proposal.	8	1578
/55a	Nov 6	09 22	Hsü Kuang-chin to Bonham. Present Provincial Treasurer no longer has additional duty to deal with foreign affairs. Colonel [K'un-shou, who had dealt with foreign affairs] had rank equal to that of Provincial Treasurer and was deputed to see Consul J. Bowring, but Bowring did not respond. Colonel [K'un-shou] now being in Peking, Hsü will ask Acting Colonel and Colonels from other regiments as well as Prefects, to see Bowring.	6	1579
/55b	Nov 6	09 22	Hsü Kuang-chin to Bonham. Refutes Bonham's claim that Magistrate of P'an-yü is to blame for pirate attack on British opium clipper. Chinese law requires Magistrates to arrest criminals within four months; Magistrate of P'an-yü has done so within one month. Again Chinese law does not provide for compensation for victims.	6	1580
/56	Nov 6	09 22	Hsü Kuang-chin to Bonham. Viceroy of Min-Che and Governor of Fukien have	8	1581

. ./ 32	Date 1849	TK 29	Description	pp F.O.	Old Ref. F.O. 682/
			jointly communicated objections to proposal by British Consul at Amoy to build houses in Hu-li-she: area is dangerously near the sea, near barracks and surrounded by graves. Encl. Memo from Viceroy of Min-Che and Governor of Fukien, 8 Oct 1849.	5	
	Nov 9	09 25	Bonham to Hsü Kuang-chin. Is pleased to read that Hsü has not seen any erection of monuments commemorating settlement of city question. Enquires if Lord Palmerston's letter has been forwarded to Peking.	1	[F.O. 677/26]
	Nov 9	09 25	Bonham to Hsü Kuang-chin. Although Colonel [K'un-shou] may hold rank equal to that of Provincial Treasurer, there is no evidence to suggest that he has additional duty to deal with foreign affairs.	1	[F.O. 677/26]
	Nov 9	09 25	Bonham to Hsü Kuang-chin. Insists that Magistrate of P'an-yü is guilty of negligence. Accuses Hsü of using character i in his communication with Fukien authorities.	2	[F.O. 677/26]
7	Nov 9	09 25	Bonham to Hsü Kuang-chin. Acknowledges receipt of memo, transmitted by Hsü, from Fukien authorities that people of Amoy object to Britons building houses at Hu-li-she where there are many graves. Consul at Amoy has reported to same effect. Will reconsider the matter.	6	1560
8	Nov 12	09 28	Hsü Kuang-chin to Bonham. Is delighted that Royal Navy has annihilated pirate fleet near Annam. Fishermen near Hu-men might plunder every now and then out of desperation but have not formed themselves into pirate fleet. Is only too pleased that Chinese were able to help shipwrecked British sailors near P'eng-hu.	7	1583
9	Nov 12	09 28	Hsü Kuang-chin to Bonham. Colonel [K'un-shou] was present in the negotiations at Hu-men on 28 Apr 1848 and again on board British warship on 1 Feb 1849, while Governor Yeh, during his years of office as	9	1584

F.O. 682/ 1982	Date 1849	TK 29	Description	pp	Old R F.O. 682/
			Provincial Treasurer, never receiv- ed a Consul. In receiving Consuls, it is rank and not position that matters.		
/60	Nov 12	09 28	Hsü Kuang-chin to Bonham. Agrees that henceforth he will request extradition of Chinese criminals hiding in Hong Kong [instead of sending detectives into the colony]. Has notified Magistrate of Hsin-an and Colonel of Ta-p'eng to this effect.	5	1585
/61	Nov 12	09 28	Hsü Kuang-chin to Bonham. Joint communication from Viceroy of Min- Che and Governor of Fukien contain- ed improper language because they are not yet familiar with diplomatic language. Is anxious to know Bonham's verdict on proposal by British Consul at Amoy to build houses at Hu-li-she.	6	1586
/62	Nov 13	09 29	Bonham to Hsü Kuang-chin. Consul J. Bowring at Canton reports that houses to west of factories, which foreigners used to rent, are being demolished to build Chinese style houses. This will aggravate housing situation of foreigners. Requests assistance to stop demolition.	8	1562
	Nov 14	09 30	Bonham to Hsü Kuang-chin. Has instructed Consul at Amoy to refer all decisions concerning building projects to treaty provisions.	2	[F.O. 677/
	Nov 15	10 01	Bonham to Hsü Kuang-chin. Colonel [K'un-shou] was present during negotiations on 28 Apr 1848 and 7 Feb 1849 only as *aide-de-camp*. Although his rank is equal to that of Provincial Treasurer, it is well known that ranks in military hierarchy are far less prestigious than those in civil hierarchy. Insists that Consul J. Bowring be treated with same pomp as Acting Consul A.W. Elmslie had been.	2	[F.O. 677/
	Nov 17	10 03	Bonham to Hsü Kuang-chin. Has heard that Howqua *et al.* had asked for permission to monopolise tea trade	1	[F.O 677

O. 2/ 82	Date 1849	TK 29	Description	pp	Old Ref. F.O. 682/
			in Canton. This contravenes the treaty.		
63	Nov 17	10 03	Bonham to Hsü Kuang-chin. Boat in which Vice-Consul at Whampoa has been living is no longer suitable for habitation. More permanent residence must be found. Requests assistance in leasing land from inhabitants to build consulate and prison in order to control three to four thousand British sailors who come and go.	10	1561
64	Nov 19	10 05	Hsü Kuang-chin to Bonham. Houses to west of foreign factories had been vacant for over a year for lack of foreign trade and were therefore pulled down. Over ten shops have been built in past two months on same site. Foreigners should rent other houses in the area.	6	1582
	Nov 22	10 08	Bonham to Hsü Kuang-chin. Requests that British goods, having paid import duties in one port, may be sold in another port.	1	[F.O. 677/26]
	Nov 22	10 08	Bonham to Hsü Kuang-chin. Again requests that owner of Hong Kong vessel sunk on way to Shanghai by Chinese fishermen be paid compensation.	8	[F.O. 677/26]
65	Nov 23	10 09	Hsü Kuang-chin to Bonham. Colonel [K'un-shou] was not *aide-de-camp*; he was too senior to assume that role. If official is not in charge of foreign affairs, he has no access to foreign correspondence and is not equipped to receive diplomats.	8	1587
66	Nov 23	10 09	Hsü Kuang-chin to Bonham. Chinese tea merchants have replied that the manner in which tea commission is put to use is an internal matter and does not affect prices of tea. If British Vice-Consul at Whampoa wishes to lease land, he should do so himself as Chinese government never interferes in such matters.	9	1588

F.O. 682/ 1982	Date 1849	TK 29	Description	pp	Old Re F.O. 682/
	Nov 29	10 15	Bonham to Hsü Kuang-chin. Has reported to London that Hsü has refused to treat Consul J. Bowring with same civility as Acting Consul A.W. Elmslie had been treated.	1	[F.O. 677/2
/67	Nov 29	10 15	Hsü Kuang-chin to Bonham. If import duties on cargo are paid at one port and cargo allowed to be transferred freely to other ports, complications will arise as ports are too far apart. Suggests that if cargo is to be transferred, certificate from Consul should be obtained. Has urged Magistrate of Hsiang-shan to speed up payment of compensation for Hong Kong vessel sunk on its way to Shanghai by Chinese fishermen.	8	1589
	Dec 1	10 17	Bonham to Hsü Kuang-chin. Complications can be avoided if all five ports use common seal to stamp goods for which import duties have been paid.	1	[F.O. 677/:
	Dec 1	10 17	Bonham to Hsü Kuang-chin. Hong Kong resident testifies that his vessel had been plundered by Chinese fishermen who sank it afterwards. Compensation of $500 is too little.	1	[F.O. 677/:
/68	Dec 7	10 23	Hsü Kuang-chin to Bonham. Cannot make any official seal without Emperor's permission: therefore Bonham's suggestion to stamp imports for which duties have been paid is out of question. Issuing certificates for taxed imports is best solution. $500 compensation for Hong Kong vessel is ample, considering the fact that opium was among its cargo.	7	1590
/69	Dec 11	10 27	Bonham to Hsü Kuang-chin. Requests assistance in overcoming local resistance to Vice-Consul's attempt to lease land in Whampoa to build his official residence and to build prison for British sailors who should break the law.	8	1522
/70	Dec 18	11 05	Hsü Kuang-chin to Bonham. Has sent agents to Whampoa to investigate; inhabitants are terrified by idea of a prison in their area and are	7	1591

0. 2/ 82	Date 1849	TK 29	Description	pp	Old Ref. F.O. 682/
			therefore opposed to it.		
	Dec 20	11 07	Bonham to Hsü Kuang-chin. Britain has right by treaty to lease land for building; unless Hsü quickly finds another site in Whampoa, will report matter to London.	2	[F.O. 677/26]
71	Dec 23	11 10	Hsü Kuang-chin to Bonham. Leasing of houses and land is matter purely for parties concerned and has nothing to do with Chinese government. Bonham's accusation is most unreasonable and is perhaps caused by bad translation of official despatches.	9	1592
	Dec 26	11 13	Bonham to Hsü Kuang-chin. Suggests that Chinese government should lease land from local inhabitants in Whampoa area and then re-lease it to Vice-Consul for building official residence and prison.	1	[F.O. 677/26]
	Dec 27	11 14	Hsü Kuang-chin to Bonham. Dr Bettelheim has persisently refused to leave Liu-ch'iu.	1	[F.O. 677/26]
72	Dec 30	11 17	Hsü Kuang-chin to Bonham. According to Chinese custom , when one leases land or a house one must specify in lease what the land or house is going to be used for. Breach of such undertaking may lead to law suits or even armed conflicts.	6	1593

F.O. 682/ 1983	Date 1850	TK 29	Description	pp	Old Ref F.O. 682/

NOTE: *For the year 1850, all but six of the in-coming despatches and all*
the out-going despatches appear to be missing; but, like their
counterparts in the year 1849, their contents were copied into an
entry-book [F.O. 677/26]. They are hereby summarised. To
maintain a consistent format, their valid reference as provided
in the last column continues to be put in square brackets. It
goes without saying that their first column remains blank.

	Jan 4	11 [22]	Bonham to Hsü Kuang-chin. If Vice-Consul is withdrawn from Whampoa for lack of proper residence for him and his staff as well as prison for British sailors who break the law, chaos will ensue.	1	[F.O. 677/2
	Jan 5	11 23	Bonham to Hsü Kuang-chin. Wonders why Chinese government should be concerned about Britons staying at Liu-ch'iu since Liu-ch'iu does not belong to China.	2	[F.O. 677/2
/1	Jan 7	11 25	Hsü Kuang-chin to Bonham. Repeats that he cannot force landlord in Whampoa to lease out land to British Vice-Consul.	6	1601
	Jan 12	11 30	Bonham to Hsü Kuang-chin. New [guarantee] system for tea trade as proposed by Howqua *et al.* is not different from monopoly, which directly contravenes treaty.	2	[F.O. 677/2
/2	Jan 13	12 01	Hsü Kuang-chin to Bonham. Liu-ch'iu *is* vassal state of China and has always left her decisions on foreign policy to China. It is futile for Dr Bettelheim to stay on in Liu-ch'iu as inhabitants do not want his medical service.	7	1602
	Jan 21	12 09	Bonham to Hsü Kuang-chin. Demands speedy reply from Hsü that new [guarantee] system for tea trade is not going to be instituted. Howqua *et al.* must not go to see Consul J. Bowring again on this matter, as Consul must refer everything to Bonham himself.	2	[F.O. 677/2
/3	Jan 21	12 09	Hsü Kuang-chin to Bonham. Prices of tea are governed by supply and demand, and have nothing to do with tea commission which is in fact	8	1603

Date		Description	pp	Old Ref. F.O. 682/
3 1850	TK 29			

		lower than before. Agrees not to institute guarantee system for tea trade if Bonham suspects that it may become monopolistic.		
Jan 21	12 09	Bonham to Hsü Kuang-chin. Is pleased that Hsü will not institute guarantee system for tea trade but points out that tea commission will push up prices of tea.	2	[F.O. 677/26]
4 Jan 25	12 13	Hsü Kuang-chin to Bonham. Howqua was sent to speak to Consul J. Bowring because Howqua had been appointed to assist in handling foreign affairs. As Bowring does not speak any Chinese, Howqua had to write out what he said. Bonham contradicts himself by insisting on the one hand that Bowring must see senior Chinese officials to settle matters, and on the other that Bowring does not have power to settle matters but must refer everything to Bonham himself.	7	1604
Jan 28	12 16	Bonham to Hsü Kuang-chin. Howqua has no official position and therefore must not participate in negotiations. Consul will be empowered to make certain decisions if asked to settle specific matters; otherwise Consul does not have access even to correspondence between senior diplomats of the two countries.	2	[F.O. 677/26]
5 Jan 31	12 19	Hsü Kuang-chin to Bonham. Has already abandoned guarantee system in tea trade in order to please Bonham, who must not pursue subject of tea commission any further since such action constitutes interference in Chinese domestic matters.	8	1605
6 Feb 4	12 23	Hsü Kuang-chin to Bonham. Is surprised that Bonham should regard his usage of *p'i-ju* [for example] as discourteous. Renting of houses should be left to parties concerned and should not be allowed to continue to trouble officials.	6	1568

F.O. 682/	Date		Description	pp	Old Re F.O.
1983	1850	TK 30			682/

	Feb 15	01 04	Bonham to Hsü Kuang-chin. Requests release of Hong Kong resident Han Tsan-shuan, who was arrested on his way to Canton.	1	[F.O. 677/
	Feb 23	01 12	Hsü Kuang-chin to Bonham. Han Tsan-shuan has tried to smuggle salt into Canton. Encl. Depositions by Han Tsan-shuan *et al.*, n.d.	3 3	[F.O. 677/
	Mar 8	01 25	Bonham to Hsü Kuang-chin. Three days ago Colonel of Ta-p'eng sent messenger to Hong Kong with intelligence that pirate fleet had been spotted to east of Hong Kong. As east wind was strong his vessel could not get there quickly. He requested that steamer be sent, offering to pay for coal. Accordingly, steamer was despatched with said Colonel on board and pirate fleet was dispersed. Declines offer of payment for coal but will appreciate permission to mine coal in Taiwan or for Taiwanese to bring coal to Hong Kong for sale.	2	[F.O. 677/
	Mar 14	02 01	Hsü Kuang-chin to Bonham. Appreciates British assistance in dispersing pirate fleet but cannot help in getting coal from Taiwan as Taiwan is outside his jurisdiction. Coal is daily necessity and is sold in five treaty ports. Has requested Commander-in-Chief of marines to reward Royal Navy.	1	[F.O. 677/
	Mar 15	02 02	Bonham to Hsü Kuang-chin. The presents for Royal Navy are returned herewith as Royal Navy is not allowed to accept presents [from foreign governments] and in any case steamer in question has returned to England.	1	[F.O. 677/
	Mar 18	02 05	Bonham to Hsü Kuang-chin. The two steamers of Hong Kong and Canton Steam Co. have made ninety trips to Canton in past six months carrying mainly passengers. In only six out of the ninety trips did they carry goods as freight because they were charged $20 tonnage dues as soon as they carried any freight, however	2	[F.O. 677/

O. 2/ 83	Date 1850	TK 30	Description	pp	Old Ref. F.O. 682/

			small. As a result, Chinese Customs obtained on average $20 per month and steamers had to decline small freights. Suggests that flat rate of $50 per month be charged to each steamer for permission to carry freight.		
	Mar 20	02 07	Bonham to Hsü Kuang-chin. Has received instructions from London. Consul J. Bowring must not be received by any Chinese official junior to Provincial Treasurer who received [Acting] Consul A.W. Elmslie, and certainly not by a military officer.	1	[F.O. 677/26]
	Mar 21	02 08	Bonham to Viceroy Liu Yün-k'o of Min-Che. More than once Royal Navy has helped Chinese authorities suppress piracy in Chinese waters; but steamers need coal, and coal on sale in treaty ports is not suitable. Hsü Kuang-chin said he could not help get coal from Taiwan because Taiwan is outside his jurisdiction. Requests Liu's help [as Taiwan is under Liu's jurisdiction].	1	[F.O. 677/27]
	Mar 24	02 11	Hsü Kuang-chin to Bonham. Hoppo has testified that no tonnage dues have ever been charged to any steamer. Treaty does not provide for steamers to carry goods and therefore they must not do so.	1	[F.O. 677/26]
	Mar 26	02 13	Hsü Kuang-chin to Bonham. Is surprised that London should complain about senior military officers being asked to meet Consul J. Bowring. Provincial Treasurer Huang En-t'ung received [Acting] Consul A.W. Elmslie only because he had additional duty to help in foreign affairs; his successors Fu and Li never saw any foreigner in their lives. Present Provincial Treasurer, Po-kuei, is charged with additional duty to help in foreign affairs and will make an appointment to see Consul J. Bowring after the hundred days of mourning for death of Empress Dowager are over.	1	[F.O. 677/26]
	Mar 27	02 14	Bonham to Hsü Kuang-chin. Po-kuei assumed duties as Provincial	1	[F.O. 677/26]

F.O. 682/ 1983	Date 1850	TK 30	Description	pp	Old Re F.O. 682/
			Treasurer almost two months ago. Much argument could have been avoided if only Hsü had informed Bonham at the time that Po-kuei had the additional duty of helping in foreign affairs.		
	Mar 28	02 15	Bonham to Hsü Kuang-chin. Consul J. Bowring reports that Hoppo has forbidden steamer to unload at Canton. Although treaty does not provide for steamers carrying cargo, Ch'i-ying has given such consent.	2	[F.o. 677/2
	Apr 2	02 20	Hsü Kuang-chin to Bonham. Since Ch'i-ying has given his consent, steamers may carry cargo as well as passengers. Requests that no more steamers than present two be allowed to ply between Hong Kong and Canton to avoid accidents and loss of lives in crowded Canton River.	1	[F.O. 677/2
	Apr 4	02 22	Bonham to Hsü Kuang-chin. Is pleased that Hsü will abide by Ch'i-ying's decision to admit steamers into Canton. Although treaty refers to one-masted and two-masted vessels etc., steamers should not be discriminated against. As long as steamers pay full tonnage dues on arrival at Canton, treaty has not been breached. No distinction should be made between steamers carrying passengers and mail, and steamers carrying cargo.	2	[F.O. 677/2
	Apr 8	02 26	Bonham to Hsü Kuang-chin. Apologises for delay in sending despatch of 27 Mar 1850.	1	[F.O. 677/
	Apr 10	02 28	Hsü Kuang-chin to Bonham. There is difference between steamers carrying passengers and mail, and steamers carrying cargo, as latter increases frequency of visits to Canton. Steamers have run down junks causing scores of deaths near Hu-men, which is least congested part of river, and nobody has admitted responsibility. Bonham must specify what he proposes to do	2	[F.O. 677/

Date		Description	pp	Old Ref. F.O. 682/
1850	TK 30			

if more junks are run down by
steamers.

Apr [13]	03 02	Bonham to Hsü Kuang-chin. There is no question of steamers not being allowed to carry cargo into Canton. Furthermore, steamer delayed for seven days in Canton because Hoppo refused to accept its tonnage dues has claimed compensation of $1,188. Hsü should send deputy to British Consulate to examine claims and request Hoppo to pay compensation.	2	[F.O. 677/26]
Apr 19	03 08	Hsü Kuang-chin to Bonham. Steamer was delayed while debate on question of cargo was going on. Therefore compensation is out of question. Bonham should not allow himself to be obsessed with small sums of money as this is not best way to inspire respect. Again urges Bonham to specify what he proposes to do if more junks are run down by steamers.	2	[F.O. 677/26]
Apr 20	03 09	Bonham to Hsü Kuang-chin. Although sum is small, compensation must be paid in accordance with treaty. If British steamers run down Chinese junks, will make sure that compensation is paid.	2	[F.O. 677/26]
Apr 26	03 15	Bonham to Hsü Kuang-chin. Will be absent from Hong Kong for thirty to forty days in order to inspect other treaty ports.	2	[F.O. 677/26]
Apr 29	03 18	Hsü Kuang-chin to Bonham. Will request Hoppo to compensate the steamer once delayed at Canton as he sees fit. Is pleased that Bonham undertakes to compensate for loss of property and lives if more junks are run down by steamers. It goes without saying that lost property will be compensated with property and lost lives with lives. Will strive to maintain peace and order while Bonham is away.	2	[F.O. 677/26]
May 13	04 02	Bonham to Grand Secretary Ch'i-ying. Previous communications with Peking had to be delivered by steamer at	2	[F.O. 677/26]

F.O. 682/ 1983	Date 1850	TK 30	Description	pp	Old R F.O. 682/
			Tientsin. Such procedure can be spared if local authorities at Shanghai are instructed to receive such communications in accordance with treaty.		
	May 13	04 02	Bonham to Viceroy Lu Chien-ying of Liang-Chiang. Requests that the enclosed two despatches from Lord Palmerston be forwarded to Peking so as to make it unnecessary for steamer to deliver them at Tientsin. Will wait in Shanghai for answer which he expects to receive within twenty days.	2	[F.O. 677/
	May 19	04 08	Liu Yün-k'o to Bonham. Agrees that mining coal in Taiwan is mutually beneficial but local gentry have remonstrated strongly against it, and mining forcibly will only lead to rebellion.	2	[F.O 677/
	May 20	04 09	Bonham to Lu Chien-ying. Cannot wait in Shanghai any longer but is despatching steamer to Tientsin to await reply from Peking.	2	[F.O. 677/
	May 21	04 10	Bonham to Ch'i-ying. Intendant at Shanghai has told him that reply will take over one month to reach Shanghai instead of reliable estimate of twenty days. Therefore, has despatched steamer to deliver copies of Lord Palmerston's despatches to Grand Secretary Ch'i-ying and Grand Councillor Mu-chang-a at Tientsin. Steamer will wait there until reply is received.	2	[F.O. 677/
	May 22	04 11	Lu Chien-ying to Bonham. Tientsin is not treaty port and steamer must not go there in contravention of treaty. Has forwarded despatches to Mu-chang-a and Ch'i-ying, and will transmit replies immediately on receipt.	1	[F.O. 677/
	May 23	04 12	Lu Chien-ying to Bonham. Even if Bonham thinks Shanghai Intendant's estimate of one month is too long, he should try other means to speed up procedure rather than contravene treaty by despatching steamer	2	[F.O 677.

Date			Description	pp	Old Ref. F.O.
3	1850	TK 30			682/

			to Tientsin. If possible, steamer should be recalled so as not to become laughing stock of French and Americans.		
Jun	1	04 21	Bonham to Lu Chien-ying. Cannot understand why despatching steamer to Tientsin should arouse derision of French and Americans. Had not planned to send steamer initially but Chinese obstruction has made it necessary.	1	[F.O. 677/26]
Jun	3	04 23	Bonham to Lu Chien-ying. Lu's reply on 22 May was not delivered until today while Lu's reply of 23 May requesting recall of steamer had been delivered on 27 May. This shows how unreliable Chinese messenger service is, and how wise it has been to send steamer to Tientsin which in no way contravenes treaty.	1	[F.O. 677/26]
Jun	6	04 26	Bonham to Hsü Kuang-chin. Urges Hsü to send deputy quickly to British Consulate to examine claims of steamer once delayed at Canton as a result of Hoppo refusing to accept its payment of tonnage dues. Cases of steamers colliding with junks causing loss of property and lives should be treated in same way as other sea-going vessels colliding with junks.	2	[F.O. 677/26]
Jun	7	04 27	Lu Chien-ying to Bonham. Chinese messenger service is affected by weather and not by deliberate delay. Peking has reacted to Palmerston's communications to Mu-chang-a and Ch'i-ying: courtiers are not allowed to correspond with foreigners.	2	[F.O. 677/26]
Jun	10	05 01	Bonham to Lu Chien-ying. Treaty provides for communication with courtiers in Peking. Has sent for another steamer from Hong Kong. If no replies are received from Mu-chang-a and Ch'i-ying by the time steamer arrives at Shanghai, will board it and go to Tientsin.	1	[F.O. 677/26]
Jun	11	05 02	Bonham to Hsü Kuang-chin. Invites China to participate in London	1	[F.O. 677/26]

F.O. 682/ 1983	Date 1850	TK 30	Description	pp	Old R F.O. 682/

Exposition of 1851.

| Jun 12 | 05 03 | Lu Chien-ying to Bonham. Bonham's intended trip to Tientsin will not change Chinese regulation forbidding courtiers from communicating with foreigners. Treaty provides that correspondence between the two countries takes the form of *chao-hui*, not that courtiers as well as the Imperial Commissioner for Foreign Affairs may communicate with foreigners. Bonham should go to Canton to settle matters there with the Imperial Commissioner for Foreign Affairs. | 1 | [F.O.
677/ |

| Jun 14 | 05 05 | Bonham to Lu Chien-ying. Will wait in Shanghai until second steamer arrives from Hong Kong and then decide what to do. | 2 | [F.O.
677/ |

| Jun 22 | 05 13 | Hsü Kuang-chin to Bonham. Insists that taking Sunday and time on debate etc. into consideration, steamer was delayed for only five days. Ch'i-ying had paid $700 compensation for delay of more than sixty days, averaging $10 per day. Therefore steamer should get only $50. As regards London Exposition in 1851, Chinese government cannot publicise British invitation but Chinese artisans may do what they like. | 2 | [F.O.
677/ |

| Jul 20 | 06 12 | Bonham to Hsü Kuang-chin. Consul J. Bowring has transmitted proclamation by Magistrates of Nan-hai and P'an-yü stipulating that all dealers in tea must pay commission of 0.2 tael per 100 catties to pay for debt to nation and that new dealers must obtain licence from Howqua. This contravenes the treaty. | 1 | [F.O.
677/ |

| Jul 27 | 06 19 | Hsü Kuang-chin to Bonham. Co-hong used to pay lump sums to the state for right of trade. Its abolition meant loss of this revenue. But 0.5 tael per 100 catties of tea has always been charged, 0.2 tael of which is now earmarked to compensate for this loss of revenue. | 1 | [F.O
677 |

). 2/ 33	Date 1850	TK 30	Description	pp	Old Ref. F.O. 682/
			New proceeding does not represent increase in tea commission and in any case this is a domestic affair with which Bonham may not concern himself.		
	Jul 31	06 23	Bonham to Hsü Kuang-chin. Will resort to other means of seeking compensation for steamer once delayed at Canton if Hsü will neither send deputy to examine claims nor pay $1,188 as claimed.	2	[F.O. 677/26]
	Aug 3	06 26	Bonham to Hsü Kuang-chin. Former tea commission of 0.5 tael has been reduced by 0.2 to 0.3 tael. Therefore recent introduction of 0.2 tael commission is definitely new and will push up prices of tea. Putting former Co-hong merchants in control of new licensing system is a return to monopoly which definitely contravenes treaty. If Hsü is worried about rampant smuggling, British Consul is always ready to discuss preventive measures.	2	[F.O. 677/26]
	Aug 5	06 28	Hsü Kuang-chin to Bonham. Again cites precedent of Ch'i-ying having paid compensation of $700 for steamer's delay of more than sixty days averaging $10 per day. Offers to double average to $20 per day and increase days of delay from five to six, making total of $120. Cannot send any deputy to examine claims because all former deputies have left Canton.	1	[F.O. 677/26]
	Aug 11	07 04	Hsü Kuang-chin to Bonham. Even if former tea commission were reduced by 0.2 to 0.3 tael, new [additional] commission of 0.2 tael does not make total exceed old commission of 0.5 tael. New commission will not affect prices of tea, which are governed by supply and demand. British merchants may be honourable but Chinese merchants are known to have engaged in smuggling, in which case only Hsü himself can deal with them; there is no need, therefore, to confer with British Consul about preventive measures.	2	[F.O. 677/26]

F.O. 682/ 1983	Date 1850	TK 30	Description	pp	Old Re F.O. 682/
	Aug 19	07 12	Bonham to Hsü Kuang-chin. Will hold Hsü personally responsible if he does not withdraw new 0.2 tael of tea commission and new tea licensing system.	2	[F.O. 677/
	Aug 21	07 14	Liu Yün-k'o to Bonham. Shen-kuang-ssu was built with funds donated by gentry and citizens of Foochow, who are therefore entitled to deny right of monks therein to let part of it to missionaries. Is surprised by Bonham's claim that treaty allows Britons of all descriptions to live in cities because Chinese version of treaty allows only consular officials to do so.	2	[F.O. 677/
	Aug 25	07 18	Hsü Kuang-chin to Bonham. Prices of tea have actually come down this year, which proves that new tea commission does not push up prices of tea. New licensing system bears no resemblance to Co-hong and in no way contravenes treaty. It was indeed Chinese merchants who initiated these new measures and therefore Hsü himself cannot be held personally responsible.	2	[F.O. 677/
	Sep 3	07 27	Bonham to Hsü Kuang-chin. Encloses copy of what is believed to be an Imperial Edict and asks Hsü to certify its authenticity. Encl. Imperial Edict decreeing that henceforth foreign affairs are to be handled by Imperial Commissioner Hsü Kuang-chin at Canton and by him alone, n.d.	1 2	[F.O. 677/
	Sep 7	08 02	Hsü Kuang-chin to Bonham. Has never received or read in Peking Gazette the Imperial Edict similar to the copy forwarded by Bonham. If Bonham wants to find out its origin, he should interrogate his informant.	2	[F.O. 677/
	Sep 11	08 06	Bonham to Liu Yün-k'o. Treaty does specify that all Britons may live in cities. If consular officials are taken ill at night they will not be able to see the [missionary] doctors if latter are not allowed to live in cities as well, because city gates	2	[F.O. 677/

Date		Description	pp	Old Ref. F.O. 682/
1850	TK 30			

are closed at night.

Oct 10	09 06	Hsü Kuang-chin to Bonham. Has received memo from Fukien authorities requesting him to protest about Interpreter W.R. Gingell having travelled by land from Foochow to Amoy. This contravenes treaty and Gingell runs risk of being attacked by bandits. Encl. Memo from Fukien authorities, 21 Aug 1850.	1 2	[F.O. 677/26]
Oct 15	09 11	Bonham to Hsü Kuang-chin. W.R. Gingell was granted sick leave to return to England and he had to catch the Mail [steamer]. He has breached treaty with good reasons. Indeed he has reported on kind and civil treatment by local authorities and people during his journey, although he found it objectionable that secret attempts should have been made by his sedan-chair bearers to take him back to Foochow.	2	[F.O. 677/26]
Oct 18	09 14	Bonham to Hsü Kuang-chin. The ship of Singapore resident Li Shun-fa, which had goods and treasure worth $12,000 on board, was plundered by pirates in presence of Chinese marines on shore and with Chinese naval vessels not far away.	3	[F.O. 677/26]
Oct 24	09 20	Hsü Kuang-chin to Bonham. Has ordered thorough investigation into Li Shun-fa's allegations.	1	[F.O. 677/26]
Oct 25	09 21	Liu Yün-k'o to Bonham. Bonham does not seem to understand that Liu cannot force gentry and citizens of Foochow to agree to missionaries living in Shen-kuang-ssu.	2	[F.O. 677/26]
Dec 31	11 28	Bonham to Hsü Kuang-chin. In addition to the controversial 0.2 tael of tea commission, other charges including 0.2 tael of licence fee, 0.05 tael of registration fee and 0.05 tael of broker's fee are now levied at Canton. New Chinese tea dealers are also required to find guarantors among former Co-hong merchants. All these are serious breaches of treaty.	2	[F.O. 677/26]

F.O. 682/	Date		Description	pp	Old Re F.O. 682/
1984	1851	TK 30			

NOTE: *If the entry-book F.O. 677/26 may be regarded as a yardstick, then it appears that only the first three documents of 1851 are missing. Following the format of 1849 and 1850, they are not given any new reference in the first column but their reference F.O. 677/26 as provided in the last column in square brackets should continue to be used by searchers. The symbol HF in the third column stands for Emperor Hsien-feng's year of reign.*

	Jan 8	12 07	Hsü Kuang-chin to Bonham. Bonham's arguments are obviously influenced by dishonest Chinese merchants against whom new licensing system is designed. Whatever fees and commissions are levied on tea, the total does not exceed traditional 0.5 tael, therefore complaints about tea charges cannot stand.	1	[F.O. 677/
	Jan 11	12 10	Bonham to Hsü Kuang-chin. Ch'en Ch'ing-chen, British subject born in Singapore and employed as scribe in British Consulate at Amoy, was accused of being member of Small Sword Society, arrested and tortured to death by Amoy authorities. This is a serious breach of treaty. Demands reparation.	3	[F.O. 677/
			Encl. Deposition by Li Hung-pu, n.d.	1	
	Jan 19	12 18	Hsü Kuang-chin to Bonham. Has ordered investigation into death of Ch'en Ch'ing-chen.	2	[F.O. 677/
		HF 1			
/1	Mar 11	02 09	Bonham to Hsü Kuang-chin. Consul J. Bowring at Canton has been investigating case of smuggling by British merchants and has invited Hoppo to Consulate to discuss preventive measures. Hoppo responds by saying that each should mind his own business. This is not best way to ensure full receipt of taxes. Requests information on results of investigation into death of Ch'en Ch'ing-chen.	9	1606
/2	Mar 15	02 13	Hsü Kuang-chin to Bonham. Hoppo has written that Chinese collaborating with foreigners to evade taxes are dealt with by Chinese officials, and foreigners by Consuls. This	6	1626

). 2/ 34	Date 1851	HF 1	Description	pp	Old Ref. F.O. 682/
			division of duties is clear and there is no need for Consul and Hoppo to hold meetings to discuss joint action. Will write again as soon as report on Ch'en Ch'ing-chen's death is received from Amoy.		
'3	Mar 19	02 17	Bonham to Hsü Kuang-chin. Consul J. Bowring has, in accordance with treaty, fined steamer $200 for having failed to deposit its sailing letters to Consulate after its arrival at Canton on 19 February, but Hoppo declines to receive money. Asks Hsü to send courier to fetch it as soon as possible.	7	1607
'4	Mar 24	02 22	Hsü Kuang-chin to Bonham. On being notified on 28 February [by Consul Bowring] of steamer having arrived on 19 February, and having tried to avoid paying customs duties, Hoppo sent officers to steamer which then paid full customs duties on its consignment of coral. Since customs duties have been fully paid, fine is unnecessary.	6	1627
5	Apr 3	03 02	Bonham to Hsü Kuang-chin. Is surprised that Hsü still cannot offer information on death of Ch'en Ch'ing-chen. Amoy authorities must pay special attention to list of names, prepared by British Consul, of various Singapore-born Chinese who are trading in Amoy.	8	1609
6	Apr 5	03 04	Bonham to Hsü Kuang-chin. According to treaty Chinese government must accept $200 fine paid by British steamer. Blames Hoppo for declining to hold meeting with Consul J. Bowring to discuss preventive measures against smuggling and evasion of taxes. Should Chinese customs officials connive with merchants of other nations to evade taxes, will take measures to protect British merchants.	10	1610
7	Apr 9	03 08	Hsü Kuang-chin to Bonham. Acting Viceroy of Min-Che has replied that Ch'en Ch'ing-chen, alleged to be	8	1628

F.O. 682/ 1984	Date 1851	HF 1	Description	pp	Old Re F.O. 682/
			Singapore-born Chinese, has confess- ed to being native of Amoy and to have attempted to establish Small Sword Society with intention to rebel. Encl. Memo from Acting Viceroy of Min-Che to Hsü, n.d.	7	
/8	Apr 10	03 09	Hsü Kuang-chin to Bonham. Decision not to accept fine of British ship that broke port regulations was intended to be an act of benevolence to foreigners. Case of Ch'en Ch'ing- chen has been dealt with the day before. Does not wish to pursue either subject any further.	6	1629
/9	Apr 18	03 17	Hsü Kuang-chin to Bonham. Encloses joint memo from Viceroy of Min-Che and Governor of Fukien: re list of sixty Chinese, born in British colonies but now residing in Amoy, suggest that criteria for deciding whether one is Chinese citizen or not should be one's dress and hair style. Encl. 1. Memo *op. cit.*, 20 Mar 1851. Encl. 2. List of sixty Chinese names, n.d.	6 3 2	1630
/10	Apr 19	03 18	Bonham to Hsü Kuang-chin. As ports of Foochow and Ningpo are not prosper- ing as expected, proposes to exchange them for Soochow and Hangchow (or Chen-chiang). Demands Hoppo puts his house in order so that merchants of all nations pay same taxes.	14	1611
/11	Apr 24	03 23	Hsü Kuang-chin to Bonham. British proposal to exchange Foochow and Ningpo for Soochow and Hangchow (or Chen-chiang) makes complete nonsense of Treaty of Nanking (1842) and Supplementary Treaty (1843).	13	1631
/12	Apr 26	03 25	Bonham to Hsü Kuang-chin. Refutes Chinese denial that Ch'en Ch'ing- chen was born in Singapore and consequently under British protect- ion. Consul at Amoy has submitted list of Singapore Chinese at Amoy. Has instructed Royal Navy to proceed to Amoy should any more Singapore Chinese there be harassed.	8	1612

O. 2/ 84	Date 1851	HF 1	Description	pp	Old Ref. F.O. 682/
13	Apr 28	03 27	Bonham to Viceroy Yü-t'ai of Min-Che. London has decreed that all Britons have treaty right to live in all five cities of treaty ports. Therefore British missionaries must be allowed to stay in city of Foochow.	5	1613
14	Apr 30	03 29	Bonham to Hsü Kuang-chin. Hsü has replied to question of exchange of treaty ports but not to those of corrupt Chinese customs officials and of smuggling in treaty ports. Requests that all three questions be brought to attention of Peking.	5	1614
15	May 2	04 02	Hsü Kuang-chin to Bonham. Ch'en Ch'ing-chen is not British according to his own deposition and testimonies given by witnesses. His hair style and dress are nothing but Chinese. If place of birth decides one's citizenship, are all British babies born in China to be regarded as Chinese? Considers British concentration of warships at Amoy as unfriendly act and contrary to spirit of treaty.	10	1632
16	May 5	04 05	Hsü Kuang-chin to Bonham. Troubling Emperor with small matters such as corrupt customs officials is out of the question: these matters are dealt with by local officials. Will take action if Bonham can provide specific cases of corruption; otherwise Bonham should stop complaining.	6	1633
17	May 16	04 16	Hsü Kuang-chin to Bonham. Asks if British merchant P'i-erh [Mr Beale] has been authorised to become Portuguese Consul at Shanghai.	8	1634
18	May 26	04 26	Bonham to Hsü Kuang-chin. Confirms that Briton P'i-erh [Mr Beale] has been appointed Portuguese Consul at Shanghai by authorities in Macao but does not know if he has authority from Portuguese government.	6	1615
19	May 29	04 29	Yü-t'ai to Bonham. Both Buddhist monastery of Shen-kuang-ssu where two British missionaries lived, and Taoist monastery of Tao-shan-kuan, where they lived subsequently, are	20	1636

F.O. 682/ 1984	Date 1851	HF 1	Description	pp	Old Re F.O. 682/
			inside city of Foochow where non-diplomatic personnel have no right to be. Magistrate who endorsed initial renting of Shen-kuang-ssu by mistake has now been dismissed by Emperor.		
/20	Jun 9	05 10	Bonham to Hsü Kuang-chin. Portuguese lorchas have been plundering Chinese shipping along coast. Urges that Briton P'i-erh [Beale] be accepted as Portuguese Consul at Shanghai and Briton Tien-ti [Dent] as Portuguese Consul at Canton.	8	1616
/21	Jun 11	05 12	Bonham to Yü-t'ai. Protests about refusal to accept letters from Acting British Consul at Foochow. Reminds Yü-t'ai that it was such refusal that led to China's humiliating defeat in Opium War.	14	1617
/22	Jun 13	05 14	Hsü Kuang-chin to Bonham. Agrees to let British merchants P'i-erh [Beale] become Portuguese Consul at Shanghai, and Tien-ti [Dent] become Portuguese Consul at Canton.	6	1635
/23	Jun 14	05 15	Bonham to Hsü Kuang-chin. Tea commission etc., now totalling 0.5 tael per 100 catties, and licensing system, definitely contravene Treaty of Nanking and Supplementary Treaty. London is indignant and will hold China responsible for all consequences. Requests that these facts be made known to Peking.	12	1618
/24	Jun 14	05 15	Bonham to Hsü Kuang-chin. Has been instructed by London to demand that matter of tea commission be brought to Emperor's attention.	8	1619
/25	Jun 22	05 23	Hsü Kuang-chin to Bonham. Total of tea commission etc. does not exceed traditional rate of 0.5 tael per 100 catties and is designed to foil attempts at smuggling by merchants whose complaints, therefore, should not be allowed to form basis for Bonham's protests. Besides, tea commission is earmarked for re-imbursing Imperial Treasury for sums paid to Britain as war indemnity.	2	1637

). 2/ 84	Date 1851	HF 1	Description	pp	Old Ref. F.O. 682/
26a	Jul -	06 -	Draft of next entry.	1	137/1/33
26b	Jul 3	06 05	Bonham to Hsü Kuang-chin. If tea commission is not abolished, China will be guilty of breach of treaty and will be held responsible for all the consequences. Again requests that matter be brought to attention of Emperor.	8	1620
27	Jul 10	06 12	Bonham to Hsü Kuang-chin. At Shanghai, dishonest merchants have been evading customs duties with connivance of corrupt customs officials, jeopardising position of honest British merchants. Unless this is promptly stopped, will consider tax agreement with China null and void.	19	1621
28	Jul 10	06 12	Hsü Kuang-chin to Bonham. Emperor had been consulted when tea commission was introduced. Declines to trouble Emperor again on this subject alone, but agrees to mention it along with other matters when opportunity arises.	6	1638
29	Jul 10	06 12	Yü-t'ai to [Bonham]. Will deal with correspondence with H.M. Plenipotentiary, but communications from British Consul will continue to be handled by Prefect of Foochow.	20	1641
30	Jul 18	06 20	Hsü Kuang-chin to Bonham. Appreciates Bonham's concern about rampant tax evasions at Shanghai but cannot understand why, with such outrageous irregularities, customs revenue there still increases from year to year. Nor can he understand how British merchants are jeopardised as taxes apply to all nations. As Imperial Commissioner, his responsibility for five treaty ports is limited to preparing annual reports on customs revenue, and can only, therefore, refer Bonham's complaints about Shanghai to Governor of Kiangsu.	6	1639
31	Jul 21	06 23	Hsü Kuang-chin to Bonham. Is proceeding to Kao-chou to prevent Kwangsi rebels invading Kwangtung. Governor Yeh Ming-ch'en will be Acting Viceroy.	6	1640

F.O. 682/ 1984	Date 1851	HF 1	Description	pp	Old Re F.O. 682/
/32	Aug 30	08 04	Bonham to Governor Yeh Ming-ch'en of Kwangtung. Has reason to believe attempts are being made by accomplices to bribe Chinese officials to release two pirates extradited from Hong Kong.	12	1622
/33	Sep 12	08 17	Hsü Kuang-Chin and Yeh Ming-ch'en to Bonham. Two of five pirate suspects have confessed and rest have been proved innocent. Endorses Bonham's view that no pirates should be treated leniently.	8	1642
/34	Dec 2	10 10	Bonham to Yeh Ming-ch'en. A-Chou, head of garrison at Lan-ts'un Fort near Hu-men, has been extorting $2 per month from messenger ships between Canton and Hong Kong, and has now increased his demands to $6 per month.	7	1623
/35	Dec 8	10 16	Bonham to Yeh Ming-ch'en. Four months have lapsed since Viceroy Hsü promised to transmit to Peking British objections to tea commission. Wonders if Yeh has heard from Peking.	6	1624
/36	Dec 10	10 18	Hsü Kuang-chin and Yeh Ming-ch'en to Bonham. British and U.S. Consuls *et al.* have made excursion into Chang-chou's hinterland, contrary to treaty stipulations. They also measured city wall of Chang-chou.	8	1643
/37	Dec 15	10 [23]	Bonham to Hsü Kuang-chin and Yeh Ming-ch'en. Chang-chou is within a day's journey from Amoy and there is no reason why Britons should not go there. Measuring city wall of Chang-chou is not commendable and will instruct Consul to restrain Britons.	9	1625
/38	Dec 25	11 04	Hsü Kuang-chin and Yeh Ming-ch'en to Bonham. Have ordered investigations into allegations that A-Chou of Lan-ts'un Fort in Hu-men area has been demanding fees of $6 per month from each of the [four] messenger boats.	5	1644

).	Date		Description	pp	Old Ref.
2/					F.O.
35	1852	HF 1			682/

E: *All but one document of 1852 seem to be missing. To fill in the gap, therefore, the documents of 1852 that were copied into the entry-books (F.O. 230/74 for out-going despatches and F.O. 230/75 for in-coming despatches) at the time are herewith summarised. As in previous years, they are not given new reference numbers in the first column while the existing references as provided in the last column in square brackets should continue to be used by searchers.*

Jan 3	11 13	Viceroy Hsü Kuang-chin of Liang-Kuang and Governor Yeh Ming-ch'en of Kwangtung to Bonham. Cannot refer question of tea commission to Emperor on its own but may append it to annual report on customs revenue, which is due shortly.	1	[F.O. 230/75]

| Jan 10 | 11 20 | Bonham to Hsü Kuang-chin and Yeh Ming-ch'en. Since their reply of 25 Dec 1851 promising investigations, A-Chou has demolished houses of sailors of messenger ships, who complained about extortions. Even the letter of reply from British Consul at Canton on same subject has been opened while being carried to Hong Kong by said relay messenger ships. | 1 | [F.O. 230/74] |

| Jan 10 | 11 20 | Bonham to Hsü Kuang-chin and Yeh Ming-ch'en. Is shocked that question of tea commission has not been referred to Emperor. Demands that enclosed objections from London be quickly transmitted to Peking, as prescribed by treaty. | 1 | [F.O. 230/74] |

| Jan 16 | 11 26 | Bonham to Hsü Kuang-chin and Yeh Ming-ch'en. Has been instructed by London to declare that Great Britain will seek compensation from Chinese government for losses suffered by British merchants as result of institution of tea commission etc., which contravenes treaty. | 2 | [F.O. 230/74] |

| Jan 31 | 12 11 | Hsü Kuang-chin and Yeh Ming-ch'en to Bonham. Investigations show that neither A-Chou nor Lan-ts'un Fort, garrison of which A-Chou is supposed to be head, exists. The relay messenger ships ply between Hong Kong and Hu-men, and then between Hu-men and Whampoa where the mail | 2 | [F.O. 230/75] |

F.O. 682/ 1985	Date 1852	HF 1	Description	pp	Old Re F.O. 682/
			is transferred to fast boat for Canton. It is at Hu-men that sailors of messenger ships rent an abode for total of 5.2 taels per month. This will now be stopped.		
	Jan 31	12 11	Hsü Kuang-chin and Yeh Ming-ch'en to Bonham. Tea commission was decided upon voluntarily by Chinese merchants and has nothing to do with foreign merchants, let alone treaty and must not, therefore, be discussed any further. Nonetheless, has appended Bonham's objections in recent annual report to Peking on customs revenue and will inform Bonham of Emperor's reaction.	2	[F.O. 230/
		HF 2			
	Mar 29	02 09	Bonham to Hsü Kuang-chin and Yeh Ming-ch'en. Has been granted leave for nine months. During his absence, General K.H. Jervois will be Acting Governor of Hong Kong and Consul J. Bowring will be H.M. Acting Plenipotentiary and Acting Superintendent of Trade.	2	[F.O. 230/
	Apr 13	02 24	Major-General K.H. Jervois to Hsü Kuang-chin and Yeh Ming-ch'en. Chinese merchants in Hong Kong have jointly petitioned about rampant piracy in waters around Hong Kong, which has made it increasingly difficult to conduct trade with mainland. Chinese officials should make greater efforts at pirate suppression.	2	[F.O. 230/
	Apr 15	02 26	Major-General K.H. Jervois to Hsü Kuang-chin and Yeh Ming-ch'en. Official letter from London appointing Consul J. Bowring to be H.M. Acting Plenipotentiary and Acting Superintendent of Trade has now been received. Consul Bowring assumes these duties today and will write separately.	1	[F.O 230/
	Apr 16	02 27	Bowring to Hsü Kuang-chin and Yeh Ming-ch'en. For three years as Consul at Canton he has been fair and just. Now that he is appointed	1	[F.O 230

).	Date		Description	pp	Old Ref. F.O.
?/					
35	1852	HF 2			682/

by his monarch to be Acting Plenipotentiary and Acting Superintendent
of Trade, will exhort all Britons to
observe treaty, expecting all
Chinese officials to do the same.
Looks forward to pleasure of meeting
Hsü and Yeh personally.

Apr 25	03 07	Hsü Kuang-chin and Yeh Ming-ch'en to Bowring. Are pleased that Bowring has been appointed H.M. Acting Plenipotentiary. At present Hsü is busy suppressing rebellion at Kao-chou and Yeh is busy supplying him with provisions. Will be glad to see Bowring after rebellion is suppressed and Hsü has returned to Canton.	1	[F.O. 230/75]

Jun 8	04 21	Hsü Kuang-chin and Yeh Ming-ch'en to Bowring. Hsü will go to Kwangsi, and Yeh to Lo-ting today, to suppress rebellions there. Provincial Treasurer Po-kuei, who has just been promoted Governor of Honan, will remain in Canton to look after foreign affairs.	2	[F.O. 230/75]

Jul 20	06 04	Bowring to Hsü Kuang-chin, Yeh Ming-ch'en and Po-kuei. Acting Consul A.W. Elmslie at Canton has reported on proclamation by Magistrate of Nan-hai, in which foreigners are referred to as i. Traditionally, character i has been used to describe tribes on borders of China. As Great Britain is a Power equal to China, Britons must not be described as i.	2	[F.O. 230/74]

Jul 27	06 11	Hsü Kuang-chin and Po-kuei to Bonham. Hsü is away in Kwangsi; and Po-kuei, confessing ignorance of the classics and dictionaries, finds it novel to read that character i can be source of anger and dispute. Will instruct local officials that henceforth when character i might have been used, another character must be employed.	1	[F.O. 230/75]

Aug 31	07 17	Hsü Kuang-chin and Yeh Ming-ch'en to Bowring. Yeh has suppressed rebellion in Lo-ching and has returned to Canton on 26 Aug 1852.	1	[F.O. 230/75]

F.O. 682/ 1985	Date 1852	HF 2	Description	pp	Old R F.O. 682/
			Henceforth communications may be addressed to him directly.		
	Sep 1	07 18	Bowring to Hsü Kuang-chin and Po-kuei. Acting Consul A.W. Elmslie at Canton complains that no reply has been received from Magistrate Li of P'an-yü to his request for arrest of culprit A-pao who fled to Ho-nan.	2	[F.O. 230/
	Sep 7	07 24	Bowring to Hsü Kuang-chin and Yeh Ming-ch'en. Is pleased to know that Yeh has suppressed rebellion at Lo-ching and has returned to Canton to resume duties as Acting Imperial Commissioner for Foreign Affairs. Expects that henceforth peace and order will be restored to Kwangtung and Kwangsi and that trade will continue as usual.	2	[F.O. 230/
	Sep 8	07 25	Hsü Kuang-chin and Yeh Ming-ch'en to Bowring. Since Acting Consul A.W. Elmslie has written to Magistrate Li of P'an-yü, the said Magistrate will have sent detectives to Ho-nan to arrest A-pao and if he has any news he will have informed Elmslie directly.	1	[F.O. 230/
/1	Oct 7	08 24	Bowring to Hsü Kuang-chin and Yeh Ming-ch'en. Acting Consul A.W. Elmslie has negotiated contract to lease land in Whampoa for building Vice-Consulate and prison to detain rowdy British sailors, but local inhabit-ants have again threatened to dis-rupt construction work. Notice is hereby given that Royal Navy will proceed to Whampoa to stand guard. Encl. 1. Contract for lease of land for thirty years at $100 per annum, n.d. Encl. 2. Proclamation objecting to lease, 31 Aug 1852.	2 2 1	253A
	Oct 8	08 25	Yeh Ming-ch'en to Bowring. Has been appointed Acting Viceroy of Liang-Kuang concurrently in charge of foreign affairs and has assumed duties on 4 Oct 1852. When he has cleared backlog of work, will go to Shao-chou to forestall invasion by rebels from Hunan.	1	[F.O 230

Date		Description	pp	Old Ref. F.O.
1852	HF 2			682/

Oct 11	08 28	Bowring to Yeh Ming-ch'en. Acknowledges Yeh's despatch of 8 Oct 1852 indicating that he was going to Shao-chou next month to forestall invasion by rebels from Hunan. Wonders to whom despatches should be sent during Yeh's absence.	1	[F.O. 230/74]
Oct 24	09 12	Yeh Ming-ch'en to Bowring. Officials cannot intervene in leasing of land which has to be agreed upon by parties concerned. Block of land in question belongs not to one but three clans and consent of other two must be obtained. No contract has been signed, no rents paid. Therefore inhabitants of Whampoa do not feel they have wronged Britons in any way, regarding presence of Royal Navy in Whampoa as quite superfluous.	1	[F.O. 230/75]
Oct 24	09 12	Yeh Ming-ch'en to Bowring. Has been ordered by Emperor to go to Shao-chou to organise defence against rebels from Hunan. Will go there on 30 Oct 1852. In his absence Acting Governor Po-kuei will be in charge of affairs.	1	[F.O. 230/75]
Oct 27	09 15	Bowring to Yeh Ming-ch'en. Non-intervention is not good enough: Chinese officials are obliged by treaty to give assistance to Britons in leasing land. Requests immediate release of landlord Tseng Ping-kao, and despatch of Chinese officials to Whampoa to oversee leasing of land.	2	[F.O. 230/74]
Oct 27	09 15	Bowring to Yeh Ming-ch'en. Notes that Yeh will be going to Shao-chou on 19 Nov 1852 to forestall invasion by rebels from Hunan, and that all despatches should be sent to Acting Governor Po-kuei.	1	[F.O. 230/74]
Nov 15	10 04	Bowring to Po-kuei. Is shocked to learn that landlord Tseng Ping-kao died shortly after being released from detention. Po-kuei must issue proclamation to pacify inhabitants of Whampoa, otherwise London will be very upset.	2	[F.O. 230/74]

F.O. 682/ 1985	Date 1852	HF 2	Description	pp	Old Re F.O. 682/
	Nov 22	10 11	Yeh Ming-ch'en and Po-kuei to Bowring. The report that Tseng Ping-kao died shortly after release from detention cannot be true. He was never detained because there was not sufficient cause for such action to be taken: his fellow clansmen testified that he had never signed contract to lease out land without consent of his clansmen nor had he received any rents.	1	[F.O. 230/
	Dec 20	11 10	Bowring to Po-kuei. British Consulate at Canton has requested Chinese government to take action against pirates who plundered British merchants in Hu-men area. Requests information on action taken.	2	[F.O. 230/

).	Date		Description	pp	Old Ref.
2/					F.O.
36	1853	HF 2			682/

ᴛᴇ: *By comparing the documents extant and the entries in F.O. 230/74 and F.O. 230/75 for the year 1853, it appears that all those documents copied into these two entry-books have survived.*

√1	Jan 2	11 23	Yeh Ming-ch'en and Po-kuei to Bowring. Have again urged Commander-in-Chief of marine forces to speed up capture of pirates who attacked British merchants near Hu-men.	4	1659

HF 3

√2	Feb 28	01 21	Bonham to Po-kuei. Has returned to Hong Kong on 13 Feb 1853 and has resumed duties as H.M. Pleni-potentiary, Superintendent of Trade, and Governor of Hong Kong. Consul J. Bowring will return to his original post at Canton.	4	1645
√3	Mar 25	02 16	Yeh Ming-ch'en and Po-kuei to Bonham. Crown Prince of Liu-ch'iu has asked Viceroy of Min-Che to transmit request to Bonham that Dr Bettelheim be withdrawn.	8	1660
√4	Mar 26	02 17	Governor Yang Wen-ting of Kiangsu to Bonham. In view of Taiping threat to Nanking, was hoping to borrow British warships as a deterrent. Intendant at Shanghai reported that Bonham would proceed to Nanking immediately, and that French and American envoys be asked to send vessels as well.	8	1661
√5	May 3	03 26	Major-General K.H. Jervois [Acting Governor of Hong Kong] to Yeh Ming-ch'en. Chinese law prohibiting export of rice to foreign countries must not apply to Hong Kong, which should have access to Chinese rice.	6	1646
√6	May 9	04 02	Yeh Ming-ch'en to Major-General K.H. Jervois. There are no plans to stop normal supply of rice from Canton area to Hong Kong.	4	1662
√7	[May 26]	4 [19]	Bonham to Yeh Ming-ch'en. Has returned to Hong Kong on 26 May 1853 from tour of inspection of other treaty ports.	4	1647

F.O. 682/ 1986	Date 1853	HF 3	Description	pp	Old Re F.O. 682/
/8	May 27	04 20	Bonham to Yeh Ming-ch'en. Consul J. Bowring has been granted leave of absence for one year. Consul D.B. Robertson will be acting in his place.	2	1648
/9	Jun 3	04 27	Yeh Ming-ch'en to Bonham. Notes that Bonham has returned to Hong Kong from his tour of other treaty ports, that Consul J. Bowring is going on leave, and that Consul D.B. Robertson will be Acting Consul at Canton.	6	1663
/10	Jun 3	04 27	Bonham to Po-kuei. British position remains unchanged: Liu-ch'iu does not belong to China, and therefore China has no right to request departure of Dr Bettelheim from Liu-ch'iu.	6	1649
/11	Aug 10	07 06	Bonham to Yeh Ming-ch'en. Chinese sailors led by P'an A-yen of Shun-te have attacked master and other sailors of ship on which they were employed, plundered it and then fled. Requests immediate action.	10	1650
			Encl. 1. Names of Chinese sailors and comprador who employed them, n.d.	1	
			Encl. 2. Names of victims on board, n.d.	1	
/12	Aug 20	07 16	Yeh Ming-ch'en to Bonham. Has instructed Magistrates of P'an-yü, Hsin-an, Shun-te and Hsiang-shan to arrest P'an A-yen et al.	6	1664
/13	Aug 27	07 23	Bonham to Yeh Ming-ch'en. In two recent operations to west of Hong Kong, Royal Navy has destroyed twelve pirate vessels with total of seventy cannon on board, and has dispersed numerous pirates. Again requests vigorous action against pirates who attacked two British vessels.	7	1651
/14	Sep 5	08 03	Yeh Ming-ch'en to Bonham. Since his return to Canton from Shao-chou, has instructed marine forces to suppress piracy. Subsequently six to seven hundred pirates have been killed or arrested. Is pleased to read that	7	1665

. /	Date		Description	pp	Old Ref. F.O.
6	1853	HF 3			682/
			Royal Navy has also been vigorous in suppressing piracy.		
5	Sep 17	08 15	Bonham to Yeh Ming-ch'en. Endorses Yeh's decision to accept silver dollars other than Spanish dollars.	6	1652
6	Sep 28	08 26	Bonham to Yeh Ming-ch'en. Urges speedy payment of debts by Chinese merchants Ts'ui A-hsi *et al.*	8	1653
7	Oct 13	09 11	Yeh Ming-ch'en to Bonham. Decision to urge merchants to accept silver dollars other than Spanish dollars was made to facilitate trade. Has instructed Magistrate of Nan-hai to make Ts'ui A-hsi *et al.* pay their debts.	6	1666
3	Oct 21	09 19	Bonham to Yeh Ming-ch'en. Tseng A-chang has attempted to set fire to Vice-Consul's ship which is his official residence at Whampoa. Unless Tseng is arrested quickly, any subsequent damage he should cause to Vice-Consul's ship will have to be paid for by Chinese government.	7	1654
9	Nov 8	10 08	Bonham to Yeh Ming-ch'en. Tseng A-chang, who attempted to set fire to Vice-Consul's ship at Whampoa, has been seen wandering freely in Canton. As Chinese authorities have been so slack about his arrest, Bonham will act unilaterally. Will hold Yeh personally responsible, and considers Chinese Government liable to pay compensation if Tseng A-chang should damage Vice-Consul's ship while still at large.	8	1655
0	Nov 10	10 10	Yeh Ming-ch'en to Bonham. Tseng A-chang's wife, A-ts'ai, was persuaded to go to Vice-Consul for payment of board and lodging owed her by British sailors. Later, her dead body was found floating in river with wound on her back. Case of murder must be settled before Tseng A-chang's alleged arson may be investigated.	9	1667
4	Nov 15	10 15	Bonham to Yeh Ming-ch'en. Tseng A-chang was wanted for questioning	8	1656

F.O. 682/ 1986	Date 1853	HF 3	Description	pp	Old R< F.O. 682/
			for having repeatedly offered refuge to deserters from British ships. His wife, A-ts'ai, was detained overnight in Vice-Consul's ship when she refused to reveal his whereabouts. She was subsequently drowned when she fell into river while attempting to escape. Then Tseng A-chang tried to avenge her death by attempting to set fire to Vice-Consul's ship. Will take unilateral action if Chinese authorities still refuse to act.		
/22	Nov 25	10 25	Bonham to Yeh Ming-ch'en. Again urges speedy settlement of debts owed by Chinese merchants Ts'ui A-hsi *et al.* Encl. Petition from British creditor to Acting British Consul at Canton seeking assistance in recovering money owed by Chinese merchants, n.d.	7 1	1657
/23	Dec 8	11 08	Yeh Ming-ch'en to Bonham. Viceroy I-liang of Liang-Chiang has reported capture of British merchants supplying Taipings with arms. Demands explanation of the report that [Bonham himself] went to dine with Taipings at Nanking and signed treaty with them. Requests that Britons stop supplying Taipings with arms. Encl. Petition by British merchants to Taiping authorities, n.d.	14 1	1668
/24	Dec 8	11 08	Yeh Ming-ch'en to Bonham. It is not fair of Bonham to try to silence Tseng A-chang on question of A-ts'ai's death. In any case, Tseng A-chang has given himself up to Chinese authorities and has undertaken not to cause any more trouble, which is why he was released. Cannot understand what Bonham means by taking unilateral action against Tseng A-chang.	6	1669
/25	Dec 8	11 08	Yeh Ming-ch'en to Bonham. Has instructed new Magistrate of Nan-hai to summons Chinese merchants and to make them pay debts they owe British merchants.	6	1670
/26	Dec 14	11 14	Bonham to Yeh Ming-ch'en. Will instruct Consul R. Alcock to punish	8	1658

No. 2/	Date		Description	pp	Old Ref. F.O. 682/
86	1853	HF 3			

Britons who supply arms to Taipings.
Has been to Nanking not to negotiate
treaty with Taipings, but to
ascertain their intentions towards
Shanghai and to warn them against
harming British subjects and trade.

F.O. 682/ 1987	Date 1854	HF 3	Description	pp	Old Ref F.O. 682/

NOTE: *Of all the documents copied into the entry-books F.O. 230/74 and*
F.O. 230/75 for the year 1854, three in-coming despatches appear
to be missing. As before, they are summarised herewith, but no
new reference numbers are given to them in the first column and
their reference as provided in square brackets in the last column
should be used by searchers.

/1	Jan 9	12 11	Bonham to Yeh Ming-ch'en. Protests against intended establishment of tea monopoly in Foochow. It is serious breach of treaty and China will be held entirely responsible for all consequences. Encl. Proclamation by Magistrate of Foochow inviting bids for tea monopoly, 12 Nov 1853.	10 1	1671
/2	Jan 17	12 19	Yeh Ming-ch'en to Bonham. Will write to Viceroy of Min-Che about alleged establishment of tea monopoly in Foochow.	6	1691A
/3	Jan 19	12 21	Bonham to Yeh Ming-ch'en. Mr Jui-man [W. Schwemann] has been appointed Consul for Han-na-wa [Hanover] at Canton.	8	1672
/4	Jan 23	12 25	Yeh Ming-ch'en to Bonham. Has accepted papers presented by Mr Jui-man [W. Schwemann], newly appointed Consul of Han-na-wa [Hanover].	5	1691B

HF 4

/5	Mar 17	02 19	Bonham to Yeh Ming-ch'en. Interpreter [M.C. Morrison of Consulate at Canton] and two other Britons have been assaulted and robbed during excursion near Hsi-ch'iao-shan. Encl. Consul Elmslie to Magistrate of Nan-hai, 15 Mar 1854.	9 5	1673
/6	Mar 27	02 29	Yeh Ming-ch'en to Bonham. When notified by M.C. Morrison of pending visit to Hsi-ch'iao-shan, Chinese police tried to stop him as inhabitants there are notorious for hostility towards outsiders, Chinese and aliens alike. But Morrison *et al.* would neither listen nor wait for police escort.	8	1692
/7	Mar 28	02 30	Bonham to Yeh Ming-ch'en. Repeats demands for redress for assault on	7	1674

O. 32/ 987	Date 1854	HF 4	Description	pp	Old Ref. F.O. 682/
			three Britons. P.S. Yeh's of 27 March has just arrived. Even if three Britons were to blame for not having waited for Chinese police escort, there was no reason for Chinese villagers to attack them.		
/8	Apr 1	03 04	Bonham to Yeh Ming-ch'en. Protests against Cantonese mob attempting to remove Dr Hobson from his rented house in Canton, and against detention of Hobson's landlord.	8	1675
/9	Apr 6	03 09	Yeh Ming-ch'en to Bonham. If all inhabitants of same street agree, [Dr Hobson] may rent the house.	6	1693
10	Apr 6	03 09	Yeh Ming-ch'en to Bonham. M.C. Morrison *et al.* were to blame because they would neither listen to advice nor wait for police escort. Estimate of $500 for worth of lost property is obviously exaggerated.	6	1694
11	Apr 8	03 11	Bonham to Yeh Ming-ch'en. Petition by Cantonese must not be allowed to interfere with Dr Hobson's right by treaty to rent house in Canton.	6	1676
12	Apr 8	03 11	Bonham to Yeh Ming-ch'en. Even if three Britons were to blame for not having waited for Chinese police escort, there is no reason why their attackers should not be punished. Encl. List of lost property, n.d.	8 1	1677
13	Apr 17	03 20	Bowring to Yeh Ming-ch'en. Has taken over as H.M.Plenipotentiary. Will write again for appointment to meet.	5	1678
14	Apr 25	03 28	Yeh Ming-ch'en to Bowring. Is pleased with Bowring's appointment as H.M. Plenipotentiary. Will be glad to see Bowring but this may have to wait a while because military campaigns being conducted simultaneously in several provinces are taking up all his time.	6	1695
15	Apr 25	03 28	Bowring to Yeh Ming-ch'en. Has been instructed to revise Treaty of	28	1679

F.O. 682/ 1987	Date 1854	HF 4	Description	pp	Old Re F.O. 682/
			Nanking, gain entry into Canton city, acquire abolition of tea commission, lease land in Ho-nan for merchants, establish regular meetings with Chinese officials, secure payment of debts owed by Chinese to British merchants, obtain redress for Britons attacked by Chinese. Insists meeting with Yeh be held in Yeh's *yamen*.		
/16	Apr 27	04 01	Bowring to Yeh Ming-ch'en. Insists that meeting with Yeh should take priority over Yeh's involvement with military campaigns in several provinces.	6	1680
/17	Apr 28	04 02	Bowring to Yeh Ming-ch'en. Urges payment of debt by Feng Sung-mao to Indian merchants.	6	1681
/18	May 7	04 11	Yeh Ming-ch'en to Bowring. Government cannot force Cantonese to admit foreigners into city; tea commission was introduced by tea merchants, not by government; leasing of land should be left to parties concerned and officials should not interfere; Chinese officials are not avoiding foreign envoys: witness Hsü's receptions for Bonham and Yeh's own willingness to see Bowring. Will write separately about meeting Bowring. Points out that Bowring's letter has no official stamp.	16	1696
/19	May 7	04 11	Yeh Ming-ch'en to Bowring. Proposes to meet Bowring on 22 May at Jen-hsin-chan.	5	1698
/20	May 7	04 11	Yeh Ming-ch'en to Bowring. Has commanded Magistrate of P'an-yü to despatch additional police to Whampoa to hunt down Feng Sung-mao.	5	1697
/21	May 9	04 13	Bowring to Yeh Ming-ch'en. Is sending W.H. Medhurst to Canton to put back official stamp on last despatch. Will resort to force if request for interview continues to be ignored.	8	1682
/22	May 11	04 15	Bowring to Yeh Ming-ch'en. Repeats instructions from London regarding	22	1683

0. 2/ 37	Date 1854	HF 4	Description	pp	Old Ref. F.O. 682/
			settlement of questions of treaty revision, entry into Canton city etc.		
23	May 11	04 15	Bowring to Yeh Ming-ch'en. Rejects Yeh's proposal to hold meeting at Jen-hsin-chan and insists that meeting be held in Yeh's *yamen* within walled city of Canton.	6	1684
24	May 12	04 16	Yeh Ming-ch'en to Bowring. Wonders why Bowring has not responded to suggestion to meet on 22 May at Jen-hsin-chan.	7	1720
25	May 17	04 21	Yeh Ming-ch'en to Bowring. Sub-Magistrate Hsü Wen-shen went to Consulate to meet W.H. Medhurst on 11 and 12 May but was told that Medhurst had not arrived. Hsü went again on 13 May but Medhurst refused to see him, demanding to be met by a higher official [i.e., a Magistrate]. Finally sent Magistrate Li, although Hsü had always been in charge of foreign correspondence; but Medhurst still refused to hand over Bowring's letter. Wonders why for over ten days Bowring has not responded to proposal to meet on 22 May.	12	1699
			Encl. Yeh to British Consul: is sending Magistrate Li to meet Medhurst, 16 May 1845.	2	
26	May 19	04 23	Bowring to Yeh Ming-ch'en. Reiterates refusal to be met in any place other than Yeh's *yamen*. Requests copies of correspondence be forwarded to Peking.	10	1685
27	May 22	04 26	Yeh Ming-ch'en to Bowring. Raising Canton city question only harms trade and in any case Sir George Bonham has abandoned it. Chinese merchants do willingly pay tea commission, and present flourishing tea trade benefits everybody. Had written to Bowring three times about meeting on 22 May 1854 before Bowring wrote to decline invitation, which is evidence that Bowring does not want meeting at all. Has always informed Emperor of all foreign affairs and there is no need for Bowring to tell him to do so.	16	1700

F.O. 682/ 1987	Date 1854	HF 4	Description	pp	Old Re F.O. 682/
/28	May 24	04 28	Bowring to Yeh Ming-ch'en. Is surprised that Yeh should attempt to change his intention to be received inside Canton city. Will depart immediately [to North China] with British Admiral [Sir James Stirling].	6	1686
/29	May 26	04 30	Yeh Ming-ch'en to Bowring. Predecessors Ch'i-ying and Hsü Kuang-chin had always met Davis and Bonham either at Hu-men or on board steamer. Proposes to meet Bowring at Hu-men.	7	1701
/30	Jun 10	05 1-5	Bowring to Yeh Ming-ch'en. Forwards impression of his seal of office [in fact Bowring's own coat of arms], henceforth to be used in official correspondence.	4	1687
/31	Jun 20	05 25	Bowring and Stirling to Provincial Treasurer Chi-erh-hang-a of Kiangsu. Ask him to come to British Consulate [at Shanghai] for interview tomorrow.	5	1688A
/32	Jun 20	05 25	Bowring and Stirling to Governor Hsü Nai-chao of Kiangsu. Ask him to come to British Consulate [at Shanghai] for interview tomorrow.	5	1688B
/33	Jun 21	05 26	Governor Hsü Nai-chao of Kiangsu to Bowring. Has a bad cold and must not go out. Is sending Provincial Treasurer Chi-erh-hang-a as deputy to meeting.	7	1702
/34	Jun 22	05 27	Hsü Nai-chao to Bowring and Stirling. Has the report from Chi-erh-hang-a about meeting in British Consulate. Is pleased that they propose to dis-arm rebels in Shanghai city, to drive them away and to hand over city to Chinese authorities. How-ever, British authorities must specify where they plan to send rebels, and must persuade leaders P'an Hsiao-ching and Hsieh An-pang to surrender whereupon they will be exempted from death penalty, or to arrest them should they refuse, because these two have killed government officials. Only then will it be possible to request	4	1703

O. 2/ 87	Date 1854	HF 4	Description	pp	Old Ref. F.O. 682/
			Emperor to endorse such a plan. Regrets that he is still unwell but will send Chi-erh-hang-a to negotiate these conditions.		
35	Jun 26	06 02	Bowring to Hsü Nai-chao. Has not replied earlier as he was waiting for outcome of negotiations with Chi-erh-hang-a. Is willing to change unhappy situation at Shanghai, to revive trade there and to help China according to treaty and to collect customs duties. However, Britain has adopted position of neutrality and will not intervene unless British subjects and property are in danger. Therefore he must be given complete freedom of action if he were to dislodge rebels from Shanghai city and thereby spare Hsü Nai-chao from difficult task of controlling rowdy Chinese soldiers. Is pleased with the way Chi-erh-hang-a handled the Chinese soldiers who went into foreign settlement on 21 Jun 1854 and attacked foreign sailors.	8	1689
	Jun 26	06 02	Hsü Nai-chao to Bowring. Is very pleased that Bowring plans to send rebels away from Shanghai city so that customs duties may be collected normally. Will, accordingly, comply with Bowring's requests, and will not be so inflexible as to contradict Bowring on point which does not seriously compromise Chinese law and precedents.	2	[F.O. 230/75]
36	Jun 30	06 06	Bowring to Hsü Nai-chao. Is doing all he can to ensure effective collection of customs duties. As for question of [dislodging rebels from Shanghai] city, Hsü had better come to British Consulate on 3 Jul 1854 to discuss it in person.	6	1690
37	Jul 1	06 07	Hsü Nai-chao to Bowring. Is gratified that Bowring and Consul R. Alcock agree to enforce payment of back duties since 7 Sep 1853. Is certain Emperor will be greatly pleased too. All other matters concerning customs duties should be referred to	9	1704

F.O. 682/ 1987	Date 1854	HF 4	Description	pp	Old Re F.O. 682/
			Intendant Wu [Chien-chang] who is fully authorised to consider them.		
/38	Jul 10	06 16	Bowring to Yeh Ming-ch'en. Rejects Yeh's proposal to see him at Hu-men: will hold meeting only within walled city of Canton. Has arrived with Royal Navy at Shanghai, where he has helped Chinese officials collect customs duties and in other ways in accordance with treaty. Will inform Emperor of grievances and that matters at Canton are seriously endangering peaceful relations between the two countries.	8	1722
/39	Jul 10	06 16	Bowring to Viceroy I-liang of Liang-Chiang. Is glad to learn from Intendant Wu [Chien-chang] that I-liang is pleased with Bowring's proceedings at Shanghai. In fact, has come to Shanghai to try to present state papers to Emperor because Imperial Commissioner Yeh at Canton has been most discourteous. Wonders if I-liang has been specially empowered to see him because he cannot see anybody, however exalted, except representatives of Emperor.	8	1723
/40	Jul 11	06 17	Yeh Ming-ch'en to Bowring. Acknowledges receipt of impression of Bowring's official seal [in fact, Bowring's own coat of arms].	5	1705A
/41	Jul 11	06 17	Yeh Ming-ch'en to Bowring. Copy of previous entry.	3	1705B
/42			Number not used.		
/43	Jul 18	06 24	I-liang to Bowring. As regards Bowring's resolve not to meet any Chinese official, however high-ranking, who is not empowered by Emperor to meet him, has to admit that I-liang himself has not been so empowered. Since Bowring has denounced Yeh Ming-ch'en as being discourteous, believes that Bowring must be very courteous and cultured.	12	1706
/44	Jul 26	[07 02]	Bowring to Emperor of China. Time has come to revise Treaty of Nanking. Requests special envoy to be sent to	12	1724

.	Date		Description	pp	Old Ref. F.O.
7	1854	HF 4			682/

			Shanghai for discussions. Because rebellions have disrupted normal pattern of trade, foreign trade should be allowed in places other than five treaty ports. If such places have already fallen to rebels or are weak in defence, will send troops there to protect trade.		
5	Aug 4	07 11	Governor Chi-erh-hang-a of Kiangsu to Bowring. Intendant Wu [Chien-chang] has been dismissed and Lan [Wei-wen] is now acting in his position.	5	1707
6	Aug 5	07 12	Bowring to Chi-erh-hang-a. Will leave for Hong Kong next day. Hopes Chinese authorities will assist British Consul in maintaining peaceful trade in Shanghai.	5	1725
7	Aug 10	07 17	Bowring to Viceroy Wang [I-te] of Min-Che. Is passing through Foochow and in hurry to go back to Hong Kong. Requests interview on following day or at the latest the day after.	4	1726
8	Aug 11	07 18	Wang I-te to Bowring. Appreciates Bowring's desire for interview but is too busy with military affairs. According to regulations, Prefect of Foochow is responsible for foreign affairs. Suggests British Consul at Foochow approaches said Prefect.	7	1708
9	Aug 12	07 19	Bowring to Wang I-te. Is offended by Wang's rejection of request for interview and will include this in list of grievances to be communicated to Peking.	8	1727
0	Aug 13	07 20	Wang I-te to Bowring. Has written before that military affairs are taking all his time, but since Prefect Lou came in person to say that Bowring has extremely urgent matters to see him about, will be pleased to see Bowring next morning.	5	1709
1	Aug 22	07 29	Bowring to Yeh Ming-ch'en. News of rebellions in Canton area has brought him back to Hong Kong, having been received cordially on his way by Viceroy Wang I-te at Foochow and local officials at Amoy. While	10	1728

F.O. 682/ 1987	Date 1854	HF 4	Description	pp	Old R F.O. 682/

NOTE: *The symbol ℓ in the third column stands for intercalary month.*

			at Shanghai, had tried to enforce payment of back duties. Time for revising Treaty of Nanking has come. Is sending Interpreter W.H. Medhurst to Canton to inquire if Yeh has received instructions from Emperor to negotiate.		
/52	Aug 25	ℓ7 02	Yeh Ming-ch'en to Bowring. Is pleased Bowring has tried to enforce payment of back duties at Shanghai. As regards treaty revision, will send official to meet W.H. Medhurst at Consulate.	6	1721
/53	[Aug] 28	ℓ7 05	Bowring to Yeh Ming-ch'en. Asks Yeh to specify if Yeh has power from Emperor to revise treaty; if not, interview with Yeh is unnecessary.	8	1729
/54	Sep 1	ℓ7 09	Yeh Ming-ch'en to Bowring. Has sent official to meet W.H. Medhurst twice. Regarding inquiry as to whether he has been authorised by Emperor to revise treaty, has to stress that he has been instructed to observe treaty to the letter and not to change it in any substantial manner.	7	1710
/55	Sep 4	ℓ7 12	Bowring to Yeh Ming-ch'en. Is bitterly disappointed that Yeh has taken all these months to say that he is not empowered to make major changes to existing treaties. Will report frustrations to London and will ask Peking to send another Imperial Commissioner for negotations.	12	1730
/56	Sep 8	ℓ7 16	Bowring to Yeh Ming-ch'en. Pirates along Pearl River have caused British merchants to spend extra money on self-protection. Chinese government must compensate British merchants for this. Asks Yeh to send deputy to British Consulate to examine claims by British merchants.	7	1731
/57	Oct 6	08 15	Governor Chi-erh-hang-a of Kiangsu to Bowring. A trench was dug by labourers hired by Chinese	7	1711

. / 7	Date 1854	HF 4	Description	pp	Old Ref. F.O. 682/
			government under protection of blue-jackets, to prevent Chinese soldiers trespassing on to the foreign settle-ment while pursuing fleeing rebels. Trench is now in disrepair. Wishes to hire labourers to repair it but wonders if British protection is forthcoming while repair is under way.		
8	Oct 7	08 16	Chi-erh-hang-a to Bowring. Rebels occupying Shanghai city have managed to hold out for a year because they continue to receive supplies through the foreign settlement. Requests co-operation in cutting off supplies.	8	1712
9	Oct 7	08 16	Chi-erh-hang-a to Bowring. Is grate-ful that Bowring has written to London arguing against Sir George Bonham's recommendation to cancel back duties between 7 Sep 1853 and 9 Feb 1854. Urges that back duties between 9 Feb 1854 and 12 Jul 1854 be paid without delay.	7	1713
0	Oct 9	08 18	Bowring to Chi-erh-hang-a. Final settlement of back duties will have to wait for decision in London.	8	1732
1	Oct 9	08 18	Bowring to Chi-erh-hang-a. Agrees to co-operate in effort to stop supplies being smuggled into rebel-occupied Shanghai city.	7	1733
2	Oct 16	08 25	Document in which Bowring certified that W.H. Medhurst has been sent to arrange with local Chinese officials for meeting between Bowring and Chinese Imperial Commissioner.	6	1734
3	[Oct -]	[08 -]	Bowring to Peking authorities. Asks them to transmit to Emperor the British demand for treaty revision, a demand shared by France and America. Present rebellion in China has made revision even more necessary. Has come to Tientsin for negotiations because Commissioner Yeh indicated that he had not been empowered to do so. Requests that another Imperial Commissioner be sent to Tientsin for negotiations.	8	1735

F.O. 682/ 1987	Date 1854	HF 4	Description	pp	Old R F.O. 682/
/64	[Nov 3]	09 13	List of demands to be met in revision of treaties.	8	1736
/65	[Nov 3]	09 13	Alternative demands if first three demands listed in previous document cannot be met.	3	1737
/66	Nov 8	09 18	Imperial Commissioner Ch'ung-lun to Bowring. Treaties are signed to be kept. Rejects all Bowring's demands under guise of treaty revision, except three reasonable ones which will be referred to Emperor.	17	1714
/67	Nov 9	09 19	Bowring to Ch'ung-lun. Is disappointed at Ch'ung-lun's reply. Ch'ung-lun must make it clear whether he has already transmitted, or is going to transmit all British demands to Emperor.	1	1738
/68	Nov 10	09 20	Ch'ung-lun to Bowring. Has referred three of Bowring's requests to Emperor. Suggests Bowring returns to Canton or Shanghai as reply will take some time to come.	6	1715
	Dec 4	10 15	Chi-erh-hang-a to Bowring. Hopes Bowring has had pleasant trip back to Hong Kong. Two-thirds of brick wall has now been built under protection of French and American troops. Expects British authorities to keep promise and send troops to give protection while remaining section of brick wall is built so as to cut communications with rebels in Shanghai city.	2	[F.O. 230/
/69a	Dec 7	10 18	Yeh Ming-ch'en to Bowring. Received, not long ago, request from D.B. Robertson [Acting Consul at Canton] for co-operation to suppress piracy near Kao-lan in Hsiang-shan waters. This request was granted and Chinese marines sent in joint operation with Royal Navy. As result numerous pirates were captured. Now that the river pirates are threatening foreign settlement in Canton, has sent troops for their defence; but as Royal Navy is also in Canton waters for same purpose, the two forces should again co-operate to attack said pirates.	6	143

	Date		Description	pp	Old Ref. F.O. 682/
7	1854	HF 4			
9b	Dec 11	10 22	Bowring to Yeh Ming-ch'en. British foreign policy forbids interference in domestic affairs of other nations, unless safety of British subjects is in question. As situation seems pressing, will come to Canton with Admiral [Sir James Stirling] and several men-of-war.	5	1739
0	Dec 15	10 26	Yeh Ming-ch'en to Bowring. Is glad that Bowring is responding to request for co-operation of Royal Navy with Chinese forces to protect foreign settlement in Canton. Has despatched Sub-Magistrate Hsü [Wen-shen] of Nan-hai to wait upon Bowring at British Consulate.	6	1716
1	Dec 20	11 01	Bowring to Yen Ming-ch'en. W.H. Medhurst has received two Chinese officials sent to wait on Bowring, and has communicated Bowring's desire to meet Yeh at Yeh's *yamen* or at Consulate. Has made arrangements jointly with French and U.S. representatives for protection of foreign community. Will soon return to Hong Kong with warships not need-ed for protection of foreign community.	6	1740
2	Dec 20	11 01	Bowring to Wang l-te. Volume of trade in Foochow has increased because of disturbances in other ports. The demands for homes by foreign merchants has increased accordingly but local inhabitants have created difficulties in way of renting houses.	6	1741
3	Dec 23	11 04	Chi-erh-hang-a to Bowring and Stirling. France and America honoured agree-ment and gave protection while walls were built to stop supplies being smuggled into rebel-occupied Shanghai city. Royal Navy did not do so and half-built wall was pulled down by rebels, leading to clash between French navy and rebels.	12	1718
4	Dec 23	11 04	Bowring to Yeh Ming-ch'en. Encloses defence measures for foreign community in Canton, jointly devised by British and U.S. Admirals. Encl. Defence measures *op. cit.* n.d.	5 7	1742

F.O. 682/ 1987	Date 1854	HF 4	Description	pp	Old Ref. F.O. 682/
/75	Dec 26	11 07	Yeh Ming-ch'en to Bowring. Has investigated and carefully consider-ed Bowring's proposals for security of foreign settlement: none of them is necessary.	12	
/76	Dec 29	11 10	Bowring to Yeh Ming'ch'en. Yeh must allow British and U.S. navy to act on proposed defence measures. Is not unable to use force to seek entry into Canton city but unwilling to compound Yeh's difficulties at present.	14	1743
/77	Dec 29	11 10	Chi-erh-hang-a to Bowring and Stirling. Wonders why Royal Navy has still not honoured agreement to offer protect-ion while wall is being built to isolate Shanghai rebels.	8	1719

Date		Description	pp	Old Ref. F.O.
1855	HF 4			682/

*Of the documents copied into the entry-books F.O. 230/74 and
F.O. 230/75, only two out-going despatches appear to be missing
and they are dealt with as for previous year, e.g. 1854.*

| 1 | Jan 3 | 11 15 | Bowring to Yeh Ming-ch'en. London has requested verification of report that China has ceded large tract of territory in Heilungkiang to Russia. Has also heard that Nepal is about to make war on China in Tibet next spring. Requests comments. | 6 | 1745 |

| 2 | Jan 20 | 12 03 | Wang I-te to Bowring. Consul's complaints about difficulties in leasing land in Foochow are no longer valid. Lists cases of satisfactory leasing of land. | 16 | 1763 |

| 3 | Jan 27 | 12 10 | Chi-erh-hang-a to Bowring. Refusal to honour back duties on the ground that Chinese did not give sufficient protection to foreigners against rebels cannot stand, because foreigners have been helping rebels to fight government troops. At least forty foreigners are still employed by rebels in Shanghai city. | 17 | 1764 |

| 4a | Feb 10 | 12 24 | Bowring to Wang I-te. Is glad that Wang has instructed local officials to observe treaty and to be co-operative. As volume of trade at Foochow is increasing daily, has decided to appoint Interpreter W.H. Medhurst to be British Consul there. | 7 | 1746 |

| 4b | Feb [10] | 12 [24] | Draft of previous entry. | 6 | 1744 |

| 5 | Feb 12 | 12 26 | Bowring to Taiwan local authorities. Captain Richards, commanding HMS *Saracen* is going to survey waters around Taiwan. Requests co-operation. | 5 | 1747 |

| 6a | Feb 15 | 12 29 | Chi-erh-hang-a to Bowring. Is pleased that R. Alcock will remain in Shanghai as Consul. Recommends H.N. Lay to succeed T. Wade as Foreign Inspector of Customs. | 8 | 1765 |

| 6b | [Feb 15] | 12 [29] | Private letter from Chi-erh-hang-a and Wu Chien-chang to [Bowring]. Acknowledge receipt of [Bowring's] | 1 | 386/1/7 |

F.O. 682/ 1988	Date 1855	HF 5	Description	pp	Old Re F.O. 682/
			letter and endorse [Bowring's] draft terms of an agreement. The Governor has examined the draft and has nothing to add to it except polishing its language. Return herewith the polished draft for [Bowring's] perusal. Point out that only Emperor has power to spare lives of Liu [Li-ch'uan?] and Lin [A-ming?] but if, according to the draft agreement, they do manage to detain P'an [Hsiao-ching] and Hsieh [An-pang], there is no question of their lives not being spared, witness the case of Chang Kuo-liang. Emphasize that they will keep their part of the agreement.		
/7	Feb 19	01 03	Bowring to Chi-erh-hang-a. Will forward London's verdict on back duties as soon as it is received. Has instructed Consul to expel any Briton found to be in the employ of rebels in Shanghai city, and to arrest them if they are re-employed by rebels.	7	1748
/8	Feb 22	01 06	Bowring to Chi-erh-hang-a. W.R. Gingell is even more suitable than H.N. Lay as successor to T. Wade as Foreign Inspector of Customs at Shanghai. However, this is a domestic matter and Bowring will not interfere, but hopes that Chi-erh-hang-a will discuss the matter with Consul R. Alcock. Whoever is to be appointed, he expects to be informed.	6	1749
/9	Mar 7	01 19	Bowring to Wang-I-te. Has just received despatch from London appointing W.H. Medhurst to be Consul at Foochow. Medhurst is well acquainted with Chinese language and customs and is certain to get on well with local Chinese officials.	7	1750
/10	Mar 8	01 20	Chi-erh-hang-a to Bowring. Shanghai rebels are now dispersed, their leader killed, and city recovered. Thanks Bowring for his help in having stopped foreign supplies reaching rebels.	9	1766
/11	Mar 8	01 20	Chi-erh-hang-a to Bowring. Again urges	6	1767

	Date		Description	pp	Old Ref. F.O. 682/
3	1855	HF 5			

			speedy settlement of Shanghai back duties. Also requests punishment of Britons who have helped Shanghai rebels.		
2	Mar 8	01 20	Chi-erh-hang-a to Bowring. W.R. Gingell may be very able, but he is in Foochow and may not know Shanghai as well as H.N. Lay. Maintains that Lay would be best candidate to succeed T. Wade.	7	1768
3	Mar 17	01 29	Wang I-te to Bowring. Notes that W.H. Medhurst has been appointed Consul at Foochow. Will instruct local officials to co-operate with him in accordance with treaty.	8	1769
4	Mar 29	02 12	Agreement on sale of British barque *Black River Packet*.	4	1784
5	Apr 5	02 19	Wang I-te to Bowring. Has received W.H. Medhurst on 3 Apr 1855. Has reports on two recent cases of Britons venturing into hinterland: one to Lung-yen[-chou] to prospect for coal, the other to Ning-yang for sightseeing. These cases contravene the treaty and cause alarm among local populace.	14	1770
6	Jun 11	04 27	Bowring to Yeh Ming-ch'en. R. Alcock, whose proceedings at Shanghai have earned praises from the Emperor, has been transferred to be Consul at Canton. Hopes to come with him to Yeh's office to pay respects. Otherwise Yeh should send Provincial Treasurer to Consulate to meet him.	9	1751
7	Jun 22	05 09	Wang-I-te to Bowring. Has no way of knowing whether or not Foreign Inspectorate of Customs at Shanghai in fact complies with treaty until he has full details from Kiangsu authorities. Rejects Bowring's request to let Britons travel freely in hinterland as this contravenes the treaty.	13	1771
8	Jul 9	05 26	Yeh Ming-ch'en to Bowring. Has become even busier since Bowring's rejection of Yeh's offer to meet at Jen-hsin-lou last year because he has to	7	1772

F.O. 682/ 1988	Date 1855	HF 5	Description	pp	Old Re F.O. 682/
			make all decisions about suppress- ion of rebellions throughout the province. There is no precedent for a British Consul being received by a Provincial Treasurer. When Bowring himself was Consul at Canton, he was never received by any Chinese official . Normally, Provincial Treasurer of Kwangtung is not charg- ed with management of foreign affairs. In any case present Provincial Treasurer has just died so there is no question of his receiving new British Consul.		
/19	Jul 12	05 29	Bowring to Yeh Ming-ch'en. Complains that Yeh has taken one month to reply to previous despatch, and then only to reject request for interview inside Canton city and to decline sending Provincial Treasurer to meet R. Alcock at Consulate.	5	1752
/20	Jul 16	06 03	Bowring to Wang I-te. Again requests that Foreign Inspectorate of Customs similar to that at Shanghai be established at Foochow as this is best way to prevent smuggling by foreign merchants. Among foreigners alleged to have gone to Lung-yen- chou to prospect for coal, there were no Britons. Asks Wang to interpret treaty liberally when deal- ing with Britons travelling in hinter- land of China.	10	1753
/21	Aug 15	07 03	Wang I-te to Bowring. Will consider question of establishing Foreign Inspectorate of Customs at Foochow once replies from Governor of Kiangsu and Imperial Commissioner Yeh Ming- ch'en at Canton are received. Treaty clearly stipulates that Britons must not venture into hinterland and Bowring must instruct Consuls to observe it.	13	1773
/22	Oct 10	08 30	Bowring to Wang I-te. Consul W.H. Medhurst has complained that Prefect at Foochow persistently ignores his communications regarding leasing of land. If this is allowed to continue, peaceful relations will be in danger.	6	1760

0. 2/ 88	Date 1855	HF 5	Description	pp	Old Ref. F.O. 682/

23	Nov 5	09 26	Bowring to Wang I-te. Exportation of Chinese girls for sale has now ceased not because of vigilance of Chinese officials but because of British Consul's initiative. Proclamation by Magistrate of Min-hsien prohibiting exportation of girls is praiseworthy but it refers to foreigners as *i*, which is intolerable.	·8	1755
24	Nov 6	09 27	Bowring to Wang I-te. Missionaries must be allowed to build churches inside city of Foochow. Wang is playing with fire if he continues to allow local officials to be hostile to foreigners. Has banned Chinese rebels from gathering in Hong Kong and does not expect Chinese officials to respond by referring to British officials as rebel or barbarian chiefs.	14	1756
25	Nov 21	10 12	Wang I-te to Bowring. Bowring must cite specific incidents rather than make general accusations that Prefect of Foochow persistently ignores communications from Consul W.H. Medhurst regarding leasing of land.	9	1774
26	Nov 21	10 12	Bowring to Yeh Ming-ch'en. Hoppo is entitled to confiscate the cargo of the Hong Kong lorcha caught smuggling but cannot detain the vessel itself. Has asked Royal Navy to secure its release. Yeh cannot argue that lorcha is Chinese because it has been registered in Hong Kong and according to a law passed in Hong Kong this year, all residents there, Chinese or foreign, may have their vessels registered and thereby enjoy protection offered by British flag. Encl. Regulations governing registration of ships in Hong Kong, n.d.	12 6	1757
27	Nov 22	10 13	Bowring to Yeh Ming-ch'en. Consul R. Alcock has forwarded copy of proclamation by Provincial Judge Shen [Ti-hui] prohibiting Chinese from building lorchas and from obtaining registers in Hong Kong.	10	1758

F.O. 682/ 1988	Date 1855	HF 5	Description	pp	Old Re F.O. 682/
			In this proclamation foreigners are referred to as 亿 which is most objectionable.		
/28	Nov 22	10 13	Bowring to Yeh Ming-ch'en. Because of upheavals in China, members of secret societies have swollen ranks of pirates in South China Sea. Requests co-operation in suppressing piracy.	6	1759
	Nov 28	10 19	Bowring to Yeh Ming-ch'en. Great Britain and France are at war with Russia and are together clearing Chinese and Japanese waters of Russian vessels. Recently, Royal Navy has encountered Russian troops in Kirin, which is Chinese territory and where Russians have no right to be. Requests that Emperor be informed of this.	1	[F.O. 230/
/29	Dec 12	11 04	Yeh Ming-ch'en to Bowring. Last June he despatched marine forces to suppress piracy in South China Sea. Since then several thousand pirates have been captured and several hundred pirate vessels sunk. South China Sea is now, [in fact], quite free of pirates. Is pleased that Bowring shares view of his predecessor Sir George Bonham that China and Great Britain should co-operate to suppress piracy because Yeh himself was personally involved in such co-operation with Bonham in 1851 and 1853.	4	1776
/30	Dec 12	11 04	Yeh Ming-ch'en to Bowring. Provincial Judge Shen Ti-hui has never beeen involved in foreign affairs and his staff are therefore unfamiliar with diplomatic language. Has instructed Shen to caution his staff to choose words with care when foreign affairs are involved.	4	1775
/31	Dec 12	11 04	Yeh Ming-ch'en to Bowring. Acknowledges copy of Hong Kong legislation on granting registers. According to Chinese salt legislation, only licensed merchants may carry salt and only in Chinese junks. Lorchas are	8	1777

0. 32/ 88	Date 1855	HF 5	Description	pp	Old Ref. F.O. 682/
			foreign vessels and must carry only foreign goods. When lorchas are used by Chinese to smuggle salt, they must be dealt with strictly according to Chinese legislation on salt-smuggling. Not even Hong Kong registers can protect them from punishment prescribed for such an offence.		
32	Dec 12	11 04	Yeh Ming-ch'en to Bowring. China never takes sides in conflicts between Great Britain and Russia, therefore Bowring must not think that China ever gave permission to Russia to use Chinese territory to ambush British soldiers. It is quite possible that shipwrecked Russian sailors took refuge on Chinese soil.	8	1779
	Dec 16	10 [08]	Bowring to Chi-erh-hang-a. Transmitted to London last February Chi-erh-hang-a's request for permission to employ H.N. Lay as Foreign Inspector of Customs at Shanghai. London has now granted request, adding that such an Inspector must be regarded as being entirely in Chinese employ and that his home government must not be held responsible for his actions in any way. Urges that Foreign Inspectorate of Customs be established in Foochow as well.	2	[F.O. 230/74]
33	Dec 22	11 14	Wang I-te to Bowring. Thanks for co-operation in stopping exportation of Chinese girls and for prohibiting elements subversive of Chinese government from gathering in Hong Kong. Has instructed all junior officials not to use character 夷 in any document . Britons already have church at Nan-t'ai, which is centre for foreign trade, therefore they should not press for another church inside city which would antagonise citizens.	24	1778

F.O. 682/	Date		Description	pp	Old Re F.O.
1989	1856	HF 5			682/

NOTE: *Like the year 1849, all the original out-going despatches appear to be missing. Summaries are made of entries in F.O. 230/74, as in previous years.*

	Jan 8	12 01	Bowring to Wang I-te. Is pleased that Wang has instructed junior officials not to use character *i*. Notes that Wang [no longer] argues that treaty prohibits missionaries building church in city of Foochow but that citizens are opposed to it. Thus citizens should be instructed to observe treaty. Gives notice that Royal Navy is about to suppress piracy in South China Sea.	2	[F.O. 230/7
/1	Jan 22	12 15	Wang I-te to Bowring. Acting Prefect Yeh of Foochow, being new to his job, might well have used improper diplomatic language but Vice-Consul F.H. Hale was most impetuous in tearing up letter.	10	129/1
			Encl. Consul W.H. Medhurst to Prefect Pao of Foochow, 19 Oct 1855.	5	
/2	Feb 3	12 27	Wang I-te to Bowring. Is pleased to read that Royal Navy is about to suppress piracy in South China Sea. As citizens of Foochow object to missionaries building churches in city, *vox populi vox Dei*.	11	129/2
	Feb 5	12 29	Bowring to Wang I-te. Has instructed Vice-Consul F.H. Hale to be patient with Chinese officials. Encloses Consul W.H. Medhurst's list of matters that Chinese officials have ignored. Setting up Foreign Inspectorate of Customs at Foochow similar to that at Shanghai will help Chinese revenue and benefit honest merchants.	2	[F.O. 230/
		HF 6			
	Feb 8	01 03	Bowring to Yeh Ming-ch'en. Again urges that Feng Sung-mao be made to pay his debt.	2	[F.O. 230/
	Feb 25	01 20	Bowring to Yeh Ming-ch'en. On 4 Aug 1855, Royal Navy annihilated entire pirate fleet near Kao-lan. On 18 Aug 1855, it dispersed large pirate fleet near Liao-tung. On 16 Jan	2	[F.O. 230/

O. 2/ 89	Date 1856 HF 6		Description	pp	Old Ref. F.O. 682/
			1856, it wiped out another near Chusan, and yet another on 31 Jan 1856 near Amoy.		
	Feb 27	01 22	Bowring to Wang I-te. At Foochow in 1855, foreign trade increased by 60% but customs revenue decreased by 25% when compared to previous year. This shows how corrupt and inefficient Foochow Customs Office is. Again urges that Foreign Inspectorate of Customs be set up along lines of that at Shanghai, where annual customs revenue has more than doubled since Inspectorate of Customs was established. Collecting customs revenue is entirely a Chinese domestic affair, and Bowring would not have offered his opinion but for strong desire to protect honest merchants.	2	[F.O. 230/74]
3	Mar 1	01 25	Wang I-te to Bowring. Has written three times to Kiangsu authorities for details of Foreign Inspectorate of Customs at Shanghai. Cannot implement same at Foochow until reply is received.	13	129/3
4	Mar 19	02 13	Bowring to Wang I-te. Consul at Foochow reports that tax evasion has become so serious that a new customs house has been established down-stream to search all vessels, caus-ing a great deal of complaint among foreign merchants. If Wang really wants to set up Foreign Inspectorate of Customs, both British and American Consuls can provide information about the one in Shanghai and can give whatever assistance is needed.	2	[F.O. 230/74]
4	Mar 27	02 21	Wang I-te to Bowring. Has received details of Shanghai Inspectorate of Customs from Kiangsu authorities and has written to Commissioner Yeh at Canton about implementing the same at Foochow. Suggests Bowring discusses matter with Yeh himself.	19	129/4
	Mar -	02 -	Bowring to Yeh Ming-ch'en. Again urges settlement of debt owed by Feng Sung-mao.	1	[F.O. 230/74]

F.O. 682/ 1989	Date 1856	HF 6	Description	pp	Old R F.O. 682/
/5	Apr 7	03 03	Yeh Ming-ch'en to Bowring. Has issued strict order to wipe out piracy along coast and many pirates have been captured. Is pleased to read that Royal Navy has been engaged in similarly successful expeditions. Will be happy to give any assistance to clear Hong Kong of outlaws to make island better place for foreigners to live in.	6	129/6
/6	Apr 7	03 03	Yeh Ming-ch'en to Bowring. Efforts to track down Feng Sung-mao have so far failed. Will instruct Magistrate of Nan-hai to intensify search. Declines to victimise firms in which Feng has shares.	8	129/5
/7	Apr 11	03 07	Wang I-te to Bowring. Has received from Kiangsu authorities details about Foreign Inspectorate of Customs at Shanghai, but cannot implement the same at Foochow without Commissioner Yeh's consent. Matter has been referred to Yeh but no reply has been received so far. Again suggests that Bowring discusses matter with Yeh himself.	14	129/7
	Apr 17	03 13	Bowring to Yeh Ming-ch'en. Has no intention of interfering with Chinese domestic policy on collecting customs revenue, but if all other treaty ports follow example of Shanghai by setting up Foreign Inspectorate of Customs, both foreign merchants and Chinese coffers will benefit. Returns herewith Yeh's despatch of 7 Apr 1856 as Yeh has no right to offer to clear Hong Kong of outlaws.	2	[F.O. 230/
	May 16	04 13	Bowring to Yeh Ming-ch'en. Art. 34 of Sino-American Treaty provides for revision on 3 Jul 1856. Most-favoured-nation principle as contained in Art. 8 of Anglo-Chinese Supplementary Treaty entitles Britain to same claim. Is fully empowered to negotiate revision of Anglo-Chinese Treaty. Requests these details be conveyed to Emperor.	2	[F.O. 230.

Date		Description	pp	Old Ref. F.O.
1856	HF 6			682/

May 25	04 [22]	Bowring to Yeh Ming-ch'en. [Crimean War] has ended. Britain has ceased all military action against Russia.	1	[F.O. 230/74]
Jun 16	05 14	Bowring to Yeh Ming-ch'en. Britain has signed treaty with Siam on 5 Apr 1856.	1	[F.O. 230/74]
Jun 30	05 28	Yeh Ming-ch'en to Bowring. Acknowledges receipt of Bowring's letter concerning end of hostilities between Britain and Russia. China has never concerned herself with such hostilities.	6	129/10
Jun 30	05 28	Yeh Ming-ch'en to Bowring. There is provision for treaty revision in Sino-American Treaty, but not in Anglo-Chinese Treaty. Bowring's demand for treaty revision is therefore groundless. Most-favoured-nation clause applies only to privileges granted, and Bowring should know that China has given no privilege to any nation recently.	6	129/8
Jun 30	05 28	Yeh Ming-ch'en to Bowring. Foreign Inspectorate of Customs is tolerated in Shanghai because of rebel occupation of that city. Other treaty ports have not found it necessary to resort to this and must not do so now as this contravenes treaty. Best way to protect honest merchants is to appoint just Consuls. Fukien authorities agree that it is not appropriate to establish Foreign Inspectorate of Customs in Foochow and Amoy. The offer to help clear Hong Kong of outlaws was made in spirit of mutual assistance and co-operation as in pirate suppression, after reports were received of several hundred houses having been set on fire by outlaws in Hong Kong.	6	129/11
Jun 30	05 28	Yeh Ming-ch'en to Bowring. Acknowledges receipt of Bowring's letter concerning signing of Anglo-Siamese Commercial Treaty. Has previous knowledge of such a treaty.	6	129/9

F.O. 682/ 1989	Date 1856	HF 6	Description	pp	Old R F.O. 682/
	Jul 3	06 02	Bowring to Yeh Ming-ch'en. Is report- ing to London on Yeh's refusal to comply with British demand for treaty revision.	2	[F.O. 230/
	Jul 3	06 02	Bowring to Yeh Ming-ch'en. Is report- ing to London on Yeh's refusal to set up in other treaty ports Foreign Inspectorates of Customs similar to that in Shanghai. Accepts both Yeh's explanation and his despatch in which he offered to help clear Hong Kong of outlaws.	2	[F.O. 230/
	Oct 3	09 05	Bowring to Yeh Ming-ch'en. Has heard rumours that China is going to let Russians use Chusan or islands near- by. Reminds Yeh of agreement between Sir John Davis and Ch'i-ying on 4 Apr 1846 that after British evacuat- ion, Chusan was never to be ceded to another Power.	2	[F.O. 230/
/12	Oct 10	09 12	Yeh Ming-ch'en to Bowring. Denies rumour that Russians have been allow- ed to use Chusan Islands.	6	129/
	Oct 12	09 14	Bowring to Yeh Ming-ch'en. [Acting] Consul [H. Parkes] at Canton has reported on hauling down of British flag and detention of crew of [lorcha Arrow]. Gives Yeh two days to apologise, after which Royal Navy will take coercive measures.	2	[F.O. 230/
	Oct 16	09 18	Bowring to Yeh Ming-ch'en. After ultimatum of two days expired, Royal Navy took Chinese Imperial junk hostage.	1	[F.O 230
/13	Oct 21	09 23	Yeh Ming-ch'en to Bowring. Chinese marines have testified that no flags were flying when they boarded lorcha Arrow; sailors have testified that lorcha belongs to Chinese who bought register in Hong Kong. Re- quests that treaty be observed by prohibiting further sales of foreign registers to Chinese ships.	10	129/
/14	Oct 21	09 23	Yeh Ming-ch'en to Bowring. Protests against seizure by Royal Navy of merchant ship in Canton River and wonders which article in peace	7	129/

	Date		Description	pp	Old Ref. F.O. 682/
9	1856	HF 6			

			treaty stipulates that Royal Navy may do so.		
	Oct 30	10 02	Rear-Admiral Sir Michael Seymour to Yeh Ming-ch'en. Canton city is being bombarded because this is only city among five treaty ports that does not admit foreign officials. This additional demand is made because Yeh has obstinately refused to acceed to original demand. Present crisis can only be resolved by Yeh meeting Seymour [inside city of Canton].	2	[F.O. 230/74]
5	Oct 31	10 03	Yeh Ming-ch'en to Seymour. Has returned to [Arrow] all sailors but Consul H. Parkes refused to accept them. As a rule British ships in port have all flags lowered. Since [Arrow] was moored during incident, it is not possible that British flag could have been flying and then lowered. After British bombardment of Canton, citizens are even more hostile to British intention to enter their city.	11	100/1/1
	Nov 1	10 04	Seymour to Yeh Ming-ch'en. Present demand to enter Canton city is not related in any way to previous agreements and promises. Unless this demand is met, more severe measures will be taken.	2	[F.O. 230/74]
	Nov 3	10 06	Yeh Ming-ch'en to Seymour. Has returned all sailors to ship as requested but H. Parkes still refused to receive them. City question is separate issue and was dropped by Bonham in 1849. British bombardment of Canton has caused great resentment.	12	100/1/2
	Nov 5	10 08	Yeh Ming-ch'en to Seymour. Cantonese strongly object to Britons' entering their city. Objection has become even stronger after British bombardment of city, causing many casualties. *Vox populi vox Dei.*	9	100/1/3
	[Nov 5]	10 08	Cantonese to Bowring. British bombardment of Canton has caused much destruction and many deaths. Even if British forces manage to force their way into the city, relatives of victims are bound to take revenge	3	[F.O. 230/74]

F.O. 682/ 1989	Date 1856	HF 6	Description	pp	Old Re F.O. 682/
			and British authorities cannot station troops in city permanently for self-protection. Officials come and go but Cantonese live and die in Canton. Therefore Britons should not make perpetual enemies of Cantonese.		
	Nov 6	10 09	Seymour to Yeh Ming-ch'en. Has nothing to add to his previous communication.	2	[F.O. 230/7
/18	Nov 7	10 10	Yeh Ming-ch'en to Seymour. *Vox populi vox Dei.*	6	100/1
	Nov 9	10 12	Seymour to Yeh Ming-ch'en. It is Yeh's disregard of treaty obligations that has forced Seymour to take military action. Strongly protests about Yeh's attempt to stir up Cantonese by putting a price on every British head. Will resume attack on Canton the day after tomorrow.	2	[F.O. 230/7
	Nov 10	10 13	Bowring to Yeh Ming-ch'en. Accuses Yeh of distorting Sir George Bonham's despatch of 9 Apr 1849 to justify refusing British entry into Canton city. Present difficulties can only be resolved if Yeh agrees to receive Sir Michael Seymour inside city of Canton.	3	[F.O. 230/
	Nov 10	10 13	Bowring to Cantonese. Royal Navy will stop bombarding Canton city only when Yeh Ming-ch'en agrees to admit foreigners into it, and Cantonese may save their city by putting pressure on Yeh.	3	[F.O. 230/
/19	Nov 11	10 14	Yeh Ming-ch'en to Seymour. He has not stirred up Cantonese but British bombardment of civilians and houses has. Such bombardment is unbecoming of a great nation, and is un-civilised.	9	100/1.
	Nov 12	10 09	Seymour to Cantonese. Has power to destroy entire city but so far has reserved shelling for government buildings only. Yeh Ming-ch'en is source of present difficulties. Cantonese must urge him to accept British demands.	2	[F.O. 230/

. ./ 9	Date 1856	HF 6	Description	pp	Old Ref. F.O. 682/
0	Nov 12	10 15	Yeh Ming-ch'en to Bowring. Chinese authorities have every right to arrest Chinese offenders. British flag has never been insulted. To use the dispute over these matters as an excuse to bombard civilian dwellings is an action which only Bowring can justify. Bombardment has made Cantonese even more determined to keep foreigners out of their city.	16	129/15
	Nov 14	10 17	Bowring to Yeh Ming-ch'en. [The Arrow] has a register from Hong Kong and is therefore entitled to fly British flag. Insists that British flag on board has been insulted, and that present difficulties can only be resolved by Yeh admitting foreigners into city of Canton.	3	[F.O. 230/74]
	Nov 15	10 18	Seymour to Yeh Ming-ch'en. On 12 and 13 Nov 1856, Royal Navy captured strategic forts and Chinese soldiers therein, in Hu-men area. Chinese soldiers were later released. If Yeh still refuses to yield, Royal Navy will blow up these forts and attack others in same area.	2	[F.O. 230/74]
1	Nov 16	10 19	Yeh Ming-ch'en to Seymour. Forts at Hu-men were built with money donated by Cantonese for protection against pirates. British destruction of them has antagonised Cantonese further. *Vox populi vox Dei.* Wonders what Britons do while worshipping God every Sunday.	8	100/1/6
	Nov 17	10 20	Seymour's proclamation to Cantonese. Present military measures are not related in any way to negotiations in 1849 to enter Canton city, but related to the insult to British flag and the arrest of people under British protection. These disputes could have been settled easily if Yeh Ming-ch'en had allowed foreign officials into city for negotiations. If Cantonese want to save their city from destruction, they should put pressure on Yeh to meet British demands.	3	[F.O. 230/74]

F.O. 682/ 1989	Date 1856	HF 6	Description	pp	Old R F.O. 682/
/22	Nov 17	10 20	Yeh Ming-ch'en to Bowring. Is surprised to read that Hong Kong law allows Hong Kong registers to be sold to Chinese vessels. Royal Navy bombardment of Canton has so antagonised inhabitants that it has become impossible, for time being at least, for him to go out of the city to meet Bowring, let alone to allow Bowring to enter it.	16	129/1
	Nov 18	10 21	Bowring to Yeh Ming-ch'en. Does not want to go over previous arguments but will ask Rear-Admiral Sir Michael Seymour to stop military operations if Yeh agrees to meeting in Canton city where Bowring, if admitted, has sufficient means for self-protection.	2	[F.O. 230/
/23	Nov 19	10 22	Yeh Ming-ch'en to Bowring. Cannot disobey successive Imperial Edicts forbidding foreigners from entering Canton. Best protection for British merchants is peaceful co-existence with Cantonese, not bombarding them.	8	129/1
	Nov 20	10 23	Bowring to Yeh Ming-ch'en. Regrets that Yeh still refuses to take his advice about meeting in Canton city. Is handing matter back to Rear-Admiral Sir Michael Seymour to do what is necessary and Yeh must accept all consequences. Is reporting to London about present proceedings.	2	[F.O. 230/
/24	Nov 21	10 24	Yeh Ming-ch'en to Bowring. Fact that Emperor, in view of Cantonese opposition, has twice rejected Bowring's request to enter city, shows that Yeh himself is not responsible for Bowring's frustration.	10	129/1
	Dec 6	11 09	Bowring to Yeh Ming-ch'en. Briton has been murdered in village near Canton. Yeh's public proclamation putting a price on any British head must be responsible for this. Severe reprisal will follow.	2	[F.O. 230/
	Dec 9	11 12	Bowring to Viceroy of Liang-Chiang [I-liang] *et al.* Yeh's refusal to	3	[F.O. 230/

apologise for insult to British
flag has led to capture of Imperial
junk, bombardment of Canton city
and destruction of forts in Hu-men
area. Even then Yeh still rejects
meeting in the city. Chinese
rebels have repeatedly asked to be
British allies but have invariably
been turned away. Requests that
these details be made known to
Emperor.

F.O. 682/ 1990	Date 1857	HF 6	Description	pp	Old R F.O. 682/

NOTE: For the year 1857, all the out-going despatches and one of the in-coming despatches appear to be missing. Summaries are made from entries in F.0.230/74 and F.0.230/75, as in previous years.

/1   Jan 6   12 11   Viceroy Wang I-te of Min-Che to Bowring. Cannot write to Emperor about dispute at Canton because he does not know reasons why Bowring has suddenly decided to start hostilities and because it is not possible to find out exactly what happened at Canton which is so far away. Nor can he transmit Bowring's statement to Emperor because it is written in language [English] he does not know. Urges Bowring to keep peace treaty.   12   465/1

/2   Jan 13   12 18   Viceroy I-liang of Liang-Chiang to Bowring. Is pleased to read that Bowring has refrained from causing suffering to Chinese civilians, and has refused to meet rebel leaders. As treaty is meant to preserve eternal peace, memorial to Emperor about Bowring having started the war on the pretext of an alleged insult to British flag will put Bowring in an unfavourable light. Urges Bowring to settle dispute with Commissioner Yeh Ming-ch'en at Canton.   9   465/2

/3   Jan 22   12 27   Governor Chao Te-ch'e of Kiangsu to Bowring. Has not received any document which Bowring asked Consul to forward. Is pleased that Bowring refused to meet rebel leaders and did not allow their boats to approach his, which is evidence of Bowring's determination to observe treaty and to keep peace. Does not know details of hostilities in Canton and therefore cannot write to Emperor about them. Advises Bowring to settle dispute with Commissioner Yeh Ming-ch'en at Canton.   8   465/3

HF 7

  Apr 17   03 23   Bowring to I-liang *et al.* Yeh Ming-ch'en has lied to Emperor about Chinese victories over British   2   [F.0 230

D. 2/ 90	Date 1857	HF 7	Description	pp	Old Ref. F.O. 682/
			forces and about French and American disapproval of British actions. His military tactics are not worthy of a civilized nation. Will keep peace in other four treaty ports unless local Chinese authorities decide otherwise.		
4	May 15	04 22	Chao Te-ch'e to Bowring. Bowring's intention not to allow hostilities in Canton to affect other four treaty ports and to achieve settlement of differences is evidence of his desire for eternal peace. Has received no memo from Yeh Ming-ch'en about his management of affairs in Canton and is therefore not in a position to write to Emperor. Wishes to see speedy return to peace.	7	465/4
5	May 18	04 25	Wang I-te to Bowring. Concerning Bowring's letter denying Yeh Ming-ch'en's claims of Chinese victories over British forces and condemning Yeh's use of guerilla tactics, cannot express opinion as no memo from Yeh is to hand. Declines to forward Bowring's statement to Emperor.	16	465/5
	Dec 10	10 25	Bowring to Yeh Ming-ch'en. Lord Elgin has been appointed H.M. Plenipotentiary with instructions to go to Peking to see Emperor and settle all differences.	2	[F.O. 230/74]
6	Dec 12	10 27	Yeh Ming-ch'en to Bowring. Acknowledges Bowring's letter of 10 Dec 1857 announcing arrival of Lord Elgin, H.M. Plenipotentiary.	5	465/5
	Dec 12	10 27	Elgin to Yeh Ming-ch'en. Demands: (1) entry into Canton city; (2) compensation for losses caused by events subsequent to insult to British flag. Canton is hereby blockaded. If Yeh accepts demands, blockade will be lifted but Ho-nan and all forts in Canton River will be occupied as guarantee. Will attack Canton if Yeh rejects demands or remains silent.	4	[F.O. 230/74]
7	Dec 14	10 29	Yeh Ming-ch'en to Elgin. Entry into	24	465/7

F.O. 682/ 1990	Date 1857	HF 7	Description	pp	Old Re F.O. 682/
			Canton city is not provided for by either Treaty of Nanking or Supplementary Treaty and in any case Sir George Bonham wrote explicitly to abandon any claim for it. Emperor has already rejected successive requests by Bonham and Bowring for treaty revision because treaty was signed to be kept. British flag has never been insulted. Cannot allow Royal Navy to be stationed in Ho-nan because of local opposition.		
	Dec 24	11 09	Rear-Admiral Sir Michael Seymour *et al.* to Yeh Ming-ch'en *et al.* All military personnel must leave Canton and repair to places no less than ninety *li* from city. They must specify where they intend to go, and name places where they wish to hand over the keys to the city gates before leaving.	2	[F.O. 230/
	Dec 24	11 09	Elgin to Yeh Ming-ch'en. Regrets that Yeh shows no sign of yielding. Has ordered attack on Canton.	2	[F.O. 230/
/8	Dec 25	11 10	Yeh Ming-ch'en to Elgin. Was hopeful, when Elgin first arrived six months ago, that he would punish H. Parkes for having started war. As he has not, Cantonese have planned to organise mass petition to Hong Kong but have been stopped by Yeh himself who does not want to put Elgin in a difficult position. Has answered all of Elgin's questions in previous letter. Endorses Elgin's desire for speedy return to peaceful trade.	10	465/8
	Dec 25	11 10	Yeh Ming-ch'en *et al.* to Elgin *et al.* All civil officials, military officers, gentry and people of Canton agree unanimously with Yeh's views as expressed in his various despatches.	2	[F.O. 230/

O.	Date		Description	pp	Old Ref.
2/					F.O.
91	1858	HF 7			682/

TE: *It appears that communication in the form of letters began to be used much more frequently in 1858 than in previous years. Their summaries are therefore prefixed by the word* Letter *in square brackets to differentiate them from the official despatches.* [See the *Introduction for the difference between despatches and letters*]. *Furthermore, four documents summarised herewith were not recorded in the entry books F.O. 230/74 and F.O. 230/75. They were related to affairs in Canton after H.M. Plenipotentiary, Lord Elgin, had gone to North China for negotiations* [see the note to 1859].

/1   Jan 5   11 21   Po-kuei *et al.* to Elgin. Request   7   121A/1
that all future correspondence be
addressed to them.

/2   Jan 9   11 25   Seymour *et al.* to Po-kuei. Propose   10   499/1
four regulations for administration
of Canton: (1) English and French
deputies will be appointed to form
Bureau of Occupation in Governor's
yamen which will henceforth be
guarded by English and French
soldiers; (2) crimes committed
inside military zone will be dealt
with by military court; those out-
side and involving Chinese only
will be dealt with by Chinese
officials, those involving foreigners
and Chinese will be dealt with by
said Bureau of Occupation; (3) all
official notices must bear seal of
Bureau of Occupation; (4) all
weapons and military equipments
must be handed over to occupying
forces.

/3   Jan 9   11 25   Copy of previous entry.   7   499/11

/4   Jan 9   11 25   Po-kuei to Seymour *et al.* Agrees to   6   121A/2
comply with all four proposals.

/5   Jan 9   11 25   Seymour *et al.* to Tartar-General Mu-   6   499/2
k'e-te-na of Canton. Grant his
request to let Banner soldiers remain
in Manchu quarters on condition they
do not carry weapons or go out in
groups.

/6   Jan 9   11 25   Copy of previous entry.   5   499/12

/7   Jan 9   11 25   Mu-k'e-te-na to Seymour. Agrees to   5   121A/3
comply with Seymour's conditions.

/8   Jan 13   11 29   Po-kuei to Elgin. Requests that trade   8   121A/4
be resumed and Allied Forces

F.O. 682/ 1991	Date 1858	HF 7	Description	pp	Old Re F.O. 682/
			withdrawn from Canton as soon as possible.		
/9	Jan 20	12 06	Elgin to Po-kuei. Will evacuate Canton only after peace agreement is reached with Peking. Establishment of Bureau of Occupation to govern foreigners, leaving administration of Chinese to Chinese officials, is evidence of good intention of British and French authorities and is quickest way to resume normal trade.	10	499/3
/10	Jan 20	12 06	Copy of previous entry. Encl. Copy of report on meeting between Elgin and Po-kuei [on 9 Jan 1858].	10 2	499/13 499/13
/11	Jan 24	12 10	Po-kuei to Elgin. Is pleased that Elgin agrees to resume trade immediately.	8	121A/5
/12	Jan 31	12 17	Po-kuei to Elgin. Feels extremely humiliated by H. Parkes' arbitrary action of taking six Chinese prisoners from Nan-hai prison and twenty-one from P'an-yü together with the chief warder. Threatens to commit suicide if insult is not redressed.	10	121A/6
/13	Jan 31	12 17	Elgin to Po-kuei. Rejects Po-kuei's claim that officials of Bureau of Occupation have no right to inspect prison cells of Nan-hai and P'an-yü. Chinese prisoners who have offered clues to whereabouts of some foreign captives are now under foreign protection. Urges Po-kuei to publicise widely his notice of amnesty to all Chinese who have been employed by foreigners.	8	499/4
/14	Jan 31	12 17	Copy of previous entry.	7	499/1
/15	Jan 31	12 17	Elgin to Po-kuei. Was shocked by what he saw while inspecting prisons of Nan-hai and P'an-yü. Has consulted Baron Gros and both have decided to set up clinic to treat sick prisoners and charge all expenses to Canton government.	8	499/5

). 2/ 91	Date 1858	HF 7	Description	pp	Old Ref. F.O. 682/
16	Jan 31	12 17	Copy of previous entry.	7	499/15
17	Feb 4	12 21	Elgin to Po-kuei. Has decided together with Baron Gros, to lift blockade of Canton River and to re-open trade. Cantonese should be urged to co-exist peacefully with foreigners.	10	499/6
18	Feb 4	12 21	Copy of previous entry.	10	499/16
19	Feb 8	12 25	Elgin to Po-kuei. Customs duties cannot be levied at Canton by Chinese authorities as city is under foreign occupation. Suggests that temporary Chinese customs office be established at Whampoa to collect duties.	5	499/7
20	Feb 8	12 25	Copy of previous entry.	5	499/17
21	Feb 8	12 25	Po-kuei to Elgin. Is pleased that Elgin has decided to resume trade on 10 Feb 1858. Requests Elgin to send deputy to work in conjunction with Hoppo.	6	121A/7
22	Feb 9	12 26	Po-kuei to Elgin. Has appointed Yü Ssu-i to Whampoa to work in conjunction with British [Vice-] Consul on customs matters.	6	121A/8
23	Feb 10	12 27	Elgin to Yü-ch'eng. Has arrived at Shanghai after capturing Canton. Demands appointment of Imperial Commissioner within seven days to negotiate new treaty which should give free access to Peking by foreign envoys, free travel in interior of China, free trade in all ports along coast and rivers; heavy transit dues and exactions should be abolished; piracy should be suppressed; and Christians should no longer be persecuted.	26	499/8
24	Feb 10	12 27	Copy of previous entry.	30	499/18
25	Feb 10	12 27	Elgin to Viceroy Ho Kuei-ch'ing of Liang-Chiang and Governor Chao Te-ch'e of Kiangsu. Requests them to forward his letter to Grand Secretary Yü-ch'eng.	6	499/9

F.O. 682/ 1991	Date 1858	HF 7	Description	pp	Old Re F.O. 682/
/26	Feb 10	12 27	Copy of previous entry.	6	499/19
/27	Feb 13	12 30	Elgin to Po-kuei. Lists names of two clerks and three constables of Hsiang-shan magistracy, who have blackmailed families of those employed by foreign merchants in Macao and Hong Kong; requests that action be taken against them.	6	499/10
/28	Feb 13	12 30	Copy of previous entry.	6	499/20
		HF 8			
/29	Feb 16	01 03	Po-kuei to Elgin. Agrees to order Hsiang-shan authorities to stop harassing families of Chinese employed by foreigners in Hong Kong and Macao, and to punish the five [two clerks and three constables] guilty of such harassment.	6	121A/9
/30	Mar 3	01 18	Po-kuei to Elgin. Commissioner Yeh Ming-ch'en has been dismissed. Huang Tsung-han is new Commissioner and before his arrival at Canton, Po-kuei is to act in his place. Chiang Kuo-lin is to become Acting Governor.	6	121A/
/31a	Mar 21	02 07	Ho Kuei-ch'ing and Chao Te-ch'e to Elgin. Transmit Grand Councillor Wen-hsiang's reply to Elgin on Yü-ch'eng's behalf: Yü-ch'eng is not in charge of foreign affairs and is therefore not allowed to communicate with Elgin; urges Elgin to return to Canton as new Imperial Commissioner for Foreign Affairs has been appointed and is on his way to Canton.	9	121A/
/31b	Apr -	02 -	C.A. Winchester [Vice-Consul in charge at Canton] to Po-kuei. Encloses two leases of land [both missing] at Whampoa, one for building Vice-Consulate and the other for building dockyard.	6	327/5/

). 2/ 91	Date 1858	HF 8	Description	pp	Old Ref. F.O. 682/
32	Apr 1	02 18	Elgin to Yü-ch'eng. Is returning to Ho Kuei-ch'ing and Chao Te-ch'e their joint despatch in which they transmitted message from Wen-hsiang to the effect that Yü-ch'eng is not in charge of foreign affairs and therefore cannot communicate with Elgin. Regards such reply as breach of treaty and insult to Great Britain. Will proceed north to contact courtiers directly.	8	499/21
33a	Apr 1	02 18	Elgin to Ho Kuei-ch'ing and Chao Te-ch'e. Returns herewith their joint despatch of 21 Mar 1858 in which they transmitted Wen-hsiang's reply, as such reply is unacceptable. Requests that enclosed despatch to [Yü-ch'eng] be forwarded to Peking.	5	499/22
33b	Apr 22	03 09	Colonel Chang of Ta-p'eng to Hong Kong authorities. Inquiries concerning Hong Kong vessel detained near Ningpo should be directed to Chinese authorities at Ningpo.	7	1124B/2
34	Apr 24	03 11	Elgin to Yü-ch'eng. Has arrived at Tientsin. Demands appointment of Imperial Commissioner within six days to treat.	8	499/23
35	Apr 24	03 11	Elgin to Viceroy T'an T'ing-hsiang of Chihli. Requests that letter to Yü-ch'eng be forwarded.	5	499/24
36	Apr 26	03 13	Ch'ung-lun and Wu-le-hung-o to Elgin. Have been appointed Imperial Commissioners to negotiate with Elgin at Tientsin.	6	121A/12
37	Apr 29	03 16	T'an T'ing-hsiang to Elgin. Has been appointed Joint Imperial Commissioner with Ch'ung-lun and Wu-le-hung-o to negotiate with Elgin at Tientsin. Requests Elgin to appoint date for meeting. PS. Has ordered scribe to correct format of communication.	7	121A/13
38	Apr 30	03 17	Elgin to T'an T'ing-hsiang. Is pleased to read that T'an has been asked by Emperor to meet him at Taku. Inquires if T'an has plenipotentiary	7	499/25

F.O. 682/ 1991	Date 1858	HF 8	Description	pp	Old Re F.O. 682/
			powers. Demands answer within two hours. If there is no answer or if answer is negative, will regard China as having refused to appoint Imperial Commissioner to treat.		
/39	Apr 30	03 17	T'an T'ing-hsiang to Elgin. Proposes a meeting tomorrow.	5	121A/1
	[May 1]	[03] 18	[Letter] Elgin to [T'an T'ing-hsiang]. Is not satisfied with T'an's reply and therefore declines meeting. Will write official despatch later.	1	[F.O. 230/7
/40	May 6	03 23	Elgin to T'an T'ing-hsiang. Regrets T'an does not possess plenipotentiary powers. Demands appointment, within six days, of officials with powers similar to those enjoyed by Ch'i-ying and I-li-pu in 1842. Encl. Imperial edict appointing Ch'i-ying and I-li-pu Joint Plenipotentiaries, 26 Jul 1842.	8 1	499/26
/41	May 10	03 27	T'an T'ing-hsiang *et al.* to Elgin. Assures Elgin that they possess plenipotentiary powers equivalent to those formerly enjoyed by Ch'i-ying and I-li-pu.	9	121A/1
	May 19	04 07	Elgin to T'an T'ing-hsiang. As T'an T'ing-hsiang, Ch'un-lun and Wu-le-hung-o have to refer decisions to Emperor, they are obviously not accredited with plenipotentiary powers. Will sail up [Peiho]. Demands evacuation of all forts guarding river as allied Anglo-French forces are going to occupy them.	3	[F.O. 230/7
/42	May 20	04 08	Elgin to T'an T'ing-hsiang. Regrets that Emperor has allowed himself to be led to believe that the Russian Minister can persuade Anglo-French forces to withdraw. Has decided to sail up Peiho all the way to Peking. Demands that all forts guarding the river be evacuated as Anglo-French forces are going to occupy them.	14	499/27
	May 24	04 12	T'an T'ing-hsiang *et al.* to Elgin. They want to pacify the people while Britons want to trade.	1	[F.O. 230/7

). 2/ 31	Date 1858	HF 8	Description	pp	Old Ref. F.O. 682/
			British ships entering Peiho will [cause consternation among the people]. Will go to Peking to plead with Emperor to [consider British demands].		
43	May 29	04 17	T'an T'ing-hsiang *et al.* to Elgin. Kuei-liang and Hua-sha-na have been sent by Emperor to Tientsin for negotiations.	4	121A/16
44a	May 31	04 19	Elgin to Yü-ch'eng. Has listed demands before, and if Imperial Commissioner with plenipotentiary powers is still not appointed, China must bear full responsibility for what is going to happen.	6	499/28
44b	Jun 1	04 20	Intendant Ssu-t'u at Ch'üan-chou to Acting Consul W.R. Gingell at Amoy. Declines to change rate of *likin* on opium.	11	112/4B/3
45	Jun 3	04 22	Kuei-liang and Hua-sha-na to Elgin. Have been appointed Joint Imperial Commissioners to treat; arrived at Tientsin yesterday; propose meeting tomorrow.	4	291/1
46	Jun 4	04 23	Elgin to Kuei-liang and Hua-sha-na. Wonders if they possess plenipotentiary powers; wishes to see their seals during meeting.	8	499/29
47	Jun 5	04 24	Kuei-liang and Hua-sha-na to Elgin. Cannot understand conditions set down in Elgin's communication to Grand Secretary Yü-ch'eng dated 10 Feb 1858. Request that H.N. Lay be sent over to interpret them.	4	121A/18
48	Jun 5	04 24	Copy of previous entry.	4	291/2
49	Jun 6	04 25	Kuei-liang and Hua-sha-na to Elgin. Imperial Edict of appointment as Joint Imperial Commissioners gives them plenipotentiary powers. China does not issue seals to Imperial Commissioners.	8	121A/17
50	Jun 6	04 25	Copy of previous entry.	8	291/3
51	Jun 7	04 26	Elgin to Kuei-liang and Hua-sha-na. Is surprised to read that they do	8	499/30

F.O. 682/ 1991	Date 1858	HF 8	Description	pp	Old R F.O. 682/
			not possess the seal of Imperial Commissioners. Encloses copies of two letters from I-li-pu on 10 Aug 1842 indicating that he possessed such a seal. [Enclosures wanting]		
/52	Jun 9	04 28	Ch'i-ying to Elgin. Has arrived, charged with management of foreign affairs. Hopes to visit Elgin in a day or two.	5	121A/
/53	Jun 9	04 28	Copy of previous entry.	4	291/4
/54	Jun 9	04 28	Kuei-liang and Hua-sha-na to Elgin. Ch'i-ying's appointment as Viceroy of Liang-Kuang, charged with additional duty of managing foreign affairs was a permanent one. Imperial Commissioners are, as a rule, temporary appointments; but since Elgin insists on their having a seal, have requested Emperor to issue one to them.	8	121A/
/55	Jun 9	04 28	Copy of previous entry.	8	291/!
/56	Jun 11	05 01	Elgin to Kuei-liang and Hua-sha-na. Has sent H.N. Lay to explain and discuss terms of peace, but after three days Chinese still cannot produce draft treaty. Is most un- happy and is sending T. Wade and H.N. Lay to fetch draft tomorrow.	10	499/.
/57	Jun 11	05 01	Ch'i-ying to Elgin. Has been appoint- ed Joint Imperial Commissioner with Kuei-liang and Hua-sha-na, sharing same seal.	4	121A/
/58	Jun 11	05 01	Copy of previous entry.	4	291/
/59	Jun 11	05 01	Kuei-liang et al. to Elgin. Blue- jackets who arrived last night went ashore this afternoon to plunder. Request that they be restrained.	4	121A.
/60	Jun 11	05 01	Copy of previous entry.	4	291/
/61	Jun 11	05 01	Kuei-liang et al. to Elgin. Outline result of meetings with Lay: (1) tax may be fixed to satisfaction of both parties; (2) China has never persecut- ed, and will never persecute missionaries; (3) will co-operate	16	121A

. / 1	Date 1858	HF 8	Description	pp	Old Ref. F.O. 682/
			in suppression of piracy; (4) Britons going into interior of China will only cause endless trouble; (5) cannot accept that henceforth all correspondence be written in English; (6) war and hence indemnity is entirely responsibility of Canton; (7) residence in Peking may be found for British envoy, but to be used only as occasions arise.		
2	Jun 11	05 01	Copy of previous entry.	17	291/8
3	Jun 11	05 01	Kuei-liang *et al.* to Elgin. Reply to Elgin's seven demands, rejecting most of them. Endorsement: copy made, original returned.	16	121A/24
4	Jun 11	05 01	Copy of previous entry.	12	291/9
5	Jun 12	05 02	Elgin to Kuei-liang *et al.* Acknow-ledges that Ch'i-ying has also been appointed Imperial Commissioner. Will read draft treaty carefully, hoping that it will soon be final-ised and signed.	6	499/32
6	Jun 13	05 03	Kuei-liang *et al.* to Elgin. Will send deputies to meet those of Elgin at 3 p.m. tomorrow at Feng-shen-miao. Have received seal of Imperial Commissioner.	5	121A/25
7	Jun 13	05 03	Copy of previous entry.	5	291/10
8	Jun 21	05 11	Kuei-liang and Hua-sha-na to Elgin. Last night, Anglo-French soldiers again terrorised Chinese civilians. Request restraint.	6	121A/26
9	Jun 21	05 11	Copy of previous entry.	6	291/11
0	Jun 21	05 11	Kuei-liang and Hua-sha-na to Elgin. Emperor has decreed: (1) trade in Yangtze area should wait till rebellion is suppressed; (2) travel by foreigners in Chinese hinterland is fraught with danger; (3) periodic visits to Peking are better than a permanent residence by envoys; (4) foreigners taking over domestic trade will deprive Chinese merchants of	14	121A/27

F.O. 682/ 1991	Date 1858	HF 8	Description	pp	Old R F.O. 682/
			their livelihood and is certain to result in disaffection.		
/71	Jun 21	05 11	Copy of previous entry.	12	291/1
/72	Jun 22	05 12	Elgin to Kuei-liang *et al.* Requests that a time be appointed tomorrow for signing the treaty.	5	499/3
/73	Jun 30	05 20	Kuei-liang and Hua-sha-na to Elgin. Emperor has read treaties with Britain, France, America and Russia, all signed on 28 Jun 1858.	5	121A/
/74	Jun 30	05 20	Copy of previous entry.	6	291/1
/75	Jul 1	05 21	Kuei-liang and Hua-sha-na to Elgin. Will send treaties to Shanghai once they are ratified by Emperor. Agree to ask Emperor to appoint Governor Chao Te-ch'e and Provincial Judge Hsüeh Huan, both of Kiangsu, to settle at Shanghai details of tariff regulations.	8	121A/
/76	Jul 1	05 21	Copy of previous entry.	8	291/1
/77	Jul 1	05 21	Elgin to Kuei-liang *et al.* As Emperor has read treaty, Elgin expects Emperor to approve it soon.	4	499/3
/78	Jul 2	05 22	Elgin to Kuei-liang and Hua-sha-na. Is shocked by their request that he waits in Shanghai for Emperor's approval of treaty. Encloses copy of Imperial Edict, which shows how quickly Emperor Tao-kuang approved the Treaty of Nanking and how quickly news of that approval was relayed to Nanking. If Emperor should vacillate further, troops newly arrived from Hong Kong will be transferred to Tientsin.	9	499/3
/79	Jul 2	05 22	Kuei-liang and Hua-sha-na to Elgin. Acknowledge receipt of copy of Imperial Edict by former Emperor, Tao-kuang. In view of this, will send treaty to Peking for Emperor's approval and should have answer in three to four days.	5	121A/
/80	Jul 2	05 22	Copy of previous entry.	6	291/

). 2/ 31	Date 1858	HF 8	Description	pp	Old Ref. F.O. 682/
31	Jul 3	05 23	Elgin to Kuei-liang and Hua-sha-na. They should, in accordance with Art. 26 of treaty, promptly go to request Emperor to appoint Governor Chao Te-ch'e and Provincial Judge Hsüeh Huan, both of Kiangsu, to thrash out details of tariff regulations as provided for by Art. 28.	6	499/36
32	Jul 4	05 24	Kuei-liang and Hua-sha-na to Elgin. Transmit Imperial Edict. Encl. Imperial Edict in which Emperor has endorsed treaties with vermilion pen, 3 July 1858.	5 2	121A/31
33	Jul 4	05 25	Copy of previous entry.	4	291/16
34	Jul 4	05 24	Kuei-liang and Hua-sha-na to Elgin. Once back in Peking, they will request Emperor to appoint Governor Chao Te-ch'e and Provincial Judge Hsüeh Huan, both of Kiangsu to settle at Shanghai details of tariff regulations.	5	121A/32
35	Jul 4	05 24	Copy of previous entry.	6	291/19
36	Jul 5	05 25	Elgin to Kuei-liang and Hua-sha-na. Has asked T. Wade to make two copies of treaty and three copies of agreement. He will take them tomorrow to Kuei-liang and Hua-sha-na to be signed. Chinese may keep one copy of each and return the rest to Elgin.	6	499/37
37	Jul 5	05 25	Kuei-liang and Hua-sha-na to Elgin. Will sign both copies of treaty and special stipulation and return one of each to Elgin.	6	121A/34
38	Jul 5	05 25	Copy of previous entry.	6	291/21
39	Jul 5	05 25	Elgin to Kuei-liang and Hua-sha-na. Is leaving Tientsin soon. Hopes to see them before leaving. Proposes to meet tomorrow but leaves them to fix a time.	5	499/38
0	Jul 5	05 25	Kuei-liang and Hua-sha-na to Elgin. Agree to meet and propose to do so at 6 a.m. tomorrow.	6	121A/33
1	Jul 5	05 25	Copy of previous entry.	6	291/20

F.O. 682/ 1991	Date 1858	HF 8	Description	pp	Old Re F.O. 682/
/92a	Jul 5	05 25	Elgin to Kuei-liang and Hua-sha-na. Is pleased to read that Emperor has approved treaty; thanks them for their labour and expects lasting peace.	6	499/3S
/92b	Jul 6	05 26	Receipt for two boxes containing copies of old treaties with Great Britain and with Sweden.	1	386/1,
/93	Jul 22	06 12	Elgin to Kuei-liang and Hua-sha-na. Has arrived at Shanghai for ten days but has still not heard that Chao Te-ch'e and Hsüeh Huan have been appointed to negotiate tariff agreement. Royal Navy in Tientsin will not be withdrawn until such agreement is reached.	6	499/4
/94	Jul 24	06 14	Ho Kuei-ch'ing to Elgin. Has been ordered to proceed to Shanghai to settle trade and tariff regulations jointly with Kuei-liang, Hua-sha-na, Chi-p'u and Ming-shan. Will arrive at Shanghai early next month.	7	121A/
/95	Jul 24	06 14	Copy of previous entry.	6	291/1
/96	Jul 30	06 20	Elgin to Ho Kuei-ch'ing. As Imperial Commissioners will not arrive for another ten days, will leave Shanghai for time being. T. Wade will deal with correspondence during Elgin's absence.	6	499/4
/97	Aug 12	07 04	Copy of next entry.	6	291/1
/98	Aug 12	07 04	Kuei-liang and Hua-sha-na to Elgin. Acknowledge that Elgin has been wait-ing at Shanghai for ten days. Have been ordered by Emperor to investigate tariff arrangements in Kiangsu first and therefore do not expect to arrive at Shanghai until September. Mean-while Provincial Judge Hsüeh Huan of Kiangsu has been authorized to begin preliminary negotiations.	7	121A/
/99	Sep 6	07 29	Ho Kuei-ch'ing to Elgin. Regrets that Elgin has been kept waiting at Shanghai. Has despatched messengers to urge Kuei-liang to come soon. Pleads with Elgin to wait till Kuei-liang's arrival before departing for England.	7	121A/
/100	Sep 6	07 29	Copy of previous entry.	8	291/2

). */)1	Date		Description	pp	Old Ref. F.O.
	1858	HF 8			682/
)1	Sep 7	08 01	Elgin to Kuei-liang *et al.* Is shocked to read that they will not reach Shanghai until end of month. Proposes to negotiate at Tientsin instead of Shanghai.	8	499/42
)2	Sep 7	08 01	Elgin to Kuei-liang and Hua-sha-na. Protests against use of word *i* in recent Imperial Edict.	10	499/43
*3	Sep 22	08 16	Ho Kuei-ch'ing to Elgin. Kuei-liang and Hua-sha-na have arrived at Ch'ing-chiang-p'u and are about to board ship for Shanghai.	5	121A/37
*4	Sep 22	08 16	Copy of previous entry.	4	291/23
*5	Sep 25	08 19	Elgin to Ho Kuei-ch'ing. Thanks him for having despatched messenger to urge Kuei-liang and Hua-sha-na to speed up their journey.	4	499/44
*6	Oct 6	08 30	Kuei-liang *et al.* to Elgin. Have all arrived at Shanghai. Request Elgin to send deputies to meet theirs for a preliminary discussion.	7	121A/38
*7	Oct 6	08 30	Copy of previous entry.	6	291/24A
*8	Oct 6	08 30	[Letter] Kuei-liang and Hua-sha-na to Elgin. Arrived two days ago and had wanted to pay courtesy visit immediately but could not do so as they had to settle official matters first. Have appointed deputies for preliminary negotiations and hope Elgin will do same.	2	291/24B
*9	[Oct 6] [08 30]	n.d.	Incomplete original of previous entry.	1	121A/44
*0	Oct 6	08 30	Elgin to Kuei-liang and Hua-sha-na. Is pleased that they have finally arrived at Shanghai. Protests that Viceroy Huang Tsung-han of Liang-Kuang *et al.* are inviting donations, organising militia against foreigners, and placing 30,000 taels on the head of H. Parkes. Hong Kong authorities attempted to spread word of Tientsin Treaty but their small boat was fired upon by militia from Hsin-an. Consequently Royal Navy launched an attack on Hsin-an.	8	499/45

F.O. 682/ 1991	Date 1858	HF 8	Description	pp	Old Re F.O. 682/
/111	Oct 9	09 03	Elgin to Kuei-liang and Hua-sha-na. Insists that Huang Tsung-han *et al.* must be dismissed.	8	499/46
/112	Oct 9	09 03	Kuei-liang and Hua-sha-na to Elgin. Regret delay in arrival at Shanghai caused by illness of one Commissioner who subsequently had to be replaced. Will order scribes in Peking never to use word *i* again.	6	121A/3
/113	Oct 9	09 03	Copy of previous entry.	6	291/25
/114	Oct 9	09 03	Kuei-liang and Hua-sha-na to Elgin. Huang Tsung-han *et al.* are still preparing for defence against foreigners, obviously because news of peace has not yet reached Kwangtung. Will notify them immediately. Will also proclaim peace to local populace. Encl. Copy of proclamation of peace.	12 1	121A/L
/115	Oct 9	09 03	Copy of previous entry.	10	291/2
/116	Oct 11	09 05	Elgin to Kuei-liang and Hua-sha-na. Is pleased to read that they will try to have Huang Tsung-han *et al.* dismissed and requests copy of Imperial Edict to this effect when it is issued. Will send deputies to negotiate tariff agreement.	6	499/4
/117	Oct 11	09 05	Kuei-liang and Hua-sha-na to Elgin. Had impeached Huang Tsung-han *et al.* even before arrival at Shanghai. Are certain that Imperial Edict dismissing them will come soon.	7	121A/
/118	Oct 11	09 05	Kuei-liang *et al.* to Elgin. Will notify Elgin as soon as Imperial Edict dismissing Huang Tsung-han *et al.* is received. Requests Elgin to send deputy of rank equal to Provincial Treasurer for meeting tomorrow at 2 p.m.	7	121A/
/119a	Oct 12	09 06	Elgin to Kuei-liang *et al.* Is sending R. Alcock, T. Wade and H.N. Lay as his deputies to negotiate tariff agreement.	6	499/4
/119b	Oct 15	09 09	[Letter: Kuei-liang *et al.*] to Elgin. Propose to visit him on 16 Oct 1858	1	386/1

.O. 82/ 991	Date 1858	HF 8	Description	pp	Old Ref. F.O. 682/
			at noon.		
	Oct 16	09 10	[Letter] Elgin to Kuei-liang *et al.* Agrees to receive them at noon.	1	[F.O. 230/74]
	Oct 17	09 11	[Letter] Elgin to Kuei-liang and Hua-sha-na. Proposes to return visit tomorrow at noon.	1	[F.O. 230/74]
119c	Oct 18	09 12	[Letter: Kuei-liang *et al.* to Elgin.] Will await his visit at noon.	1	386/1/1
120	Oct 22	09 16	Kuei-liang *et al.* to Elgin. Had agreed to all demands at Tientsin because of enormous military pressure. After reporting to Peking, they feel that the permanent residence of British envoy in Peking will damage reputation of dynasty irreparably and will cause even worse rebellions. Plead with Elgin to choose any place other than Peking as permanent residence.	18	121A/43
121	Oct 25	09 19	Elgin to Kuei-liang *et al.* Rejects request to change Art. 3 of Treaty which provides for permanent residence of foreign envoys in Peking.	10	499/49
122	Oct 28	09 22	Kuei-liang *et al.* to Elgin. Elgin had declared that none of his demands was intended to harm China in any way; but his demand for permanent or even periodic residence in Peking would. Request Elgin to reconsider this demand but will of course abide by treaty if Elgin rejects request.	10	121A/45
123a	Oct 29	09 23	Elgin to Kuei-liang *et al.* Will consider requesting H.M. Government not to have envoy permanently resident in Peking, but to have him make periodic visits there as occasions require.	10	499/50
123b	Oct 30	09 24	[Letter: Kuei-liang and Hua-sha-na to Elgin.] Propose to visit Elgin at 2 [p.m.].	1	386/1/8
	Oct 30	09 24	[Letter] Elgin to Kuei-liang and Hua-sha-na. Will await their visit at 2 [p.m.].	1	[F.O. 230/74]

F.O. 682/ 1991	Date 1858	HF 8	Description	pp	Old Ref. F.O. 682/
/124a	Oct 30	09 24	Bowring to Po-kuei. Is sending R. Alcock to Canton as Consul.	8	327/5/113
/124b	Oct 30	09 24	Elgin to Kuei-liang *et al*. Plans to make tour of inspection in Yangtze area.	4	499/51
/125	Oct 31	09 25	Kuei-liang *et al*. to Elgin. Have notified authorities in Yangtze area of Elgin's pending visit and sent deputy with appropriate papers to accompany Elgin.	6	121A/46
/126	Oct 31	09 25	Copy of previous entry.	6	291/27
/127	Nov 5	09 30	Kuei-liang *et al*. to Elgin. Request: (1) specifications of passports for Britons travelling in interior of China; (2) that merchants must not be allowed to become Consuls; (3) that since past Consuls have proved to be arrogant and reckless, their ranks and Chinese equivalents must now be specified, and they must be required to consult their seniors instead of stampeding them; (4) that foreign flags must no longer be issued to Chinese boats.	15	121A/47
/128a	Nov 5	09 30	Copy of previous entry.	16	291/28
/128b	Nov 5	09 30	[Letter] Kuei-liang and Hua-sha-na to Elgin. Scribes cannot cope with transcription of lengthy tariff agreement. Request one day's grace, postponing the signing of tariff agreement from 6 Nov to 7 Nov 1858.	1	386/1/2
/129	Nov 6	10 01	Kuei-liang *et al*. to Elgin. Ask Elgin to specify how the two million taels of indemnity for which Canton is responsible may be paid, whether or not he wishes to follow French example of payment by six annual instalments.	8	121A/48
/130	Nov 6	10 01	Copy of previous entry.	8	291/29
/131	Nov 6	10 01	Kuei-liang *et al*. to Elgin. Urge payment of Shanghai back duties.	8	121A/49
/132	Nov 6	10 01	Copy of previous entry.	8	291/30
/133a	Nov 7	10 02	Po-kuei to Bowring. Notes that R. Alcock is being sent to Canton as Consul.	6	327/5/11♦

F.O. 82/ 991	Date 1858	HF 8	Description	pp	Old Ref. F.O. 682/
133b	n.d. [Dec 8]	n.d. [11 04]	[Letter] Elgin to [Viceroy Kuan-wen of Hu-Kuang]. Proposes to visit him tomorrow at 2 p.m.	1	68/1/18
134	Dec 9	11 05	[Letter] Viceroy Kuan-wen of Hu-Kuang to Elgin. Invites Elgin to a feast inside the city. Will put four viceregal sedan-chairs [and their bearers] at his disposal.	1	386/1/10

F.O. 682/ 1992	Date 1859	HF 8	Description	pp	Old Ref F.O. 682/

NOTE: *Quite a few documents of the year 1859 were not copied into the entry-*
books F.O. 230/74 and F.O. 230/75. They were despatches between the
Allied Forces occupying Canton and the Chinese authorities in that city
A possible explanation is that the Chinese Secretary was part of the
establishment of H.M. Plenipotentiary and he recorded only the
communications to and from the Plenipotentiary, who was negotiating in
North China at this time. They are summarised herewith ·to give a
fuller picture of the period.

/1a   Jan 6   12 03   [Letter: Kuei-liang *et al.* to Elgin.]   1   386/1/5
Are pleased to hear that Elgin has
returned from Hankow. Propose to
come tomorrow to wish him a Happy
New Year.

/1b   Jan 9   12 06   [Letter: Elgin to Kuei-liang *et al.*]   1   386/1/9
Received their letter only today.
Will be pleased to receive them
tomorrow at 2 pm.

/1c   Jan 12   12 09   Elgin to Kuei-liang *et al.* Report   8   121A/50
from Canton indicates that Vice-
roy Huang Tsung-han and gentry are
still actively engaged in anti-
foreign activities.

/2   Jan 13   12 10   Kuei-liang *et al.* to Elgin.   7   458/1
Enclose Imperial Edict. Testify
that what Elgin enclosed before
must be a false edict.
Encl. Imperial Edict: whether or not
Huang Tsung-han should be dismissed
if he did disobey Imperial
Edict is for Emperor to decide and
it is not up to Kuei-liang *et al.*
to impeach him, 21 Oct 1858.

/3   Jan 13   12 10   Elgin to Kuei-liang *et al.* Only   16   121A/5
vessels with British register and
a British captain or owner can fly
British flag; agrees that Consuls
should not take military action
but should consult superiors on
important matters; cannot answer
question of other nations employing
merchants as Consuls; China should
send envoys abroad to see the world.

/4   Jan 14   12 11   Elgin to Kuei-liang *et al.* Complains   7   121A/5
that no action has been taken
against Huang Tsung-han and gentry.
If special provision agreed upon at
Tientsin is not promptly acted upon,

O.	Date		Description	pp	Old Ref.
•2/					F.O.
92	1859	HF 8			682/

			all Chinese officials in Canton will be expelled and customs duties taken over to pay garrison in city.		
/5	Jan 17	12 14	Kuei-liang *et al.* to Elgin. Are pleased Elgin agrees that: (1) passports for travel in interior of China should be issued only to respectable Britons; suggest that such passports be printed in both languages and stamped with both Chinese official and British consular seals, and that they be cancelled when trip is completed; (2) British flags be issued only to British ships; (3) Consuls should report to superiors if in doubt instead of taking arbitrary action; (4) foreigners without treaty relations with China be dealt with separately.	14	458/2
/6	Jan 17	12 14	Kuei-liang *et al.* to Elgin. Re-iterate that they did impeach Huang Tsung-han *et al.* and that Imperial Edict was true version. It is up to Emperor, and not to them, to decide if Huang Tsung-han *et al.* should be dismissed.	9	458/3
/7	Jan 20	12 17	Elgin to Kuei-liang *et al.* British soldiers have been attacked by Chinese militia in villages near Canton. Will order Allied Forces to punish militia severely. Protests against Emperor's refusal to dismiss Viceroy Huang Tsung-han and gentry. Will settle account with Emperor on arrival at Peking to exchange treaties.	12	121A/53
/8	Jan 21	12 18	Kuei-liang *et al.* to Elgin. Are certain that their impeachment of Huang Tsung-han *et al.* will bring desired result. Are equally incensed by Kwangtung militia firing on British soldiers and will request Emperor to issue strict orders to restrain them.	9	458/19
/9	Jan 23	12 20	Elgin to Kuei-liang *et al.* Is pleased that Kuei-liang *et al.* are going to make another request to Emperor to dismiss Huang Tsung-han	10	121A/54

F.O. 682/ 1992	Date 1859	HF 8	Description	pp	Old Re F.O. 682/
			and gentry. Will go to Canton for thirty to forty days to pacify Cantonese before returning to Shanghai to discuss remaining matters on agenda.		
/10	Jan 23	12 20	Elgin to Kuei-liang *et al*. Allied Forces at Canton have captured the militia base of An-liang-chü at Shih-ching, and seized papers which implicate Kuei-liang *et al*.	6	121A/5
/11	Jan 24	12 21	Kuei-liang *et al*. to Elgin. Appreciate Elgin's intention to spend thirty to forty days in Canton, but request that he does not do so, promising that they have effective ways of dealing with problems at Canton.	9	458/18
/12	Jan 25	12 22	Elgin to Kuei-liang and Hua-sha-na. Will not change plans to go to Canton, plans made necessary by in-ability of Kuei-liang and Hua-sha-na to control situation at Canton.	10	121A/5
		HF 9			
/13	Feb 14	01 12	Kuei-liang *et al*. to Elgin. Emperor has transferred the traditional office of Imperial Commissioner for Foreign Affairs at Canton from Vice-roy Huang Tsung-han of Liang-Kuang to Viceroy Ho Kuei-ch'ing of Liang-Chiang. Henceforth all [routine] foreign affairs will be dealt with by Ho Kuei-ch'ing. Encl. Imperial Edict, 29 Jan 1859.	6 2	458/1
/14	Mar 3	01 29	Elgin to Kuei-liang *et al*. Is pleased that Huang Tsung-han has been dis-missed. Is about to return to England, and his successor, Bruce, will arrive soon. London has agreed not to insist on permanent residence of British envoy in Peking but such provision must remain in treaty and will be invoked if necessary.	10	121A/
/15	Apr 5	03 03	Cantonese merchants to Vice-Consul [in charge] C.A. Winchester. Hundreds of thousands of Cantonese have been kidnapped by foreigners to be sold	4	39/36

0. 2/ 92	Date 1859	HF 9	Description	pp	Old Ref. F.O. 682/
			as coolies overseas, leaving their dependants to die. Request action to be taken to stop such inhumane trade.		
16	May 15	04 13	Acting Governor Pi Ch'eng-chao of Kwangtung to H. Parkes *et al.* Acknowledges receipt of Yeh Ming-ch'en's body and belongings, which arrived at Canton yesterday.	4	1789
17	May 16	04 14	Bruce to Kuei-liang. Has been appointed H.M. Plenipotentiary to go to Peking to exchange treaties. Requests that authorities at Tientsin be commanded to make all necessary preparations for journey to Peking, and that a spacious residence in Peking be selected for his stay there.	9	121A/58
18	May 19	04 17	Pi Ch'eng-chao to H. Parkes. As regards demand for indemnity of two million taels to be paid by Canton, has not heard from Imperial Commissioner for Foreign Affairs and will await his instructions.	8	1787
19	May 27	04 25	Kuei-liang *et al.* to Bruce. Have been waiting in Shanghai since receipt of Elgin's letter of 25 Jan 1859 saying that he had to go to Canton but would return to Shanghai in thirty to forty days. Elgin's further letter of 3 Mar 1859 stated that he was returning to England and would be succeeded by Bruce. Are pleased that Bruce has now arrived and are prepared to hold meeting as soon as possible.	9	458/16
20	May 28	04 26	Kuei-liang *et al.* to Bruce. Have received on 27 May Bruce's letter of 16 May in which he stated that he had been appointed H.M. Plenipotentiary and was proceeding to Peking for exchange of treaties. Have waited in Shanghai as Elgin said he was returning there. But now that Bruce wants to go to Peking, it will take them two months to travel there by land. Suggest that they meet in Shanghai first to make arrangements to go to Peking.	9	458/15

F.C. 682/ 1992	Date 1859	HF 9	Description	pp	Old R F.O. 682/
/21	May 28	04 26	Kuei-liang *et al.* to Bruce. Inform Bruce of state of negotiations where Elgin has left them: H.M. Plenipotentiary will go to Peking to exchange treaties but will not live there permanently; Elgin has inspected Yangtze area; Chinese have no way of ascertaining respectability of Britons to whom passports are issued for travel in the hinterland of China; return of Canton city has yet to be settled. Again request Bruce to stay in Shanghai for further discussion.	12	458/1
/22	[c. May]		Chinese pamphlet entitled *The Emperor's Great Wrath* containing garbled version of Tientsin treaties.	6	1783
/23	Jun 8	05 08	Bruce to Kuei-liang. Rejects proposal to meet at Shanghai. Will proceed to Peking immediately where he will stay until all treaty provisions are fulfilled.	18	121A.
/24	Jun 11	05 11	Bruce to Kuei-liang. Regrets that Kuei-liang has not replied to previous communication. Is despatching this as final notice of plan to proceed immediately to Tientsin and then to Peking in order to satisfy stipulation for exchange of treaties within one year of their signing.	8	121A.
/25a	Jun 12	05 12	Kuei-liang *et al.* to Bruce. Note Bruce's refusal to change his mind. Will send letter to Emperor by express, requesting despatch of high-ranking official to receive Bruce at Tientsin, and will hurry back to Peking themselves. Request that on arrival at Tientsin, Bruce leave his steamer outside that port and do not proceed to Peking with all his soldiers. Guarantee Bruce's safety as peace has now been reached.	10	458.
/25b	Jun 24	05 24	Viceroy Heng-fu to British authorities. Has arrived at Pei-t'ang to prepare the way for H.M. Plenipotentiary to go to Peking.	1	68/1
			Encl. Draft comment on this despatch: Chinese characters for H.M. Plenipotentiary are not elevated.	1	68/1

	Date		Description	pp	Old Ref. F.O. 682/
	1859	HF9			

5c	Jul 6	06 07	Parkes and Martineau to Pi ch'eng-chao. British and French merchants have been deprived of a proper place in which to live and trade in Canton ever since the foreign factories were burnt down in 1856. There are two possible sites for a new factory area which will meet all the needs of the merchants. One is Hsi-hao-k'ou area adjoining the former factory area to the east, where all local houses were also burnt down in 1856. The other is Shameen [Sha-mien] which submerges at high tide. The former involves compensation to landlords; the latter has to be reclaimed, which will take up to eighteen months. If Chinese authorities can guarantee completion of reclamation to the satisfaction of the Chief Engineer from Hong Kong within eighteen months, then Hsi-hao-k'ou will not be forcibly bought. Estimated cost of reclamation is $264,000, which will be deducted from indemnity to be demanded from China. Chinese authorities should prohibit the rebuilding of houses in Hsi-hao-k'ou area until reclamation of Shameen is completed.	8	769/3/10
a	Jul 8	06 09	Pi Ch'eng-chao to H. Parkes and M. Martineau. Shameen is government land and when reclaimed, British and French authorities should lease it and pay rent in the same way as they do in Shanghai for the land they have leased.	2	769/3/8
b	Jul 9	06 10	Hoppo to Consul C.A. Winchester. Urges that back duties for 1856 in Canton be promptly paid.	4	1786
c	Jul 14	06 15	Acting Viceroy Lao Ch'ung-kuang of Liang-Kuang to H. Parkes and M. Martineau. Thanks them for their visit two days ago when he took office as Governor of Kwangtung and as Acting Viceroy of Liang-Kuang. Will do all he can to facilitate reclamation of Shameen but rents must be paid once British and French merchants begin to occupy it.	3	769/3/1

F.O. 682/ 1992	Date 1859	HF9	Description	pp	Old F.O. 682/
/26d	Jul 16	06 17	H. Parkes and M. Martineau to Lao Ch'ung-kuang. Will refer matter of rents for Shameen to their Plenipotentiaries. Request that contracts for reclaiming Shameen be sent to them for safe keeping.	6	40/5
/26e	Jul 23	06 24	Lao Ch'ung-kuang to H. Parkes and M. Martineau. A cheque for $20,000 from Hoppo's Treasury is hereby delivered by Acting Magistrate Fang Chien-yüan of Nan-hai as part of the expenses involved in reclaiming Shameen. Requests receipt.	2	769/
/26f	Jul 26	06 27	H. Parkes and M. Martineau to Lao Ch'ung-kuang. Acknowledge receipt of cheque for $20,000 and of contract prepared by the Cantonese gentry and the developer Ho-chi. The twelve sub-contractors of Ho-chi signed the contract on 23 July, whereupon they were handed the cheque for $20,000. They then acknowledged receipt of the same amount in writing. This receipt, the contract, as well as the specifications and the two plans prepared by the Chief Engineer of Hong Kong are all triplicated: one copy is enclosed herewith for Lao's reference, the other two will be forwarded to the British and French Plenipotentiaries. It is only fair that Chief Engineer of Hong Kong and his assistants should be rewarded with 3% of the $20,000 and they are hereby paid $600.	7	769/
/27	Aug 1	07 03	Ho Kuei-ch'ing to Bruce. U.S. envoy has gone to Peking to exchange treaties. Wonders if Bruce and Gros wish to do the same; if so, will request Emperor to notify Keui-liang *et al.* as well as Viceroy of Chihli to provide all facilities on way to Peking.	9	458/
/28	Aug 9	07 11	Bruce to Ho Kuei-ch'ing. Declines to discuss with Ho question of exchange of treaties because Ho is in charge of trade in five treaty ports only, but *does* wish Ho in his capacity as Viceroy of Liang-Chiang to settle	8	121/

Date		Description	pp	Old Ref. F.O. 682/
1859	HF 9			

the problems raised by the disturbance in Shanghai [on 29 Jul 1859]
in which one Briton was killed and
several others seriously injured.

| Aug 13 | 07 15 | Ho Kuei-ch'ing to Bruce. Is surpris-
ed to read that Bruce regards him
as Imperial Commissioner in charge
only of foreign trade with nothing
to do with exchange of treaties,
and will therefore not reply to his
letter. Ho himself was Joint
Imperial Commissioner with Kuei-
liang *et al.*, who negotiated treaty
with Elgin, and all correspondence
then bore his name and title. Even
Bruce's first despatch on arrival
at Shanghai was addressed to Ho *et
al.* Disturbance in Shanghai on 29
July was caused by foreigners press-
ganging Chinese to ship them
abroad. | 11 | 458/11 |

| Aug 22 | 07 24 | Ho Kuei-ch'ing to Bruce. Although
Taiwan is included in new treaty
ports to be opened, treaties have
yet to be exchanged and British
merchants should not, therefore, go
and trade there yet. Hopes Bruce
will reply. | 5 | 458/10 |

| Aug 28 | 08 01 | Bruce to Ho Kuei-ch'ing. Points out
that in his first despatch to Ho he
referred to Ho as Grand Secretary
only. Cannot believe that Chinese
authorities could have failed to
capture criminals after a whole
month if they had been in earnest.
Allegations of Britons press-ganging
Chinese are only excuses not to take
action. | 10 | 121A/62 |

| Sep 1 | 08 05 | Ho Kuei-ch'ing to Bruce. Will
intensify search for those respons-
ible for killing one Briton and
wounding others during disturbance
in Shanghai. | 9 | 458/9 |

| Sep 5 | 08 09 | Ho Kuei-ch'ing to Bruce. Has executed
four Chinese who hired fellow
countrymen ostensibly as sailors
and then sold them as labourers
overseas. Has instructed local
officials in coastal areas to | 13 | 458/8 |

F.O. 682/ 1992	Date 1859	HF 9	Description	pp	Old F. F.O. 682/
			proclaim prohibition against hiring Chinese to sail on high seas and requests that Bruce instruct Consuls to do same.		
/34a	Sep 5	08 09	Hoppo to C.A. Winchester. Again urges that back duties for 1856 in Canton be paid promptly.	4	39/39
/34b	Sep 7	08 11	C.A. Winchester to Hoppo. Arrears of 1856 export duties were caused by Commissioner Yeh Ming-ch'en's closing Customs Office. Consul kept record of taxes due and let ships leave Canton. There are glaring discrepancies between these records and sum now demanded by Chinese. In any case cannot pay arrears until specific instructions have been received from London.	4	1788
/35a	Sep 20	08 24	Bruce to Ho Kuei-ch'ing. Chinese who attacked Britons in Shanghai must be punished in Shanghai to serve as deterrent to future attacks; it is pointless to transfer them to provincial seat of government for punishment. Cannot comment on rules governing Chinese going overseas, but agrees that press-gangs are detestable and will suggest best way of dealing with them at appropriate time in future.	8	121A
/35b	Sep 25	08 29	Lao ch'ung-kuang to H. Parkes *et al.* Agrees to request Hoppo to deliver $4,000 to Bureau of Occupation for its expenses of following month. Also agrees to request Hoppo to reimburse the Bureau, in three instalments within three months, the sum of $61,803.96 which the Bureau had expended in last twenty months or so.	2	769
/36	Sep 26	09 01	Ho Kuei-ch'ing to Bruce. Those responsible for killing Briton and wounding others have been captured but he cannot execute them summarily because according to Chinese law, execution for murder may be author- ised only by Emperor; others will be punished according to seriousness of wounds they have caused. All offenders will, according to	7	458

) 2/ 92	Date 1859	HF 9	Description	pp	Old Ref. F.O. 682/
			Chinese law, be transported to provincial seat for trial.		
37	Oct 11	09 16	Proclamation by Acting Magistrate Kao feng-p'o of Lu-ling-hsin: the preaching and practising of Catholicism are prohibited.	7	1793/1
8a	Oct 12	09 17	H. Parkes *et al.* to Lao Ch'ung-kuang. Prefect Designate Tuan Chi *et al.* have been levying *likin* in western Canton. The Commanders-in-Chief of the Allied Forces occupying Canton have instructed H. Parkes *et al.* to act as specified in the enclosed proclamation.	2	40/5/2
			Encl. Proclamation [by the Joint Commanders of the Allied Forces occupying Canton]: Tuan Chi *et al.* who have been collecting *likin* in western Canton, are hereby expelled from the city; the 4,000 taels or so collected by them will be confiscated and used for charity in Canton. 12 Oct 1859.	2	40/5/1
38b	Oct 12	09 17	Lao Ch'ung-kuang to H. Parkes *et al.* Agrees to the expulsion from Canton of Tuan Chi *et al.* who have been levying *likin* [in the western part of the city]. The 4,000 taels or so collected as *likin*, as well as the three other colleagues of Tuan Chi are handed over herewith.	2	40/5/3
38c	Oct 13	09 18	Hoppo to C.A. Winchester. Inspector- General H.N. Lay of Imperial Maritime Customs has come with order from Imperial Commissioner to re- organise Canton Customs Office along Shanghai lines. After consultation with Viceroy and Governor, has decided to follow example of Shanghai and employ T. Wade *et al.* as inspectors.	4	1785
39a	Oct 26	10 01	H. Parkes *et al.* to Lao Ch'ung-kuang. Late Governor Po-kuei of Kwangtung conferred with Commanders-in-Chief of Anglo-French forces. They all agreed that abduction of Chinese males for sale overseas should be strictly prohibited, and that voluntary emigration should be	7	289/4/13

F.O. 682/ 1992	Date 1859	HF 9	Description	pp	Old Re F.O. 682/

			legislated. Now a British Officer O-ssu-tien [Austin] has been appointed to organise recruitment of coolies for British West Indies. He has drawn up five regulations, copy of which is enclosed herewith. Lao Ch'ung-kuang should depute an official to act in co-operation with [Austin].		
/39b	Oct 28	10 03	Tax Commissioner Ching of Nan-t'ai to Consul W.H. Medhurst. Requests an appointment to discuss tax regulat-ions regarding opium imports.	4	1790/4
/39c	Oct 29	10 04	Proclamation by Lao Ch'ung-kuang. Brit-ish authorities have set up an office at Canton to recruit labourers for working in the West Indies. Interested parties should go to these to sign a contract specifying tenure, annual pay, etc.	3	769/1
/39d	n.d. [Oct -]	n.d. [10 -]	Proclamation drafted [by H. Parkes] to be issued in the name of Acting Viceroy [Lao Ch'ung-kuang]. Cantonese should conduct their business as usual and should not listen to agitators.	2	391/1
/40	Oct 29	10 04	Tartar-General [Tung-ch'un] of Foochow to Tax Commissioner Ching of Nan-t'ai. Henceforth opium imports will be taxed at treaty ports only.	3	1790/2
/41	n.d.	n.d.	Copy of memorial from Tartar-General Tung-ch'un of Foochow *et al*. to Emperor. All *likin* stations in Fukien have been abolished and all transit dues will be collected hence-forth by proper authorities.	3	1790/:
/42	Nov 10	10 16	Five regulations, endorsed by H. Parkes, concerning export of Chinese labourers to West Indies.	3	1782
/43	n.d.	n.d.	Proclamation by Austin about rules governing migration of Chinese labourers to West Indies.	8	1793/:
/44a	Nov 14	10 20	Acting Consul C.A. Winchester to Viceroy Lao Ch'ung-kuang of Liang-	3	1791

	Date		Description	pp	Old Ref. F.O.
2	1859	HF 9			682/

			Kuang. Denies categorically that any kidnapped coolie can be on board any British ship, on the ground that Great Britain has long-standing policy of prohibiting coolie trade; but will request Consuls of other nations to investigate their ships.		
+b	Nov 14	10 20	Lao Ch'ung-kuang to [H. Parkes *et al.*] The hundred copies of proclamation received earlier have been distributed by Magistrate of Nan-hai in his own district only, which explains why none of them has appeared in P'an-yü district. Requests additional hundred copies for distribution in other parts of Canton area. Received fifty copies of another proclamation yesterday; requests additional two hundred copies for distribution. Encloses his own draft proclamation prohibiting abduction [of Chinese males for sale as coolies overseas] for the perusal of [Parkes *et al.*]	1	327/5/167
	Nov 28	11 05	Bruce to Ho Kuei-ch'ing. Rumour-mongers and agitators must be severely punished on the spot to prevent Chinese taking the law into their hands, or British authorities will take unilateral action.	11	121A/68
	Dec 5	11 12	Ho Kuei-ch'ing to Bruce. Chinese agitators [during disturbance in Shanghai] will be paraded in public.	9	458/6
	Dec 5	11 12	Bruce to Ho Kuei-ch'ing. Consul at Shanghai reports that new low tonnage due of 0.4 tael per ton has been granted to U.S.A. According to most-favoured-nation principle, Great Britain should also enjoy new rate.	6	121A/65
	Dec 8	11 15	Ho Kuei-ch'ing to Bruce. Will request permission from Emperor to let British and French ships enjoy same low tonnage due of 0.4 tael per ton just granted to U.S. shipping.	9	458/5
	Dec 27	12 04	Ho Kuei-ch'ing to Bruce. Emperor has agreed that the new low tonnage due of 0.4 tael per ton may be enjoyed	7	458/4

F.O. 682/ 1992	Date 1859	HF 9	Description	pp	Old R F.O. 682/
			by British and French shipping.		
/50	n.d.	n.d.	Copy of memo from three anonymous officials to Emperor, detailing tax on opium.	3	1790/
/51	n.d.	n.d.	Monthly expenditure of Bureau of Occupation at Canton for thirteen months from Jan 1858 to Jan 1859 inclusive: $28,687.32 for office expenses and $33,116.64 for patrolling the streets, making a total of $61,803.96. In addition, expenses involved in repairing *yamen* of Bureau of Occupation and repairing city gates garrisoned by soldiers amount to $10,637.60.	3	327/5

.	Date		Description	pp	Old Ref.
/					F.O.
3	1860	HF 9			682/

e: *As before, summaries made from the entry-books of F.O. 230/74 and F.O. 230/75 are not given new reference numbers in the first column but their references in square brackets in the last column should continue to be used by searchers.*

a   Jan 6   12 14   Consul C.A. Winchester to Hoppo. H.M.   336/4
Plenipotentiary Sir Frederick Bruce
has instructed that foreign cargo
in transit in Canton must not be
taxed. Hoppo would be held responsible for losses consequent on delays
if Hoppo should continue to insist
on taxing such cargo.

b   Jan 10   12 18   H.M. Plenipotentiary Sir Frederick Bruce   8   392/1
to Ho Kuei-ch'ing. On 13 Oct 1857
British vessel [*Laura*] found another
British vessel with more than three
hundred Chinese soldiers and treasure
on board foundering in heavy seas.
[*Laura*] was damaged in rescue
operation which took three days and
incurred extra expenses in delivering
soldiers and treasure to Fukien.
Apart from half of treasure received
according to Western practice,
Chinese government still owes [*Laura*]
3,500 taels for damages and extra
expenses. Chinese authorities in
Fukien must be instructed to pay
promptly.
Encl. Extra expenses incurred, *op.*   3
cit., n.d.

     Jan 10   12 18   Bruce to Ho Kuei-ch'ing. British   8   392/2
Consul at Foochow received request
from Prefect of Foochow for help
to rescue one hundred and thirty
Chinese merchant ships surrounded
by pirates not far from Foochow.
Two warships of the Royal Navy
were despatched on 16 Dec 1859 to
the scene. The pirates seemed to
have heard about the despatch of
the warships and fled before
arrival of warships. On their
return voyage the warships encountered five Kwangtung boats which
local fishermen said were part
of pirate fleet. Pirates fled
after exchange of fire and their
boats ran aground. Two pirates
were captured by local people
and delivered to Royal Navy, which

F.O. 682/ 1993	Date 1860	HF	9	Description	pp	Old R F.O. 682/

in turn handed them over to
Chinese authorities at Foochow.
Three captives kept by pirates
were set free. Intense efforts
by Royal Navy to suppress piracy
in Chinese waters is in stark
contrast to failure by Chinese
government to take action.

/3 Jan 17 12 25 Bruce to Ho Kuei-ch'ing. Consul   8   392/
W.H. Medhurst at Foochow has
complained about the four months'
delay in Chinese government's
dealing with four cases of
Chinese merchants not paying
their debts or not honouring
their contracts. Requests that
Chinese authorities at Foochow
be instructed to act more
vigorously.

/4 Jan 17 12 25 Ho Kuei-ch'ing to Bruce. Received   9   248
on 15 Jan 1860 Bruce's despatch
of 10 Jan 1860. Expresses
appreciation of Royal Navy having
frightened away pirates who
surrounded one hundred and thirty
Chinese merchant ships; and for
having wiped out five pirate ships
subsequently, delivered two
pirates to Foochow authorities,
and set free three captives who had
been kept by pirates. Has not
received similar report from
Foochow authorities. Is annoyed
that naval authorities of Foochow
have been so slack in pirate-
suppression. Has written to Viceroy
of Min-Che requesting an inquiry.

/5 Jan 17 12 25 Ho Kuei-ch'ing to Bruce. Has no record   9   248
of demand for compensation for British
ship which saved two hundred and forty
Chinese soldiers and treasure in ship
which was foundering near Fukien in
1857. Wonders if Viceroy of Liang-
Kuang [Yeh Ming-ch'en] was notified as
he was in charge of foreign affairs at
the time. However, [as Yeh Ming-ch'en
and his archives have been captured by
the Allied Anglo-French forces], there
is no way of knowing if Yeh Ming-ch'en
had been so informed. In the circumstances, the only thing Ho Kuei-ch'ing
himself can do is to inform Viceroy

). 2/ 33	Date 1860	HF 10	Description	pp	Old Ref. F.O. 682/
			of Min-Che of what happened and to ask him to take action.		
6	Jan 30	01 08	Ho Kuei-ch'ing to Bruce. Has written to Viceroy of Min-Che urging speedy settlement of debt owed by Chinese to British merchants.	6	248/3
7	Feb 24	02 03	Hoppo to C.A. Winchester. All Chinese goods arriving at Canton in foreign vessels will be taxed at 2.5% *ad valorem*. Such tax will be refunded if goods are originally meant for export and if there is no reason to suspect that consignments have been opened during stay of up to four months in Canton.	4	1792
8	Mar 8	02 16	Bruce to Grand Councillor P'eng Wen-chang *et al*. Kuei-liang *et al*. did not inform him of Imperial Edict specifying that British envoy should go to Peking via Pei-t'ang and not via Taku; nor did Taku soldiers, who said they had put barricade across river on their own initiative. Demands: (1) redress for Taku attack on Royal Navy; (2) British entry to Peking to be made via Taku with appropriate pomp; (3) indemnity of four million taels for what happened in Canton; (4) permanent residence for British envoy in Peking.	32	392/4
9	Mar 8	02 16	Bruce to Ho Kuei-ch'ing. Requests that the enclosed letter to Grand Councillors in Peking be forwarded immediately as it requires reply within thirty days.	6	392/5
0	Mar 14	02 22	Ho Kuei-ch'ing to Bruce. Has forward-ed Bruce's letters to Peking.	5	248/4
1	Mar 28	03 07	Ho Kuei-ch'ing to Bruce. Hsüeh Huan, Provincial Treasurer of Kiangsu, has been awarded title of Governor to help in management of trade in five treaty ports.	5	248/5
2	Apr 2	03 12	Bruce to Ho Kuei-ch'ing. Acknowledges receipt of letter conveying news that Provincial Treasurer Hsüeh Huan of Kiangsu has been granted title of	6	392/6

F.O. 682/ 1993	Date 1860	HF 10	Description	pp	Old R. F.O. 682/

NOTE: The symbol *ι* in the third column stands for intercalary month.

			Governor to assist in supervising trade in five treaty ports.		
/13	Apr 5	03 15	Ho Kuei-ch'ing to Bruce. Transmits letter from Grand Council to Bruce.	7	248/6
			Encl. Grand Council to Ho Kuei-ch'ing for Bruce: reject all Bruce's demands and accusations, n.d.	5	
/14	Apr 13	03 23	Bruce to Ho Kuei-ch'ing. His writing to Grand Councillors P'eng Wen-chang *et al.* is permitted by Treaty of Nanking. Their refusal to reply directly, asking, instead, Ho to transmit the message, is an unaccept-able mode of communication. As reply is unsatisfactory, has placed matter in hands of Admiral and General.	10	392/7
/15	Apr 17	03 27	Ho Kuei-ch'ing to Bruce. Will write to Emperor as requested but pleads with Bruce not to resort to arms.	8	248/7
/16	May 5	*ι*3 15	Hoppo to C.A. Winchester. Complains about two British vessels having been allowed to come and go at Whampoa without registering with Vice-Consul as specified by treaty.	5	1796
/17	May 18	*ι*3 28	Ho Kuei-ch'ing to Bruce. Requests that Consul C.A. Winchester at Canton be reprimanded for having allowed British ship that had not paid duty on its tea to set sail. Demands that back duties be paid.	9	248/8
/18	May 22	04 02	Bruce to Ho Kuei-ch'ing. Returns Ho's despatch in which the characters that stand for the British Monarch and her Empire were not given the appropriate elevated position signifying respect, when reference was made to them.	6	392/8
			Encl. List of five places where format of Ho's despatch was wrong.	1	
/19	[May -]	n.d.	Acting Magistrate [Chu Hsieh] of Nan-hai to Howqua *et al.* If they are found guilty of mixing tea with im-purities they will be punished heavily and required to pay compen-sation.	4	1795

. / 3	Date 1860	HF 10	Description	pp	Old Ref. F.O. 682/
0	Jun 13	04 24	Ho Kuei-ch'ing to Bruce. Has been ordered to proceed to Shanghai to negotiate peace treaties with Great Britain and France.	7	248/9
1	Jun 16	04 27	Ho Kuei-ch'ing to Bruce. Macao, un-like Hong Kong, is Chinese territory. British merchants exporting Chinese goods from Macao should pay export duties. The two British vessels that loaded tea in Macao and then came to Whampoa must therefore pay export duties before they sail again.	10	248/10
2a	Jun 28	05 10	Hsüeh Huan to Bruce. Has been appointed Acting Imperial Commissioner for Foreign Affairs in place of Ho Kuei-ch'ing and has today received the seal for this office.	5	248/50
2b	n.d.	n.d.	Parts of two variant drafts of a despatch [from Bruce?] to [Hsüeh Huan]. Bowring had ignored his instructions from London when he made promises to [Hsüeh Huan when Hsüeh Huan was Intendant at Shanghai, Jul 1857-Dec 1859] about [payment of Shanghai back duties]. That is why Bowring was recalled [in fact Bowring was simply superseded by Elgin as H.M. Plenipotentiary in 1857; when Elgin left on 3 Mar 1859 Bowring resumed office as Plenipotentiary, but again lost this position to Bruce on Bruce's arrival at Hong Kong on 19 Apr 1859; Bowring remained Governor of Hong Kong until his retirement on 5 May 1859]. Whatever agreement Bowring had made with [Hsüeh Huan] must be overturned and new agreement reached. [It is not clear whether this despatch was ever sent to the Chinese.]		289/3B /3+8
3	Aug 6	06 20	Viceroy Heng-fu of Chihli to Elgin. Has withdrawn defence of Pei-t'ang to let Elgin come for peace talks. Requests Elgin to appoint time and place to meet.	9	248/42
4	Aug 8	06 22	Elgin to Heng-fu. Has resumed military action because Grand	9	392/20

F.O. 682/ 1993	Date 1860	HF 10	Description	pp	Old F.O. 682/
			Council's reply to Bruce's letter of last March was unsatisfactory. Will not cease fire until Imperial Commissioner is appointed to grant all British demands. Cannot forward Heng-fu's letter to French Plenipotentiary: Heng-fu must write to him directly.		
/25	Aug 14	06 28	Heng-fu to Elgin. Emperor has appointed Imperial Commissioner who will wait for Elgin at Peking for negotiations.	7	248/
/26	Aug 15	06 29	Heng-fu to Elgin. Urges Elgin to respond to Emperor's appointment of Imperial Commissioner, who is waiting at Peking for Elgin to go for peace talks.	7	248/
/27	Aug 16	06 30	Heng-fu to Elgin. Further to his communications of previous two days, has now been told by Emperor that Imperial Commissioner(s) have been ordered to proceed to Tientsin to meet Elgin. Pleads for armistice.	5	248/
/28	Aug 17	07 01	Heng-fu to Elgin. Emperor has sent Wen-chün and Heng-ch'i to come to Pei-t'ang to accompany Elgin to Peking for exchanges of treaties. Requests Elgin to appoint date and place to start journey. Returns two prisoners of war.	6	248/
/29	Aug 17	07 01	Elgin to Heng-fu. Will wait until British forces have occupied all forts on both sides of river and paved way for entry into Tientsin city, and Chinese have agreed to all British demands, before he can request British Commanders-in-Chief to stop military action.	8	392/
/30	Aug 18	07 02	Wen-chün and Heng-ch'i to Elgin. Have arrived at Tientsin to accompany Elgin to Peking to exchange treaties.	6	248/
/31	Aug 18	07 02	Heng-fu to Elgin. Has transmitted Elgin's reply to Emperor.	6	248/
/32	Aug 20	07 04	Wen-chün and Heng-ch'i to Elgin. Emperor has appointed Imperial Commissioner who is waiting in	7	248/

F.O. 82/ 993	Date 1860	HF 10	Description	pp	Old Ref. F.O. 682/
			Peking for Elgin to go there to exchange treaties and to discuss Bruce's four new demands.		
/33	Aug 20	07 04	Elgin to Wen-chün and Heng-ch'i. Has nothing to add to his previous letter to Heng-fu.	6	392/22
/34	Aug 21	07 05	Heng-fu to Elgin. Admits defeat and pleads with Elgin not to fight any more. Imperial Commissioner has been appointed to hold necessary discussions with Elgin, who may go north via Taku.	5	248/51
	Aug 23	07 07	Heng-fu to Elgin. Has returned from Taku to Tientsin, where he has withdrawn all soldiers guarding the walls, ditches, forts and cannon. Pleads with Elgin not to bring too many battleships to Tientsin.	1	[F.O. 230/75]
/35	Aug 25	07 09	Wen-chün and Heng-fu to Elgin. Heng-fu and Kuei-liang have been appointed Joint Imperial Commissioners and Heng-ch'i their assistant, to conduct negotiations at Tientsin. Wen-chün himself is recalled to Peking.	6	248/11
/36	Aug [25]	07 [09]	Heng-fu to Elgin. Has been appointed Joint Imperial Commissioner with Kuei-liang. Kuei-liang is due to arrive from Peking on 31 Aug with seal of Imperial Commissioner. Forwards letter from Kuei-liang.	6	248/12
/37	Aug 25	07 09	Kuei-liang to Elgin. Has been appointed Joint Imperial Commissioner with Viceroy of Chihli, Heng-fu. Will arrive at Tientsin on 31 August to discuss British demands made five months ago.	5	248/13
/38	Aug 29	07 13	Heng-fu and Heng-ch'i to Elgin. Heng-ch'i has been appointed Assistant Imperial Commissioner.	4	248/14
/39	Aug 29	07 13	Elgin to Kuei-liang. Has captured all Taku forts and occupied Tientsin city. Will stop military action until all demands are met. In addition to four million taels of indemnity originally agreed upon,	12	392/23

F.O. 682/ 1993	Date 1860	HF 10	Description	pp	Old Re F.O. 682/
			China now must pay another four million taels before Allied Forces will evacuate Tientsin and Teng-chou [in Shantung].		
/40	Aug 30	07 14	Elgin to Kuei-liang *et al.* Acknowledges receipt of letter transmitting Imperial Edict by which Kuei-liang *et al.* were appointed Joint Imperial Commissioners to deal with question of exchanging treaties.	5	392/24
/41	Sep 2	07 17	Kuei-liang *et al.* to Elgin. Accept all British demands as contained in treaty of 1958, in communications of 8 Mar 1860 and 29 Aug 1860. Propose meeting to decide on proportions of customs revenue to be earmarked for payment of indemnity, and on exchange of treaties in Peking.	7	248/15
/42	Sep 3	07 18	Elgin to Kuei-liang *et al.* It is good to know that they have agreed to all his demands. Will request Commanders-in-Chief to stop all military action on day treaty is signed. After details about reception in Peking are thrashed out, will proceed there to exchange treaties.	7	392/25
/43	Sep 5	07 20	Elgin to Kuei-liang *et al.* Fair copy of treaty is ready and will be taken to them by T. Wade and H. Parkes for signing at appropriate date.	5	392/26
	Sep 6	07 21	[Letter] Kuei-liang to Elgin. Proposes to visit Elgin tomorrow. Requests Elgin to appoint a time.	1	[F.O. 230/7
/44	Sep 7	07 22	Kuei-liang *et al.* to Elgin. Have reported to Emperor on meeting of yesterday with T. Wade and H.N. Lay. Request Elgin to wait at Tientsin for three days or so.	6	248/16
/45	Sep 7	07 22	Elgin to Kuei-liang *et al.* Is surprised to hear that they have to consult Emperor about additional demands. Will not waste any more time but will ask Commanders-in-Chief to open way to T'ung-chou where he expects them	8	392/27

O. 2/ 93	Date		Description	pp	Old Ref. F.O. 682/
	1860	HF 10			
			to sign the treaty on the spot.		
'46a	Sep 8	07 23	[Letter] Kuei-liang to Elgin. Has heard that Elgin is about to lead his troops to go north. Ordinary people are bound to be greatly alarmed. Proposes to visit Elgin to plead with him personally to postpone his departure.	1	386/1/6
'46b	Sep 8	07 23	Elgin to Kuei-liang *et al.* Declines request to remain at Tientsin, but will proceed to T'ung-chou.	5	392/28
'47	Sep 8	07 23	General Sir Hope Grant to Heng-fu. Is leading troops to escort Elgin from Tientsin to T'ung-chou. All Chinese forts and encampments *en route* must be evacuated or face destruction.	6	392/29
48	Sep 10	07 25	Prince I and Grand Councillor Mu-yin to Elgin. Disapprove of manner in which Kuei-liang *et al.* have conducted negotiations. Have now received order from Emperor to proceed to Tientsin to take over negotiations. Plead with Elgin to wait at Tientsin and not to proceed to T'ung-chou.	8	248/17
	Sep 11	07 26	Prince I and Mu-yin to Elgin. Cannot proceed to Tientsin unless Elgin abandons plan to go to T'ung-chou with his troops.	2	[F.O. 230/75]
49	Sep 11	07 26	Elgin to Prince I and Mu-ying. Refuses to remain at Tientsin but will proceed to T'ung-chou as planned.	10	392/30
50	Sep 12	07 27	Kuei-liang *et al.* to Elgin. Plead with Elgin not to lead troops further towards T'ung-chou but to withdraw to Tientsin to await arrival of new Imperial Commissioners.	7	248/19
51	Sep 12	07 27	Prince I and Mu-yin to Elgin. Have already left T'ung-chou to board ship for Tientsin. Returning to T'ung-chou to meet Elgin will waste more time. Propose to meet Elgin at Tientsin or mid-way between Tientsin and T'ung-chou.	11	248/20

F.O. 682/ 1993	Date 1860	HF 10	Description	pp	Old Re F.O. 682/
/52	Sep 12	07 27	Prince I and Mu-yin to Elgin. Plead with Elgin to withdraw troops to Tientsin to show his sincere desire for peace talks.	10	248/18
/53	Sep 13	07 28	Prince I and Mu-yin to Elgin. Regret that neither of their despatches has been replied to. If Elgin proceeds any further with his troops, he is bound to meet with resistance from Chinese troops guarding approaches to Peking. Suggest Elgin goes with his personal guards but not entire army to T'ung-chou where they may finalise treaty.	11	248/2
/54	Sep 14	07 29	Prince I and Mu-yin to Elgin. Agree to all of Elgin's demands and to meet T. Wade and H. Parkes at T'ung-chou for preliminary talks. If Elgin still insists on going to T'ung-chou himself, he should be accompanied by no more than 1,000 soldiers.	8	248/2
/55a	Sep 16	08 02	Elgin to Prince I and Mu-yin. Agrees to stop troops five miles short of Chang-chia-wan. Chinese must bring food to encampment for sale or soldiers will help themselves to whatever provisions they can lay their hands on. Will be accompanied by 1,000 soldiers to T'ung-chou to sign treaty and afterwards to Peking to exchange treaties and present his credentials to Emperor.	10	392/3
/55b	n.d.	n.d.	[Letter: Prince I and Mu-yin to Elgin]. Note Elgin's appreciation of their presents. Praise T. Wade and H.N. Lay for their labour. Wish Elgin happy journey to [T'ung-chou and Peking].	1	386/1
/56	Sep 21	08 07	Prince Kung to Elgin. Has been appointed Imperial Commissioner to succeed Prince I and Mu-yin.	5	248/2
/57	Sep 22	08 08	Elgin to Prince Kung. Has asked Prefect of T'ung-chou to forward order to British and French soldiers [captured by the Chinese] to return to their bases immediately. Hostilities will not cease until all missing soldiers are accounted for.	6	392/3

). 2/ 93	Date 1860	HF 10	Description	pp	Old Ref. F.O. 682/
58	Sep 23	08 09	Prince Kung to Elgin. Cannot release prisoners of war or foward Elgin's letter to them until peace is concluded. Question of Elgin having audience with Emperor to present his credentials has yet to be decided.	9	248/24
59	Sep 25	08 11	Elgin to Prince Kung. Gives three-day ultimatum for: (1) release of messengers taken prisoners while travelling between T'ung-chou and Peking; (2) safe passage of Allied personnel from Peking back to their bases; (3) signing of treaty at T'ung-chou; (4) provision for Elgin to present credentials to Emperor in Peking.	14	392/33
60	Sep 27	08 13	Prince Kung to Elgin. Has agreed to all British demands and hence threats of war should no longer be made. Offers to receive Elgin's credentials in Peking. Assures him that H. Parkes is safe and well, enclosing Parkes' name card as evidence.	14	248/25
61	Sep 28	08 14	Elgin to Prince Kung. Reminds him that he has one more day to release hostages and to sign treaty before three-day ultimatum expires. Reiterates that credentials may be presented to Emperor only in person.	10	392/9
62	Sep 29	08 15	Prince Kung to Elgin. Will release prisoners of war and meet to sign treaty after foreign troops have retreated from vicinities of Peking to Chang-chia-wan. Emperor has gone hunting as he usually does in autumn and hence is not available to receive Elgin's credentials in person. Again offers to receive them himself in Peking.	12	248/26
63	Sep 30	08 16	Elgin to Prince Kung. Prince Kung is wasting his time demanding withdrawal of Allied Forces before signing treaty which is to be followed by release of hostages. As three-day ultimatum has expired, will leave matter in hands of General [Sir Hope Grant].	7	392/34

F.O. 682/ 1993	Date 1860	HF 10	Description	pp	Old Re F.O. 682/
/64	Oct 1	08 17	Prince Kung to Elgin. Reiterates that prisoners of war cannot be released until peace is concluded. Suspects that incompetent translation is cause of Elgin's impression that his demands have not been granted in full.	7	248/27
/65	Oct 2	08 18	Prince Kung to Elgin. Forwards H. Parkes' letter and H. Parkes' request for winter clothes.	5	248/28
	Oct 2	08 18	Elgin to Prince Kung. British forces have started their journey to Peking. If China wants peace, she must send official with full pleni- potentiary powers to negotiate and must return all hostages.	1	[F.O. 230/7
/66	Oct 2	08 18	Elgin to Prince Kung. Has asked Prince Kung's messenger to take to Parkes *et al.* their clothes and other personal effects.	4	392/35
/67	Oct 3	08 19	Prince Kung to Elgin. With help of H. Parkes and French interpreter, who both know Chinese, terms of treaties have been finally settled. Has ordered withdrawal of Chinese troops, expecting Elgin to order withdrawal of British troops as well. Has forwarded letter and two bags of clothes to H. Parkes.	10	248/29
/68	Oct 3	08 19	Prince Kung to Elgin. Forwards four letters from Parkes *et al.* Re- iterates desire for mutual with- drawal of troops.	6	248/30
/69	Oct 4	08 20	Elgin to Prince Kung. Endorses Chinese desire for peace but this cannot be achieved when they are still holding British hostages in Peking and refus- ing to yield to British demands. Requests that enclosures and clothes for Parkes *et al.* be forwarded.	7	392/36
/70	Oct 6	08 22	Prince Kung to Elgin. Parkes has helped finalise treaties which will be signed within two or three days and sent to Elgin. Parkes also agrees that presentation of credentials to Emperor is of second- ary importance, and hence there	13	248/31

.O. 82/ 993	Date 1860	HF 10	Description	pp	Old Ref. F.O. 682
			seems no further major obstacle to peace. Has ordered Chinese troops to withdraw and expects Elgin to order withdrawal of Allied Forces.		
1	Oct 6	08 22	Prince Kung to Elgin. Elgin's complete lack of response to Chinese overtures, and the continued advance on Peking by Allied Forces, are not best ways to achieve peace. Offers to meet Elgin two days later and to return all prisoners of war.	6	248/32
2a	Oct 10	08 26	General Grant to Prince Kung. Has chosen An-ting-men as point of entry into Peking. Any resistance will be crushed. Guarantees Prince Kung's safety on his return journey to Peking.	9	392/37
2b	Oct 12	08 28	Prince Kung to Elgin. Pleads with Elgin to stop soldiers sacking and burning palaces. Agrees to let Allied Forces guard city gate of An-ting-men but Elgin must elaborate on how it is to be guarded. Will fix date to hand over prisoners of war.	14	248/33
3	Oct -	08 -	[Heng-ch'i] to H. Parkes and T. Wade. Has been reprimanded by Prince Kung for the sacking and burning of Summer Palace by Allied Forces. Requests them to specify how An-ting-men is to be guarded, and when treaties are to be signed.	17	248/41
4	Oct 14	09 01	Prince Kung to Elgin. Is pleased with report that Allied Forces appear to be well-behaved in city of Peking. Has sent Heng-ch'i to meet Elgin's deputy to sign treaties. Requests Elgin to fix date to meet for exchanging treaties.	6	248/34
5a	Oct 16	09 03	Elgin to Prince Kung. Yüan-ming-yüan was partly and will be completely destroyed in retaliation for ill-treatment of British and French hostages: demands compensation of 300,000 taels to be delivered by 22 Oct 1860. Demands treaty be altered to provide for Anglo-French occupation of Tientsin until war	13	392/38

F.O. 682/ 1993	Date 1860	HF 10	Description	pp	Old Ref F.O. 682/
			indemnity is paid, that treaty be signed on 23 Oct 1860. Otherwise palace [inside city of Peking] will be destroyed.		
/75b	Oct 16	09 03	General Grant to Prince Kung. Demands to know the whereabouts of five missing hostages.	5	392/39
/76	Oct 19	09 06	Prince Kung to Elgin. Agrees to compensate for thirteen dead prisoners of war with 300,000 taels. Date for exchange of treaties may be fixed by deputies who are going to sign them.	7	248/35
/77	Oct 21	09 08	Prince Kung to Elgin. Agrees to sign [Peking Convention] and exchange Treaty of Tientsin on 23 Oct 1860. Requests Elgin to specify time of day to do so.	6	248/36
/78	Oct 22	09 09	Prince Kung to Elgin. Is sending herewith 300,000 taels as compensation for thirteen dead prisoners of war. Requests receipt.	5	248/37
/79	Oct 23	09 10	Elgin to Prince Kung. Silver ingots are being counted. Will issue receipt once counting is complete. Demands meeting at 2 p.m. next day in Ministry of Rites to exchange treaties and sign [Peking Convention].	4	392/40
/80	Oct 27	09 14	Elgin to Prince Kung. Counting of silver ingots is complete. Acknowledges receipt of 300,000 taels.	3	392/41
/81	Oct 29	09 16	Prince Kung to Elgin. Encloses copies of letters to coastal authorities detailing Arts. 3, 5 and 6 of [Peking Convention].	5	248/38
			Encl. Copies of Prince Kung's letters to Hoppo, Viceroys of Liang-Kuang, Min-Che, Liang-Chiang and Prefect of Feng-t'ien, n.d.	12	
/82	Nov 1	09 19	Prince Kung to Elgin. Transmits Imperial Edict.	5	248/39
/83	Nov 8	09 26	Prince Kung to Elgin. Proposes to meet Elgin and Bruce this afternoon at 4 p.m. at Kuang-hua-ssu.	4	248/40

). 2/ 93	Date 1860	HF 10	Description	pp	Old Ref. F.O. 682/
84	Nov 8	09 26	Bruce to Prince Kung. Has found suit-able house in Peking, at 1,000 taels per annum. As house is in disrepair, will use rent of first two years to renovate it. Landlord is out of Peking on official duty; requests Prince Kung to see to complete removal of sundry items from house.	7	392/10
85	Nov 9	09 27	Prince Kung to Bruce. Agrees to Bruce's plan to rent Liang-kung-fu as residence.	6	233/1
86	Nov 16	10 04	Prince Kung to Bruce. Has signed and put his seal on 2,500 copies of the proclamation prepared by Bruce: 200 of which have now been posted up throughout Peking, 300 are reserved for putting up in Chihli and Feng-t'ien, 1000 to be transmitted by Royal Navy to Chinese authorities in Kwangtung and other coastal provinces, 1000 are returned here-with. Has also put his seal on 2000 of 4000 copies of the treaty prepared by Bruce for distribution. Requests that 250 copies of the treaty prepared by Prince Kung him-self, 1200 copies of Peking Gazette and five official letters be trans-mitted by Royal Navy to Chinese authorities in Kwangtung and other coastal provinces.	8	233/2
87	Nov 21	10 09	Bruce to Prince Kung. Is going to send Consuls to additional treaty ports as specified in Treaty of Tientsin in 1858; requests co-operation of local authorities. Proposes that only Hankow and Kiukiang in the Yangtze area be opened to trade for time being; suggests that taxes be paid at Shanghai or Chen-chiang and that ships be allowed to carry a fixed amount of arms for self-protection.	9	392/11
88	Nov 24	10 12	Bruce to Prince Kung. First instal-ment of indemnity is due on 9 Jan 1861. Requests that customs authorities at Canton, Ch'ao-chou, Amoy, Foochow, Ningpo and Shanghai be notified of this, that the money at Ch'ao-chou be transferred to	10	392/12

F.O. 682/ 1993	Date 1860	HF 10	Description	pp	Old Re F.O. 682/
			Canton, that at Amoy to Foochow, and that at Ningpo to Shanghai, for delivery to British Consuls.		
/89	Nov 25	10 13	Prince Kung to Bruce. Although Yangtze area is still troubled by rebels, he will comply with Bruce's intention to open Hankow and Kiukiang for trade; details of customs payments should be thrashed out, however, by British and Chinese officials at Shanghai; endorses Bruce's proposal that British merchant ships going to Hankow and Kiukiang should not be allowed to carry more arms than what is necessary for self-protection.	11	233/3
/90	Nov 26	10 14	Prince Kung to Bruce. Permission for foreign envoys to be stationed at Peking will ensure that all matters will be settled promptly. Therefore Emperor should not be required to see foreign envoys, unless he wishes to do so.	6	233/4
/91	Nov 27	10 15	Prince Kung to Bruce. Agrees that money in small treaty ports should be transferred to major treaty ports for payment of indemnity; has notified authorities concerned.	5	233/5
/92	Dec 3	10 21	Acting Imperial Commissioner Hsüeh Huan to Bruce. Endorses proposal by Acting Prefect Liu of Foochow to restrict all Cantonese junks, whether they have British flags, papers or personnel on board, to mooring place of their guildhall. Foreign ships however, will be allowed into Foochow freely provided they possess genuine papers.	15	233/6
/93	Dec 4	10 22	Bruce to Prince Kung. Wishes to lease permanently area of 440 *mou* to south of Tientsin at 1.5-2 taels per *mou*. Inhabitants of area must move out, but they will be compensated at 30 taels per *mou*, with additional 10 taels removal expenses, their houses and other buildings will also be compensated for.	10	392/13

0. 2/ 93	Date 1860	HF 10	Description	pp	Old Ref. F.O. 682/
94	Dec 4	10 22	Bruce to Prince Kung. Is going to send Acting Consul to Tientsin: requests co-operation in opening of port for foreign trade.	6	392/15
95	Dec 4	10 22	Bruce to Prince Kung. Is going to send Acting Consul to Taiwan: requests co-operation in selection of best port for trading purposes.	6	392/14
96	Dec 4	10 22	Bruce to Prince Kung. Is going to send Acting Consul to Teng-chou: requests co-operation in selecting best port for foreign trade.	6	392/16
97	Dec 8	10 26	Prince Kung to Bruce. Will request Viceroy of Chihli to co-operate with British representatives in Tientsin to settle matter of leasing land for building British consulate and for establishing a foreign settlement. Will also notify authorities in Chihli, Shantung and Fukien of despatch of British [Acting] Consuls to Tientsin, Teng-chou and Taiwan respectively.	9	233/7
98	Dec 10	10 28	Bruce to Prince Kung. Is pleased to read that Prince Kung agrees that it is necessary for foreign envoys to be stationed at Peking permanently and that Emperor is willing to see him: in West, monarchs receive foreign envoys and their credentials as sign of mutual trust and respect.	13	392/17
99	Dec 13	11 02	Bruce to Prince Kung. Has received first instalment of indemnity, sum of 500,947.4 taels of silver, and has employed Chinese silversmiths to weigh the ingots. Chinese officials, who delivered the silver, ordered the silversmiths to keep quiet over ingots deficient in weight. Will issue formal receipt only after true weight of silver is ascertained.	10	392/18
100	Dec 19	11 08	Bruce to Prince Kung. Returns Prince Kung's letter in which character Ch'in-ch'ai, referring to H.M. Plenipotentiary, was not put in elevated position.	5	392/19

F.O. 682/ 1993	Date 1860	HF 10	Description	pp	Old Re F.O. 682
/101	Dec 21	11 10	Prince Kung to Bruce. Heng-ch'i has been appointed Superintendent of Trade, and Ch'ung-hou as his deputy, both to be stationed at Tientsin.	6	233/8
/102	Dec 23	11 12	Prince Kung to Bruce. Regrets that Tientsin officials have intimidated Chinese silversmiths employed to inspect the silver paid as indemnity. Will send two honest silversmiths from Peking to inspect silver in conjunction with Magistrate Chang Yü-ch'ing to Tientsin.	12	233/9

CROSS REFERENCES

A Guide to the Original Piece-Numbers of Materials
in F.O. 682, which has been Re-arranged.
Addenda may be found at the end of this section.

Old Reference	New Reference	Old Reference	New Reference
F.O. 682/	F.O. 682/	F.O. 682/	F.O. 682/
39/4	1973/1	104/24	1977/20
39/10/1	1972/21b	104/25	1977/26
39/10/2	1972/23b	104/26	1977/28
39/35	1992/34a	104/27	1977/29
40/5/1	1992/38a Encl.	104/28	1977/15
40/5/2	1992/38a	104/29	1977/36
40/5/3	1992/38b	104/30	1977/30
40/5/4	1992/26d	104/31	1977/27
68/1/18	1991/133b	104/32	1977/31
68/1/19-20	1992/25b	104/33	1977/32
68/3B/1	1979/109b	104/34	1977/33
68/3B/2	1979/114b	104/35	1977/34
68/3B/3	1976/118b	104/36	1977/35
68/3B/4	1976/110b	104/37	1977/38
68/3B/5	1979/119b	104/38	1977/37
68/3B/6	1976/123b	104/39	1977/40
68/3B/7	1976/123c	104/40	1977/41
68/3B/8	1979/57c	104/41	1977/42
68/3B/9	1979/57b	104/42	1977/43
68/3B/10	1979/68c	104/43	1977/44
100/1/1	1989/15	104/44	1977/39
100/1/2	1989/16	104/45	1977/45
100/1/3	1989/17	104/46	1977/47
100/1/4	1989/18	104/47	1977/46
100/1/5	1989/19	112/4B/1	1980/7b
100/1/6	1989/21	112/4B/3	1991/44b
102	1973/8	113/1	1975/1
104/1	1977/1	113/2	1975/4
104/2	1977/2	113/3	1975/6
104/3 A-B	1977/3	113/4	1975/7
104/4	1977/4	113/5	1975/11
104/5	1977/6	113/6	1975/13
104/6	1977/5	113/7	1975/15
104/7	1977/7b	113/8	1975/18
104/8	1977/8	113/9	1975/23
104/9	1977/10	113/10	1975/21
104/10	1977/9	113/11	1975/25
104/11	1977/11	113/12	1975/37
104/12 A-B	1977/12	113/13	1975/39
104/13	1977/13	113/14	1975/44
104/14	1977/14	113/15	1975/49
104/15	1977/16	113/16	1975/45
104/16	1977/17	113/17	1975/52
104/17	1977/18	113/18	1975/54
104/18	1977/21	113/19	1975/58
104/19	1977/22	113/20	1975/62
104/20	1977/23	113/21	1975/60
104/21	1977/24	113/22	1975/67
104/22	1977/7a	113/23	1975/69
104/23	1977/19	113/24	1975/71

Old Reference	New Reference	Old Reference	New Reference
F.O. 682/	F.O. 682/	F.O. 682/	F.O. 682/
113/25	1975/72	114/23	1975/59
113/26	1975/73	114/24	1975/63
113/27	1975/74a	114/25	1975/64
113/28	1975/80	114/26	1975/65
113/29A	1975/84	114/27	1975/66
113/29C	1975/86	114/28	1975/70
113/30	1975/87	114/29	1975/77
113/31	1975/90	114/30	1975/78
113/32	1975/92	114/31	1975/79
113/33	1975/94a	114/32	1975/82
113/34	1975/99	114/33	1975/83
113/35	1975/105	114/34	1975/89
113/36	1975/110	114/35	1975/96
113/37	1975/113	114/36	1975/97
113/39	1975/117	114/37	1975/98
113/40	1975/121	114/38	1975/101
113/41	1975/124	114/39	1975/102
113/42	1975/132	114/40	1975/103
113/43	1975/136	114/41	1975/104
113/44	1975/137a	114/42	1975/109
113/45	1975/140	114/43	1975/115
113/46	1975/145	114/44	1975/116
113/47	1975/148	114/45	1975/120
113/48	1975/150	114/46	1975/123
113/49	1975/160	114/47	1975/126
113/50	1975/158	114/48	1975/127
113/51	1975/162	114/49	1975/128
113/52	1975/164	114/50	1975/130
113/53	1975/166	114/51	1975/129
113/54	1975/170	114/52	1975/139
113/55	1975/174	114/53	1975/138
113/56	1975/177	114/54	1975/152
114/1	1975/3	114/55	1975/153
114/2	1975/2	114/56	1975/143
114/3	1975/5	114/57	1975/131
114/4	1975/8	114/58	1975/134
114/5	1975/10	114/59 A-B	1975/142
114/6	1975/17	114/60	1975/168
114/7	1975/30	114/61	1975/176
114/8	1975/31	114/62	1975/155
114/9	1975/32	114/63	1975/179
114/10	1975/29	114/64	1975/173
114/11	1975/33	114/65	1975/154
114/12	1975/34	114/66	1975/169
114/13	1975/35	116/2	1972/1a
114/14 A-B	1975/36	116/3	1972/1b
114/15	1975/41	116/4	1972/1c
114/16	1975/42	116/5	1979/39 Enc
114/17	1975/48	121A/1	1991/1
114/18	1975/28	121A/2	1991/4
114/19	1975/53	121A/3	1991/7
114/20	1975/55	121A/4	1991/8
114/21 A-B	1975/56	121A/5	1991/11
114/22	1975/57	121A/6	1991/12

Old Reference	New Reference	Old Reference	New Reference
F.O. 682/	F.O. 682/	F.O. 682/	F.O. 682/
121A/7	1991/21	121A/60	1992/24
121A/8	1991/22	121A/61	1992/28
121A/9	1991/29	121A/62	1992/31
121A/10	1991/30	121A/63	1992/35a
121A/11	1991/31	121A/65	1992/47
121A/12	1991/36	121A/68	1992/45
121A/13	1991/37	129/1	1989/1
121A/14	1991/39	129/2	1989/2
121A/15	1991/41	129/3	1989/3
121A/16	1991/43	129/4	1989/4
121A/17	1991/49	129/5	1989/6
121A/18	1991/47	129/6	1989/5
121A/19	1991/52	129/7	1989/7
121A/20	1991/54	129/8	1989/9
121A/21	1991/57	129/9	1989/11
121A/22	1991/59	129/10	1989/8
121A/23	1991/61	129/11	1989/10
121A/24	1991/63	129/12	1989/12
121A/25	1991/66	129/13	1989/13
121A/26	1991/68	129/14	1989/14
121A/27	1991/70	129/15	1989/20
121A/28	1991/73	129/16	1989/22
121A/29	1991/75	129/18	1989/24
121A/30	1991/79	129/19	1989/23
121A/31	1991/82	137/1/33	1984/26a
121A/32	1991/84	233/1	1993/85
121A/33	1991/90	233/2	1993/86
121A/34	1991/87	233/3	1993/89
121A/35	1991/94	233/4	1993/90
121A/36A	1991/98	233/5	1993/91
121A/36B	1991/99	233/6	1993/92
121A/37	1991/103	233/7	1993/97
121A/38	1991/106	233/8	1993/101
121A/39	1991/112	233/9	1993/102
121A/40	1991/114	248/1	1993/4
121A/41	1991/118	248/2	1993/5
121A/42	1991/117	248/3	1993/6
121A/43	1991/120	248/4	1993/10
121A/44	1991/109	248/5	1993/11
121A/45	1991/122	248/6	1993/13
121A/46	1991/125	248/7	1993/15
121A/47	1991/127	248/8	1993/17
121A/48	1991/129	248/9	1993/20
121A/49	1991/131	248/10	1993/21
121A/50	1992/1c	248/11	1993/35
121A/51	1992/3	248/12	1993/36
121A/52	1992/4	248/13	1993/37
121A/53	1992/7	248/14	1993/38
121A/54	1992/9	248/15	1993/41
121A/55	1992/10	248/16	1993/44
121A/56	1992/12	248/17	1993/48
121A/57	1992/14	248/18	1993/52
121A/58	1992/17	248/19	1993/50
121A/59	1992/23	248/20	1993/51

Old Reference	New Reference	Old Reference	New Reference
F.O. 682/	F.O. 682/	F.O. 682/	F.O. 682/
248/21	1993/53	253B/10	1975/47
248/22	1993/54	253B/11	1975/40
248/23	1993/56	253B/12	1975/61
248/24	1993/58	253B/13	1975/68
248/25	1993/60	253B/14	1975/81
248/26	1993/62	253B/15	1975/167
248/27	1993/64	253B/17	1975/165
248/28	1993/65	253B/18	1975/125
248/29	1993/67	253B/19	1975/24
248/30	1993/68	253B/20	1975/14
248/31	1993/70	253B/21	1975/12
248/32	1993/71	253B/22	1975/43
248/33	1993/72	253B/23	1975/16
248/34	1993/74	253B/24	1975/135
248/35	1993/76	253B/25	1975/74b
248/36	1993/77	253B/26	1975/75
248/37	1993/78	253B/27	1975/85
248/38	1993/81	253B/29	1975/19
248/39	1993/82	253B/30	1975/76
248/40	1993/83	253B/31	1975/122
248/41	1993/73	253B/32	1975/157
248/42	1993/23	253B/32	1975/157
248/43	1993/25	253B/33	1975/137b
248/44	1993/26	253B/34	1975/108
248/45	1993/27	253B/35	1975/118
248/46	1993/28	253B/36	1975/94b
248/47	1993/31	253B/37	1975/146
248/48	1993/30	253B/38	1975/133
248/49	1993/32	253B/39	1975/112
248/50	1993/22a	253B/40	1975/144
248/51	1993/34	253B/41	1975/141
253A/4B/2	1975/20a	253B/42	1975/151
253A/4B/3	1979/27a	253B/43	1975/149
253A/4B/4	1979/66b	253B/44	1975/106
253A/4B/5	1979/66c	253B/45	1975/111
253A/4B/6	1979/66d	253B/46	1975/114
253A/4B/7	1979/66e	253B/47	1975/100
253A/4B/8	1976/112	253B/48	1975/93
253A/4B/9	1979/68b	253B/49	1975/95
253A/4B/10	1979/70b	253B/50	1975/88
253A/4B/11	1979/45b	253B/51	1975/91
253A/4B/12	1979/45c	253B/52	1975/147
253A/4B/13	1979/45d	253B/53	1975/178
253A/4B/14	1985/1	253B/54	1975/175
253A/4B/15	1974/49	253B/55	1975/51
253B/1	1975/156	253B/56 A-B	1975/46
253B/2	1975/161	253B/58	1975/163
253B/3	1975/171	258	1975/1a
253B/4	1975/159	259	1975/1b
253B/5	1975/22	260	1975/1c
253B/6	1975/27	261	1975/1d
253B/7	1975/38	262	1975/1e
253B/8	1975/26	263	1975/1g
253B/9	1975/50	264	1971/1f

Old Reference	New Reference	Old Reference	New Reference
F.O. 682/	F.O. 682/	F.O. 682/	F.O. 682/
265	1975/1h	327/5/63	1978/50c
266	1975/5b	327/5/66	1978/48b
267	1975/6b	327/5/71	1978/48c
268	1975/7a	327/5/73	1978/48d
269	1975/11a	327/5/80	1978/46b
270	1975/11c	327/5/113	1991/124a
271	1975/54a	327/5/114	1991/133
272	1975/58a	327/5/115	1975/20b
273A	1975/71a	327/5/119	1991/31b
273B	1975/69a	327/5/120	1978/66
289/3B/3+8	1993/22b	327/5/167	1992/44b
289/4/1	1979/15a	327/5/168	1992/51
289/4/13	1992/39a	336/4	1993/1a
290/2	1973/6	352/1	1976/107b
290/3	1973/7	352/2	1976/107c
291/1	1991/45	352/3	1976/126
291/2	1991/48	352/4	1979/50a
291/3	1991/50	386/1/1	1991/119c
291/4	1991/53	386/1/2	1991/128b
291/5	1991/55	386/1/3	1993/55b
291/6	1991/58	383/1/4	1991/119b
291/7	1991/60	386/1/5	1992/1a
291/8	1991/62	386/1/6	1993/46a
291/9	1991/64	386/1/7	1988/6b
291/10	1991/67	386/1/8	1991/123b
291/11	1991/69	386/1/9	1992/1b
291/12	1991/71	386/1/10	1991/134
291/13	1991/74	386/1/11	1991/92b
291/14	1991/76	391/1/17	1992/39d
291/15	1991/80	392/1	1993/1b
291/16	1991/83	392/2	1993/2
291/17	1991/95	392/3	1993/3
291/18	1991/97	392/4	1993/8
291/19	1991/85	392/5	1993/9
291/20	1991/91	392/6	1993/12
291/21	1991/88	392/7	1993/14
291/22	1991/100	392/8	1993/18
291/23	1991/104	392/9	1993/61
291/24A	1991/107	392/10	1993/84
291/24B	1991/108	392/11	1993/87
291/25	1991/113	392/12	1993/88
291/26	1991/115	392/13	1993/93
291/27	1991/126	392/14	1993/95
291/28	1991/128a	392/15	1993/94
291/29	1991/130	392/16	1993/96
291/30	1991/132a	392/17	1993/98
327/5/5	1980/9c	392/18	1993/99
327/5/6	1980/20b	392/19	1993/100
327/5/8	1980/9b	392/20	1993/24
327/5/16	1980/44b	392/21	1993/29
327/5/23	1979/8b	392/22	1993/33
327/5/55	1981/33c	392/23	1993/39
327/5/57	1981/33b	392/24	1993/40
327/5/59	1978/50b	392/25	1993/42

Old Reference	New Reference	Old Reference	New Reference
F.O. 682/	F.O. 682/	F.O. 682/	F.O. 682/
392/26	1993/43	499/8	1991/23
392/27	1993/45	499/9	1991/25
392/28	1993/46	499/10	1991/27
392/29	1993/47	499/11	1991/3
392/30	1993/49	499/12	1991/6
392/31	1993/55	499/13A	1991/10
392/32	1993/57	499/14	1991/14
392/33	1993/59	499/15	1991/16
392/34	1993/63	499/16	1991/18
392/35	1993/66	499/17	1991/20
392/36	1993/69	499/18	1991/24
392/38	1993/75	499/19	1991/26
392/40	1993/79	499/20	1991/28
392/41	1993/80	499/21	1991/32
426/1-41 Encl.	1972/1d-41 Encl.	499/22	1991/33a
426/42	1972/43	499/23	1991/34
426/43	1972/42	499/24	1991/35
458/1	1992/2	499/25	1991/38
458/2	1992/5	499/26	1991/40
458/3	1992/6	499/27	1991/42
458/4	1992/49	499/28	1991/44a
458/5	1992/48	499/29	1991/46
458/6	1992/46	499/30	1991/51
458/7	1992/36	499/31	1991/56
458/8	1992/33	499/32	1991/65
458/9	1992/32	499/33	1991/72
458/10	1992/30	499/34	1991/77
458/11	1992/29	499/35	1991/78
458/12	1992/27	499/36	1991/81
458/13	1992/25a	499/37	1991/86
458/14	1992/21	499/38	1991/89
458/15	1992/20	499/39	1991/92a
458/16	1992/19	499/40	1991/93
458/17	1992/13	499/41	1991/96
458/18	1992/11	499/42	1991/101
458/19	1992/8	499/43	1991/102
465/1	1990/1	499/44	1991/105
465/2	1990/2	499/45	1991/110
465/3	1990/3	499/46	1991/111
465/4	1990/4	499/47	1991/116
465/5	1990/5	499/48	1991/119a
465/6	1990/6	499/49	1991/121
465/7	1990/7	499/50	1991/123a
465/8	1990/8	499/51	1991/124b
483/2/1	1973/2	769/1/18	1992/39c
483/2/2	1973/3	769/2/12	1992/26f
483/2/3	1973/4	769/3/1	1992/26c
499/1	1991/2	769/3/2	1992/26e
499/2	1991/5	769/3/7	1992/35b
499/3	1991/9	769/3/8	1992/26b
499/4	1991/13	769/3/10	1992/25c
499/5	1991/15	845	1973/5
499/6	1991/17		
499/7	1991/19		

Old Reference	New Reference	Old Reference	New Reference
F.O. 682/	F.O. 682/	F.O. 682/	F.O. 682/
846	1974/75	901	1974/42
847	1974/73	902	1974/45
848	1974/67	903	1974/46
849	1974/66	904	1974/47
850	1974/72	905	1974/48
851	1974/69	906	1975/56
852	1974/63	907	1974/52
853	1974/37	908	1974/54
854	1974/53	909	1974/55
856	1974/30	910	1974/57
857	1974/24	911	1974/58
858	1974/25	912	1974/60
859	1974/17	913	1974/59
860	1974/20	914	1974/61
861	1974/16	915	1974/65
862	1974/14	916	1974/64
863	1974/11	917	1974/62
864	1974/10	918	1974/68
865	1974/7	919	1974/70
866	1974/4	920	1974/71
867	1974/1	921	1974/74
868	1974/81	922	1974/76
869	1974/80	923	1974/78
870	1974/51	924	1974/77
871	1974/81	925	1974/12
872	1974/82	926	1974/15
873	1974/84	927	1975/180
874	1974/27	928	1975/183
875	1974/21	929	1975/9
876	1974/22	930	1975/181
877	1974/23	931	1975/172
878	1974/26	932	1976/2
879	1974/28	933	1976/3
880	1974/29	934	1976/7
881	1974/32	935	1976/8
882	1974/33	936	1976/11
883	1974/33 Encl.	937	1976/12
884	1974/34	938	1976/17
885	1974/35	939	1976/16
886	1974/2	940	1976/18
887	1974/3	941	1976/19
888	1974/6	942	1976/20
889	1974/5	943	1976/21
890	1974/9	944	1976/26
891	1974/8	945	1976/27
892	1974/13	946	1976/29
893	1974/18	947	1976/30
894	1974/19	948	1976/35
895	1974/36	949	1976/36
896	1974/38	950	1976/37
897	1974/40	951	1976/38
898	1974/39	952	1976/40
899	1974/41	953	1976/39
900	1974/43	954	1976/41

Old Reference	New Reference	Old Reference	New Reference
F.O. 682/	F.O. 682/	F.O. 682/	F.O. 682/
955	1976/45	1009	1976/31
956	1976/44	1010	1976/51
957	1976/46	1011	1976/53
958	1976/52	1012	1976/54
959	1976/57	1013	1976/55
960	1976/59	1014	1976/56
961	1976/61	1015	1976/58
962	1976/62	1016	1976/48
963	1976/68	1017	1976/60
964	1976/70	1018	1976/50
965	1976/73	1019	1976/63
966	1976/74	1020	1976/64
967	1976/75	1021	1976/65
968	1976/80	1022 A-B	1976/69
969 A-B	1976/81	1023	1976/71
970	1976/83	1024	1976/66
971	1976/87	1025	1976/72
973	1976/89	1026	1976/76
974	1976/90	1027	1976/77
975	1976/92	1028	1976/67
976	1976/93	1029	1976/78
977	1976/94	1030	1976/79
978	1976/95	1031	1976/82
979	1976/99	1032	1976/84
980	1976/99 Encl.	1033	1976/85
981	1976/102	1034	1976/86
982	1976/103	1035	1976/96
983	1976/116	1037	1976/98
984	1976/115	1038	1976/100
985	1976/113	1039	1976/101
986	1976/117	1040	1976/104
987	1976/1	1041	1976/105
988	1976/6	1042	1976/106
989	1976/5	1043	1976/107a
990	1976/4	1044	1976/108
991	1976/9	1045	1976/108 En
992	1976/10	1046	1976/108 En
993	1976/13	1047	1976/108 En
994	1975/182	1048	1976/109a
995	1976/15	1049	1976/110a
996A	1976/14	1050	1976/111
996B	1974/83	1051	1976/114a
997	1976/22	1052	1976/118a
998	1976/23	1053	1976/119a
999	1976/24	1054	1976/120
1000	1976/25	1055	1976/121
1001	1976/28	1056	1976/122
1002	1976/32	1057	1976/123a
1003	1976/33	1058	1976/124
1004	1976/34	1059	1976/125a
1005	1976/42	1060	1977/162
1006	1976/43	1061	1977/161
1007	1976/47	1062	1977/163
1008	1976/49	1063	1977/166

Old Reference	New Reference	Old Reference	New Reference
F.O. 682/	F.O. 682/	F.O. 682/	F.O. 682/
1064	1977/171	1116	1977/65
1065	1977/155	1117	1977/66
1066	1977/154	1118	1977/67
1068	1977/172	1119	1977/68
1069	1977/169	1120	1977/72
1070	1977/173	1121	1977/73
1071	1977/117	1122	1977/80
1072	1977/100	1123	1977/81
1073	1977/102	1124A	1977/82
1074A	1977/104	1124B/2	1991/33b
1074B	1977/106	1125	1977/83
1075	1977/105	1126	1977/84
1076	1977/107	1127	1977/85
1077	1977/109	1128	1977/86
1078	1977/110	1129	1977/88
1079	1977/111	1130	1977/89
1080	1977/116	1131	1977/93
1081	1977/119	1132	1977/133
1082	1977/120	1133	1977/124
1083	1977/122	1134	1977/125
1084	1977/126	1135	1977/50
1085	1977/127	1136	1977/49
1086	1977/128b	1137	1977/54
1087	1977/130	1138	1977/55
1088	1977/135	1139	1977/56
1089	1977/136	1140	1977/57
1090	1977/137	1141	1977/62
1091	1977/141	1142	1977/63
1092	1977/142	1143	1977/64
1093	1977/146	1144	1977/69
1094A	1977/147	1145	1977/71
1094B	1977/148	1146	1977/70
1095	1977/149	1147	1977/74
1096	1977/156	1148	1977/75
1097	1977/157	1149	1977/76
1098	1977/159a	1150	1977/77
1099	1977/164	1151	1977/78
1100	1977/165	1152	1977/87
1101	1977/167	1153	1977/90
1102	1977/168	1154	1977/91
1103	1977/170	1155	1977/92
1104	1977/174	1156	1977/94
1105	1977/175	1157	1977/95
1106	1977/176	1158	1977/96
1107A	1977/177	1159	1977/97
1107B	1977/178	1160	1977/98
1108	1977/48	1161	1977/112
1109	1977/51	1162	1977/108
1110	1977/52	1163	1977/114
1111	1977/53	1164	1977/115
1112	1977/58	1165	1977/99
1113	1977/59	1166	1977/103
1114	1977/60	1167	1977/113
1115	1977/61	1169	1977/128a

Old Reference	New Reference	Old Reference	New Referen
F.O. 682/	F.O. 682/	F.O. 682/	F.O. 682/
1170	1977/121	1227	1978/8
1171	1977/118	1228	1978/9
1172	1977/123	1229	1978/12
1173	1977/131	1230	1978/14
1176	1977/79	1231	1978/15
1177	1977/129	1232	1978/20
1178	1977/134	1233	1978/21
1179	1977/138	1234	1978/25
1180	1977/140	1235	1978/26
1181	1977/143	1236	1978/27
1182	1977/145	1237	1978/28
1183	1977/151	1238	1978/31
1184	1977/132	1239	1978/34
1185	1977/152	1240	1978/35
1186	1977/153	1241	1978/36
1187	1977/150	1242	1978/42
1188	1977/158a	1243	1978/50a
1189	1977/160	1244	1978/51
1190	1977/101	1245	1978/52
1191	1977/139	1246	1978/54
1192	1977/144	1247	1978/58
1193	1978/1	1248	1978/59
1194	1978/3	1249	1978/60
1195	1978/4	1250	1978/61
1196	1978/6	1251	1978/62
1197	1978/10	1252	1977/181
1198	1978/11	1253	1978/64
1199	1278/13	1254	1978/65
1200	1978/16	1255A	1978/44
1201	1978/17	1255B	1978/45
1202	1978/18	1255C	1978/46a
1203	1978/19	1255D	1978/48a
1204	1978/22	1255E	1978/47
1205	1978/23	1255F	1978/49
1206	1978/24	1256	1979/1
1207	1978/30	1257	1979/2
1208	1978/32	1258	1979/3
1209	1978/33	1259	1979/4a
1210	1978/37	1260	1979/5
1211	1978/38	1261	1979/6
1212	1978/39	1262	1979/7b
1213	1978/40	1263	1979/8a
1214	1978/41	1264	1979/9
1215	1978/43	1265	1979/10
1216	1978/53	1266	1979/11
1217	1978/55	1267	1979/13
1218	1978/56	1268	1979/15b
1219	1978/57	1269	1979/22
1220	1978/63	1270	1979/23
1221	1978/29	1271	1979/24
1222	1977/179	1272	1979/28
1223	1977/180	1273	1979/21
1224	1978/2	1274	1979/31
1225	1978/5	1275	1979/33
1226	1978/7	1276	1979/32

Old Reference	New Reference	Old Reference	New Reference
F.O. 682/	F.O. 682/	F.O. 682/	F.O. 682/
1277	1979/38	1331	1979/30
1278	1979/46	1332	1979/14
1279	1979/50b	1333	1979/47
1280	1979/53	1334	1979/48
1281	1979/54	1335	1979/76
1282	1979/63	1336	1979/73
1283	1979/84b	1337	1979/35
1284	1979/16	1338	1979/43
1285	1979/17	1339	1979/44
1286	1979/18	1340	1979/42
1287	1979/19	1341	1979/59
1288	1979/20	1342	1979/93
1289	1979/25	1343	1979/70a
1290	1979/29	1344	1979/88
1291	1979/34	1345	1979/60
1292	1979/36	1346A	1979/12
1293	1979/37	1346B	1979/26
1294	1979/39	1346C	1979/94
1295	1979/40	1346D	1979/55
1296	1979/41	1346E	1979/45a
1297	1979/51	1346F	1979/49
1298	1979/57a	1347	1979/56
1299	1979/52	1348	1979/98
1300	1979/64	1349	1980/1
1301	1979/58	1350	1980/2
1302	1979/62	1351	1980/4
1303	1979/65	1352	1980/5
1304	1979/66a	1353	1980/6
1305	1979/67	1354	1980/7a
1306	1979/68a	1355	1979/97
1307	1979/69	1356	1980/8a
1308	1979/71	1357A	1980/9a
1309A	1979/72	1357B	1980/3
1309B	1979/61	1357C	1980/14
1310	1979/74	1357D	1980/21
1311	1979/77	1358	1980/10
1312	1979/80	1359	1980/11
1313	1979/81	1360	1980/12
1314	1979/82	1361	1980/13
1315	1979/83	1362	1980/15
1316	1979/83 Encl.	1363	1980/16
1317	1979/85	1364	1980/17
1318	1979/86	1365	1980/18
1319	1979/79	1366	1980/19
1320	1979/87	1367	1980/20a
1321	1979/89	1368	1980/22
1322	1979/90	1369	1980/23
1323	1979/91	1370	1980/24
1324	1979/91 Encl.	1371	1980/25
1325	1979/92	1372	1980/27
1326	1979/95	1373	1980/28
1327	1979/96	1374	1980/29
1328	1979/78	1375	1980/30
1329	1979/75	1376	1980/31
1330	1979/27b	1377	1980/32

Old Reference	New Reference	Old Reference	New Reference
F.O. 682/	F.O. 682/	F.O. 682/	F.O. 682/
1378	1980/33	1431	1981/41
1379	1980/34	1432	1981/42
1380	1980/35	1433	1981/43
1381	1980/36	1434	1981/46
1382	1980/37	1435	1981/47
1383	1980/38	1436	1981/48
1384	1980/39	1438/2	1972/18b
1385	1980/40	1438/3	1977/159b
1386	1980/41	1438/7	1987/69a
1387	1980/42	1439	1981/53
1388	1980/43	1440	1981/54
1389	1980/44a	1441	1981/56
1390	1980/45	1442	1981/57
1391	1980/46	1443	1981/60
1392	1980/47	1444	1981/63
1393	1980/48	1445	1981/65
1394	1980/49	1446	1981/66
1395	1980/50	1447	1981/67
1396	1980/51	1448	1981/69
1397	1980/52	1449	1981/72
1398	1980/53	1450	1981/73
1399	1980/54	1451	1981/74
1400	1980/55	1452	1981/76
1401	1980/56	1453	1981/79
1402	1980/57	1454	1981/82
1403	1980/58	1455	1981/84
1404	1980/59	1456	1981/86
1405	1980/60	1457	1981/87
1406	1980/61	1458	1981/88
1407	1980/62	1459	1981/92
1408	1980/63	1460	1981/94
1409	1980/64a	1461	1981/97
1410	1980/65	1462	1981/98
1411	1980/66	1463	1981/100
1412	1980/67	1464	1981/101
1413	1980/26	1465	1981/104
1414	1981/1	1466	1981/105
1415A	1981/2	1467	1981/108
1415B	1980/64b	1468A/9/1	1979/4b
1416A	1981/4	1468A/9/2	1979/7a
1416B	1981/4 Encl. 1	1468A/14/1	1979/84a
1416C	1981/4 Encl. 2	1468A/14/2	1980/8b
1417	1981/8	1468B	1981/3
1418	1981/9	1470	1981/6
1419	1981/12	1471	1981/7
1420	1981/14	1472	1981/10
1421	1981/15	1473	1981/11
1422	1981/21	1474	1981/13
1423	1981/22	1475	1981/16
1424	1981/24	1476	1981/17
1245	1981/27	1477	1981/18
1426	1981/28	1478	1981/19
1427	1981/29	1479	1981/20
1428	1981/32	1480	1981/23
1429	1981/39	1481	1981/25
1430	1981/40	1482	1981/26

Old Reference	New Reference	Old Reference	New Reference
F.O. 682/	F.O. 682/	F.O. 682/	F.O. 682/
483	1981/30	1538	1982/19
484	1981/31	1539	1982/20
485	1981/33a	1540	1982/18
486	1981/34	1541	1982/21
487	1981/35	1542	1982/22
488	1981/36	1543	1982/23
489	1981/37	1544	1982/24
490	1981/38	1545	1982/25
491	1981/44	1546	1982/26
492	1981/45	1547	1982/27
493	1981/51	1548	1982/29
494	1981/49	1549	1982/30
495	1981/50	1550	1982/32
496	1981/52	1551	1982/31
497	1981/55	1552	1982/34
498	1981/58	1553	1982/35
499	1981/59	1554	1982/36
500	1981/62	1555	1982/37
501	1981/64	1556	1982/38
502	1981/68	1557	1982/39
503	1981/70	1558	1982/40
504	1981/71	1559	1982/41
505	1981/75	1560	1982/57
506	1981/77	1561	1982/63
507	1981/78	1562	1982/62
508	1981/80	1563A	1982/6
509	1981/81	1563B	1982/28
510	1981/83	1564	1982/16
511	1981/85	1565	1982/33
512	1981/89	1566	1982/43
513	1981/91	1567	1982/44
514	1981/93	1568	1983/6
515	1981/95	1569	1982/45
516	1981/96	1570	1982/46
517	1981/99	1571	1982/47
518	1981/102	1572	1982/48a
519	1981/103	1573	1982/48b
520	1981/106	1574	1982/49
521	1981/107	1575	1982/51
522	1982/69	1576	1982/52
523	1981/61	1577	1982/53
524	1981/90	1578	1982/54
525	1982/1	1579	1982/55a
526	1982/2	1580	1982/55b
527	1982/3	1581	1982/56
528	1982/4	1582	1982/64
529	1982/5	1583	1982/58
530	1982/7	1584	1982/59
531	1982/8	1585	1982/60
532	1982/10	1586	1982/61
533	1982/11	1587	1982/65
534	1982/12	1588	1982/66
535	1982/13	1589	1982/67
536	1982/14	1590	1982/68
537	1982/17	1591	1982/70

Old Reference	New Reference	Old Reference	New Reference
F.O. 682/	F.O. 682/	F.O. 682/	F.O. 682/
1592	1982/71	1646	1986/5
1593	1982/72	1647	1986/7
1594	1982/42	1648	1986/8
1595A	1981/109	1649	1986/10
1595B	1974/79	1650	1986/11
1596	1981/110	1651	1986/13
1597	1982/9	1652	1986/15
1598	1982/15	1653	1986/16
1599A	1974/44	1654	1986/18
1599B	1974/50	1655	1986/19
1600	1982/50	1656	1986/21
1601	1983/1	1657	1986/22
1602	1983/2	1658	1986/26
1603	1983/3	1659	1986/1
1604	1983/4	1660	1986/3
1605	1983/5	1661	1986/4
1606	1984/1	1662	1986/6
1607	1984/3	1663	1986/9
1609	1984/5	1664	1986/12
1610	1984/6	1665	1986/14
1611	1984/10	1666	1986/17
1612	1984/12	1667	1986/20
1613	1984/13	1668	1986/23
1614	1984/14	1669	1986/24
1615	1984/18	1670	1986/25
1616	1984/20	1671	1987/1
1617	1984/21	1672	1987/3
1618	1984/23	1673	1987/5
1619	1984/24	1674	1987/7
1620	1984/26b	1675	1987/8
1621	1984/27	1676	1987/11
1622	1984/32	1677	1987/12
1623	1984/34	1678	1987/13
1624	1984/35	1679	1987/15
1625	1984/37	1680	1987/16
1626	1984/2	1681	1987/17
1627	1984/4	1682	1987/21
1628	1984/7	1683	1987/22
1629	1984/8	1684	1987/23
1630	1984/9	1685	1987/26
1631	1984/11	1686	1987/28
1632	1984/15	1687	1987/30
1633	1984/16	1688A	1987/31
1634	1984/17	1688B	1987/32
1635	1984/22	1689	1987/35
1636	1984/19	1690	1987/36
1637	1984/25	1691A	1987/2
1638	1984/28	1691B	1987/4
1639	1984/30	1692	1987/6
1640	1984/31	1693	1987/9
1641	1984/29	1694	1987/10
1642	1984/33	1695	1987/14
1643	1984/36	1696	1987/18
1644	1984/38	1697	1987/20
1645	1986/2	1698	1987/19

Old Reference	New Reference	Old Reference	New Reference
F.O. 682/	F.O. 682/	F.O. 682/	F.O. 682/
1699	1987/25	1753	1988/20
1700	1987/27	1755	1988/23
1701	1987/29	1756	1988/24
1702	1987/33	1757	1988/26
1703	1987/34	1758	1988/27
1704	1987/37	1759	1988/28
1705A	1987/40	1760	1988/22
1705B	1987/41	1763	1988/2
1706	1987/43	1764	1988/3
1707	1987/45	1765	1988/6a
1708	1987/48	1766	1988/10
1709	1987/50	1767	1988/11
1710	1987/54	1768	1988/12
1711	1987/57	1769	1988/13
1712	1987/58	1770	1988/15
1713	1987/59	1771	1988/17
1714	1987/66	1772	1988/18
1715	1987/68	1773	1988/21
1716	1987/70	1774	1988/25
1717	1987/75	1775	1988/30
1718	1987/73	1776	1988/29
1719	1987/77	1777	1988/31
1720	1987/24	1778	1988/33
1721	1987/52	1779	1988/32
1722	1987/38	1780	1979/67 Encl.
1723	1987/39	1781A	1977/158b
1724	1987/44	1781B	1977/163b
1725	1987/46	1781C	1977/160b
1726	1987/47	1781D	1977/150b
1727	1987/49	1781E	1977/176b
1728	1987/51	1782	1992/42
1729	1987/53	1783	1992/22
1730	1987/55	1784	1988/14
1731	1987/56	1785	1992/38c
1732	1987/60	1786	1992/26a
1733	1987/61	1787	1992/18
1734	1987/62	1788	1992/34b
1735	1987/63	1789	1992/16
1736	1987/64	1790/1	1992/50
1737	1987/65	1790/2	1992/40
1738	1987/67	1790/3	1992/41
1739	1987/69b	1790/4	1992/39b
1740	1987/71	1791	1992/44a
1741	1987/72	1792	1993/7
1742	1987/74	1793/1	1992/37
1743	1987/76	1793/2	1992/43
1744	1988/4b	1795	1993/19
1745	1988/1	1796	1993/16
1746	1988/4a	1869	1981/5
1747	1988/5		
1748	1988/7		
1749	1988/8		
1750	1988/9		
1751	1988/16		
1752	1988/19		

Addenda on next page.

Addenda to CROSS REFERENCES

Old Reference	New Reference
F.O. 682/	F.O. 682/
113/38	1975/107
253B/16	1975/166
327/5/75	1978/48e
392/37	1993/73b
392/39	1993/75b
855	1974/31
972	1976/88
1036	1976/97

BIBLIOGRAPHY OF WORKS CONSULTED

(I) *WORKS IN WESTERN LANGUAGES*

Baark, Erik. *Catalogue of Chinese Manuscripts in Danish Archives: Chinese diplomatic correspondence from the Ch'ing dynasty (1644-1911).* London, Curzon Press, 1979.

Beeching, Jack. *The Chinese Opium Wars.* London, Hutchinson & Co., 1975.

Bonner-Smith, D. and Lumby, E.W.B. (eds.) *The Second China War 1856-1860.* Navy Records Society, London, 1954

Bowring, Sir John. *Autobiographical Recollections of Sir John Bowring.* London, 1877.

Brunnert, H.S. and Hagelstrom, V.V. *Present Day Political Organization of China.* Beltchenko, A. and Morgan, E.E. (trs.) Taipei (reprinted), 1963.

Chang, Hsin-pao. *Commissioner Lin and the Opium War.* Camb., Mass., Harvard University Press, 1964.

Clark, Arthur Hamilton. *The Clipper Ship Era 1843-1869.* New York, 1910.

Costin, W.C. *Great Britain and China, 1833-60.* Oxford, Oxford University Press, 1937.

Couling, S. *The Encyclopaedia Sinica.* Shanghai, Kelly and Walsh, 1917.

Cunynghame, Capt. A. *The Opium War, Being Recollections of Service in China.* London, 1844.

Davis, Sir John. *China during the War and since the Peace.* (2 vols.) London, 1852.

Eitel, E.J. *Europe in China: The history of Hong Kong from the beginning to the year 1882.* London, 1895.

Endacott, G.B. *A History of Hong Kong.* Hong Kong, Oxford University Press, 1958.

Fairbank, J.K. *Trade and Diplomacy on the China Coast: The opening of the treaty ports, 1841-1854.* Camb., Mass., Harvard University Press, 1953.

Fay, Peter Ward. *The Opium War, 1840-1841.* Chapel Hill, University of North Carolina Press, 1975.

Forbes, Lt. F.E., RN. *Five Years in China, from 1841 to 1847.* London, 1848.

Forbes, R.B. *Personal Reminiscences*. Boston, 1878.

Fox, Grace. *British Admirals and Chinese Pirates, 1832-1869*. London, 1940.

Gerson, Jack J. *Horatio Nelson Lay and Sino-British Relations, 1854-1864*. Camb., Mass., 1972.

Graham, G.S. *The China Station: War and diplomacy, 1830-1860*. Oxford, Oxford University Press, 1978.

Grant, General Sir Hope and Knollys, Capt. H. *Incidents in the China War of 1860*. Edinburgh and London, 1875.

Greenberg, M. *British Trade and the Opening of China, 1800-1842*. Cambridge, Cambridge University Press, 1951.

Gulick, Edward V. *Peter Parker and the Opening of China*. Camb., Mass., Harvard University Press, 1974.

Hao, Yen-p'ing. *The Comprador in Nineteenth Century China*. Camb., Mass., Harvard University Press, 1970.

Hay, Admiral Rt. Hon. Sir John C.D. *The Suppression of Piracy in the China Sea, 1849*. London, 1889.

Holt, Edgar. *The Opium Wars in China*. London, 1964.

Hsü, I.C.Y. *China's Entrance into the Family of Nations: The diplomatic phase, 1858-1880*. Camb., Mass., Harvard University Press, 1960.

Hummel, A.W. (ed.) *Eminent Chinese of the Ch'ing Period (1644-1912)*. (2 vols.) Washington, D.C., U.S. Government Printing Office, 1943-44.

Hurd, Douglas. *The Arrow War: An Anglo-Chinese confusion, 1856-1860*. London, 1967.

Inglis, Brian. *The Opium War*. London, Hodder and Stoughton, 1976.

Iwao, Seiichi (comp.) *List of Foreign Office Records Preserved in the Public Record Office in London, Relating to China and Japan*. Tokyo, 1959.

Jardine, Matheson & Co. *An Outline of the History of a China House for a Hundred Years, 1832-1932*. Hong Kong (privately printed), 1934.

Jocelyn, Lord Robert. *Six months with the Chinese Expedition, or, Leaves from a soldier's note-book*. London, 1841.

Johnson, R.E. *Far China Station: The U.S. Navy in Asian waters, 1800-1898*. Annapolis, Maryland, Naval Institute Press, 1979.

Lane-Poole, S. *The Life of Sir Harry Parkes* (vol. 1), *Consul in China*. London, 1894.

Lay, H.N. 'Our Interests in China' - a letter to the Rt. Hon. Earl Russell K.G. (H.M.'s Principal Secty. of State for Foreign Affairs). London, 1864.

Notes on the Opium Question, and Brief Survey of our Relations with China. London, 1893.

Lindsay, H.H. ['A Resident in China']. *Remarks on Occurrences in China since the Opium Seizure in March 1839 to the Latest Date*. London, 1840.

Loch, Capt. G.G., RN. *The Closing Events of the Campaign in China: The operations in the Yang-Tse-Kiang; and the Treaty of Nanking*. London, 1843.

McPherson, D. (M.D.) *Two Years in China: Narrative of the Chinese expedition from its formation in April 1840 till April 1842*. London, 1842.

The War in China, 1840-42. London, 1843.

Mancall, Mark. 'Major-General Ignatieff's Mission to Peking 1859-1860'. *Papers on China for the East Asian Regional Studies Seminar, Harvard University*. Camb., Mass., 1956.

Martin, R.M. *China: Political, commercial and social; in an official report to Her Majesty's Government*. London, 1847.

Reports, Minutes and Despatches on the British Position and Prospects in China. London, 1846.

Maxwell, Rt. Hon. Sir Herbert. *The Life and Letters of George William Frederick, Fourth Earl of Clarendon*. (2 vols.) London, 1913.

Mayers, W.F. (ed.) *Treaties between the Empire of China and Foreign Powers....* Taipei (reprinted), 1966.

Mayers, W.F., Dennys, N.B. and King, C. *The Treaty Ports of China and Japan: A complete guide to the open ports of those countries, together with Peking, Yedo, Hong Kong and Macao*. London, 1867.

Michie, A. *The Englishman in China during the Victorian Era: The career of Sir Rutherford Alcock*. London, 1900.

Moges, Marquis de. *Recollections of Baron Gros' Embassy to China in 1857-8*. (Authorized translation.) London and Glasgow, 1860.

Morison, J.L. *The Eighth Earl of Elgin: A chapter in nineteenth century imperial history*. London, 1928.

Morse, H.B. *The International Relations of the Chinese Empire*. (Vol. 1) Shanghai, 1910.

Mundy, W.W. *Canton and the Bogue: The narrative of an eventful six months in China.* London, 1875.

Murray, Lt. Alexander. *Doings in China: Being the personal narrative of an officer engaged in the late Chinese expedition.* London, 1843

Nolde, J.J. 'The False Edict of 1849', *Journal of Asian Studies,* Vol. 20, no. 3 (1960): pp. 299-351.

'Xenophobia in Canton, 1842-1849', *Journal of Oriental Studies,* vol. 13, no. 1 (1975): pp. 1-22.

Oliphant, L. *Narrative of the Earl of Elgin's Mission to China and Japan in the Years 1857, 1858 and 1859.* 2nd ed. London, 1860.

Owen, D.E. *British Opium Policy in China and India.* New Haven, Conn., Yale University Press, 1934.

Playfair, G.M.H. *The Cities and Towns of China: A geographical dictionary.* 2nd ed. Shanghai, 1910.

Pong, D. 'The Kwangtung Provincial Archives at the Public Record Office of London: A progress report', *Journal of Asian Studies,* Vol. 28, no. 1 (1968): pp. 139-143.

'Correspondence Between the British and the Chinese in the 19th and the 20th Centuries: Chinese language manuscripts from the British Legation at Peking deposited in the Public Record Office, London', *Ch'ing-shih wen-t'i,* Vol. 2, No. 4 (1970): pp. 40-63.

A Critical Guide to the Kwangtung Provincial Archives Deposited at the Public Record Office of London. Camb., Mass., 1975.

Rait, Robert S. *The Life and Campaigns of Hugh, Field Marshal, Viscount Gough.* (2 vols.) London, 1903.

Sargent, A.J. *Anglo-Chinese Commerce and Diplomacy.* Oxford, 1907.

Scott, Beresford. *An Account of the Destruction of the Fleets of the Celebrated Pirate Chieftains Chui-Apoo and Shap-ng-tsai, in September and October, 1849.* London, 1881.

Swinhoe, Robert. *Narrative of the North China Campaign of 1860....* London, 1861.

Swisher, E. *China's Management of the American Barbarians: A study of Sino-American relations, 1841-1861, with documents.* New Haven, Conn., Yale University Press, 1953.

Tan, Chung. *China and the Brave New World: A study of the origins of the Opium War (1840-41).* New Delhi, Allied Publishers Private, 1978.

Taylor, E.S. 'Hong Kong as a Factor in British Relations with China, 1834-1860'. M.A. thesis, University of London, 1967.

Tong, Te-kong. *United States Diplomacy in China 1844-60*. Seattle, University of Washington Press, 1964.

Wakeman, F. Jr. *Strangers at the Gate: Social disorder in South China, 1839-1861*. Berkeley, University of California Press, 1966.

Webster, C.K. *The Foreign Policy of Palmerston, 1830-1841*. (2 vols.) London, 1951.

Wolseley, Lt. Col. G.J. *Narrative of the War with China in 1860*. London, 1862.

Wong, J.Y. 'Sir John Bowring and the Canton City Question', *Bulletin of the John Rylands University Library of Manchester*, Vol. 56, no. 1 (1973): pp. 219-45.

'The *Arrow* Incident: A reappraisal', *Modern Asian Studies*, Vol. 8, no. 3 (1974): pp. 373-89.

'Harry Parkes and the *Arrow* War in China', *Modern Asian Studies*, Vol. 9, no. 3 (1975): pp. 303-20.

Yeh Ming-ch'en: Viceroy of Liang-Kuang, 1852-8. Cambridge, Cambridge University Press, 1976.

'Lin Tse-Hsü and Yeh Ming-ch'en: A comparison of their roles in the two Opium Wars', *Ch'ing-shih wen-t'i*, Vol. 3, Supplement (1977): pp. 63-85.

(II) WORKS IN CHINESE AND JAPANESE

*Note: Like authors, editors and compilers are usually
put at the beginning of each entry. In cases of works
that are commonly referred to by their titles rather
than by the compilers or editors, however, the titles
are put at the beginning of the entry for easy
reference.*

Chang, Po-feng 章伯鋒   (ed.) *Ch'ing-tai ko-ti chiang-chün tu-t'ung
ta-ch'en teng nien-piao, 1796-1911* 清代各地將軍都統大臣等年表
(A table of Tartar-Generals and Brigadier-Generals of the Ch'ing
period, 1796-1911). Peking, 1965.

Ch'ao-chou fu-chih 潮州府志   (Gazetteer of Ch'ao-chou prefecture).
Chou Shih-hsün 周碩勛   *et al.* (comps.) 1893.

Ch'en, Hsi-ch'i 陳錫祺   . *Kuang-tung San-yüan-li jen-min te
k'ang-Ying tou-cheng* 廣東三元里人民的抗英鬥爭   (The
resistance to British incursion by the people of San-yüan-li in
Kuang-tung). Canton, 1956.

Ch'en, Te-yün 陳德芸 (comp.) *Ku-chin jen-wu pieh-ming so-yin*
古今人物別名索引   (An index to the aliases of Chinese persons
from early to modern times). Taipei, 1965.

Ch'i, Ssu-ho 齊思和   *et al.* (eds.) *Ya-p'ien chan-cheng* 鴉片戰爭
(The Opium War). (6 vols.) Shanghai, 1954.

(eds.) *Ti-erh-tz'u ya-p'ien chan-cheng* 第二次鴉片戰爭
(The Second Opium War). (6 vols.) Shanghai, 1978.

Chiang, Meng-yin 蔣孟引   . *Ti-erh-tz'u ya-p'ien chan-cheng*
第二次鴉片戰爭   (The Second Opium War). Peking, 1965.

Chiang, T'ing-fu 蔣廷黻 (comp.) *Chin-tai Chung-kuo wai-chiao-shih
tzu-liao chi-yao* 近代中國外交史資料輯要   (Selected
materials on modern Chinese diplomatic history). (2 vols.)
Taipei, 1959.

Ch'ien, Shih-fu 錢實甫 (comp.) *Ch'ing-chi chung-yao chih-kuan
nien-piao* 清季重要職官年表 (A table of important officials
of late Ch'ing). Peking, 1961.

Ch'ing-shih 清史 (History of the Ch'ing dynasty). Ch'ing-shih
pien-tsuan wei-yüan-hui 清史編纂委員會 (comp.) (8 vols.)
Taipei, 1961.

Ch'ing-shih lieh-chuan 清史列傳 (Biographies in Ch'ing history).
Chung-hua shu-chü 中華書局 (ed.) Shanghai, 1928.

Ch'iung-chou fu-chih 瓊州府志 (Gazetteer of Ch'iung-chou
prefecture). Ming-i 明誼 *et al.* (comps.) 1890.

Ch'ou-pan i-wu shih-mo 籌辦夷務始末 (A complete account of
the management of foreign affairs). Peking, 1930.

Ch'ou-pan i-wu shih-mo pu-i 籌辦夷務始末補遺 , see
Tao-kuang Hsien-feng liang-ch'ao ch'ou-pan i-wu shih-mo pu-i
道光咸豐兩朝籌辦夷務始末補遺.

Chung-kuo jen-ming ta tz'u-tien 中國人名大辭典 (Biographical
dictionary of China). Fang I 方毅 *et al.* (comps.) Hong
Kong, 1931.

Chung-kuo ku-chin ti-ming ta tz'u-tien 中國古今地名大辭典
(A dictionary of Chinese place names from early to modern times).
Tsang Li-ho 臧勵龢 *et al.* (comps.) Hong Kong, 1931.

Fang, Shih-ming 方詩銘. *Shang-hai Hsiao-tao-hui ch'i-i*
上海小刀會起義 (The uprising of the Small Sword Society at
Shanghai). Kwangsi (reprinted), 1972.

Hsiang-shan hsien-chih 香山縣志 (Gazetteer of Hsiang-shan
magistracy). T'ien Ming-yao 田明曜 and Ch'en Li 陳澧
et al. (comps). 1879.

Hsiao, I-shan 蕭一山 . Ch'ing-tai t'ung-shih 清代通史 (A general history of the Ch'ing dynasty). (5 vols.) Taipei, 1963.

Hsin-hui hsien-chih 新會縣志 (Gazetteer of Hsin-hui magistracy). Lin Hsing-chang 林星章 et al. (comps.) 1841.

Huang, Chia-mo 黃嘉謨 . Mei-kuo yü T'ai-wan 美國與台灣 (The United States and Taiwan, [1784-1895]). Nan-kang [near Taipei], 1966.

Huang, Fo-i 黃佛頤 . Kuang-chou ch'eng fang-chih 廣州城坊志 (Gazetteer of the city of Canton). (6 vols.) Reprinted, 1948.

Jung Meng-yüan 榮孟源 . Chung-kuo chin-tai-shih li-piao 中國近代史曆表 (A cross-reference of Chinese and Western calendars, [1830-1949]). Hong Kong, 1962.

Kuang-chou fu-chih 廣州府志 (Gazetteer of Kuang-chou prefecture). Tai Chao-ch'en 戴肇辰 and Shih Ch'eng 史澄 et al. (comps.) 1879.

Kuang-tung t'ung-chih 廣東通志 (Gazetteer of Kwangtung province). Juan Yüan 阮元 et al. (comps,) 1818.

Kuang-tung yü-ti t'u-shuo 廣東輿地圖說 (An atlas of Kwangtung province, with descriptions). Liao T'ing-ch'en 廖廷臣 (comp.) 1909.

Kuo T'ing-i 郭廷以 . Chin-tai Chung-kuo shih-shih jih-chih 近代中國史事日誌 (A chronology of modern Chinese history). (2 vols.) Taipei, 1963.

Lin Ch'ung-yung 林崇墉 . Lin Tse-hsü chuan 林則徐傳 (A biography of Lin Tse-hsü). Taipei, 1967.

Ming-Ch'ing li-k'o chin-shih t'i-ming pei-lu 明清歷科進士題名碑錄
(A list of successful *chin-shih* examination candidates in Ming
and Ch'ing times). Taipei (reprinted), 1969.

Nan-hai hsien-chih 南海縣志 (Gazetteer of Nan-hai magistracy).
Cheng Meng-yü 鄭夢玉 and Liang Shao-hsien 梁紹獻 *et al.*
(comps.) 1872.

P'an-yü hsien-chih 番禺縣志 (Gazetteer of P'an-yü
magistracy). Li Fu-t'ai 李福泰 *et al.* (comps.) 1871.

San-yüan-li jen-min k'ang-Ying tou-cheng shih-liao 三元里人民抗英鬥爭史料
(Sources on the resistance to British incursion by the people of
San-yüan-li). Kuang-tung wen-shih-kuan 廣東文史館 (comp.)
Revised and expanded edition. Peking, Chung-hua shu-chü, 1978.

Sasaki, Masaya 佐々木正哉 (comp.) *Ahen sensō no kenkyū, shiryō hen*
鴉片戰爭の研究資料篇 (Materials for research on
the Opium War). Tokyo, 1964.

(comp.) *Ahen sensō go no Chū-Ei kōsō, shiryō henkō* 鴉片戰爭
後の中英抗爭資料篇稿(Draft collection of materials on Anglo-
Chinese confrontations after the Opium War). Tokyo, 1964.

(comp.) *Ahen sensō zen Chū-Ei kōshō monjo* 鴉片戰爭前中英交涉文書
(Documents on Anglo-Chinese relations before the Opium War).
Tokyo, 1967.

Shun-te hsien-chih 順德縣志 (Gazetteer of Shun-te
magistracy). Chou Ch'ao-huai 周朝槐 *et al.* (comps.) 1929.

Ssu-kuo hsin-tang 四國新檔 (New archives concerning our
relations with America, England, France and Russia). (4 vols.)
Nan-kang [near Taipei], 1966.

Ta-Ch'ing li-ch'ao shih-lu 大清歷朝實錄 . (Veritable records of the successive reigns of the Ch'ing dynasty). Mukden, 1937-1938.

Tao-kuang Hsien-feng liang-ch'ao ch'ou-pan i-wu shih-mo pu-i 道光咸豐兩朝籌辦夷務始末補遺 (Supplements to *Ch'ou-pan i-wu shih-mo*, Tao-kuang and Hsien-feng periods). Nan-kang [near Taipei], 1966.

Ts'ai Kuan-lo 蔡冠洛 . *Ch'ing-tai ch'i-pai ming-jen chuan* 清代 七百名人傳 (Biographies of seven hundred famous persons of the Ch'ing period). (3 vols.) Shanghai, 1937.

Tung-kuan hsien-chih 東莞縣志 (Gazetteer of Tung-kuan magistracy). Ch'en Po-t'ao 陳伯陶 *et al.* (comps.) 1921.

Wei Hsiu-mei 魏秀梅 (comp.) *Ch'ing-chi chih-kuan-piao fu jen-wu-lu* 清季職官表附人物錄 (A table of Ch'ing officials with biographies). (2 vols.) Nan-kang [near Taipei], 1979.

Yang Chia-lo 楊家駱 (ed.) *Li-tai jen-wu pieh-shu chü-ch'u ming t'ung-chien.* 歷代人物別署居處名通檢 (A cross-reference of historical persons and their names taken after their residences, studies and villas). Taipei, 1962. [This was originally compiled by Ch'en Nai-ch'ien 陳乃乾 and published in 1957 by Chung-hua shu-chü in Peking under the title *Shih-ming pieh-hao so-yin* 室名別號索引 .]

(ed.) *Li-tai jen-wu nien-li t'ung-p'u* 歷代人物年里通譜 (Index of dates and places of birth of figures in Chinese history). Taipei, 1963. [This was originally compiled by Chiang Liang-fu 姜亮夫 and published in 1937 by the Commercial Press in Shanghai (first edition) under the title *Li-tai ming-jen nien-li pei-chuan tsung-piao* 歷代名人年里碑傳總表 and again in 1959 by Chung-hua shu-chü in Peking (second edition) under the title *Li-tai ming-jen nien-li pei-chuan tsung-piao* 歷史名人年里碑傳綜表 .]

INDEX-GLOSSARY

B

Balfour, G. 巴富
    Captain
      29 Sep 1843
    Consul at Shanghai
      29 Sep 1843
      1 Dec 1843
      21 Jul 1844

      24 Nov 1844
      4 Dec 1844
      17 Jul 1846
      18 Aug 1846
      24 Aug 1846
      7 Oct 1846
      31 Oct 1846

Banner soldiers 旗兵
    9 Jan 1858

barter 現貨兌換
    24 Jan 1843

Beale, Mr 友爾
    Portugese Consul at Shanghai
      16 May 1851
      26 May 1851
      9 Jun 1851
      13 Jun 1851

Bettelheim, Dr 咟噫哈醫生
    British medical practitioner
      25 Feb 1849
      28 Feb 1849
      27 Dec 1849
      13 Jan 1850
      25 Mar 1853
      3 Jun 1853

Black River Packet
    barque
      29 Mar 1855

blackmail 訛索
    17 Sep 1842
    7 Jul 1847
    16 Jul 1847
    13 Feb 1858
    16 Feb 1858

bluejackets 水手
    6 Jul 1842
    1 Dec 1843
    29 Nov 1845
    16 Dec 1845
    9 Feb 1846
    21 Feb 1846
    6 Mar 1846
    6 Oct 1854
    11 Jun 1858

Bogue, The 虎門
    see Hu-men

bond servants
    28 Feb 1844
    12 Mar 1844

Bonham, Sir George 文翰
    argues against payment
      of Shanghai back duties
      7 Oct 1854
    H.M. Plenipotentiary
      20 Mar 1848ff.
      1 Jan 1849ff.
      4 Jan 1850ff.
      8 Jan 1851ff.
      3 Jan 1852ff.
      28 Feb 1853ff.
      9 Jan 1854ff.
    inspection of treaty ports
      23 Jun 1848
      27 Jun 1848
      15 Jul 1848
      26 Apr 1850
      29 Apr 1850
      26 May 1853
      3 Jun 1853
    leave of absence
      29 Mar 1852
      28 Feb 1853
    met Hsü Kuang-chin
      6 Apr 1848
    retirement
      17 Apr 1854
      12 Dec 1855
    visit to Nanking
      [26 May 1853]
      8 Dec 1853
      14 Dec 1853
    see also
      meetings

28 Jan 1846
2 Feb 1846
5 Feb 1846
7 Feb 1846
8 Feb 1846
14 Feb 1846
18 Feb 1846
1 Mar 1846
9 Mar 1846
13 Mar 1846
14 Mar 1846
26 Mar 1846
28 Mar 1846
31 Mar 1846
5 Apr 1847
18 May 1847
7 Jun 1848
17 Jun 1848
21 Jun 1848
27 Jun 1848
22 Dec 1848
29 Dec 1848
5 Jan 1849
20 Jan 1849
27 Jan 1849
21 Feb 1849
27 Feb 1849
13 Mar 1849
18 Mar 1849
21 Mar 1849
1 Apr 1849
2 Apr 1849
6 Apr 1849
21 Aug 1849
27 Aug 1849
30 Aug 1849
4 Sep 1849
10 Sep 1849
13 Sep 1849
17 Sep 1849
31 Oct 1849
6 Nov 1849
9 Nov 1849
[see Bowring for the years 1852-1855]
30 Oct 1856
31 Oct 1856
1 Nov 1856
3 Nov 1856
5 Nov 1856
10 Nov 1856
12 Nov 1856
14 Nov 1856
17 Nov 1856
18 Nov 1856
19 Nov 1856

20 Nov 1856
21 Nov 1856
9 Dec 1856
6 Jan 1857
12 Dec 1857
14 Dec 1857
Convention
26 May 1841
27 May 1841
9 Jun 1841
17 Jun 1841
Foreign Inspectorate of
Customs
13 Oct 1859
indemnity
11 Jun 1858
6 Nov 1858
19 May 1859
8 Mar 1860
opening [as treaty port] of
24 Jul 1843
ransom for
26 May 1841
riots
13 Dec 1842
15 Dec 1842
- Dec 1842
6 Jan 1843
9 Jan 1843
21 Jan 1843
29 Jan 1843
18 Feb 1843
30 Mar 1843
29 May 1843
1 Jun 1843
20 Jun 1844
28 Jun 1844
26 Aug 1844
22 Sep 1845
8 Jan 1846
18 Jan 1846
22 Jan 1846
26 Jan 1846
5 Feb 1846
28 Mar 1846
4 Aug 1846
9 Aug 1846
14 Aug 1846
23 Aug 1846
26 Aug 1846
6 Sep 1846
11 Sep 1846
19 Sep 1846
23 Sep 1846
26 Sep 1846
3 Oct 1846

9 Oct 1846
19 Oct 1846
31 Oct 1846
7 Nov 1846
10 Nov 1846
29 Nov 1846
30 Jan 1847
8 Feb 1847
5 Apr 1847
24 May 1847
21 Sep 1847
siege of (1841)
22 May 1841
see also
smuggling

cassia bark 桂皮
4 Nov 1844
11 Nov 1844
15 Nov 1844
24 Nov 1844
13 May 1848
19 May 1848
30 May 1848
10 Jun 1848
21 Jun 1848
4 Nov 1848
10 Nov 1848
2 Dec 1848
10 Dec 1848
14 Dec 1848
20 Dec 1848
22 Dec 1848
29 Dec 1848
8 Jan 1849
15 Jan 1849
19 Jan 1849
27 Jan 1849

cemetery 黄埔山猪腰岗
Whampoa
5 Apr 1847
25 Jul 1847
1 Aug 1847
5 Aug 1847
25 Aug 1847
28 Aug 1847
1 Sep 1847
4 Sep 1847
18 Sep 1847

cha 剳
30 Dec 1844
4 Aug 1846

cha 札
30 Dec 1844
4 Aug 1846

Cha-p'u 乍浦
Chekiang
24 Jul 1843

Ch'a-t'ou 茶頭
Canton area
5 Nov 1847
10 Nov 1847

Chads 札提督
British officer
13 Oct 1842
18 Oct 1842
6 Nov 1842

Chang 張
Colonel of Ta-p'eng
22 Apr 1858

Chang-chia-wan 張家灣
Chihili
16 Sep 1860
29 Sep 1860

Chang-chou 漳州
near Amoy
17 Jan 1844
30 Jan 1844
12 Feb 1844
17 Feb 1844
10 Dec 1851
15 Dec 1851

Chang Kuo-liang 張國樑
15 Feb 1855

Chang Shih-ch'un 張士淳
Ch'i-ying's deputy
12 Aug 1842
14 Aug 1842

Chang Shih-wu-tsai 張十五仔
pirate
26 Oct 1849
6 Nov 1849

Chang Yü-ch'ing 張餘慶
Magistrate at Tientsin
23 Dec 1860

Ch'ang-chou 長洲
   island near Hong Kong
    20 Jun 1844
    28 Jun 1844
    18 Jul 1844
    23 Jul 1844
    30 Aug 1844
    7 Sep 1844
   14 Sep 1844

Ch'ang-chou 長洲
   in Whampoa area
    21 Jun 1848
    9 Aug 1849
   13 Aug 1849

Chao-ch'ing 肇慶
   Kwangtung
   24 Nov 1844
   21 Jun 1848

chao-hui 照會
   12 Jun 1850
   25 Oct 1850

Chao Te-ch'e 趙德轍
   Governor of Kiangsu
   22 Jan 1857
   15 May 1857
   10 Feb 1858
   21 Mar 1858
   1 Apr 1858
   1 Jul 1858
   3 Jul 1858
   4 Jul 1858
   22 Jul 1858

Ch'ao-chou 潮州
   Kwangtung
   28 Aug 1844
   24 Nov 1860

Chekiang 浙江省
   3 Apr 1841
   16 Sep 1842
   17 Sep 1842
   7 Mar 1843
   8 Mar 1844
   3 Jul 1844

Chen-chiang 鎮江
   [Chinkiang]
   Kiangsu
   8 Jul 1842

   19 Jul 1842
   - Sep 1842
   17 Sep 1842
   19 Sep 1842
   25 Sep 1842
   27 Sep 1842
   19 Apr 1851
   24 Apr 1851
   21 Nov 1860
  see also
   Shu

Chen-hai 鎮海
   Chekiang
   5 Dec 1841
   27 Jun 1842 [Rec'd]
  blockade of
   3 Sep 1842

Ch'en 陳
   of Ho-nan
   22 Jun 1847
   2 Jul 1847

Ch'en A-an 陳亞安
   robber
   22 Mar 1845
   29 Mar 1845
   8 Apr 1845
   18 Apr 1845
   24 Apr 1845

Ch'en A-erh 陳亞二
   pirate
   17 Dec 1844

Ch'en A-t'ai 陳亞太
   aliases
    Ch'en Ta 陳大
    Ch'en Tai 陳太
   pirate
   31 May 1844
   6 Jun 1844
   20 Jun 1844
   21 Jun 1844
   24 Jun 1844
   28 Jun 1844
   7 Sep 1844
   14 Sep 1844
   21 Oct 1844
   30 Oct 1844
   7 Nov 1844
   11 Nov 1844
   15 Nov 1844

24 Nov 1844
6 Dec 1844

Ch'en Ch'ing-chen 陳慶真
   Singapore-born Chinese
   11 Jan 1851
   19 Jan 1851
   11 Mar 1851
   15 Mar 1851
    3 Apr 1851
    9 Apr 1851
   10 Apr 1851
   18 Apr 1851
   26 Apr 1851
    2 May 1851

Ch'en Hua-t'ou-men 陳花頭們
   pirate
   29 Oct 1949

Ch'en Meng-niu 陳懜牛
   pirate
   17 Dec 1844
   21 Dec 1844

Cheng-chüeh-ssu 正覺寺
   Nanking
   28 Sep 1842

Cheng Tung 鄭棟
   clerk from Hsin-an
   22 Nov 1844

Ch'eng-hai 澄海
   Kwangtung
   19 Dec 1839
    6 Jan 1840
    9 Jan 1840

Ch'eng Yü-ts'ai 程矞采
   Acting Vieroy of Liang-Kuang
   30 Jan 1844
   12 Feb 1844
   17 Feb 1844
   20 Feb 1844
   21 Feb 1844
   27 Feb 1844
   28 Feb 1844
    8 Mar 1844
   11 Mar 1844
   12 Mar 1844
   16 Mar 1844
   20 Mar 1844
   21 Mar 1844

30 Mar 1844
  5 Apr 1844
19 Apr 1844
20 Apr 1844
22 Apr 1844
27 Apr 1844
  5 May 1844
  8 May 1844
  9 May 1844
12 May 1844
15 May 1844
18 May 1844
20 May 1844
22 May 1844
24 May 1844
31 May 1844
Governor of Kiangsu
15 Oct 1842
Governor of Kwangtung
22 Jul 1843
24 Jul 1843
25 Aug 1843
14 Oct 1843
14 Nov 1843
25 Dec 1843
11 Jan 1844
17 Jan 1844
30 Jan 1844

Chi-erh-hang-a 吉爾杭阿
   Governor of Kiangsu
    4 Aug 1854
    5 Aug 1854
    6 Oct 1854
    7 Oct 1854
    9 Oct 1854
    4 Dec 1854
   23 Dec 1854
   29 Dec 1854
   27 Jan 1855
   15 Feb 1855
   19 Feb 1855
   22 Feb 1855
    8 Mar 1855
   16 Dec 1855
   Provincial Treasurer of
   Kiangsu
   20 Jun 1854
   21 Jun 1854
   22 Jun 1854

Chi-li-pu 記里布
   see
    Gribble

Chi-p'u 基溥
    Captain-General
    24 Jul 1858

Ch'i Kung 祈墳
    Viceroy of Liang-Kuang
      5 Jun 1841
      8 Jun 1841
    10 Jun 1841
    11 Jun 1841
    17 Jun 1841
    19 Jun 1841
    13 Dec 1842
    15 Dec 1842
     4 Jan 1843
     6 Jan 1843
     9 Jan 1843
    12 Jan 1843
    16 Jan 1843
    17 Jan 1843
    19 Jan 1843
    21 Jan 1843
    29 Jan 1843
    18 Feb 1843
     6 Mar 1843
     9 Mar 1843
    13 Mar 1843
    14 Mar 1843
    17 Mar 1843
    18 Mar 1843
    19 Mar 1843
    20 Mar 1843
    25 Mar 1843
    30 Mar 1843
    12 Apr 1843
    13 Apr 1843
    14 Apr 1843
    16 Apr 1843
    20 Apr 1843
    23 Apr 1843
    27 Apr 1843
    12 May 1843
    29 May 1843
     1 Jun 1843
    22 Jul 1843
     1 Aug 1843
     4 Aug 1843
    25 Aug 1843
    14 Oct 1843
    14 Nov 1843
    25 Dec 1843
     2 Jan 1844
    11 Jan 1844
    17 Jan 1844

    24 Jan 1844
    30 Jan 1844
    31 Jan 1844
     3 Feb 1844
    12 Feb 1844
    19 Feb 1844
    resignation of
    12 Feb 1844

Ch'i-shan 琦善
    Imperial Commissioner and
    Viceroy of Liang-Chiang
     2 Jan 1841
     5 Jan 1841
     8 Jan 1841
     9 Jan 1841
    10 Jan 1841
    11 Jan 1841
    13 Jan 1841
    14 Jan 1841
    15 Jan 1841
    16 Jan 1841
    17 Jan 1841
    18 Jan 1841
    20 Jan 1841
    30 Jan 1841
     1 Feb 1841
     5 Feb 1841
     7 Feb 1841
    13 Feb 1841
    16 Feb 1841
    18 Feb 1841
     7 Mar 1841
     9 Mar 1841
    16 Mar 1841
    Imperial Resident, Lahsa
    18 Nov 1846 Encl.
    punished by Emperor
     9 Aug 1842
    Viceroy of Chihli
    13 Sep 1840
     1 Oct 1840

Ch'i-ying 耆英
    17 Oct 1841
    arrival at Canton as
    Imperial Commissioner while
    being Viceroy of Liang-Chiang
     4 Jun 1843
    final departure from Canton
    28 Feb 1848
    Grand Secretary
    13 May 1850
    21 May 1850

22 May 1850
7 Jun 1850
10 Jun 1850
Hong Kong, visiting
13 Jun 1843
15 Oct 1845
29 Nov 1845
3 Dec 1845
Imperial Commissioner at
Canton
3 Nov 1842
21 Nov 1842
19 Jan 1843
7 Mar 1843
17 Mar 1843
20 Mar 1843
25 Mar 1843
30 Mar 1843
31 Mar 1843
23 Apr 1843
12 May 1843
4 Jun 1843ff.
11 Jan 1844ff.
1 Jan 1845ff.
8 Jan 1846ff.
13 Jan 1847ff.
3 Jan 1848ff.
Joint Imperial Commissioner at
Nanking
4 Aug 1842
6 Aug 1842
8 Aug 1842
10 Aug 1842
11 Aug 1842
12 Aug 1842
14 Aug 1842
16 Aug 1842
- Aug 1842
1 Sep 1842
7 Sep 1842
9 Sep 1842
13 Sep 1842
14 Sep 1842
- Sep 1842
16 Sep 1842
17 Sep 1842
18 Sep 1842
19 Sep 1842
20 Sep 1842
22 Sep 1842
23 Sep 1842
25 Sep 1842
26 Sep 1842
27 Sep 1842
28 Sep 1842

Joint Imperial Commissioner
at Tientsin
9 Jun 1858
11 Jun 1858
12 Jun 1858
Macao, visiting
28 Jun 1844
Tartar-General of Canton but
negotiation at Nanking
27 Jun 1842
- Jul 1842
3 Aug 1842
Viceroy of Liang-Chiang
17 Oct 1841
- Oct 1841
3 Nov 1842
14 Dec 1842
30 Dec 1842
4 Jan 1843
6 Jan 1843
18 Jan 1843
19 Jan 1843
21 Jan 1843
19 Feb 1843
20 Feb 1843
22 Feb 1843
20 Mar 1843
25 Mar 1843
31 Mar 1843
23 Apr 1843
Viceroy of Liang-Kuang
8 May 1844ff.

Chia-li-yin   喋哩唔
foreign ship
21 May 1839

Chiang Li-ang 蔣立昂
Acting Sub-Magistrate of
Macao
7 Jun 1839
8 Jun 1839
20 Sep 1839
28 Sep 1839
16 Feb 1841
17 Feb 1841

Chiang Kuo-lin 江國霖
Acting Governor of
Kwangtung
3 Mar 1858

Chiao-t'ang-ssu 茭塘司
P'an-yü
28 Aug 1843

14 Nov 1843
25 Dec 1843

Chien-sha-tsui 尖沙咀
   Kowloon area
     11 Jan 1841
     14 Jan 1841
     15 Jan 1841
     5 Mar 1841

Chihli 直隸
     8 Oct 1843
     24 Apr 1858
     16 Nov 1860
     8 Dec 1860

Chin-hsing-men 金星門
   Hong Kong waters
     2 Oct 1849

ch'in 欽
     19 Dec 1860

ch'in-ch'ai 欽差
     19 Jan 1849
     19 Dec 1860

Ch'in-ch'ai ta-ch'en 欽差大臣
     3 Aug 1842

China Station, RN 東南洋並各島
     24 Aug 1843   岸水師
     15 Oct 1843
     17 Apr 1845
     13 Sep 1845
     17 Sep 1845
     5 Aug 1846
     9 Aug 1846
     13 Aug 1846

Ching 景
   Tax Commissioner of Nan-t'ai
     28 Oct 1859
     29 Oct 1859

Ching-chiang 靖江
   Kiangsu
     23 Sep 1842
     25 Sep 1842

Ching-hai-ssu 靜海寺
   Nanking
     5 Aug 1842

Ch'ing-chiang-p'u 清江蒲
   Kiangsu
     22 Sep 1858

Chinkiang 鎭江
   see
     chen-chiang

Ch'iung-chou 瓊州
   Kwangtung
     - Apr 1843
     12 Apr 1843
     20 Apr 1843
     12 May 1843
     19 Dec 1845
     24 Jan 1849
     26 Oct 1849
     6 Nov 1849

Chou 周
   Magistrate at Shanghai
     24 Aug 1847
     1 Sep 1847

Christianity 天主教
   see   英國所崇之教門
   religious toleration

Chu-erh-hang-a 珠爾杭阿
   Prefect of Canton
     25 Mar 1839
     26 Mar 1839
     27 Mar 1839
     28 Mar 1839
     1 Apr 1839
     5 Apr 1839
     8 Apr 1839
     13 Apr 1839
     4 May 1839
     8 May 1839
     9 May 1839
     10 May 1839
     12 May 1839
     13 May 1839
     21 May 1839
     24 May 1839
     1 Jan 1840

Chu Hsieh 朱燮
   Acting Magistrate of
   Nan-hai
     - May 1860

Ch'üan-chou 泉州
  Fukien
    1 Jun 1858

ch'üan-ch'üan 全權
    3 Aug 1842

Ch'ung-hou 崇厚
  Deputy Superintendent of Trade
    at Tientsin
    21 Dec 1860

Ch'ung-lun 崇綸
  Imperial Commissioner [sometime
  Salt Commissioner]
    8 Nov 1854
    9 Nov 1854
    10 Nov 1854
  Joint Imperial Commissioner
    26 Apr 1858ff.

churches 禮拜堂
  Canton
    5 Apr 1847
    4 May 1847
    28 May 1847
    22 Jun 1847
  see also
    Foochow

Chusan 舟山
  occupation of
    17 Jan 1841
    16 Oct 1841
    17 Sep 1842
    15 Nov 1842
    1 Jul 1843
    18 Jul 1843
    13 Aug 1844
    19 Aug 1844
  return of
    13 Aug 1844
    19 Aug 1844
    24 Dec 1844
    3 Dec 1845
    8 Dec 1845
    15 Dec 1845
    20 Dec 1845
    21 Dec 1845
    27 Dec 1845
    8 Jan 1846
    15 Jan 1846
    21 Jan 1846
    22 Jan 1846

    2 Feb 1846
    5 Feb 1846
    7 Feb 1846
    8 Feb 1846
    14 Feb 1846
    18 Feb 1846
    1 Mar 1846
    13 Mar 1846
    14 Mar 1846
    26 Mar 1846
    10 May 1846
    15 May 1846
    16 May 1846
    18 May 1846
    21 May 1846
    23 Jun 1846
    25 Jun 1846
    14 Jul 1846
    16 Jul 1846
    17 Jul 1846
    22 Jul 1846
    2 Aug 1846
    7 Aug 1846
    30 Aug 1846
    20 Oct 1846

Cleland, Mr 克蘭
  British merchant
    26 Sep 1848

clipper
    7 Jun 1839

cloth imports 洋布
  see Pei-hsin-kuan

Co-hong 公行
    21 Apr 1839
    13 Feb 1841
    5 Mar 1841
    16 Jun 1841
    5 Mar 1841
    16 Jun 1841
    22 Jan 1843
    23 Jan 1843
    28 Jan 1843
    29 Jan 1843
    6 Feb 1843
    18 Feb 1843
    27 Jul 1850
    3 Aug 1850
    25 Aug 1850
    31 Dec 1850

D

D'Aguila 大
  General
    Acting Governor of
    Hong Kong
      28 Aug 1844
      7 Sep 1844
      14 Sep 1844
      19 Sep 1844
      24 Sep 1844
      25 Sep 1844
      16 Oct 1847
      31 Oct 1847
  Commander-in-Chief
    16 May 1846

Daniells, Mr 羊爹厘
  British merchant
    13 Apr 1839

Davis, Sir John 德［惠師］
  H.M. Plenipotentiary
    8 May 1844ff.
    1 Jan 1845ff.
    8 Jan 1846ff.
    13 Jan 1847ff.
  inspection of treaty ports
    10 Aug 1844
    13 Aug 1844
  knighted
    16 Sep 1845
  retired
    20 Mar 1848

debts 拖欠
  owed by Britons
    24 Jan 1843
    29 Dec 1848
  owed by Chinese
    24 Jan 1843
    27 Jan 1843
    19 Feb 1843
    29 Jul 1847
    22 Apr 1848
    24 Apr 1848
    26 Apr 1848
    30 May 1848
    8 Dec 1853
    25 Apr 1854
    17 Jan 1860
    30 Jan 1860

  see also
    Feng Sung-mao
    Ts'ui A-hsi
    Turner
  owed by Indians
    29 Dec 1848
    8 Jan 1849
    16 Aug 1849
  see also
    Abdullah
    Hassain

Dent, Mr 嗹地
  British merchant
    26 Mar 1839
    4 May 1839

Dent, Mr 嗹地
  Portugese Consul at
  Canton
    9 Jun 1851
    13 Jun 1851

deserter 私行水手
    15 Nov 1853

diplomatic representation in Peking
  see 歐差大臣長久駐劄
  Peking

domestic trade 内地通商
  by foreigners
    21 Jun 1858

Dovecote 嘟哗嘈．二桅小商船
  foreign ship
    - Apr 1843
    12 Apr 1843
    20 Apr 1843
    12 May 1843

Dowager, Empress
  birthday
    21 Nov 1842
    6 Nov 1845
  death of
    26 Mar 1850

Driver, HMS 大威
  steamer
    17 Apr 1845

F

factory area 廣東十三行
  Canton
  execution near
    5 Mar 1839
  extension of
    20 Jul 1843
    24 Jul 1843
    5 Nov 1843
    20 Jun 1844
    28 Jun 1844
    17 Aug 1844
    19 Aug 1844
    5 Apr 1847
    7 Jul 1847
    16 Jul 1847
    12 Nov 1849
    19 Nov 1849
  siege of
    25 Mar 1839
    26 Mar 1839
    13 Apr 1839
    21 Apr 1839
    22 Apr 1839
    4 May 1839
    9 May 1839
  see also
    Hog Lane
    Shameen

Fang Chien-yüan 方臨源
  Acting Magistrate of
  Nan-hai
    23 Jul 1859

Feng-hua 奉化
  near Ningpo
    18 Feb 1846
    1 Mar 1846

Feng-shen-miao 風神廟
  near Tientsin
    13 Jun 1858

Feng Sung-mao 馮松茂
  Chinese merchant
    28 Apr 1854
    7 May 1854
    8 Feb 1856
    - Mar 1856
    7 Apr 1856

    11 Apr 1856

Feng-t'ien 奉天
    29 Oct 1860
    16 Nov 1860

fire boats 火船
    19 Jul 1842

Fo-shan 佛山
  Kwangtung
    21 Jun 1848

Foochow 福州
    17 Mar 1843
    15 Oct 1843
    16 Jul 1844
    17 Jul 1844
    24 Jul 1844
    25 Sep 1844
    3 Dec 1844
    18 Dec 1844
    4 Aug 1845
    10 Oct 1850
    15 Oct 1850
    19 Apr 1851
    24 Apr 1851
    28 Apr 1851
    10 Aug 1854
    11 Aug 1854
    22 Aug 1854
    10 Feb 1855
    8 Mar 1855
    24 Nov 1860
    3 Dec 1860
  building of churches at
    6 Nov 1855
    22 Dec 1855
    8 Jan 1856
    3 Feb 1856
  city question
    11 Sep 1850
    25 Oct 1850
    28 Apr 1851
    6 Nov 1855
  disturbance at
    1 Apr 1846
    3 Apr 1846
    10 May 1846
    12 Jun 1846
    23 Jun 1846
  Foreign Inspectorate of
  Customs
    22 Jun 1855

16 Jul 1855
15 Aug 1855
16 Dec 1855
5 Feb 1856
27 Feb 1856
1 Mar 1856
19 Mar 1856
27 Mar 1856
11 Apr 1856
17 Apr 1856
30 Jun 1856
3 Jul 1856
leasing houses and land
 by foreigners
20 Dec 1854
20 Jan 1855
10 Feb 1855
10 Oct 1855
21 Nov 1855
tea monopoly
9 Jan 1854
17 Jan 1854

Forbes 福士
U.S. Consul at Canton
19 Sep 1846 Encl.
29 Nov 1846

format 書夫縉蔦妗睹
diplomatic
8 Aug 1842
10 Aug 1842
15 Nov 1842
21 Nov 1842
26 Nov 1842
21 Dec 1842
22 Dec 1842
27 Dec 1842
20 Jan 1843
21 Jan 1843
26 Jun 1843
8 Jul 1845
8 Sep 1848
29 Apr 1858
22 May 1860
19 Dec 1860
proclmation
24 Apr 1845
3 May 1845
8 May 1845
23 Nov 1846
27 Nov 1846
19 Jan 1849

free trade [自由] 貿易
4 Nov 1844
11 Nov 1844
15 Nov 1844
24 Aug 1847
26 Jul 1854
10 Feb 1858

French Embassy
- Aug 1842

Fu 傅
Provincial Treasurer of
Kwangtung
26 Mar 1850

G

Gevant Packet 三梡洋船
foreign ship
25 Sep 1843

Gingell, W.R. 金執尔
Interpreter, Foochow
10 Oct 1850
15 Oct 1850
22 Feb 1855
8 Mar 1855

ginseng 洋参
7 Nov 1843

girls, Chiense 販賣幼女
exportation of
5 Nov 1855
22 Dec 1855

Gough, Sir Hugh 郭
General
7 Jun 1842
- Jun 1842
20 Jun 1842
19 Jul 1842
26 Jul 1842
2 Aug 1842
4 Aug 1842
5 Aug 1842
6 Aug 1842

- Sep 1842
6 Nov 1842
15 Nov 1842

Grand Council 軍機處
5 Apr 1860
13 Apr 1860

Grant, Sir Hope 克
General
8 Sep 1860
30 Sep 1860
10 Oct 1860
16 Oct 1860

Gribble, H. 記里卜
Captain
1 Jan 1840
7 Jan 1840
9 Jan 1840
Consul at Amoy
9 Jan 1840
29 Sep 1843
2 Jan 1844
17 Jan 1844
19 Feb 1844

Gros, Baron 葛 [羅熙.]
French Plenipotentiary
31 Jan 1858
4 Feb 1858
1 Aug 1859

Gutzlaff, K. Dr 郭士立
Chinese Secretary
9 Feb 1843
20 Feb 1843
5 May 1844
5 Jul 1844
n.d. 1847

H

Hai-men 海阿
Chekiang
8 Mar 1844
16 Mar 1844

Hale, F.H. 赫
Vice-Consul at Foochow
23 Jan 1856
5 Feb 1856

Han 韓
Colonel of Canton
Regiment
26 Mar 1839

Han Tsan-shuan 韓贊爽
Hong Kong resident
15 Feb 1850
23 Feb 1850

Hangchow 杭州
Chekiang
16 Oct 1841
19 Apr 1851
24 Apr 1851

Hankow 漢口
Hupei
6 Jan 1859
21 Nov 1860
25 Nov 1860

Hanover 漢挪瓦
19 Jan 1854
23 Jan 1854

Hardinge, Lord Henry 哈丁公爵
Governor-General of
India
18 Nov 1846

Hassain 娘心
Indian merchant
18 Nov 1848
23 Nov 1848
1 Dec 1848
1 Jan 1849
8 Jan 1849
11 Jan 1849
27 May 1849

Heilungkiang 黑龍江省
3 Jan 1855

Heng-ch'i 恒祺
    Director of the Imperial
    Armoury
    17 Aug 1860
    18 Aug 1860
    20 Aug 1860
    25 Aug 1860
     - Oct 1860
    14 Oct 1860
    Superintendent of trade
    at Tientsin
    21 Dec 1860

Heng-fu 恒福
    Joint Imperial Commissioner
    25 Aug 1860
    29 Aug 1860
    Viceroy of Chihli
    6 Aug 1860ff.

Heng-tang Fort 横檔砲台
    Canton River
    5 Jun 1841
    10 Jun 1841
    1 Aug 1843
    24 Aug 1843

hinterland travel 内地遠遊
    in China
    10 Oct 1850
    15 Oct 1850
    22 Jun 1855
    16 Jul 1855
    15 Aug 1855
    10 Feb 1858
    11 Jun 1858
    21 Jun 1858
    5 Nov 1858
    17 Jan 1859
    28 May 1859
    see also
    Chang-chou
    Gingell
    Lung Yen-chou

Ho 何
    Brigadier-General of
    Ch'iung-chou
    26 Oct 1849

Ho-chi 合記
    developer
    26 Jul 1859

Ho Kuei-ch'ing 何桂清
    Imperial Commissioner for
    Foreign Affairs [office
    transferred from Canton]
    14 Feb 1859
     1 Aug 1859ff.
    10 Jan 1860ff.
    Viceroy of Liang-Chiang
    10 Feb 1858ff.

Ho-nan 河南
    Canton
    5 Apr 1847
    4 May 1847
    22 May 1847
    5 Apr 1848
    8 Apr 1848
    1 Sep 1852
    8 Sep 1852
    25 Apr 1854
    12 Dec 1857
    14 Dec 1857

Ho-p'u 合蒲
    Kwangtung
    22 Jan 1848
    28 Jan 1848

Hobson, Dr 合信
    renting house in Catnon
    1 Apr 1854
    6 Apr 1854
    8 Apr 1854

Hog Lane 新荳欄
    Canton factory area
    9 Apr 1847
    28 May 1847
    22 Jun 1847
    3 Oct 1847

Holland
    10 May 1839

Honan 河南省
    8 Jun 1852

Hong Kong 香港
    27 Oct 1839
     - Sep 1842
    building of forts
    27 Feb 1844
    11 Mar 1844
    5 May 1844
    census
     - May 1843

cession of
  11 Jan 1841
  14 Jan 1841
  15 Jan 1841
  16 Jan 1841
  28 Jan 1841
  30 Jan 1841
  5 Feb 1841
  13 Feb 1841
  5 Mar 1841
fishing licence
  22 Nov 1844
  24 Nov 1844
  6 Dec 1844
  14 Dec 1844
  18 Dec 1844
free port declared
  7 Jun 1841
  10 Jun 1841
garrison of
  30 Jan 1841
  5 Feb 1841
gunboats at
  18 Jul 1843
jurisdiction of
  13 Sep 1842
  17 Sep 1842
  27 Sep 1842
  1 Feb 1843
  - Feb 1843
  20 Feb 1843
  9 Mar 1843
  26 Jun 1843
  15 Jan 1844
  28 Feb 1844
  29 Feb 1844
  5 Mar 1844
  7 Mar 1844
  9 Mar 1844
  12 Mar 1844
  21 Mar 1844
  20 Apr 1844
  5 May 1844
  6 Jun 1844
  21 Jun 1844
  24 Jun 1844
  28 Jun 1844
  6 Dec 1844
  30 Dec 1844
  25 Jan 1846
  23 Oct 1846
  28 Oct 1846
  6 Nov 1846
  13 Nov 1846
  27 Sep 1849

  2 Oct 1849
  29 Oct 1849
  3 Nov 1849
  5 Nov 1849
  12 Nov 1849
  7 Apr 1856
  17 Apr 1856
  30 Jun 1856
land tax
  20 Nov 1844
  25 Nov 1844
  24 Dec 1844
  26 Dec 1844
piracy around
  15 May 1844
  22 May 1844
  13 Apr 1852
  27 Aug 1853
see also
  Ch'ang-chou
  Lorcha No. 11
register, see
  register
secret societies
  19 Dec 1844
  21 Dec 1844
  30 Dec 1844
  30 Dec 1846
  6 Nov 1855
  22 Dec 1855
  7 Apr 1856
  17 Apr 1856
  30 Jun 1856
trade regulations
  7 Mar 1844
  21 Mar 1844
  30 Mar 1844

Hong Kong and Canton Steam Co.
  18 Mar 1850
  24 Mar 1850
  28 Mar 1850
  2 Apr 1850
  4 Apr 1850
  10 Apr 1850
  13 Apr 1850
  19 Apr 1850
  20 Apr 1850
  29 Apr 1850
  6 Jun 1850
  22 Jun 1850
  31 Jul 1850
  5 Aug 1850

Hope 胡到将
  Captain
      6 Jul 1842
     13 Jun 1843
      1 Jul 1843

Hoppo 粤海關監督
      - Jul 1843
      7 Nov 1843
     18 Apr 1845
      9 Apr 1846
     21 Jun 1848
     15 Jan 1849
     27 Jan 1849
     11 Aug 1849
     24 Mar 1850
     28 Mar 1850
     13 Apr 1850
     29 Apr 1850
      6 Jun 1850
     11 Mar 1851
     15 Mar 1851
     19 Mar 1851
     24 Mar 1851
      5 Apr 1851
     19 Apr 1851
     21 Nov 1855
      8 Feb 1858
      9 Jul 1859
     23 Jul 1859
      7 Sep 1859
     13 Oct 1859
     24 Feb 1860
      5 May 1860
     29 Oct 1860

hostages 被執人
  H. Parkes et al.
     22 Sep 1860
     25 Sep 1860
     27 Sep 1860
     28 Sep 1860
     29 Sep 1860
     30 Sep 1860
      1 Oct 1860
      2 Oct 1860
      3 Oct 1860
      4 Oct 1860
      6 Oct 1860
     12 Oct 1860
     16 Oct 1860
     19 Oct 1860
     22 Oct 1860
     [23 Oct 1860]
     [27 Oct 1860]

Howqua 伍崇曜
  see
    Wu Ch'ung-yüeh

Howqua's packhouse 仁信棧
  see
    Jen-hsin-lou

Hsi-ch'iao-shan 西樵山
  Canton area
     17 Mar 1854
     27 Mar 1854
     28 Mar 1854
      6 Apr 1854
      8 Apr 1854

Hsi-hao-k'ou 西濠口
  Canton
      6 Jul 1859

Hsiang-shan 香山
  Kwangtung
      9 Mar 1841
     22 Jul 1843
     11 May 1847
     27 Jun 1847
      7 Jul 1847
     10 Nov 1847
     27 Aug 1849
     17 Oct 1849
     29 Nov 1849
     20 Aug 1853
      7 Dec 1854
     13 Feb 1858
     16 Feb 1858

Hsiao-tao-hui 小刀會
  see
    Ch'en Ch'ing-chen

Hsieh An-pang 謝安邦
  Shanghai rebel leader
     22 Jun 1854
     15 Feb 1855

Hsieh Hsiao-chuang 謝效莊
  Sub-Magistrate of Macao
      5 Jun 1841
     10 Jun 1841
     11 Jun 1841
     15 Jun 1841
     16 Jun 1841
     17 Jun 1841
     21 Jul 1843
     28 Jul 1843

Hsien-ling 咸齡
    Intendent at Shanghai
      10 May 1846
      25 Jun 1846
      14 Jul 1846
      16 Jul 1846
      17 Jul 1846
      22 Jul 1846
      2 Aug 1846
      24 Aug 1846
      28 Feb 1848
      2 Aug 1848
      5 Aug 1848

Hsin-an 新安
    Kwangtung
      22 Jul 1843
      23 Jul 1844
      22 Nov 1844
      24 Nov 1844
      6 Dec 1844
      14 Dec 1844
      18 Dec 1844
      11 May 1847
      12 Nov 1849
      20 Aug 1853
      6 Oct 1858

Hsing 興
    Customs Officer at Amoy
      4 Apr 1846

Hsiung 熊
    Prefect in Taiwan
      13 Oct 1842
      8 Nov 1842

Hsü A-chin 徐亞進
    Chinese servant
      23 Feb 1849
      27 Feb 1849
      12 Aug 1849

Hsü A-pao 徐亞保
    murderer
      7 Mar 1849
      11 Mar 1849
      2 Aug 1849
      2 Oct 1849
      6 Oct 1849
      8 Oct 1849
      11 Oct 1849
      17 Oct 1849

Hsü Chang-pao 徐張寶
    stabbed to death by
    drunken sailor
      29 Feb 1848
      3 Mar 1848

Hsü Chi-yü 徐繼畬
    Acting Governor of Fukien
      1 Apr 1846
      - Apr 1846
    Provincial Treasurer of
    Fukien
      9 Feb 1846
      10 May 1846
      12 Jun 1846

Hsü Kuang-chin 徐廣縉
    Acting Imperial Commissioner
    at Catnon
      28 Feb 1848ff.
    at Kao-chou
      21 Jul 1851
      23 Apr 1852
    Imperial Commissioner at
    Canton and Viceroy of
    Liang-Kuang
      4 Jul 1848ff.
      1 Jan 1849ff.
      4 Jan 1850ff.
      8 Jan 1851ff.
      3 Jan 1852ff.
    in Kwangsi
      8 Jun 1852
      27 Jul 1852

Hsü Nai-chao 許乃釗
    Governor of Kiangsu
      20 Jun 1854
      21 Jun 1854
      22 Jun 1854
      26 Jun 1854
      30 Jun 1854
      1 Jul 1854

Hsü Wen-shen 許文深
    Sub-Magistrate of Nan-hai
      17 May 1854
      15 Dec 1854

Hsüeh Huan 薛煥
    Acting Imperial Commissioner
    for Foreign Affairs
      28 Jun 1860
      n.d. [1860]
      3 Dec 1860

awarded title of Governor
  28 Mar 1860
  2 Apr 1860
Provincial Judge of Kiangsu
  [the duties of which
  position he never assumed,
  as he continued to perform
  the role of Intendant at
  Shanghai]
  1 Jul 1858
  3 Jul 1858
  4 Jul 1858
  22 Jul 1858
  2 Aug 1858

Hu-li-she 湖裏社
  Amoy
  6 Nov 1849
  9 Nov 1849
  12 Nov 1849
  14 Nov 1849

Hu-men 虎門
  [The Bogue]
  11 Jan 1841
  11 Jun 1841
  26 Mar 1846
  10 Jan 1849
  20 Jan 1849
  27 Jan 1849
  8 Feb 1849
  11 Feb 1849
  14 Feb 1849
  10 Apr 1850
  2 Dec 1851
  25 Dec 1851
  31 Jan 1852
  26 May 1854
  10 Jul 1854
  burning of opium at
  28 Mar 1839
  12 Apr 1839
  13 Apr 1839
  19 Apr 1839
  22 Apr 1839
  4 May 1839
  12 May 1839
  21 May 1839
  destruction of forts at
  15 Nov 1856
  16 Nov 1856
  9 Dec 1856
  12 Dec 1857
  14 Dec 1857

piracy around
  8 Sep 1848
  14 Sep 1848
  12 Nov 1849
  20 Dec 1852
  2 Jan 1853

Hu-shu-kuan 滸墅關
  Kiangsu
  19 May 1847
  24 Aug 1847
  1 Sep 1847
  8 Feb 1848
  17 Feb 1848
  29 Apr 1848
  21 Jun 1848

Hua-sha-na 花沙納
  Joint Imperial Commissioner
  29 May 1858
  3 Jun 1858
  4 Jun 1858
  5 Jun 1858
  6 Jun 1858
  7 Jun 1858
  9 Jun 1858
  11 Jun 1858
  12 Jun 1858
  13 Jun 1858
  21 Jun 1858
  22 Jun 1858
  30 Jun 1858
  1 Jul 1858
  2 Jul 1858
  3 Jul 1858
  4 Jul 1858
  5 Jul 1858
  22 Jul 1858
  2 Aug 1858
  7 Sep 1858
  22 Sep 1858
  25 Sep 1858
  6 Oct 1858
  9 Oct 1858
  11 Oct 1858
  12 Oct 1858
  15 Oct 1858
  16 Oct 1858
  17 Oct 1858
  18 Oct 1858
  22 Oct 1858
  25 Oct 1858
  28 Oct 1858
  29 Oct 1858

30 Oct 1858
31 Oct 1858
5 Nov 1858
6 Nov 1858
6 Jan 1859
9 Jan 1859
12 Jan 1859
13 Jan 1859
14 Jan 1859
17 Jan 1859
20 Jan 1859
21 Jan 1859
23 Jan 1859
24 Jan 1859
25 Jan 1859
14 Feb 1859
3 Mar 1859
27 May 1859
28 May 1859
12 Jun 1859

Huang-chu-ch'i 黄竹岐
  Canton area
    firing incident at
    24 Aug 1847
    28 Aug 1847
    6 Sep 1847
  deaths at
    13 Dec 1847
    17 Dec 1847
    20 Dec 1847
    3 Jan 1848ff.

Huang En-t'ung 黄恩彤
  Governor of Kwangtung
    24 Mar 1845
    29 Mar 1845
    2 Apr 1845
    8 Apr 1845
    18 Apr 1845
    21 Apr 1845
    24 Apr 1845
    28 Apr 1845
    3 May 1845
    6 May 1845
    8 May 1845
    16 May 1845
    15 Jun 1845
    21 Jun 1845
    26 Jun 1845
    27 Jun 1845
    4 Jul 1845
    11 Jul 1845
    10 Sep 1845
    17 Sep 1845
    20 Sep 1845

22 Sep 1845
31 Oct 1845
21 Dec 1845
18 Jan 1846
22 Jan 1846
7 Aug 1846
9 Aug 1846
23 Aug 1846

30 Aug 1846
6 Sep 1846
19 Sep 1846
23 Sep 1846
7 Nov 1846
27 Nov 1846
29 Nov 1846
3 Dec 1846
30 Dec 1846
  Provincial Treasurer of
  Kwangtung
    22 Dec 1843
    11 Jan 1844
    24 Jan 1844
    1 Feb 1844
    4 Feb 1844
    15 Feb 1844
    14 May 1844
    20 May 1844
    5 Jul 1844
    20 Nov 1844
    25 Nov 1844
    24 Dec 1844
    26 Dec 1844
    30 Apr 1849
    26 Mar 1850

Huang Hsin-kuang 黄信光
  pirate-suspect
    2 Jul 1844

Huang Tsung-han 黄宗漢
  Imperial Commissioner
    for Foreign Affairs
    and Viceroy of Liang-Kuang
    3 Mar 1858
    6 Oct 1858
    9 Oct 1858
    11 Oct 1858
    12 Jan 1859
    13 Jan 1859
    14 Jan 1859
    17 Jan 1859
    20 Jan 1859
    21 Jan 1859
    23 Jan 1859
    24 Jan 1859

25 Jan 1859
14 Feb 1859
[dismissed]
3 Mar 1859

hulks 躉船
1 Apr 1839
5 Apr 1839
12 Apr 1839
13 Apr 1839
19 Apr 1839
21 Apr 1839
22 Apr 1839
4 May 1839
26 May 1839

Hunan 湖南省
8 Oct 1852
11 Oct 1852
24 Oct 1852
27 Oct 1852

Huntly 訓得利
foreign ship
19 Dec 1845

Huo 霍
Acting Sub-Magistrate of
Amoy
18 Dec 1845

I

i 夷
1 Feb 1843
5 Nov 1849
9 Nov 1849
12 Nov 1849
20 Jul 1852
27 Jul 1852
5 Nov 1855
6 Nov 1855
22 Nov 1855
12 Dec 1855
22 Dec 1855
8 Jan 1856
11 Dec 1856
7 Sep 1858
9 Oct 1858

I, Prince 怡親王載垣
10 Sep 1860
11 Sep 1860
12 Sep 1860
13 Sep 1860
14 Sep 1860
16 Sep 1860
21 Sep 1860

I Ch'ang-hua 易長華
Prefect of Canton
- Dec 1842
20 Dec 1842
21 Dec 1842
22 Dec 1842

I Chung-fu 易中孚
Intendant of Kao-Lien
9 Mar 1841

I-li-pu 伊里布
Acting Deputy
Lieutenant-General
20 Jun 1842
27 Jun 1842
4 Jul 1842
- Jul 1842
3 Aug 1842
Assistant to Ch'i-ying
26 May 1842
7 Jun 1842
- Jun 1842
death of
6 Mar 1843
7 Mar 1843
17 Mar 1843
20 Mar 1843
25 Mar 1843
30 Mar 1843
31 Mar 1843
23 Apr 1843
Imperial Commissioner at
Canton [first time]
17 Oct 1841
Imperial Commissioner at
Canton [second time]
and concurrently Tartar-
General of Canton
28 Dec 1842
4 Jan 1843
6 Jan 1843
9 Jan 1843
[arrival at Canton]
12 Jan 1843ff.

Joint Imperial Commissioner
[with Ch'i-ying] at
Nanking
    4 Aug 1842
    6 Aug 1842
    - Aug 1842
    8 Aug 1842
   10 Aug 1842
   11 Aug 1842
   12 Aug 1842
   15 Aug 1842
   16 Aug 1842
    5 Nov 1842
   12 Nov 1842
   21 Nov 1842
   24 Nov 1842
   27 Nov 1842
   30 Nov 1842
    - Nov 1842
   28 Dec 1842
Viceroy of Liang-Chiang
    1 Oct 1840
   17 Jan 1841

I-liang 怡良
  Governor of Kwangtung
   13 Apr 1839
   10 May 1839
  Viceroy of Liang-Chiang
    8 Dec 1853
   10 Jul 1854
   18 Jul 1854
    9 Dec 1856
   13 Jan 1857
   17 Apr 1857
  Viceroy of Min-Che
   18 Oct 1842
   27 Nov 1842
   30 Nov 1842
   30 Dec 1842
   19 Jan 1843
    5 Apr 1843
   27 Apr 1843

I-shan 奕山
  General
   14 Apr 1841
   15 Apr 1841
    2 May 1841
    5 Jun 1841

i-shih 奕翀
   13 Jun 1843

import duties 完納稅餉
  22 Nov 1849
  29 Nov 1849
   1 Dec 1849
   7 Dec 1849

indemnity 賠還使費
   5 Jan 1841
   8 Jan 1841
   9 Jan 1841
  13 Feb 1841
   5 Mar 1841
  26 May 1841
  11 Aug 1842
  14 Aug 1842
   - Aug 1842
   1 Sep 1842
   9 Sep 1842
   - Sep 1842
  16 Sep 1842
  18 Sep 1842
  20 Sep 1842
  23 Sep 1842
  24 Sep 1842
  11 Oct 1842
  15 Oct 1842
  11 Nov 1842
  27 Jan 1843
   - Feb 1843
  19 Feb 1843
   9 Mar 1843
  18 Mar 1843
  24 Jul 1843
   4 Aug 1843
  11 Jan 1844
  24 Jan 1844
   1 Feb 1844
   3 Feb 1844
   4 Feb 1844
  15 Feb 1844
  12 May 1844
  14 May 1844
  20 May 1844
  15 Jun 1844
  25 Jun 1844
  26 Jun 1844
  13 Jul 1844
  24 Jul 1844
  27 Jul 1844
  13 Aug 1844
  19 Aug 1844
   1 Sep 1844
   9 Sep 1844

K

Kan-lan 干欖
    Chekiang
      5 Nov 1842

Kao-chou 高州
    Kwangtung
      21 Jul 1851
      25 Apr 1852

Kao Feng-p'o 高峰坡
    Acting Magistrate of
    Lu-ling-hsien
      11 Oct 1859

Kao-lan 高蘭
    at mouth of Pearl River
      7 Dec 1854
      25 Feb 1856

Kao-Lien 高廉
    Kwangtung
      9 Mar 1841

Kelpie 吉苹.三板棍商船
    foreign ship
      24 Jan 1849

Kiangnan 江南
      5 Jul 1842

Kirin 吉林省
      28 Nov 1855

Kiukiang 九江
    Kiangsi
      21 Nov 1860
      25 Nov 1860

Ko 嗝
    Customs Officer at Amoy
      23 Apr 1846

Ko-ssu-ta 哥斯達
    [Calcutta?]
      12 May 1839

Kowloon 九龍
      11 Jan 1841
      13 Jan 1841
      14 Jan 1841
      15 Jan 1841
      30 Jan 1841
      5 Feb 1841
      5 Mar 1841
      17 Sep 1842
      27 Sep 1842
      20 Apr 1844
    building of forts in
      5 May 1844
      12 May 1844
      6 Jun 1844

    sheriff at
      - Feb 1843
      20 Feb 1843
      5 May 1844
      6 Jun 1844

Ku-lang-hsü 鼓浪嶼
      7 Sep 1842
      14 Nov 1842
      21 Feb 1843
      17 Jan 1844
      18 Jan 1844
      21 Jan 1844
      30 Jan 1844
      12 Feb 1844
      17 Feb 1844
      15 Jun 1844
      11 Nov 1844
      15 Nov 1844
      24 Nov 1844
      3 Dec 1844
      18 Dec 1844
      19 Dec 1844
      21 Dec 1844
      24 Dec 1844
      30 Dec 1844
    evacuation of
      2 Mar 1845
      3 Mar 1845
      6 Mar 1845
      6 May 1845
      15 Dec 1845
    feud in
      21 Dec 1844
      30 Dec 1844
      16 Mar 1845

Kua-chou 佩州
    Kiangsu
      16 Sep 1842
      24 Sep 1842

Kuan-fu 官富
   Sheriff of
     5 May 1844

Kuan T'ien-p'ei 關天培
   Commander-in-Chief of
   Kwangtung marines
     3 Nov 1839
     8 Jan 1841
     10 Jan 1841
     11 Jan 1841
     13 Jan 1841
     24 Feb 1841

Kuan-wen 官文
   Viceroy of Hu-Kuang
     8 Dec 1858
     9 Dec 1858

Kuang-hua-ssu 慶化寺
   Peking
     8 Nov 1860

Kuei-liang 桂良
   Joint Imperial Commissioner
     29 May 1858ff.
     6 Jan 1859ff.
     8 Mar 1860ff.

K'un-shou 昆壽
   Colonel
     6 Nov 1849
     9 Nov 1849
     12 Nov 1849
     15 Nov 1849
     23 Nov 1849

Kung, Prince 恭親王奕訢
     21 Sep 1860ff.

Kung Mu-chiu 宮慕久
   Intendant of Su-Sung-T'ai
     1 Dec 1843
     17 Jul 1846
     7 Oct 1846
     31 Oct 1846
     26 Dec 1846

K'ung Chi-yin 孔繼尹
   Acting Provincial Treasurer
   of Kwangtung
     4 Jul 1845
     8 Jul 1845
     13 Jul 1845

Kuo A-an 郭亞安
   murderer
     15 Oct 1849

L

Lai En-chüeh 賴恩爵
   Colonel of Ta-p'eng
     28 Jan 1841
     22 Feb 1843
     13 Mar 1843
     20 Jul 1843
     22 Jul 1843
     28 Jun 1844
   Commander-in-Chief of
   Kwangtung marines
     28 Jun 1844

Lan-ts'un 欖村
   Hu-men area
     2 Dec 1851
     25 Dec 1851
     31 Jan 1852

Lan Wei-wen 藍蔚雯
   Acting Intendant at
   Shanghai
     4 Aug 1854

language [外交詞雅]
   diplomatic
     30 Dec 1844
     1 Mar 1846
     3 Mar 1846
     4 Aug 1846
     23 Nov 1848
     11 Jun 1849
     15 Jun 1849
     25 Jun 1849
     2 Jul 1849
     4 Feb 1850
     20 Jul 1852
     22 Nov 1855
     12 Dec 1855
     22 Jan 1856
   see also
     format
     i

Lao Ch'ung-kuang 勞崇光
  Acting Viceroy of
   Liang-Kuang
    14 Jul 1859
    16 Jul 1859
    23 Jul 1859
    26 Jul 1859
    12 Oct 1859
    26 Oct 1859
  Viceroy of Liang-Kuang
    14 Nov 1859

lascar 港腳 [地名] 黑人
    16 Jan 1841
    18 Jan 1841
    20 Jan 1841

Laura 嗮啦
  foreign ship
    10 Jan 1860
    17 Jan 1860

Lay, G.T. 李太郭
  Consul at Amoy
    3 Mar 1845
    9 Mar 1845
    8 May 1845
    16 May 1845
    30 Sep 1845
  Consul at Canton
    25 Dec 1843
    18 May 1844
    24 May 1844
    31 May 1844
  Consul at Foochow
    6 Jun 1844
    21 Jun 1844
    28 Jun 1844
    21 Oct 1844
    30 Oct 1844
    24 Dec 1844
    28 Dec 1844
    8 May 1845
    19 Nov 1845
  death of
    5 Dec 1845
    12 Dec 1845
    18 Dec 1845

Lay, H.N. 李太國
  Elgin's interpreter
    5 Jun 1858
    11 Jun 1858
    12 Oct 1858
    7 Sep 1860

  Foreign Inspector of
   Customs, Shanghai
    15 Feb 1855
    22 Feb 1855
    8 Mar 1855
    16 Dec 1855
    13 Oct 1859

Layton, T.H. 賣
  Acting Consul at Amoy
    5 Dec 1845
    12 Dec 1845
    18 Dec 1845
    12 Feb 1846
    15 Feb 1846
    23 Apr 1846
    18 Aug 1846
  Consul at Ningpo
    18 Aug 1846
    24 Aug 1846

Lei-chou 雷州
  Kwangtung
    24 Jan 1849

Li 李
  Colonel of Ch'eng-hai
    19 Dec 1839
    7 Jan 1840
    9 Jan 1840

Li 李
  Magistrate of Nan-hai
    17 May 1854

Li 李
  Magistrate of P'an-yü
    1 Sep 1852
    8 Sep 1852

Li 李
  Provincial Treasurer of
   Kwangtung
    26 Mar 1850

li 華里
    26 May 1841
    5 Aug 1842
    24 Dec 1857

Li A-ch'uan 李亞船
  shopkeeper
    23 Oct 1846
    28 Oct 1846

Li A-pao 李孖係
  murderer
    15 Oct 1849

Li Hsiang-hsien 李象先
  shot dead by Britons
    27 Oct 1839

Li Hung-pu 李洪圓
  witness
    11 Jan 1851

Li Shun-fa 李順發
  overseas Chinese of the
  Straits Settlement
    23 Mar 1848
    18 Oct 1850
    24 Oct 1850

Liang-Chiang 兩江
  passim

Liang-kuang 兩廣
  passim

Liang-kung-fu 樑公府
  Peking
    9 Nov 1860

Liao-tung 遼東
    25 Feb 1856

likin 釐金
  see
    transit dues

Lin A-ming 林阿明
  Shanghai rebel leader
    15 Feb 1855

Lin Fu-tsai 林富仔
  pirate
    17 Dec 1844

Lin Tse-hsü 林則徐
  Imperial Commissioner at
  Canton
    25 Mar 1839
    26 Mar 1839
    27 Mar 1839
    28 Mar 1839
     1 Apr 1839
     5 Apr 1839
     8 Apr 1839
    12 Apr 1839
    13 Apr 1839
    19 Apr 1839
    20 Apr 1839
    21 Apr 1839
    22 Apr 1839
     4 May 1839
     8 May 1839
     9 May 1839
    10 May 1839
    12 May 1839
    13 May 1839
    18 May 1839
    21 May 1839
    26 May 1839
     1 Jun 1839
     7 Jun 1839
     8 Jun 1839
    20 Sep 1839
    28 Sep 1839
     8 Oct 1839
    27 Oct 1839
    19 Dec 1839
  dismissal of
     5 Jan 1841

Lin Wei-hsi 林維喜
  murdered by British
  sailors
    20 Sep 1839
    28 Sep 1839
     8 Oct 1839
    27 Oct 1839
     3 Nov 1839
    19 Dec 1839

linguists 通事
     1 Dec 1843
    14 Apr 1849
    30 Apr 1849

Lintin 伶仃
  at mouth of Pearl River
    28 Mar 1839
     1 Apr 1839
     5 Apr 1839

Liu 劉
  Acting Prefect of Foochow
     3 Dec 1860

Liu-ch'iu 琉球
   or Ryuku
    16 Jan 1847
    21 Jan 1847
    12 Mar 1849
    5 Jan 1850
   see also Bettelheim

Liu K'ai-yü 劉開域
   Acting Sub-Magistrate
    of Fo-shan
    26 May 1839
    1 Jun 1839
    7 Jun 1839
    8 Jun 1839

Liu Li-ch'uan 劉麗川
   Shanghai rebel leader
    15 Feb 1855

Liu Ssu 劉四
   Hong Kong resident
    10 Mar 1848
    16 Mar 1848
    18 Mar 1848
    23 Mar 1848

Liu Yün-k'o 劉韻珂
   Governor of Chekiang
    3 Apr 1841
    3 Nov 1842
    12 Nov 1842
    15 Nov 1842
    21 Nov 1842
    26 Nov 1842
    27 Dec 1842
    16 Jan 1843
    20 Jan 1843
    28 Feb 1843
   Viceroy of Min-Che
    21 Jun 1844
    11 Jul 1844
    11 Nov 1844
    4 Aug 1845
    1 Apr 1846
    - Apr 1846
    6 Jun 1849
    25 Jun 1849
    21 Mar 1850
    19 May 1850
    21 Aug 1850
    11 Sep 1850
    25 Oct 1850

Lo A-chin 盧亞錦
   Hong Kong resident
    28 Jan 1848
    31 Jan 1848

Lo-ching 羅鏡
   Kwangtung
    31 Aug 1852
    7 Sep 1852

Lo-ting 羅定
   Kwangtung
    8 Jun 1852

lorcha 西洋嘜艇
   Chinese vessel with
    Western rigging
    9 Apr 1846
    11 Apr 1846
    26 Nov 1855
    12 Dec 1855
    12 Oct 1856

Lorcha No. 11 西洋十一號華艇
   plundered
    20 Jul 1843
    21 Jul 1843
    22 Jul 1843
    25 Aug 1843
    5 Oct 1843
    14 Oct 1843

Lou 婁
   Prefect of Foochow
    13 Aug 1854

Lu Chien-ying 陸建瀛
   Viceroy of Liang-Chiang
    13 May 1850
    20 May 1850
    22 May 1850
    23 May 1850
    1 Jun 1850
    3 Jun 1850
    7 Jun 1850
    10 Jun 1850
    12 Jun 1850
    14 Jun 1850

Lu-ling-hsien 盧陵縣
   Kiangsi
    11 Oct 1859

Lu Sun-ting 陸孫鼎
    Magistrate of Hsiang-shan
    17 Jun 1847
    7 Jul 1847
    16 Jul 1847

Lu Tse-ch'ang 鹿澤長
    Intendant of Ning-Shao-
    T'ai, Chekiang
    5 Nov 1842
    6 Nov 1842
    11 Nov 1842
    15 Nov 1842
    26 Nov 1842
    27 Nov 1842

Lung-wen 隆文
    Minister
    14 Apr 1841
    15 Apr 1841
    2 May 1841
    5 Jun 1841

Lung-yen-chou 龍巖州
    Fukien
    5 Apr 1855
    16 Jul 1855

Luzon 呂宋
    23 Apr 1846

        M

Ma Chi-hsing 馬吉星
    robber-suspect
    21 Jan 1846
    25 Jan 1846

Macao 澳門
    28 Mar 1839
    13 Apr 1839
    24 May 1839
    7 Jun 1839
    8 Jun 1839
    28 Sep 1839
    8 Oct 1839
    19 Dec 1839
    16 Feb 1841
    9 Mar 1841
    29 Mar 1841

    11 May 1841
    5 Jun 1841
    10 Jun 1841
    22 Jul 1843
    24 Aug 1843
    25 Aug 1843
    28 Jun 1844
    not foreign territory
    5 May 1860
    18 May 1860
    16 Jun 1860
    see also
      Amaral
      Hsieh Hsiao-chuang
      Lorcha No. 11

Macgregor, F.C. 馬顯義
    Consul at Canton
    18 May 1844
    24 May 1844
    31 May 1844
    6 Jun 1844
    26 Apr 1845
    3 May 1845
    10 Sep 1845
    22 Sep 1845
    31 Oct 1845
    9 Apr 1846
    11 Apr 1846
    16 Apr 1846
    5 May 1846
    4 Aug 1846
    9 Aug 1846
    29 Nov 1846
    29 Apr 1847
    22 May 1847
    28 May 1847
    2 Jul 1847
    7 Jul 1847
    16 Jul 1847
    15 Jan 1848
    8 Feb 1848
    26 Feb 1848

McLinley, Dr 馬哩利
    murder of
    22 Apr 1844

McQueen, Mr 鳴嘆
    British merchant
    17 Feb 1848
    19 Apr 1848

Malcolm 麻恭
  Major, secretary to Sir
    Henry Pottinger's mission
    22 Aug 1842
    20 Mar 1843

Man 滿
  Lieutenant-Colonel
    - Sep 1842

marines, Chinese
  alleged misconduct of
    28 Aug 1844
    26 Oct 1844
    30 Oct 1844
    7 Mar 1845
    9 Mar 1845
    24 Mar 1845
    21 Jan 1846
    10 Mar 1848
    16 Mar 1848
    18 Mar 1848
    23 Mar 1848
    15 Oct 1849
    17 Oct 1849
    21 Oct 1849
    29 Oct 1849
    2 Nov 1849

Martineau, M. 馬
  of Bureau of Occupation,
    Canton
    6 Jul 1859
    8 Jul 1859
    14 Jul 1859
    16 Jul 1859
    23 Jul 1859
    26 Jul 1859

Meadows, T.T. 麥
  interpreter
    1 Dec 1848
    6 Dec 1848
    12 Dec 1848
    20 Dec 1848
    22 Dec 1848
    29 Dec 1848
    3 Jan 1849
    15 Jan 1849
    20 Jan 1849
    27 Jan 1849

Medhurst, W.H. 麥都思
  Consul at Foochow
    10 Feb 1855
    7 Mar 1855
    17 Mar 1855
    5 Apr 1855
    10 Oct 1855
    21 Nov 1855
    22 Jan 1856
    5 Feb 1856
    28 Oct 1859
    17 Jan 1860
  interpreter
    9 May 1854
    17 May 1854
    22 Aug 1854
    25 Aug 1854
    1 Sep 1854
    16 Oct 1854
    20 Dec 1854

meetings between 會敘
  Chinese Imperial Commissioners
    and Bonham, Sir George
    21 Mar 1848
    28 Mar 1848
    6 Apr 1848
    7 Jun 1848
    5 Jan 1849
    8 Jan 1849
    10 Jan 1849
    15 Jan 1849
    20 Jan 1849
    27 Jan 1849
    8 Feb 1849
    9 Feb 1849
    and Bowring, Sir John [requests fo
    16 Apr 1852
    25 Apr 1852
    17 Apr 1852
    25 Apr 1852
    17 Apr 1854
    25 Apr 1854
    27 Apr 1854
    7 May 1854
    9 May 1854
    11 May 1854
    17 May 1854
    19 May 1854
    22 May 1854
    24 May 1854
    26 May 1854
    10 Jul 1854

[cf. I-liang of
  10 Jul 1854
  18 Jul 1854
  and Wang I-te of
  10 Aug 1854
  11 Aug 1854
  13 Aug 1854]
  28 Aug 1854
  16 Oct 1854
  - Oct 1854
  20 Dec 1854
  29 Dec 1854
  11 Jun 1855
  9 Jul 1855
  12 Jul 1855
and Bruce, Hon Frederick
  27 May 1859
  28 May 1859
  8 Jun 1859
  8 Nov 1859
and Davis, Sir John
  with Ch'i-ying *et al.*
  9 May 1844
  10 May 1844
  31 May 1844
  6 Jun 1844
  26 Mar 1846
and Elgin, Lord
  20 Jan 1858
  29 Apr 1858
  30 Apr 1858
  1 May 1858
  3 Jun 1858
  4 Jun 1858
  9 Jun 1858
  5 Jul 1858
  6 Oct 1858
  11 Oct 1858
  15 Oct 1858
  16 Oct 1858
  17 Oct 1858
  18 Oct 1858
  30 Oct 1858
  8 Dec 1858
  9 Dec 1858
  6 Jan 1859
  9 Jan 1859
  6 Aug 1860
  14 Aug 1860
  15 Aug 1860
  16 Aug 1860
  6 Sep 1860
  8 Sep 1860
  6 Oct 1860

  23 Oct 1860
  8 Nov 1860
and Pottinger, Sir Henry
  with Ch'i-ying *et al.*
  27 Jun 1842
  8 Jul 1842
  - Jul 1842
  27 Sep 1842
  28 Sep 1842
  with I-li-pu *et al.*
  6 Jan 1843
  12 Jan 1843
  16 Jan 1843
  17 Jan 1843
  19 Jan 1843
  again with Ch'i-ying *et al.*
  4 Jun 1843
  13 Jun 1843
  6 Jun 1844

messenger service 書信艇
  between Hong Kong and Canton
  2 Dec 1851
  25 Dec 1851
  10 Jan 1852
  31 Jan 1852

Min-hsien 閩縣
  Fukien
  5 Nov 1855

Min River 閩江
  Fukien
  25 Jun 1849

Ming-shan 明善
  Deputy Minister
  24 Jul 1858

missionaries 傳教之師
  21 Aug 1850
  11 Sep 1850
  25 Oct 1850
  28 Apr 1851
  29 May 1851
  6 Nov 1855
  8 Jan 1856
  3 Feb 1856
  11 Jun 1858
  see also
  religious toleration

modernisation [現代化]
  British offer of help
  27 Aug 1845

Nepal 混泊爾
        3 Jan 1855

New City 新城
    Canton
        26 Mar 1839

New Territories 歸田鄉
    Hong Kong area
        24 Dec 1844

Ni Li 倪澧
    Prefect
        5 Apr 1844
        7 Jun 1844

Ning-Shao-T'ai 寧紹台
    Chekiang
        5 Nov 1842

Ning-yang 寧洋
    Fukien
        5 Apr 1855

Ningpo 寧波
        11 Aug 1840
        17 Jan 1841
        26 May 1841
        15 Nov 1842
        18 Mar 1843
        19 Mar 1843
        18 Jul 1843
        15 Oct 1843
        29 Feb 1848
        19 Apr 1851
        24 Apr 1851
        22 Apr 1858
        24 Nov 1860
    opening for trade
        31 Jan 1844
    ransom for
        - Feb 1843
        18 Mar 1843

Niu Chien 牛鑑
    Viceroy of Liang-Chiang
        26 Jul 1842
        27 Jul 1842
        30 Jul 1842
        4 Aug 1842
        5 Aug 1842
        6 Aug 1842
        7 Aug 1842
        9 Aug 1842
        10 Aug 1842
        11 Aug 1842
        14 Aug 1842
        15 Aug 1842
        16 Aug 1842
        - Aug 1842
        15 Oct 1842

                    0

opium 鴉片
    bond
        26 Mar 1839
        5 Apr 1839
        8 Apr 1839
        28 Apr 1839
        28 Sep 1839
        8 Oct 1839
        27 Oct 1839
        19 Dec 1839
    clipper
        28 Mar 1839
        13 May 1839
        7 Jun 1839
        6 Nov 1849
    death penalty
        10 May 1839
    legalisation of
        28 Jun 1842
        - Aug 1842
        26 Jun 1843
        24 Aug 1843
        22 Jun 1844
        13 Jul 1844
        13 Aug 1844
        19 Aug 1844
        25 Feb 1846
        6 Mar 1846
        7 Mar 1846
        9 Mar 1846
        13 Mar 1846
        29 Apr 1847
        18 May 1847
        18 Sep 1847
        7 Jun 1848
        17 Jun 1848
        21 Jun 1848
        29 Dec 1848
    likin
        1 Jun 1858
    official British prohibition
        24 Aug 1843
    prevention of
        7 Jun 1839
        8 Jun 1839

smuggling
    19 Apr 1839
    8 May 1839
    7 Jun 1839
    27 Oct 1839
    13 Feb 1841
    24 Aug 1843
    25 Aug 1843
    26 Apr 1845
    3 May 1845
    16 May 1845
    9 Feb 1846
    25 Feb 1846
    6 Mar 1846
    9 Mar 1846
    29 Apr 1847
    18 May 1847
    7 Dec 1849
surrender of
    25 Mar 1839
    26 Mar 1839
    27 Mar 1839
    28 Mar 1839
    1 Apr 1839
    5 Apr 1839
    12 Apr 1839
    13 Apr 1839
    19 Apr 1839
    20 Apr 1839
    21 Apr 1839
    22 Apr 1839
    4 May 1839
    9 May 1839
    12 May 1839
    21 May 1839
    26 May 1839
    8 Jun 1839
    20 Sep 1839
    13 Sep 1840
tax regulations [Nan-t'ai]
    28 Oct 1859
    29 Oct 1859
    n.d. 1859

overseas Chinese [外僑華人]
see
    Ch'en Ch'ing-chen
    Li Shun-fa

P

Pa 巴
    17 Mar 1843

Palmerston, Lord 巴
    Foreign Secretary
    16 Oct 1841
    21 Sep 1847
    4 Nov 1848
    6 Jun 1849
    25 Jun 1849
    9 Nov 1849
    13 May 1850
    21 May 1850
    7 Jun 1850

P'an A-yen 潘亞炎
    sailor from Shun-te
    10 Aug 1853
    20 Aug 1853

P'an Ho 潘河
    see Pao-ch'ang

P'an Hsiao-ching 潘小曉
    Shanghai rebel leader
    22 Jun 1854
    15 Feb 1855

P'an Shih-ch'eng 潘仕成
    Cantonese merchant
    29 Jul 1847

P'an shih-ping 潘仕炳
    Cantonese merchant
    29 Jul 1847

P'an-yü 番禺
    Kwangtung
    24 Apr 1845
    3 May 1845
    8 May 1845
    8 Jan 1848
    13 Aug 1849
    21 Oct 1849
    6 Nov 1849
    9 Nov 1849
    20 Aug 1853
    7 May 1854
    31 Jan 1858
    14 Nov 1859

Pao 保
    Prefect of Foochow
    22 Jan 1856

Pao-ch'ang 寶昌
    Cantonese firm
    8 Feb 1848

17 Feb 1848
19 Apr 1848
24 Apr 1848
27 Apr 1848
17 May 1848
21 May 1848
24 May 1848
30 May 1848

pao-chia 保甲
  8 Jun 1839

Parker, Sir William 巴駕
  Admiral
  17 Mar 1843

Parkes, H. 巴夏禮
  Acting Consul at Canton
  12 Oct 1856
  31 Oct 1856
  3 Nov 1856
  Bureau of Occupation,
  Canton
  15 May 1859
  19 May 1859
  6 Jul 1859
  8 Jul 1859
  14 Jul 1859
  16 Jul 1859
  23 Jul 1859
  26 Jul 1859
  12 Oct 1859
  26 Oct 1859
  10 Nov 1859
  14 Nov 1859
  Elgin's interpreter
  25 Dec 1857
  31 Jan 1858
  5 Nov 1858
  13 Jan 1859
  17 Jan 1859
  5 Sep 1860
  14 Sep 1860
  - Oct 1860
  30,000 taels on his head
  6 Oct 1858
  see also
  hostages

Parsee 白頭人
  11 Jan 1849
  9 Aug 1849
  11 Aug 1849
  13 Aug 1849
  16 Aug 1849

Pearl River 珠江
  Kwangtung
  27 Apr 1846
  5 May 1846
  18 May 1847
  16 Oct 1847

peasants 粵省之民
  refusal to pay taxes
  24 Aug 1847
  25 Aug 1847

Pei-hsin-kuan 北新關
  Chekiang
  25 Jan 1846
  19 Feb 1846
  21 May 1846
  22 Jun 1846
  17 Jul 1846
  18 Sep 1846
  23 Sep 1846
  26 Dec 1846
  3 Feb 1847
  19 May 1847
  1 Sep 1847
  8 Feb 1848
  17 Feb 1848
  29 Apr 1848
  4 May 1848
  17 May 1848
  17 Jun 1848
  21 Jun 1848

pei-t'ang 北塘
  Chihli
  8 Mar 1860
  6 Aug 1860
  17 Aug 1860

Peiho 白河
  Chihli
  11 Aug 1840
  19 May 1858
  20 May 1858
  24 May 1858

Peking 北京
  communication with
  24 Nov 1842
  15 Nov 1844
  29 Apr 1850
  13 May 1850
  20 May 1850
  21 May 1850
  22 May 1850

23 May 1850
1 Jun 1850
3 Jun 1850
7 Jun 1850
10 Jun 1850
12 Jun 1850
14 Jun 1850
3 Sep 1850
7 Sep 1850
19 May 1854
22 May 1854
24 May 1854
10 Jul 1854
26 Jul 1854
12 Aug 1854
4 Sep 1854
- Oct 1854
9 Dec 1856
6 Jan 1857
13 Jan 1857
22 Jan 1857
15 May 1857
18 May 1857
10 Dec 1857
10 Feb 1858
1 Apr 1858
8 Mar 1860
14 Mar 1860
13 Apr 1860
18 Aug 1860
Convention
14 Oct 1860
16 Oct 1860
19 Oct 1860
21 Oct 1860
23 Oct 1860
29 Oct 1860
free access to
10 Feb 1858
residence in
11 Jun 1858
21 Jun 1858
22 Oct 1858
25 Oct 1858
28 Oct 1858
29 Oct 1858
3 Mar 1859
16 May 1859
28 May 1859
8 Mar 1860
8 Nov 1860
9 Nov 1860

Peking Gazette 京報
5 Dec 1841

P'eng-hu 彭湖
shipwreck near
6 Nov 1849
12 Nov 1849

P'eng Wen-chang 彭蘊章
Grand Councillor
8 Mar 1860
14 Mar 1860
13 Apr 1860

Philippine ship 呂宋船
26 May 1841

Pi Ch'eng-chao 翠承昭
Acting Governor of
Kwangtung
15 May 1859
19 May 1859
6 Jul 1859
8 Jul 1859

P'i-erh 皮爾
see
Beale

p'i-ju 璧如
4 Feb 1850

pilot 引水
28 Jul 1843
1 Aug 1843
24 Aug 1843
25 Sep 1843

P'ing-nan 平南
Kwangsi
29 Dec 1848

pirates 海賊
20 Jul 1843
21 Jul 1843
5 Oct 1843
14 Oct 1843
20 Feb 1844
28 Feb 1844
15 May 1844
22 May 1844
31 May 1844
6 Jun 1844
20 Jun 1844
18 Jul 1844
7 Sep 1844
14 Sep 1844
13 Nov 1844

19 Nov 1844
19 Dec 1844
24 Dec 1844
28 Dec 1844
7 Mar 1845
9 Mar 1845
2 Apr 1845
28 Jan 1848
18 Oct 1850
British and American
  5 Aug 1846
dispute over captured
  pirates
  18 Aug 1847
in Canton River
  16 Oct 1847
  8 Sep 1854
Portugese
  9 Jun 1851
requests for co-operation
  in suppression of
  2 Aug 1849
  2 Oct 1849
  8 Mar 1850
  14 Mar 1850
  7 Dec 1854
  11 Dec 1854
  15 Dec 1854
  22 Nov 1855
  12 Dec 1855
[cf. 7 Apr 1856
  17 Apr 1856
  30 Jun 1856
  3 Jul 1856]
suppression of
  - Feb 1843
  10 Feb 1843
  19 Feb 1843
  22 Feb 1843
  13 Mar 1843
  19 Mar 1843
  26 Jun 1843
  22 May 1844
  6 Dec 1844
  13 Sep 1845
  5 Aug 1846
  18 Aug 1847
  7 Jun 1848
  17 Jun 1848
  21 Jun 1848
  2 Sep 1848
  10 Sep 1848
  29 Dec 1848
  2 Aug 1849
  12 Aug 1849

20 Sep 1849
24 Sep 1849
27 Sep 1849
2 Oct 1849
8 Oct 1849
11 Oct 1849
26 Oct 1849
6 Nov 1849
12 Nov 1849
8 Mar 1850
14 Mar 1850
15 Mar 1850
21 Mar 1850
3 Aug 1850
5 Apr 1851
13 Apr 1852
27 Aug 1853
5 Sep 1853
8 Jan 1856
3 Feb 1856
25 Feb 1856
7 Apr 1856
10 Jan 1860
17 Jan 1860

Plover 啤囉哖
  see
    surveying coast of China

plunder 搶奪
  by British forces
  11 Jun 1858
  21 Jun 1858
  see also
    bluejackets

Po-kuei 柏貴
  Acting Governor of Kwangtung
  24 Oct 1852
  27 Oct 1852
  15 Nov 1852
  22 Nov 1852
  20 Dec 1852
  2 Jan 1853
  Governor of Honan [but
    remaining in Kwangtung]
  8 Jun 1852
  27 Jul 1852
  1 Sep 1852
  Governor of Kwangtung
  28 Feb 1853
  3 Jun 1853
  Provincial Treasurer of
    Kwangtung
  26 Mar 1850
  27 Mar 1850

puppet Governor of Kwangtung
    5 Jan 1858
    9 Jan 1858
   13 Jan 1858
   20 Jan 1858
   24 Jan 1858
   31 Jan 1858
    4 Feb 1858
    8 Feb 1858
    9 Feb 1858
   13 Feb 1858
   16 Feb 1858
    3 Mar 1858
    - Apr 1858
   30 Oct 1858
    7 Nov 1858

porcelain 磁器
   12 Apr 1845
   18 Apr 1845
   21 Apr 1845
   19 Nov 1845
   12 Feb 1846
   15 Feb 1846
    4 Apr 1846
   10 Jan 1848
   16 Jan 1848
   10 May 1849
   14 May 1849
   20 May 1849
    1 Aug 1849
    4 Aug 1849
    4 Sep 1849
  see also
    Amoy customs dispute

port regulations 五口交易章程
    5 Nov 1842
   12 Nov 1842
   27 Nov 1842
    - Feb 1843
   26 Jun 1843
   30 Jun 1843
    9 Jul 1843
    - Jul 1843
   15 Jul 1843
   18 Jul 1843
   24 Jul 1843
   28 Jul 1843
   29 Jul 1843
    4 Sep 1843
    4 Apr 1846
   10 Apr 1851

pottery 瓦器
   12 Apr 1845
   18 Apr 1845
   21 Apr 1845
   19 Nov 1845
    4 Apr 1846
  see also
    Amoy customs dispute

Pottinger, Sir Henry 璞
  H.M. Plenipotentiary
   27 Jun 1842
   28 Jun 1842
    4 Jul 1842
    8 Jul 1842
    - Jul 1842
   27 Jul 1842
   30 Jul 1842
    1 Aug 1842
    3 Aug 1842
    4 Aug 1842
    5 Aug 1842
    6 Aug 1842
    - Aug 1842
    7 Aug 1842
    8 Aug 1842
    9 Aug 1842
   10 Aug 1842
   11 Aug 1842
   12 Aug 1842
   14 Aug 1842
   15 Aug 1842
   16 Aug 1842
   31 Aug 1842
    - Aug 1842
    1 Sep 1842
    3 Sep 1842
    7 Sep 1842
    9 Sep 1842
    - Sep 1842
   12 Sep 1842
   13 Sep 1842
   14 Sep 1842
    - Sep 1842
   16 Sep 1842
   17 Sep 1842
   18 Sep 1842
   19 Sep 1842
   20 Sep 1842
   22 Sep 1842
   23 Sep 1842
   24 Sep 1842
   25 Sep 1842
   26 Sep 1842
   27 Sep 1842

28 Sep 1842	20 Mar 1843
15 Oct 1842	25 Mar 1843
- Oct 1842	30 Mar 1843
3 Nov 1842	31 Mar 1843
5 Nov 1842	5 Apr 1843
6 Nov 1842	- Apr 1843
11 Nov 1842	12 Apr 1843
14 Nov 1842	13 Apr 1843
15 Nov 1842	14 Apr 1843
21 Nov 1842	16 Apr 1843
23 Nov 1842	20 Apr 1843
24 Nov 1842	23 Apr 1843
26 Nov 1842	27 Apr 1843
27 Nov 1842	12 May 1843
30 Nov 1842	29 May 1843
- Nov 1842	1 Jun 1843
13 Dec 1842	4 Jun 1843
14 Dec 1842	7 Jun 1843
15 Dec 1842	13 Jun 1843
27 Dec 1842	22 Jun 1843
28 Dec 1842	26 Jun 1843
30 Dec 1842	30 Jun 1843
4 Jan 1843	1 Jul 1843
6 Jan 1843	9 Jul 1843
9 Jan 1843	- Jul 1843
12 Jan 1843	15 Jul 1843
16 Jan 1843	18 Jul 1843
17 Jan 1843	20 Jul 1843
18 Jan 1843	2 Jan 1844
19 Jan 1843	11 Jan 1844
20 Jan 1843	15 Jan 1844
21 Jan 1843	17 Jan 1844
22 Jan 1843	18 Jan 1844
23 Jan 1843	21 Jan 1844
24 Jan 1843	24 Jan 1844
27 Jan 1843	30 Jan 1844
28 Jan 1843	31 Jan 1844
29 Jan 1843	1 Feb 1844
1 Feb 1843	3 Feb 1844
9 Feb 1843	4 Feb 1844
- Feb 1843	12 Feb 1844
18 Feb 1843	15 Feb 1844
19 Feb 1843	17 Feb 1844
20 Feb 1843	19 Feb 1844
21 Feb 1843	20 Feb 1844
22 Feb 1843	21 Feb 1844
28 Feb 1843	27 Feb 1844
6 Mar 1843	28 Feb 1844
7 Mar 1843	7 Mar 1844
13 Mar 1843	8 Mar 1844
14 Mar 1843	11 Mar 1844
17 Mar 1843	12 Mar 1844
18 Mar 1843	16 Mar 1844
19 Mar 1843	20 Mar 1844

salt 鹽
 monopoly
  19 Feb 1846
  28 Feb 1848
  3 Mar 1848
 smuggling
  23 Feb 1850
  12 Dec 1855

saltpetre 硝石
 9 Feb 1846

sampan 三板
 20 Dec 1842

San-yüan-li 三元里
 27 Feb 1849

Saracen, HMS 撒拉洵
 surveying ship
  12 Feb 1855

Schwemann, W. 瑞曼
 Consul for Hanover
  19 Jan 1854
  23 Jan 1854

seamen's hospital 水手病院
 London
  29 Nov 1845
  16 Dec 1845

Seymour, Sir Michael 西
 Rear-Admiral
  30 Oct 1856
  31 Oct 1856
  1 Nov 1856
  3 Nov 1856
  5 Nov 1856
  6 Nov 1856
  7 Nov 1856
  9 Nov 1856
  10 Nov 1856
  11 Nov 1856
  12 Nov 1856
  15 Nov 1856
  16 Nov 1856
  17 Nov 1856
  18 Nov 1856
  20 Nov 1856
  9 Dec 1856
  24 Dec 1856
  9 Jan 1858ff.

Sha-Chiao 沙角
 Hu-men area
  28 Mar 1839
  8 Jan 1841
  9 Jan 1841
  11 Jan 1841
  14 Jan 1841
  20 Jan 1841

Shameen 沙面
 [Sha-mien]
 Canton
  16 Jul 1859
  8 Jul 1859
  14 Jul 1859
  16 Jul 1859
  23 Jul 1859
  26 Jul 1859

shang 商
 10 Dec 1848

Shanghai 上海
 back duties
  1 Jul 1854
  22 Aug 1854
  25 Aug 1854
  7 Oct 1854
  9 Oct 1854
  27 Jan 1855
  19 Feb 1855
  8 Mar 1855
  6 Nov 1858
  [n.d.] 1860
 British ransom for
  see ransom
 British warship at
  9 Aug 1846
 cannon import
  16 Jul 1844
  21 Jul 1844
 customs dispute
  2 May 1849
  10 May 1849ff.
  4 Sep 1849
 Foreign Inspectorate of
  Customs
  22 Jun 1854
  26 Jun 1854
  30 Jun 1854
  1 Jul 1854
  10 Jul 1854
  15 Feb 1855

22 Feb 1855
8 Mar 1855
22 Jun 1855
16 Dec 1855
opened for trade
1 Dec 1843
premature arrival of
British merchant ship
5 Nov 1842
rebels
22 Jun 1854
26 Jun 1854
30 Jun 1854
6 Oct 1854
7 Oct 1854
9 Oct 1854
4 Dec 1854
23 Dec 1854
29 Dec 1854
27 Jan 1855
19 Feb 1855
8 Mar 1855
salt imports
19 Feb 1846
29 Feb 1848
3 Mar 1848
see also
press-gang

Shantung 山東
8 Oct 1843

Shao-chou 韶州
Kwangtung
6 Jan 1843
8 Oct 1852
11 Oct 1852
24 Oct 1852
27 Oct 1852
5 Sep 1853

She Pao-shun 余葆純
Prefect Designate
21 Apr 1839
24 Apr 1839
4 May 1839
12 May 1839
11 May 1841
27 May 1841
9 Jun 1841
11 Jun 1841
17 Jun 1841

Shen Chen-pang 沈鎮邦
Acting Colonel of
Ta-p'eng
5 Oct 1843
28 Feb 1844
29 Feb 1844
5 Mar 1844
9 Mar 1844
2 Jul 1844

Shen Chih-liang 沈志亮
murderer
17 Sep 1849

Shen-kuang-ssu 神光寺
Foochow
21 Aug 1850
25 Oct 1850
29 May 1851

Shen Ti-hui 沈棣輝
Provincial Judge of
Kwangtung
22 Nov 1855
12 Dec 1855

Shih-ching 石井
Canton area
23 Jan 1859

Shih-wei-t'ang 石圍塘
Canton area
2 Jul 1847
7 Jul 1847
16 Jul 1847
26 Jul 1847
5 Aug 1847

shipwrecked sailors 遭風水手
Chinese
Fukien coast
20 Sep 1845
foreign
Amoy
22 Jun 1843
17 Feb 1844
28 Feb 1844
Ch'iung-chou
- Apr 1843
12 Apr 1843
20 Apr 1843
20 Apr 1843
12 May 1843
19 Dec 1845

Ssu-t'u 司徒
    Intendant at Ch'üan-chou
    1 Jun 1858

Stanley 赤狂
    Hong Kong
    7 Nov 1844

Stead, Mr 吐得
    master of British ship
    3 Apr 1841

steam engine [蒸汽機]
    27 Aug 1845

steamers 火輪船
    20 Dec 1842
    9 Apr 1846
    11 Apr 1846
    16 Apr 1846
    27 Apr 1846
    5 May 1846
    18 May 1846
    21 May 1846
    1 Dec 1846
    6 Jun 1850
    fines of
    19 Mar 1851
    24 Mar 1851
    5 Apr 1851
    10 Apr 1851
    sinking junks
    17 Jan 1843
    19 Jan 1843
    19 Dec 1845
    31 Aug 1847
    20 Apr 1850
    29 Apr 1850
    6 Jun 1850
    10 Nov 1847
    2 Apr 1850
    10 Apr 1850
    19 Apr 1850
    20 Apr 1850
    29 Apr 1850
    6 Jun 1850
    see also
    Hong Kong and Canton
    Steam Co.

Stirling 撒大令
    see surveying coast of China

Stirling, Sir James 賜
    24 May 1854
    20 Jun 1854
    22 Jun 1854
    11 Dec 1854
    23 Dec 1854
    29 Dec 1854

stones 石
    cargo of
    26 Oct 1844
    30 Oct 1844
    see also
    Liu Ssu

sugar 土磺
    imports
    23 Apr 1846

Sullivan, G.G. 頊
    Acting Vice-Consul at
    Amoy
    4 Apr 1846

sulphur 硝
    smuggling of
    26 Apr 1845
    3 May 1845
    9 Feb 1846

Sung-chiang 松江
Kiangsu
    27 Jun 1842

Supplementary Treaty 善後約
    28 Sep 1842
    3 Nov 1842
    21 Nov 1842
    21 Jan 1843
    22 Jan 1843
    26 Jun 1843
    25 Jul 1843
    4 Sep 1843
    19 Oct 1843
    22 Dec 1843
    11 Apr 1846
    23 Apr 1846
    24 Apr 1851
    exchange of
    5 Jul 1844
    9 Jul 1844

29 Aug 1860

T'an Ting-hsiang 譚廷襄
    Joint Imperial Commissioner
    29 Apr 1858ff.
    Viceroy of Chihli
    24 Apr 1858ff.

T'an Ts'ai 譚才
    Hong Kong resident
    22 Jan 1848
    28 Jan 1848

Tao-shan-kuan 道山觀
    Foochow
    29 May 1851

tariff regulations 稅則
    - Aug 1842
    12 Nov 1842
    27 Nov 1842
    - Jul 1843
    15 Jul 1843
    18 Jul 1843
    24 Jul 1843
    29 Jul 1843
    4 Sep 1843
    2 Jan 1844
    1 Jul 1858
    4 Jul 1858
    22 Jul 1858
    12 Aug 1858
    11 Oct 1858
    12 Oct 1858
    5 Nov 1858
    24 Feb 1860

tax 稅
    evasions
        13 Apr 1858
        16 Apr 1843
    negotiations
        3 Jul 1858
        4 Jul 1858
        22 Jul 1858
        24 Jul 1858
        2 Aug 1858
        6 Sep 1858
        7 Sep 1858
        22 Sep 1858
        25 Sep 1858
        6 Oct 1858
        9 Oct 1858

11 Oct 1858
5 Nov 1858

Te-chu-pu 德珠卟
    Tartar-General of Nanking
    26 Jul 1842
    30 Jul 1842

tea commission 茶棧收用
    Canton
        23 Nov 1849
        12 Jan 1850
        21 Jan 1850
        25 Jan 1850
        31 Jan 1850
        20 Jul 1850
        27 Jul 1850
        3 Aug 1850
        11 Aug 1850
        19 Aug 1850
        25 Aug 1850
        31 Dec 1850
        8 Jan 1851
        14 Jun 1851
        22 Jun 1851
        3 Jul 1851
        10 Jul 1851
        8 Dec 1851
        3 Jan 1852
        10 Jan 1852
        16 Jan 1852
        31 Jan 1852
        25 Apr 1854
        7 May 1854
        11 May 1854
        22 May 1854

tea monopoly 保結茶棧
    Canton
        17 Nov 1849
        12 Jan 1850
        21 Jan 1850
        25 Jan 1850
        31 Jan 1850
        20 Jul 1850
        3 Aug 1850
        19 Aug 1850
        25 Aug 1850
        31 Dec 1850
        8 Jan 1851
        14 Jun 1851

Foochow
9 Jan 1854
17 Jan 1854

tea routes
4 Nov 1844
11 Nov 1844
24 Aug 1847

Teng 鄧
owned land in island of
Hong Kong
25 Nov 1844
24 Dec 1844

Teng Chih-p'ing 鄧治平
son of landlord in Canton
26 Sep 1848
29 Sep 1848

Teng-chou 登州
Shantung
20 Feb 1843
21 Feb 1843
29 Aug 1860
4 Dec 1860
8 Dec 1860

Teng T'ing-cheng 鄧廷楨
Viceroy of Liang-Kuang
5 Mar 1839
25 Mar 1839
28 Mar 1839
12 Apr 1839
13 Apr 1839
19 Apr 1839
20 Apr 1839
22 Apr 1839
4 May 1839
8 May 1839
9 May 1839
10 May 1839
12 May 1839
18 May 1839
21 May 1839
24 May 1839
26 May 1839
1 Jun 1839
7 Jun 1839
8 Jun 1839
20 Sep 1839
28 Sep 1839
8 Oct 1839
27 Oct 1839

19 Dec 1839
6 Jan 1840
9 Jan 1840

Thency
ran aground near Liu-ch'iu
12 Mar 1849

Thom, R. 羅伯聃
Consul at Ningpo
31 Jan 1844
18 Aug 1846
24 Aug 1846
Interpreter at Canton
- Dec 1842
20 Dec 1842
21 Dec 1842
22 Dec 1842
9 Jan 1843
12 Jan 1843
21 Jan 1843
24 Jan 1843

threatening behaviour 強悍數夷
Cantonese
24 Aug 1847
28 Aug 1847
6 Sep 1847
5 Nov 1847
10 Nov 1847
5 Apr 1848
8 Apr 1848

Tibet 西藏
British mission to
18 Nov 1846
3 Dec 1846
13 Jan 1847
16 Jan 1847
20 Jan 1847
26 Jan 1847
1 Aug 1847
3 Jan 1848
7 Jan 1848
3 Jan 1855

Tien-pai 電白
Kwangtung
20 Sep 1849
27 Sep 1849
3 Oct 1849

Tien-ti 顛地
see
Dent

10 Jul 1854
18 Jul 1854
26 Jul 1854
22 Aug 1854
25 Aug 1854
28 Aug 1854
1 Sep 1854
4 Sep 1854
16 Oct 1854
- Oct 1854
3 Nov 1854
8 Nov 1854
9 Nov 1854
10 Nov 1854
16 May 1856
30 Jun 1856
3 Jul 1856
14 Dec 1857

tributary state
25 Mar 1839
21 Apr 1839
16 Jun 1841

truce 戰災相守
of 1841
5 Mar 1841
14 Apr 1841
15 Apr 1841
11 May 1841
of 1842
26 May 1842
of 1860
17 Aug 1860

Ts'ai 蔡
Captain
20 Jul 1843

Tseng A-chang 曾亞彰
of Whampoa
21 Oct 1853
8 Nov 1853
10 Nov 1853
15 Nov 1853
8 Dec 1853

Tseng Ping-kao 曾炳高
of Whampoa
27 Oct 1852
15 Nov 1852
22 Nov 1852

Ts'ui A-hsi 崔亞禧
Chinese merchant
28 Sep 1853
13 Oct 1853
25 Nov 1853
8 Dec 1853

Tu A-te 杜亞得
pirate
17 Dec 1844

Tuan Chi 段吉
Prefect Designate
12 Oct 1859

Tung-ch'un 秉純
Tartar-General of Foochow
29 Oct 1859
n.d. (1859)

T'ung-chou 通州
Chihli
7 Sep 1860
8 Sep 1860
10 Sep 1860
11 Sep 1860
12 Sep 1860
13 Sep 1860
14 Sep 1860
16 Sep 1860
22 Sep 1860
25 Sep 1860

Turner, Mr 打拿
British merchant
8 Feb 1848
17 Feb 1848
19 Apr 1848
24 Apr 1848
27 Apr 1848
17 May 1848
21 May 1848
24 May 1848
30 May 1848

Wen-wei 文蔚
    Captain-General
        8 Oct 1842

West Fort 西砲台
    Canton
       11 May 1841

Whampoa 黃埔
       7 Jun 1839
       8 Jan 1841
     12 Jan 1843
     17 Jan 1843
     19 Jan 1843
      1 Feb 1843
      9 Mar 1843
     20 Jun 1844
     19 Nov 1844
     15 Oct 1845
      8 Feb 1849
     11 Feb 1849
     11 Aug 1849
     31 Jan 1852
      5 May 1860
     18 May 1860
     16 Jun 1860
  Anglo-Chinese conflicts at
     20 Feb 1843
     21 Feb 1843
     14 Mar 1843
      9 Feb 1846
     14 Feb 1846
     21 Feb 1846
     25 Feb 1846
      6 Mar 1846
     13 Mar 1846
  British warship at
     17 Apr 1845
     26 Jan 1846
  opium smuggling at
     28 Mar 1839
     26 Apr 1845
      8 May 1845
     16 May 1845
  piracy at
      1 Dec 1848
      6 Dec 1848
     12 Dec 1848
     20 Dec 1848
     22 Dec 1848
      3 Jan 1849
     15 Jan 1849
     20 Jan 1849
     27 Jan 1849

temporary customs office
      8 Feb 1858
      9 Feb 1858
posting of Vice-Consul
     21 Feb 1843
     14 Mar 1843
vice-consulate building
project
     17 Nov 1849
     23 Nov 1849
     11 Dec 1849
     18 Dec 1849
     20 Dec 1849
     26 Dec 1849
     30 Dec 1849
      4 Jan 1850
      7 Jan 1850
      7 Oct 1852
     24 Oct 1852
     27 Oct 1852
     15 Nov 1852
     22 Nov 1852
     - Apr 1858
vice-consulate,
  attempted arson
     21 Oct 1853
      8 Nov 1853
     10 Nov 1853
     15 Nov 1853
see also
  cemetry

West Indies 西印度
     26 Oct 1859
     10 Nov 1859
  n.d. 1859

White, Mr
  whose house was burgled
     29 Feb 1844
      9 Mar 1844

Wilson, Mr 喊唎臣
  whose house was burgled
      7 Jan 1848
     12 Jan 1848
     18 Jan 1848
     25 Jan 1848
      1 Feb 1848

Winchester, C.A. 溫
    Vice-Consul in charge
    at Canton
      - Apr 1858
      5 Apr 1859
      9 Jul 1859
      7 Sep 1859
     25 Sep 1859
     13 Oct 1859
     14 Nov 1859
     24 Feb 1859
      5 May 1860
     18 May 1860

Wu, Mr 伍
    landlord
      2 Jul 1847
      7 Jul 1847

Wu A-liu 吳亞六
    pirate
     20 May 1847
     16 Oct 1847

Wu Chien-chang 吳健彰
    Intendant at Shangahi
      1 Jul 1854
     10 Jul 1854
     [dismiised]
      4 Aug 1854
     [reinstated]
     15 Feb 1855

Wu-chou 梧州
    Kwangsi
     21 Jun 1848

Wu Ch'ung-yüeh 伍崇曜
    or Howqua
      6 Apr 1849
      9 Apr 1849
     17 Nov 1849
     12 Jan 1850
     21 Jan 1850
     25 Jan 1850
     28 Jan 1850
     20 Jul 1850
      - May 1860

Wu-hsi 無錫
    Kiangsu
      5 Aug 1842

Wu I-hsi 巫宜禊
    Intendant at Shangahi
     22 Sep 1842
     11 Oct 1842

Wu-le-hung-o 烏勒洪額
    Joint Imperial Commissioner
     26 Apr 1858
     29 Apr 1858
     19 May 1858

Wu-sung 吳淞
    Kiangsu
     20 Jun 1842 [Rec'd]
     27 Jun 1842
      6 Jul 1842
      - Aug 1842
      3 Mar 1848
    blockade of
      2 Aug 1842
      3 Sep 1842

Y

Yang Fang 楊芳
    Imperial Commissioner at
    Canton
     18 Mar 1841
     19 Mar 1841
     29 Mar 1841
     14 Apr 1841
     15 Apr 1841
      2 May 1841

Yang Wen-ting 楊文定
    Governor of Kiangsu
     26 Mar 1853

Yangchow 揚州
    Kiangsu
    ransom for
      - Aug 1842

Yangtze River 楊子江
     19 Jul 1842
      - Sep 1842
     25 Sep 1843
     25 Mar 1844
     21 Jun 1858